A+

Practice
Questions

Charles J. Brooks

A+ Practice Questions Exam Cram 2

International Standard Book Number: 0-7897-3108-8

Library of Congress Catalog Card Number: 2003113759

Printed in the United States of America

First Printing: March 2004
Reprinted with Corrections: April 2006

09   08   07   06   13   12   11   10   9

Trademarks

Warning and Disclaimer

Bulk Sales

Que Publishing offers excellent discounts on this book when ordered in quantity for bulk purchases or special sales. For more information, please contact

U.S. Corporate and Government Sales
1-800-382-3419
corpsales@pearsontechgroup.com

For sales outside of the U.S., please contact

International Sales
international@pearsoned.com

Publisher
Paul Boger

Executive Editor
Jeff Riley

Acquisitions Editor
Jeff Riley

Development Editor
Steve Rowe

Managing Editor
Charlotte Clapp

Project Editor
Tricia Liebig

Production Editor
Jessica McCarty

Proofreader
Tracy Donhardt

Technical Editor
David Eytchison

Publishing Coordinator
Pamalee Nelson

Multimedia Developer
Dan Scherf

Interior Designer
Anne Jones

Cover Designer
Anne Jones

Page Layout
Brad Chinn

CERTIFICATION

Que Certification • 800 East 96th Street • Indianapolis, Indiana 46240

A Note from Series Editor Ed Tittel

You know better than to trust your certification preparation to just anybody. That's why you, and more than two million others, have purchased an Exam Cram book. As Series Editor for the new and improved Exam Cram 2 series, I have worked with the staff at Que Certification to ensure you won't be disappointed. That's why we've taken the world's best-selling certification product—a finalist for "Best Study Guide" in a CertCities reader poll in 2002—and made it even better.

As a two-time finalist for the "Favorite Study Guide Author" award as determined by CertCities readers, I know the value of good books. You'll be impressed with Que Certification's stringent review process, which ensures the books are high-quality, relevant, and technically accurate.

We've also added a MeasureUp test engine, which is trusted by certification students throughout the world.

As a 20-year-plus veteran of the computing industry and the original creator and editor of the Exam Cram series, I've brought my IT experience to bear on these books. During my tenure at Novell from 1989 to 1994, I worked with and around its excellent education and certification department. This experience helped push my writing and teaching activities heavily in the certification direction. Since then, I've worked on more than 70 certification-related books, and I write about certification topics for numerous Web sites and for *Certification* magazine.

In 1996, while studying for various MCP exams, I became frustrated with the huge, unwieldy study guides that were the only preparation tools available. As an experienced IT professional and former instructor, I wanted "nothing but the facts" necessary to prepare for the exams. From this impetus, Exam Cram emerged in 1997. It quickly became the best-selling computer book series since "...*For Dummies*," and the best-selling certification book series ever. By maintaining an intense focus on subject matter, tracking errata and updates quickly, and following the certification market closely, Exam Cram was able to establish the dominant position in cert prep books.

You will not be disappointed in your decision to purchase this book. If you are, please contact me at etittel@jump.net. All suggestions, ideas, input, or constructive criticism are welcome!

Ed Tittel

Expand Your Certification Arsenal!

A+, Second Edition Exam Cram 2

James Jones and Craig Landes

ISBN 0-7897-3043-X

$29.99 US/$45.99 CAN/£21.99 Net UK

- Key terms and concepts highlighted at the start of each chapter
- Notes, Tips, and Exam Alerts advise what to watch out for
- End-of-chapter sample Exam Questions with detailed discussions of all answers
- Complete text-based practice test with answer key at the end of each book
- The tear-out Cram Sheet condenses the most important items and information into a two-page reminder
- A CD that includes PrepLogic Practice Tests for complete evaluation of your knowledge
- Our authors are recognized experts in the field. In most cases, they are current or former instructors, trainers, or consultants— they know exactly what you need to know!

About the Author

Charles J. Brooks is currently the president of Marcraft International Corporation, located in Kennewick, Washington, and is in charge of research and development. He is the author of several books, including *Speech Synthesis*, *Pneumatic Instrumentation*, *The Complete Introductory Computer Course*, *Radio-Controlled Car Project Manual*, and *IBM PC Peripheral Troubleshooting and Repair*. A former electronics instructor and technical writer with the National Education Corporation, Charles has taught and written on post-secondary EET curriculum, including introductory electronics, transistor theory, linear integrated circuits, basic digital theory, industrial electronics, microprocessors, and computer peripherals.

About Marcraft International Corporation

ΠLMARCRAFT Marcraft International Corporation has been producing IT training products for 20 years, supplying the hardware, software, and courseware materials for numerous technical training curricula. Marcraft sells its products worldwide from its headquarters in Kennewick, Washington. Marcraft's mission is to develop exceptional products for effectively teaching and training people the IT skills in demand both today and in the future.

Dedication

. . . .

I dedicate this book to my wife, Robbie, and my two grandsons, Michael and Joshua. It amazes me that by the time they can read this, the technology will have changed so much that they will need a new book.

Acknowledgments

I would like to acknowledge the people who have made this book a reality. First, thanks to Jeff Riley at Que Certification Publishing for having the vision to create these tools for certification. I also must thank You Wen Ho for her diligent work in maintaining our test banks. There's nothing more fun than pouring over hundreds and hundreds of test questions and answers and keeping them correct. Also, thanks to Steve Rowe, Jessica McCarty, and Tricia Liebig for their excellent review and project-management work.

Contents at a Glance

Table of Contents

Chapter 2
Hardware Domain 2.0: Diagnosing and Troubleshooting 81

Chapter 3
Hardware Domain 3.0: PC Preventive Maintenance, Safety, and Environmental Issues 115

Chapter 2
Operating System Domain 2.0: Installation, Configuration, and Upgrading 287

We Want to Hear from You!

As the reader of this book, *you* are our most important critic and commentator. We value your opinion and want to know what we're doing right, what we could do better, what areas you'd like to see us publish in, and any other words of wisdom you're willing to pass our way.

As an executive editor for Que Publishing, I welcome your comments. You can email or write me directly to let me know what you did or didn't like about this book—as well as what we can do to make our books better.

Please note that I cannot help you with technical problems related to the topic of this book. We do have a User Services group, however, where I will forward specific technical questions related to the book.

When you write, please be sure to include this book's title and author as well as your name, email address, and phone number. I will carefully review your comments and share them with the author and editors who worked on the book.

Email: feedback@quepublishing.com

Mail: Jeff Riley
             Executive Editor
             Que Publishing
             800 East 96th Street
             Indianapolis, IN 46240 USA

For information about the *Exam Cram 2* series, visit www.examcram2.com. Type the ISBN (excluding hyphens) or the title of a book in the Search field to find the page you're looking for.

Introduction

What Is This Book About?

Welcome to the *A+ Practice Questions Exam Cram 2*! The sole aim of this book is to provide you with practice questions complete with answers and explanations that will help you learn, drill, and review for the A+ certification exams.

Who Is This Book For?

If you have studied the A+ exam's content and feel you are ready to put your knowledge to the test, but not sure you want to take the real exams yet, this book is for you! Maybe you have answered other practice questions or unsuccessfully taken the real exams, reviewed, and want to do more practice questions before going to take the real exams—this book is for you, too!

What Will You Find in This Book?

As mentioned before, this book is all about practice questions! This book is separated according to the topics you will find in the A+ exams. Each chapter represents an exam topic and in the chapter you will find three elements:

➤ **Practice Questions**—These are the numerous questions that will help you learn, drill, and review.

➤ **Quick Check Answer Key**—When you have finished answering the questions, you can quickly grade your exam from this section. Only correct answers are given here. No explanations are offered yet!

➤ **Answers and Explanations**—This section offers you the correct answers as well as further explanation about the content posed in that question.

Use this information to learn why an answer is correct and to reinforce the content in your mind for exam day.

You will also find a CramSheet at the beginning of this book specifically written for this exam. This is a very popular element that is also found in the corresponding *A+ Certification Exam Cram 2, Second Edition* (ISBN: 0-7897-3043-X). This item condenses all the necessary facts found in this exam into one, easy-to-handle tearout card. The CramSheet is something you can carry with you to the exam location and use as a last-second study aid. Be aware that you can't take it into the exam room, though!

Hints for Using This Book

Because this book is a paper practice product, you might want to complete your exams on a separate piece of paper so you can reuse the questions over and over without having previous answers in your way. Also, a general rule of thumb across all practice-question products is to make sure you are scoring well into the high 80%–90% range in all topics before attempting the real exam. The higher percentages you score on practice-question products, the better your chances for passing the real exam. Of course, we can't guarantee a passing score on the real exam, but we can offer you plenty of opportunities to practice and assess your knowledge levels before entering the real exam.

Need Further Study?

Are you having a hard time correctly answering these questions? If so, you probably need further review. Be sure to see the sister product to this book, the *A+ Exam Cram 2, Second Edition* by Que Publishing (ISBN: 0-7897-3043-X). If you need even further study, check out Que's *A+ Training Guide, Fifth Edition* (ISBN: 0-7897-3044-0).

PART I

Hardware

Hardware Domain 1.0: Installation, Configuration, and Upgrading

Quick Check

Objective 1.1: Identify the names, purpose, and characteristics of system modules.

1. What type of I/O device uses a 3-row, 15-pin female connector?
   - ❑ a. Monitor
   - ❑ b. Joystick
   - ❑ c. Printer
   - ❑ d. Modem

Quick Answer: **54**
Detailed Answer: **58**

2. The normal size for a hard drive sector in a PC-compatible system is _____.
   - ❑ a. 512 bytes
   - ❑ b. 640 bytes
   - ❑ c. 512KB
   - ❑ d. 640KB

Quick Answer: **54**
Detailed Answer: **58**

3. The standard VGA resolution in graphics mode with 16 onscreen colors is _____ pixels.
   - ❑ a. 1,280×1,024
   - ❑ b. 640×480
   - ❑ c. 800×600
   - ❑ d. 1,024×768

Quick Answer: **54**
Detailed Answer: **58**

4. When a computer boots up, the first set of instructions it receives is stored in _____.
   - ❑ a. the CMOS memory
   - ❑ b. the ROM BIOS chip
   - ❑ c. RAM
   - ❑ d. the CPU

Quick Answer: **54**
Detailed Answer: **58**

. . . .

5. Which of the following is not located in the BIOS?

- ❏ a. Hardware configuration information
- ❏ b. RAM-checking routine
- ❏ c. Startup functions
- ❏ d. Master Boot Record

Quick Answer: **54**
Detailed Answer: **58**

6. An ATX-type system board supports _____.

- ❏ a. a soft power switch
- ❏ b. a total of 16 expansion slots
- ❏ c. universal expansion slots
- ❏ d. a RAM memory capacity of 256MB

Quick Answer: **54**
Detailed Answer: **58**

7. In Microsoft systems, a typical hard drive sector is _____ bytes long.

- ❏ a. 256
- ❏ b. 512
- ❏ c. 1,024
- ❏ d. 2,048

Quick Answer: **54**
Detailed Answer: **58**

8. A magnetic disk has tracks on its surface, and the tracks are divided into _____.

- ❏ a. sectors
- ❏ b. clusters
- ❏ c. FRUs
- ❏ d. magnetic spots

Quick Answer: **54**
Detailed Answer: **58**

9. PC-compatible systems use a _____ connector for the VGA video function.

- ❏ a. 9-pin, female
- ❏ b. 15-pin, male
- ❏ c. 15-pin, female
- ❏ d. 25-pin, male

Quick Answer: **54**
Detailed Answer: **58**

10. The purpose of the rechargeable battery on some system boards is to _____ in the event of a power fluctuation.

- ❏ a. back up the contents of the RAM memory
- ❏ b. keep the microprocessor's registries alive
- ❏ c. maintain the contents of CMOS RAM
- ❏ d. maintain the system's time-of-day chip

Quick Answer: **54**
Detailed Answer: **58**

11. What system structure contains the PC's time, date, and configuration information?

- ❑ a. The ROM BIOS
- ❑ b. The CMOS RAM
- ❑ c. The RAMDAC
- ❑ d. The Upper Memory Block (UMB)

Quick Answer: **54**
Detailed Answer: **58**

12. Cache memory is used to _____.

- ❑ a. increase the speed of data access
- ❑ b. increase the size of memory available to programs
- ❑ c. store data in nonvolatile memory
- ❑ d. augment the memory used for the operating system kernel

Quick Answer: **54**
Detailed Answer: **58**

13. If a new option is installed in the system and it refuses to operate, what type of problem should be assumed?

- ❑ a. Software conflict
- ❑ b. Hardware failure
- ❑ c. BIOS failure
- ❑ d. Setup/configuration conflict

Quick Answer: **54**
Detailed Answer: **58**

14. For computer bootup purposes, the first set of instructions is stored in the _____.

- ❑ a. CPU
- ❑ b. CMOS
- ❑ c. ROM BIOS
- ❑ d. RAM

Quick Answer: **54**
Detailed Answer: **59**

15. Which of the following constitutes a valid bootup sequence?

- ❑ a. Initialization, POST, bootup
- ❑ b. Initialization, bootup, POST
- ❑ c. Bootup, POST, initialization
- ❑ d. POST, initialization, bootup

Quick Answer: **54**
Detailed Answer: **59**

16. A good example of firmware is _____.

- ❑ a. ROM BIOS
- ❑ b. Windows 95
- ❑ c. DOS
- ❑ d. CONFIG.SYS

Quick Answer: **54**
Detailed Answer: **59**

17. During startup, the memory of a computer is tested by
_____.

❑   a. the CMOS setup program
❑   b. the POST
❑   c. the CPU
❑   d. the Interrupt Controller

Quick Answer: **54**
Detailed Answer: **59**

18. Which of the following connectors is used in PC compatibles for the VGA video function?

❑   a. 9-pin, female D-shell
❑   b. BNC female
❑   c. 15-pin, female D-shell
❑   d. 4-pin female

Quick Answer: **54**
Detailed Answer: **59**

19. Which type of interface would you normally expect to encounter when installing an external CD-ROM drive?

❑   a. Parallel port
❑   b. EIDE connector
❑   c. PCI slot
❑   d. SCSI port

Quick Answer: **54**
Detailed Answer: **59**

20. An optical CD-ROM disk typically contains _____ of information.

❑   a. 380MB
❑   b. 600MB
❑   c. 420MB
❑   d. upwards of 600MB

Quick Answer: **54**
Detailed Answer: **59**

21. A computer has two floppy disk drives. Which of them is the A: drive?

❑   a. The floppy drive that is first attached to the cable
❑   b. The floppy drive that is attached to the nearest connector
❑   c. The floppy drive that is attached to the connector at the end of the cable
❑   d. The floppy drive that is designated via its jumpers

Quick Answer: **54**
Detailed Answer: **59**

22. Disk tracks are composed of _____.

❑   a. clusters
❑   b. sectors
❑   c. FRUs
❑   d. magnetic spots

Quick Answer: **54**
Detailed Answer: **59**

Quick Check

23. The resolution for a video adapter operating in native VGA mode is _____ pixels.

Quick Answer: **54**
Detailed Answer: **59**

   - ❏ a. 640×480
   - ❏ b. 350×468
   - ❏ c. 800×600
   - ❏ d. 1,024×768

24. Which video standard is superior to the others listed?

Quick Answer: **54**
Detailed Answer: **59**

   - ❏ a. XGA
   - ❏ b. VGA
   - ❏ c. SVGA
   - ❏ d. HGA

25. Replacing the power supply in an AT system requires that you also _____.

Quick Answer: **54**
Detailed Answer: **60**

   - ❏ a. replace the AC power cord that attaches to the rear of the system unit
   - ❏ b. reinstall the Windows operating system using a different directory
   - ❏ c. reset the CMOS setup values to their default power-on settings
   - ❏ d. match the P8 and P9 PS connectors to the P1 and P2 motherboard connectors, respectively

26. What is the main difference between AT and ATX power supplies?

Quick Answer: **54**
Detailed Answer: **60**

   - ❏ a. ATX power supplies require 240V AC input.
   - ❏ b. The ATX power supply is controlled by a software switch on the system board.
   - ❏ c. ATX power supplies deliver more power to the system.
   - ❏ d. AT power supplies blow air onto the system board rather than out through the back of the unit.

27. Which of the following describe differences between an ISA expansion slot and a PCI expansion slot? (Select two correct answers.)

Quick Answer: **54**
Detailed Answer: **60**

   - ❏ a. PCI slots are primarily used for video graphics adapters.
   - ❏ b. PCI slots are available in 32 or 64 bits.
   - ❏ c. 32-bit PCI slots are shorter than 16-bit ISA slots.
   - ❏ d. PCI slots are longer.

28. Which pin is used to align a microprocessor for insertion?

   ❏   a. Pin 8
   ❏   b. Pin 0
   ❏   c. Pin 10
   ❏   d. Pin 1

Quick Answer: **54**
Detailed Answer: **60**

29. Which system component executes software instructions and carries out arithmetic operations for the system?

   ❏   a. The CMOS RAM
   ❏   b. The microprocessor
   ❏   c. The BIOS
   ❏   d. The U and V pipes

Quick Answer: **54**
Detailed Answer: **60**

30. Which two are legitimate names for system boards?

   ❏   a. Motherboards
   ❏   b. Planar boards
   ❏   c. Circuit boards
   ❏   d. Daughter boards

Quick Answer: **54**
Detailed Answer: **60**

31. Nonvolatile data can be stored in _____.

   ❏   a. register
   ❏   b. cache
   ❏   c. ROM
   ❏   d. RAM

Quick Answer: **54**
Detailed Answer: **60**

32. Which type of storage is volatile?

   ❏   a. RAM
   ❏   b. CD-ROM
   ❏   c. Disk
   ❏   d. ROM

Quick Answer: **54**
Detailed Answer: **60**

33. Which memory package uses a 168-pin slot or socket?

   ❏   a. SIP
   ❏   b. DIP
   ❏   c. SIMM
   ❏   d. DIMM

Quick Answer: **54**
Detailed Answer: **60**

34. Which of the following is not a function of the Basic Input Output System?

   ❏   a. Performing the Power On Self Tests
   ❏   b. Initializing the system's intelligent devices
   ❏   c. Loading an operating system
   ❏   d. Configuring printers attached to the system

Quick Answer: **54**
Detailed Answer: **60**

35. What does .28-dot pitch mean?
- ❏ a. The dots are .28cm apart.
- ❏ b. The dots are .28mm apart.
- ❏ c. The dots are .28 inches wide.
- ❏ d. The dots are .28nm apart.

Quick Answer: **54**
Detailed Answer: **60**

36. Which of the following terms is not associated with the dot information produced by a color monitor?
- ❏ a. PEL
- ❏ b. Pixel
- ❏ c. Triad
- ❏ d. Picture element

Quick Answer: **54**
Detailed Answer: **60**

37. If you were buying a new monitor, which of the following has the best dot pitch?
- ❏ a. .29
- ❏ b. .28
- ❏ c. .30
- ❏ d. .32

Quick Answer: **54**
Detailed Answer: **61**

38. What is used to prevent the spreading of the electron beam on a color monitor?
- ❏ a. Glass faceplate
- ❏ b. Color shield
- ❏ c. Shadow mask
- ❏ d. Phosphor shield

Quick Answer: **54**
Detailed Answer: **61**

39. Which interface type is normally associated with an internal CD-ROM drive in a PC-compatible computer?
- ❏ a. IEEE-1394 FireWire adapter
- ❏ b. EIDE connector
- ❏ c. USB port connector
- ❏ d. SCSI adapter

Quick Answer: **54**
Detailed Answer: **61**

40. What type of card is a SCSI adapter?
- ❏ a. Video adapter
- ❏ b. Host adapter
- ❏ c. Sound adapter
- ❏ d. Network adapter

Quick Answer: **54**
Detailed Answer: **61**

41. How much information is a typical CD-ROM disc able to store?

Quick Answer: **54**
Detailed Answer: **61**

- ❏ a. 420MB
- ❏ b. 680MB
- ❏ c. 500MB
- ❏ d. 580MB

42. The LCD display on a portable computer is powered by _____.

Quick Answer: **54**
Detailed Answer: **61**

- ❏ a. low-voltage AC
- ❏ b. high-voltage AC
- ❏ c. low-voltage DC
- ❏ d. high-voltage DC

Objective 1.2: Identify basic procedures for adding and removing field-replaceable modules for desktop systems.

1. The key to inserting a microprocessor is to _____.

Quick Answer: **54**
Detailed Answer: **61**

- ❏ a. make sure to orient the writing on the top of the chip with that of the previous processor
- ❏ b. align the notch in the chip with the notch in the socket
- ❏ c. reattach the fan unit properly
- ❏ d. look for the arrow on the chip, and align it with the arrow on the PC board

2. Which of the following activities should be avoided when the computer is in operation?

Quick Answer: **54**
Detailed Answer: **61**

- ❏ a. Removing CD-ROM disks
- ❏ b. Exchanging mice track balls
- ❏ c. Pushing the ON/OFF switch
- ❏ d. Swapping keyboards

3. What is the rule for AT system board power connections?

Quick Answer: **54**
Detailed Answer: **61**

- ❏ a. Black to black
- ❏ b. Red to red
- ❏ c. Red to black
- ❏ d. Red to orange

4. Which Windows file system provides protected-mode operations for CD-ROM drives?
   - ❏   a.   CDFAT
   - ❏   b.   CDFS
   - ❏   c.   NTFS
   - ❏   d.   MSCDEX

Quick Answer: **54**
Detailed Answer: **61**

5. What type of device is connected to a 5-pin DIN connector?
   - ❏   a.   Mouse
   - ❏   b.   Printer
   - ❏   c.   Keyboard
   - ❏   d.   Joystick

Quick Answer: **54**
Detailed Answer: **61**

6. What type of error checking can repair the defective bit in the bit stream?
   - ❏   a.   XOR
   - ❏   b.   ECC
   - ❏   c.   8-bit
   - ❏   d.   Single bit

Quick Answer: **54**
Detailed Answer: **61**

7. A 168-pin memory module is known as a _____.
   - ❏   a.   SIMM
   - ❏   b.   DIMM
   - ❏   c.   DRAM
   - ❏   d.   PRAM

Quick Answer: **54**
Detailed Answer: **62**

8. What factors must be taken into account when ordering a new power supply?
   - ❏   a.   Form factor and wattage
   - ❏   b.   Total BTUs and amperage
   - ❏   c.   Voltage and form factor
   - ❏   d.   Noise and total BTUs

Quick Answer: **54**
Detailed Answer: **62**

9. Which statement best describes the key to properly connecting an AT power supply to a baby AT–style system board?
   - ❏   a.   It does not matter which power supply connector is plugged into which circuit-board connector.
   - ❏   b.   P9 should be plugged into P1; P8 should be plugged into P2.
   - ❏   c.   P8 should be plugged into P1; P9 should be plugged into P2.
   - ❏   d.   The connectors are configured so that the power supply will only plug into the circuit board one way.

Quick Answer: **54**
Detailed Answer: **62**

10. When installing RAM memory modules, which of these potential problems is the most unlikely?

    ❑ a. Installing one stick of RAM with tin contacts and a second stick with gold contacts
    ❑ b. Installing a DIMM in a SIMM slot
    ❑ c. Installing two sticks of RAM with different bus speeds
    ❑ d. Installing two sticks of RAM with different memory sizes

Quick Answer: **54**
Detailed Answer: **62**

11. What system board feature is used to manage the installation and replacement of the microprocessor?

    ❑ a. Operating system
    ❑ b. HSF
    ❑ c. ROM BIOS
    ❑ d. ZIF sockets

Quick Answer: **54**
Detailed Answer: **62**

12. In a water cooler system, what device is used to cool the water and exhaust heat into the outside atmosphere?

    ❑ a. Water pump
    ❑ b. Water reservoir tank
    ❑ c. Condenser coil radiator
    ❑ d. CPU cooling block

Quick Answer: **54**
Detailed Answer: **62**

13. In a refrigerant-cooled microprocessor system, which cooling component is responsible for connecting directly to the microprocessor and extracting heat from it?

    ❑ a. Condenser
    ❑ b. Evaporator
    ❑ c. CPU cooling block
    ❑ d. Dynamic heat sink

Quick Answer: **54**
Detailed Answer: **62**

14. In a liquid-cooled microprocessor system, which cooling component is responsible for connecting directly to the microprocessor and extracting heat from it?

    ❑ a. Condenser
    ❑ b. CPU cooling block
    ❑ c. Evaporator
    ❑ d. Dynamic heat sink

Quick Answer: **54**
Detailed Answer: **62**

15. Which of the following connectors are used for devices that can be hot-swapped?

    ❑ a. 5-pin DIN connector
    ❑ b. 6-pin PS/2 mini-DIN connector
    ❑ c. RS-232C serial port
    ❑ d. USB port

Quick Answer: **54**
Detailed Answer: **62**

16. A BIOS with LBA can support _____.

    ❑ a. HDDs larger than 504MB

    ❑ b. HDDs no greater than 504MB

    ❑ c. more than four COM ports

    ❑ d. more than four HDDs

Quick Answer: **54**
Detailed Answer: **62**

17. What is the first step of installing a Universal Serial Bus (USB) device?

    ❑ a. Install the USB driver in the Add New Hardware Wizard.

    ❑ b. Enable the USB driver in Device Manager.

    ❑ c. Enable USB resources in CMOS.

    ❑ d. Right-click on the USB device icon in the Taskbar and select Enable.

Quick Answer: **54**
Detailed Answer: **62**

18. How many devices can be attached to a single Universal Serial Bus (USB) host?

    ❑ a. 32

    ❑ b. 64

    ❑ c. 127

    ❑ d. 255

Quick Answer: **54**
Detailed Answer: **63**

19. Which new serial interface is faster?

    ❑ a. USB 1.1

    ❑ b. ECP

    ❑ c. IrDA

    ❑ d. IEEE-1394

Quick Answer: **54**
Detailed Answer: **63**

20. After the USB function has been enabled and the device has been plugged into the system, what action must be performed to fully install the device?

    ❑ a. Run the Add New Hardware Wizard from the Control Panel.

    ❑ b. Run the Add/Remove Programs Wizard to install the drivers for the new device.

    ❑ c. Use the Have Disk option to install proprietary USB drivers from the device manufacturer's disk.

    ❑ d. Start the system and let the operating system detect it through the PnP process.

Quick Answer: **54**
Detailed Answer: **63**

21. Which standard ATX ports are often confused with each other?

    ❑ a. The serial port and the VGA/SVGA port

    ❑ b. The docking port and the parallel ports

    ❑ c. The NIC card and modem connector ports

    ❑ d. The mouse and keyboard connections

Quick Answer: **54**
Detailed Answer: **63**

22. When using Windows 98, how many partitions are required to utilize a 5GB hard drive?

    ❑ a. One
    ❑ b. Two
    ❑ c. Three
    ❑ d. Four

Quick Answer: **54**
Detailed Answer: **63**

23. What effect does the BIOS have in upgrading the system's hard disk drives?

    ❑ a. It has no effect.
    ❑ b. It allows the creation of partitions greater than 2GB.
    ❑ c. It needs LBA or ECHS support to allow drives larger than 504MB.
    ❑ d. It normally limits the size of partitions to 2GB.

Quick Answer: **54**
Detailed Answer: **63**

24. What must be done to delete the extended partition containing logical drives E and F?

    ❑ a. Format drive E and delete drive F.
    ❑ b. Format the extended partition.
    ❑ c. Delete drives E and F.
    ❑ d. Format drives E and F.

Quick Answer: **54**
Detailed Answer: **63**

25. The second thing to do after installing a new SCSI hard drive in a system is to _____.

    ❑ a. low-level format it
    ❑ b. load DOS on it
    ❑ c. partition it
    ❑ d. run SETUP to configure the drive

Quick Answer: **54**
Detailed Answer: **63**

26. What type of hardware device is the MSCDEX file used with and where should it be located in the system?

    ❑ a. CD-ROM. The execution line should be in the Autoexec.bat file.
    ❑ b. SVGA card. The video driver file is located in the C:\Windows\System directory.
    ❑ c. HDD. The file is located in the boot sector and is an extension of the BIOS.
    ❑ d. FDD. The file is located in the C:\Windows\System directory.

Quick Answer: **54**
Detailed Answer: **63**

27. What is the partition size limit for Windows 95?

    ❑ a. 8GB

    ❑ b. 528MB

    ❑ c. 32MB

    ❑ d. 2GB

Quick Answer: **54**
Detailed Answer: **64**

28. What is the highest drive letter that can be assigned to a logical drive in a FAT-based system?

    ❑ a. W

    ❑ b. Z

    ❑ c. S

    ❑ d. H

Quick Answer: **54**
Detailed Answer: **64**

29. What physical feature determines which floppy drive will be the A: drive in a two-floppy system?

    ❑ a. Connecting the FDD to the end connector of the cable

    ❑ b. Connecting the color strip to pin 34

    ❑ c. Connecting the FDD to the middle connector of the cable

    ❑ d. Connecting the color strip to pin 1

Quick Answer: **54**
Detailed Answer: **64**

30. Where does the bootstrap loader look for the operating system boot files?

    ❑ a. The dynamic partition

    ❑ b. The active partition

    ❑ c. The extended partition

    ❑ d. The primary partition

Quick Answer: **54**
Detailed Answer: **64**

31. Where is the hard drive partition table located in a PC-compatible system?

    ❑ a. In the BIOS

    ❑ b. In the Master Boot Record

    ❑ c. In RAM

    ❑ d. In the CMOS setup configuration

Quick Answer: **54**
Detailed Answer: **64**

Objective 1.3: Identify basic procedures for adding and removing field-replaceable modules for portable systems.

1. What is the maximum data throughput for a low-speed USB device?

   □   a.   1.5Mbps

   □   b.   12Mbps

   □   c.   60Mbps

   □   d.   480Mbps

   Quick Answer: **54**
   Detailed Answer: **64**

2. Which type of interface would you normally expect to encounter when installing an external CD-ROM drive? (Select two correct answers.)

   □   a.   USB

   □   b.   IDE

   □   c.   ISA

   □   d.   SCSI

   Quick Answer: **54**
   Detailed Answer: **64**

3. Why would a notebook computer only show 64MB of RAM after you have just upgraded the system to 256MB of RAM?

   □   a.   Incorrect memory type

   □   b.   CMOS needs to be configured

   □   c.   BIOS needs upgrading

   □   d.   Improper memory allocation by the operating system

   Quick Answer: **54**
   Detailed Answer: **64**

4. What item needs to be checked on an external CD-ROM drive that is not normally checked on an internal drive when installing the drive on a notebook PC?

   □   a.   Its signal cable

   □   b.   Its power supply

   □   c.   Its disk drive controller

   □   d.   Its hard drive

   Quick Answer: **54**
   Detailed Answer: **64**

5. What should you do first if you want to remove a PCMCIA card from a notebook computer?

   □   a.   Pull the card from the computer.

   □   b.   Select the command to stop the operation of the PC Card you want to remove.

   □   c.   Uninstall the PC Card driver.

   □   d.   Click on the PC Card Status indicator on the Taskbar.

   Quick Answer: **54**
   Detailed Answer: **64**

6. What device enables a notebook computer to be used with a desktop monitor, keyboard, and mouse?

- ❏ a. Portable station
- ❏ b. Desktop port
- ❏ c. Docking station
- ❏ d. Notebook port

Quick Answer: **55**
Detailed Answer: **65**

7. What internal device is usually not found in modern PC notebooks?

- ❏ a. Floppy drive
- ❏ b. CD-ROM drive
- ❏ c. USB port
- ❏ d. IrDA port

Quick Answer: **55**
Detailed Answer: **65**

8. What must occur in order for a PC Card (PCMCIA) to work properly?

- ❏ a. TCP/IP must be disabled.
- ❏ b. COM3 must be disabled.
- ❏ c. A jumper must be set on the motherboard.
- ❏ d. The system's PC Card enablers must be loaded.

Quick Answer: **55**
Detailed Answer: **65**

9. What is the most common repair for a failed LCD monitor?

- ❏ a. Replace the signal cable.
- ❏ b. Replace the LCD panel.
- ❏ c. Demagnetize the LCD screen.
- ❏ d. Replace the computer.

Quick Answer: **55**
Detailed Answer: **65**

10. What functions are performed by the external power supply of a portable computer system?

- ❏ a. Increase the voltage of commercial power for the computer.
- ❏ b. Convert commercial DC voltage into AC voltage for system usage and battery charging.
- ❏ c. Store commercial power to recharge the battery.
- ❏ d. Convert commercial AC voltage into DC voltage for system usage and battery charging.

Quick Answer: **55**
Detailed Answer: **65**

11. What type of device is designed to extend a notebook computer's expansion bus so that it can be used with a collection of desktop devices, such as an AC power source and full-sized keyboard and CRT monitor, as well as modems, mice, and standard PC port connectors?

- ❏ a. A port replicator
- ❏ b. A docking station
- ❏ c. A portable bus extender
- ❏ d. A backplane

Quick Answer: **55**
Detailed Answer: **65**

. . . .

12. Which power conservation mode typically enabled in portable computers turns off selected components, such as the hard drive and display, until a system event, such as a keyboard entry or a mouse movement occurs?

   ❑   a. Hibernate mode
   ❑   b. Suspend mode
   ❑   c. Standby mode
   ❑   d. Shutdown mode

Quick Answer: **55**
Detailed Answer: **65**

13. In networking terms, a hot spot is _____.

   ❑   a. a communication zone where wireless connectivity can be established
   ❑   b. an electrically active zone where wireless transmissions can experience interference
   ❑   c. an electrically active zone where wireless connectivity is excellent
   ❑   d. a wireless network access zone set up by businesses to enable portable wireless units to access the Internet

Quick Answer: **55**
Detailed Answer: **65**

14. You are trying to determine the best place to locate your desk in a large open office area. You communicate with the office network through a wireless 802.11b PC Card adapter in your notebook computer. There are three different Access Points (APs) positioned more or less equally around the periphery of the office. What is the easiest way to determine where to put your desk?

   ❑   a. Use the power meter in the wireless device's configuration program to view the relative signal strength as you move your portable around the office. Put the desk in the area of the room where the meter shows the highest signal strength.
   ❑   b. Use the power meter in the wireless device's configuration program to view the relative signal strengths of the different APs and then place your desk near the strongest one.
   ❑   c. Use the power meter in the wireless device's configuration program to view the relative signal strengths of the different APs and then configure your notebook card to communicate with the strongest one. You can put the desk anywhere in the office you like.
   ❑   d. Obtain a hand-held power meter to take high-quality samples of the signal strengths produced by the different APs and then configure your wireless card to communicate with the AP that has the highest signal strength. Then place the desk in the area where that AP is strongest.

Quick Answer: **55**
Detailed Answer: **65**

15. Which of the following devices cannot be used to print a document saved in a notebook computer through a standard printer?

   ❑ a. LAN adapter

   ❑ b. Concentrator

   ❑ c. Docking station

   ❑ d. Port replicator

Quick Answer: **55**
Detailed Answer: **65**

16. What is the maximum distance that an 802.11b rated wireless network card should be located away from its designated Access Point?

   ❑ a. 1 mile

   ❑ b. Less than 110 feet

   ❑ c. Less than 500 feet

   ❑ d. Up to 5 miles

Quick Answer: **55**
Detailed Answer: **66**

17. Which of the following steps are required to set up wireless networking on a portable PC? (Select two.)

   ❑ a. Insert the wireless PC Card adapter in a vacant PCMCIA slot.

   ❑ b. Load the OEM drivers for the PC Card adapter into the system.

   ❑ c. Connect the Access Point's signal cable to the notebook.

   ❑ d. Load PC Card socket services enablers in the operating system.

Quick Answer: **55**
Detailed Answer: **66**

18. Before you remove a PC Card device from a PCMCIA slot in a working computer, you should _____.

   ❑ a. Do nothing. PCMCIA devices are hot-swappable and can be removed from the system at any time.

   ❑ b. Open the Device Manager and click on the PC Card node. Then, select the option to disable the PC Card you want to remove.

   ❑ c. Access the Add New Hardware applet in the Control Panel, and start the Add New Hardware Wizard. When the wizard starts, select the option to disable the PC Card device. Then remove the card from the system.

   ❑ d. Click on the PC Card status indicator on the Taskbar and then select the option to stop the operation of the PC Card you want to remove.

Quick Answer: **55**
Detailed Answer: **66**

19. To install the PC Card (PCMCIA) Wizard on a Windows 9x system, you must _____.

Quick Answer: **55**
Detailed Answer: **66**

    ❑   a.   Navigate the Start/Settings/Control Panel path and access the Add New Hardware applet. When the Add New Hardware Wizard starts, select the Details tab. Then simply click on the PC Card component listed in the dialog box.

    ❑   b.   Navigate the Start/Settings/Control Panel path and access the Device Manager in the System applet. Right-click on the PCMCIA node and select the desired PC Card component listed in the dialog box.

    ❑   c.   Navigate the Start/Settings/Control Panel path and access the Add/Remove Programs applet. Click the Windows Setup tab, select a category, and then click on the Details tab. Then simply click on the PC Card component listed in the Add/Remove Programs dialog box.

    ❑   d.   Navigate the Start/Programs/Accessories path and access the Administrative Tools applet. Select the Computer Management option and click on the System node in the MMC. Then simply click on the PC Card component in the list on the right side of the screen.

20. At different times when you are traveling, you need to prevent the PC Card driver from being loaded. To turn off support for a PC Card in a Windows 9x machine, you must _____.

Quick Answer: **55**
Detailed Answer: **66**

    ❑   a.   Access the Add/Remove Hardware Wizard through the Control Panel, double-click on the PC Card controller option, and check the Disable in This Hardware Profile check box option.

    ❑   b.   Access the Device Manager tab and expand the PC Card slot node. Then, double-click the PC Card controller and in the Device usage area, check the Disable in This Hardware Profile check box option.

    ❑   c.   Access the Add/Remove Programs Wizard through the Control Panel, select the PC Card controller option, and check the Disable in This Hardware Profile check box option.

    ❑   d.   Access the System node in the MMC, select the PC Card controller option, and click on the Disable in This Hardware Profile entry.

Quick Check

21. Which of the following options is not a legitimate way in
which the Card Services utility in a Windows 2000–based
portable PC delivers the proper drivers to the PCMCIA card
hot-swapped into the system?

Quick Answer: 55
Detailed Answer: 66

❑ a. The operating system does not recognize the card and
requires that an external driver be loaded.

❑ b. The operating system recognizes the card and has its driver,
but needs to reboot the operating system for the driver to be
loaded.

❑ c. The Windows 2000 PC Card Wizard starts up to guide the
user through the driver installation process.

❑ d. The operating system immediately recognizes the card and
installs the driver without restarting.

22. In a portable PC that has PCMCIA slots, the _____ portion
of the operating system's socket services delivers the correct
device driver for an installed PC Card when it is hot-swapped
into the system.

Quick Answer: 55
Detailed Answer: 66

❑ a. card services

❑ b. Autodetect

❑ c. driver bank

❑ d. Universal PnP

23. The operating system must support the PCMCIA slots at two
levels. What are they?

Quick Answer: 55
Detailed Answer: 66

❑ a. At the BIOS level (built-in BIOS support for PC Cards)

❑ b. At the card level (specific drivers to handle the function of the
particular card installed)

❑ c. At the Device Manager level (a Device Manager version with
support for PC Cards)

❑ d. At the socket level (universal support for all PCMCIA
devices)

24. _____ is a redefined and enhanced 32-bit version of the PC
Card standard whose main purpose is to extend the PCMCIA
bus to higher speeds with more powerful devices, and to provide support of 32-bit I/O and memory data paths.

Quick Answer: 55
Detailed Answer: 66

❑ a. IEEE bus

❑ b. Rambus

❑ c. PCbus

❑ d. Cardbus

25. What type of expansion slot is the defacto standard for note-book PCs?

    ❏   a.   SCSI slots

    ❏   b.   PC Card slots

    ❏   c.   PCI slots

    ❏   d.   ISA slots

Quick Answer: **55**
Detailed Answer: **67**

26. The main objective of portable system manufacturers is to produce portable computers that can travel efficiently. Therefore, they are always striving to _____. (Select all that apply.)

    ❏   a.   create systems that are lighter

    ❏   b.   create systems that have greater computing power

    ❏   c.   create systems that use less energy

    ❏   d.   create systems that are smaller

Quick Answer: **55**
Detailed Answer: **67**

27. What must you do to replace a system board in a given note-book computer model?

    ❏   a.   Obtain an exact replacement for the board being removed.

    ❏   b.   Check the compatibility of the replacement board with the other components in the notebook. This can be accomplished by accessing the portable manufacturer's Web site.

    ❏   c.   Obtain a Flash program for the new BIOS to make sure that it is compatible with the existing architecture of the note-book.

    ❏   d.   Store the contents of the old BIOS configuration on a floppy before changing out the boards. This will permit you to reload your existing settings back into the new system after the installation.

Quick Answer: **55**
Detailed Answer: **67**

28. What type of electrical power does the LCD panel of a note-book computer require?

    ❏   a.   100Hz AC

    ❏   b.   Low-voltage AC

    ❏   c.   100Hz DC

    ❏   d.   Low-voltage DC

Quick Answer: **55**
Detailed Answer: **67**

Objective 1.4: Identify typical IRQs, DMAs, and I/O addresses and procedures for altering these settings when installing and configuring devices.

1. What I/O address range is typically assigned to the video controller BIOS?

   ❏ a. C0000–C7FFF

   ❏ b. C8000–CFFFF

   ❏ c. D0000–D7FFF

   ❏ d. D8000–D8FFF

Quick Answer: **55**
Detailed Answer: **67**

2. You have an older computer with only one IDE controller and you want to add another IDE device. You already have a hard drive and a CD-ROM connected to the controller. How can you add the drive?

   ❏ a. Add a SCSI controller.

   ❏ b. Get an IDE cable with an additional connector on it.

   ❏ c. Connect the hard drive to the extra connector that is also connected to the floppy disk drive.

   ❏ d. Add an IDE controller card to the system.

Quick Answer: **55**
Detailed Answer: **67**

3. What is the IRQ for a floppy disk drive controller?

   ❏ a. IRQ15

   ❏ b. IRQ6

   ❏ c. IRQ10

   ❏ d. IRQ14

Quick Answer: **55**
Detailed Answer: **67**

4. What is the standard address of the primary IDE controller?

   ❏ a. 170

   ❏ b. 168

   ❏ c. 1F0

   ❏ d. 2F0

Quick Answer: **55**
Detailed Answer: **67**

5. What IRQ does the Real-Time Clock use?

   ❏ a. 8

   ❏ b. 5

   ❏ c. 15

   ❏ d. 10

Quick Answer: **55**
Detailed Answer: **67**

6. What is the IRQ typically assigned to COM1?

❑   a.   IRQ1
❑   b.   IRQ2
❑   c.   IRQ3
❑   d.   IRQ4

Quick Answer: **55**
Detailed Answer: **67**

7. In which I/O method does the microprocessor examine the status of the peripheral under program control?

❑   a.   Polling
❑   b.   Programmed I/O
❑   c.   Interrupt-driven I/O
❑   d.   DMA

Quick Answer: **55**
Detailed Answer: **67**

8. Which port normally uses IRQ14?

❑   a.   Primary IDE controller
❑   b.   Serial port
❑   c.   FDD controller
❑   d.   Parallel port

Quick Answer: **55**
Detailed Answer: **68**

9. Which of the following is used by a device to signal the micro-processor for services?

❑   a.   UDMA
❑   b.   ECP
❑   c.   Stop code
❑   d.   IRQ

Quick Answer: **55**
Detailed Answer: **68**

10. The IRQ1 channel is used _____ and cannot be used for other devices.

❑   a.   for the system's internal time-of-day clock
❑   b.   by the system's keyboard receiver
❑   c.   by the floppy disk drive
❑   d.   by the printer for LPT1

Quick Answer: **55**
Detailed Answer: **68**

11. Which IRQ channel would you expect to be servicing an external modem in a PC system that was using a serial mouse in COM1 for input?

❑   a.   IRQ3
❑   b.   IRQ2
❑   c.   IRQ4
❑   d.   IRQ10

Quick Answer: **55**
Detailed Answer: **68**

12. Which IRQ channel is reserved for the Real-Time Clock module in an ATX system?

   □   a.   IRQ0
   □   b.   IRQ9
   □   c.   IRQ8
   □   d.   IRQ1

Quick Answer: **55**
Detailed Answer: **68**

13. Which of the following describes the bit pattern that would appear on the address bus to activate the first serial port?

   □   a.   0111110000
   □   b.   1001111000
   □   c.   1011111000
   □   d.   1111111000

Quick Answer: **55**
Detailed Answer: **68**

14. On which I/O address would you find the primary IDE controller in a PC-compatible system?

   □   a.   070
   □   b.   1F0
   □   c.   170
   □   d.   3F8

Quick Answer: **55**
Detailed Answer: **68**

15. On which I/O address would you find the second IDE controller in a PC-compatible system?

   □   a.   378
   □   b.   070
   □   c.   278
   □   d.   170

Quick Answer: **55**
Detailed Answer: **68**

16. Which standard PC device uses a DMA channel?

   □   a.   FDD
   □   b.   COM1
   □   c.   INTC1
   □   d.   LPT1

Quick Answer: **55**
Detailed Answer: **68**

17. How many DMA channels are there in an AT-compatible system?

   □   a.   2
   □   b.   4
   □   c.   8
   □   d.   16

Quick Answer: **55**
Detailed Answer: **68**

18. What is the standard port address and IRQ for COM2?

- ❏   a.   2F8 and IRQ3
- ❏   b.   3F8 and IRQ4
- ❏   c.   3E8 and IRQ2
- ❏   d.   2E8 and IRQ1

Quick Answer: **55**
Detailed Answer: **68**

19. What is the IRQ for COM1?

- ❏   a.   IRQ2
- ❏   b.   IRQ4
- ❏   c.   IRQ3
- ❏   d.   IRQ1

Quick Answer: **55**
Detailed Answer: **68**

20. A floppy disk drive uses which of the following IRQs?

- ❏   a.   IRQ6
- ❏   b.   IRQ5
- ❏   c.   IRQ2
- ❏   d.   IRQ9

Quick Answer: **55**
Detailed Answer: **68**

21. IRQ4 is normally assigned to _____.

- ❏   a.   the device connected to the LPT2 port
- ❏   b.   the device connected to the LPT1 port
- ❏   c.   the device connected to the COM2 port
- ❏   d.   the device connected to the COM1 port

Quick Answer: **55**
Detailed Answer: **68**

22. Which interrupt is cascaded with IRQ2?

- ❏   a.   IRQ7
- ❏   b.   IRQ9
- ❏   c.   IRQ5
- ❏   d.   IRQ10

Quick Answer: **55**
Detailed Answer: **68**

23. The IRQ0 channel is _____.

- ❏   a.   used by the floppy disk drive and cannot be used for other devices
- ❏   b.   used by the keyboard and cannot be used for other devices
- ❏   c.   used by the system's counter/timer clock and cannot be used for other devices that are open and can be used for any device requiring an IRQ channel
- ❏   d.   open and can be used for any device requiring an IRQ channel

Quick Answer: **55**
Detailed Answer: **69**

24. What is the maximum capacity of a double-sided, double-density 3.5" floppy disk?

- ❑ a. 1.44MB
- ❑ b. 1.2MB
- ❑ c. 720kB
- ❑ d. 2.88MB

Quick Answer: **55**
Detailed Answer: **69**

25. Which interrupt request channels are available for external use?

- ❑ a. IRQ 0–7, 14–15
- ❑ b. IRQ 3–7, 9–12, 14–15
- ❑ c. IRQ 0–15
- ❑ d. IRQ 1–4, 9–11

Quick Answer: **55**
Detailed Answer: **69**

26. What does the computer system typically use to stop the processes of the microprocessor so that attention can be given to the demands of a particular device?

- ❑ a. NMI
- ❑ b. ATA
- ❑ c. ATX
- ❑ d. IRQ

Quick Answer: **55**
Detailed Answer: **69**

27. Which two of the following system board–based conditions will create an NMI type of interrupt in the system?

- ❑ a. A Parity Check (PCK) error in the system's DRAM memory
- ❑ b. When an active IO Channel Check (IOCHCK) signal is received from an adapter card located in one of the board's expansion slots
- ❑ c. IRQ conflict between devices
- ❑ d. Overvoltage of the system board

Quick Answer: **55**
Detailed Answer: **69**

28. Which standard system device uses IRQ6?

- ❑ a. The parallel printer port
- ❑ b. The keyboard
- ❑ c. The system board's DRAM Refresh circuitry
- ❑ d. Floppy-disk drives

Quick Answer: **55**
Detailed Answer: **69**

29. You are installing a new system board and operating system in an older machine and find that it uses an ISA modem for dial-up operations. What must you do to install this device in the system?

Quick Answer: **55**
Detailed Answer: **69**

- ❑ a. Install the ISA modem and reserve system resource settings for it directly through the operating system.
- ❑ b. The old ISA modem will not operate with a modern Pentium/PCI-based system board because of its PnP function. Therefore, you must also upgrade the modem.
- ❑ c. You must access the PnP and PCI Setup screens in the CMOS Setup routine and reserve resources for the modem's configuration.
- ❑ d. Access the modem manufacturer's Web site and try to obtain PnP drivers for the old card so that it can communicate with the new system.

30. Identify the legacy ports found on a typical PC. (Select two.)

Quick Answer: **55**
Detailed Answer: **69**

- ❑ a. SPP Centronics parallel ports
- ❑ b. RS-232C serial ports
- ❑ c. PS/2 mouse and keyboard ports
- ❑ d. Infrared ports

31. What system resources do network adapter cards normally require? (Select all that apply.)

Quick Answer: **55**
Detailed Answer: **69**

- ❑ a. Interrupt request (IRQ) setting
- ❑ b. I/O port address
- ❑ c. DMA address
- ❑ d. Base memory address

32. What action normally accompanies installing an internal modem?

Quick Answer: **55**
Detailed Answer: **69**

- ❑ a. Disabling the second parallel port
- ❑ b. Pushing the reset button on the modem
- ❑ c. Disabling the second onboard COM port
- ❑ d. Rebooting the system

33. How do you configure an ISA LAN card without PnP or jumpers?

Quick Answer: **55**
Detailed Answer: **70**

- ❑ a. Try the card in different ISA slots.
- ❑ b. Use an ISA-to-PCI converter.
- ❑ c. Solder the card.
- ❑ d. Use the manufacturer's users guide.

Objective 1.5: Identify the names, purposes, and performance characteristics, or common peripheral ports, associated cabling, and their connectors.

1. What is an onboard 25-pin female port on an ATX board used for?

  ❑   a.   Video card

  ❑   b.   Parallel port

  ❑   c.   Game drive

  ❑   d.   Mouse

Quick Answer: **55**
Detailed Answer: **70**

2. Which type of system board uses a 5-pin DIN connector for the keyboard?

  ❑   a.   NTX

  ❑   b.   ATX

  ❑   c.   PC-AT

  ❑   d.   PS/2

Quick Answer: **55**
Detailed Answer: **70**

3. Which of the following combinations are correct? (Select two correct answers.)

  ❑   a.   IRQ3 is the default for COM2 and COM4.

  ❑   b.   IRQ2 is the default for COM1 and COM3.

  ❑   c.   IRQ1 is the default for COM2 and COM4.

  ❑   d.   IRQ4 is the default for COM1 and COM3.

Quick Answer: **55**
Detailed Answer: **70**

4. Which IRQ is the default assignment for the printer attached to LPT1?

  ❑   a.   IRQ13

  ❑   b.   IRQ5

  ❑   c.   IRQ3

  ❑   d.   IRQ7

Quick Answer: **55**
Detailed Answer: **70**

5. What is the IRQ for LPT2?

  ❑   a.   IRQ4

  ❑   b.   IRQ5

  ❑   c.   IRQ9

  ❑   d.   IRQ7

Quick Answer: **55**
Detailed Answer: **70**

6. A 15-pin D-shell connector would probably be used as a
   _____.
   - ❏ a. SCSI port
   - ❏ b. printer port
   - ❏ c. serial port
   - ❏ d. joystick port

Quick Answer: **55**
Detailed Answer: **70**

7. The address typically reserved for a COM4 port is _____.
   - ❏ a. 2E8
   - ❏ b. 3E8
   - ❏ c. 2F8
   - ❏ d. 3F8

Quick Answer: **55**
Detailed Answer: **70**

8. The address typically reserved for a COM1 port is _____.
   - ❏ a. 2E8
   - ❏ b. 3E8
   - ❏ c. 2F8
   - ❏ d. 3F8

Quick Answer: **55**
Detailed Answer: **70**

9. The address typically reserved for a COM2 port is _____.
   - ❏ a. 2E8
   - ❏ b. 3E8
   - ❏ c. 2F8
   - ❏ d. 3F8

Quick Answer: **55**
Detailed Answer: **70**

10. The COM port connectors on a PC are usually _____.
    - ❏ a. 5-pin DINS
    - ❏ b. 15-pin female D-shells
    - ❏ c. 9-pin male D-shells
    - ❏ d. 25-pin female D-shells

Quick Answer: **55**
Detailed Answer: **70**

11. IrLPT is described as an _____.
    - ❏ a. infrared transmission protocol that provides a high-speed serial port interface
    - ❏ b. infrared transmission protocol used between a computer and a printer
    - ❏ c. infrared transmission protocol that allows digital image transfer with image capture devices
    - ❏ d. infrared transmission protocol used as a standard serial port interface

Quick Answer: **55**
Detailed Answer: **70**

12. What is the maximum data transmission speed specified by the standard infrared protocol?

    ❏   a. 4Mbps
    ❏   b. 64Kbps
    ❏   c. 128Kbps
    ❏   d. 115Kbps

13. How far can an IrDA-compliant device be placed away from the IrDA port and be expected to operate efficiently?

    ❏   a. 10 meters
    ❏   b. 5 meters
    ❏   c. 1 meter
    ❏   d. 20 meters

14. How is power supplied to a low-power USB device?

    ❏   a. Through the USB bus
    ❏   b. From an external power supply
    ❏   c. Directly from the computer's interface
    ❏   d. Through a power cable

15. What wiring consideration must you take to create a null modem cable for use with two serial ports?

    ❏   a. Cable must be less than 3 meters long
    ❏   b. Must use a serial twisted-pair (STP) cable
    ❏   c. Must use a parallel cable
    ❏   d. Cable must have crossed-over connections

16. What IRQ is normally used for COM2?

    ❏   a. IRQ4
    ❏   b. IRQ2
    ❏   c. IRQ3
    ❏   d. IRQ5

17. Which IRQ channel and I/O address is typically used for the first serial port?

    ❏   a. IRQ6, 3F0h
    ❏   b. IRQ4, 3F8h
    ❏   c. IRQ7, 378h
    ❏   d. IRQ15, 170h

18. Which IRQ channel and I/O address is typically used for standard parallel printer ports?

❑   a. IRQ6, 3F0h
❑   b. IRQ7, 378h
❑   c. IRQ3, 3F8h
❑   d. IRQ15, 170h

Quick Answer: **55**
Detailed Answer: **71**

19. Which two types of connectors are found on the ends of a standard parallel printer cable?

❑   a. DB-25M
❑   b. DB-9F
❑   c. DB-36M
❑   d. 36-pin Centronics

Quick Answer: **55**
Detailed Answer: **71**

20. What is the maximum recommended length of a standard parallel printer cable?

❑   a. 30 feet
❑   b. 3 feet
❑   c. 20 feet
❑   d. 10 feet

Quick Answer: **55**
Detailed Answer: **71**

21. Which of these connectors can be easily confused in an ATX system? (Select two.)

❑   a. Monitor
❑   b. Keyboard
❑   c. Mouse
❑   d. Joystick

Quick Answer: **55**
Detailed Answer: **71**

22. From the figure depicting an ATX back panel, which of these connectors is a printer port?

Quick Answer: **55**
Detailed Answer: **71**

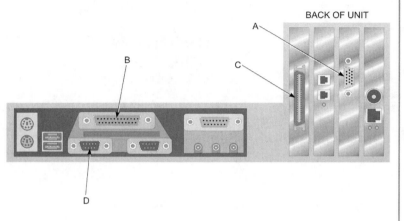

- ❑ a. B
- ❑ b. A
- ❑ c. C
- ❑ d. D

23. From the figure depicting an ATX back panel, which of these connectors is a SCSI port?

Quick Answer: **55**
Detailed Answer: **71**

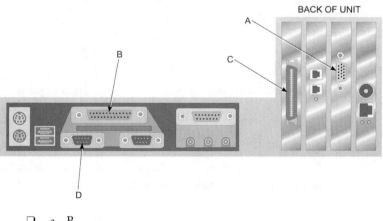

- ❑ a. B
- ❑ b. C
- ❑ c. A
- ❑ d. D

Quick Check

Quick Answer: **56**
Detailed Answer: **71**

24. Which of these connectors is a VGA port?

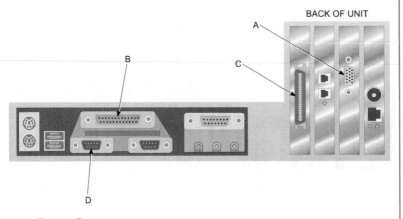

BACK OF UNIT

❑ a. B
❑ b. A
❑ c. C
❑ d. D

25. Which connectors common on both AT- and ATX-style system boards use the same number of pins but a different configuration to prevent them from being confused with each other?

Quick Answer: **56**
Detailed Answer: **71**

❑ a. Keyboard and mouse connectors
❑ b. Serial and VGA ports
❑ c. Game and VGA ports
❑ d. Parallel and serial ports

26. How long can an RS-232C serial cable be?

Quick Answer: **56**
Detailed Answer: **71**

❑ a. 50 feet
❑ b. 25 feet
❑ c. 10 feet
❑ d. 100 feet

27. Which IRQ is the default assignment for the printer attached to LPT2?

Quick Answer: **56**
Detailed Answer: **72**

❑ a. IRQ3
❑ b. IRQ7
❑ c. IRQ5
❑ d. IRQ13

28. Which device normally uses IRQ7?

☐ a. An inkjet printer

☐ b. A modem

☐ c. A floppy disk drive

☐ d. A hard disk drive

Quick Answer: **56**
Detailed Answer: **72**

29. The type of connectors usually associated with speaker and microphone ports are _____.

☐ a. 25-pin, D-shells

☐ b. RCA plugs and jacks

☐ c. RJ-11 jacks and plugs

☐ d. 15-pin, D-shells

Quick Answer: **56**
Detailed Answer: **72**

30. The type of connectors usually associated with audio-in and audio-out ports are _____.

☐ a. 15-pin, D-shells

☐ b. 25-pin, D-shells

☐ c. RJ-11 jacks and plugs

☐ d. RCA plugs and jacks

Quick Answer: **56**
Detailed Answer: **72**

31. Which peripheral connections can be confused in an ATX system?

☐ a. Modem, network

☐ b. Mouse, keyboard

☐ c. Printer, RCA

☐ d. Video, game port

Quick Answer: **56**
Detailed Answer: **72**

32. When selecting a mouse for a particular computer system, what is the most important consideration?

☐ a. The type of interface the mouse employs

☐ b. The length of the mouse cord

☐ c. The type of drivers that come with the mouse

☐ d. The number of buttons the mouse has

Quick Answer: **56**
Detailed Answer: **72**

. . . .

33. A user needs to connect a FireWire-compatible video camera with his workstation. However, before he requests a purchase for all required devices, he wants to make sure that the cable segment will be long enough so that he can place the video camera on a tripod in a specific place at his office, and still be connected to the workstation. Which of the following is the maximum segment length for an IEEE-1394 connection?

- ❏ a. 14 feet
- ❏ b. 20 feet
- ❏ c. 30 feet
- ❏ d. 63 feet

Quick Answer: **56**
Detailed Answer: **72**

Objective 1.6: Identify proper procedures for installing and configuring common IDE devices.

Choose the appropriate installation or configuration sequences in given scenarios. Recognize the associated cables.

1. How can you differentiate between an ATA-33 and an ATA-66 IDE cable?

- ❏ a. Cable width
- ❏ b. Number of conductors
- ❏ c. Connector style
- ❏ d. Connector color

Quick Answer: **56**
Detailed Answer: **72**

2. Which of these items is supported by BIOS?

- ❏ a. IDE drive
- ❏ b. Mouse
- ❏ c. Printer
- ❏ d. Scanner

Quick Answer: **56**
Detailed Answer: **72**

3. An ATAPI interface refers to which type of device?

- ❏ a. Printer
- ❏ b. CD-ROM
- ❏ c. Modem
- ❏ d. Monitor

Quick Answer: **56**
Detailed Answer: **72**

4. One advantage offered by the EIDE interface is _____.

- ❏ a. the capability to connect four HDDs in a row
- ❏ b. compatibility with SCSI devices
- ❏ c. compatibility with the ATAPI interface
- ❏ d. the capability to connect four printers in a row

Quick Answer: **56**
Detailed Answer: **72**

5. If a system contains one master and one slave hard drive, and each drive has been partitioned into two equal-sized drives, the logical assignment for the primary partition of the slave drive is _____.

Quick Answer: **56**
Detailed Answer: **72**

- ❑   a. drive C:
- ❑   b. drive D:
- ❑   c. drive E:
- ❑   d. drive F:

6. When installing an IDE drive in a system, which of the following jumper settings do not apply?

Quick Answer: **56**
Detailed Answer: **72**

- ❑   a. Cable Select
- ❑   b. Slave
- ❑   c. Master
- ❑   d. Terminal

7. How is IDE support provided for system boards that have integrated IDE controllers?

Quick Answer: **56**
Detailed Answer: **73**

- ❑   a. Through an installed driver
- ❑   b. Through the BIOS firmware
- ❑   c. Through the operating system
- ❑   d. Through an installed application

8. What distinctive feature enables you to quickly identify an Ultra ATA-66 interface cable?

Quick Answer: **56**
Detailed Answer: **73**

- ❑   a. The cable has 40 wires.
- ❑   b. The cable is blue.
- ❑   c. The cable has 80 wires.
- ❑   d. The connectors are blue.

9. Which part of the system is responsible for assigning drive letters for IDE drives?

Quick Answer: **56**
Detailed Answer: **73**

- ❑   a. Operating system
- ❑   b. User
- ❑   c. IDE controller
- ❑   d. BIOS

10. RAID5 is an example of _____.

Quick Answer: **56**
Detailed Answer: **73**

- ❑   a. Disk striping
- ❑   b. Disk mirroring
- ❑   c. Disk mirroring and duplexing
- ❑   d. Disk striping with parity

11. If you are working on an older Pentium system board that
    supports a single IDE connector, how can you install a large
    HDD, a CD-ROM drive, and an IDE tape drive?

    ❑   a. Install a SCSI adapter card.
    ❑   b. Install an IDE adapter card.
    ❑   c. This type of motherboard can only use one IDE device.
    ❑   d. This type of motherboard can only use two IDE devices.

Quick Answer: **56**
Detailed Answer: **73**

12. How many devices can an ATX Pentium system board support
    if it employs EIDE technology with ATA-2 enhancements?

    ❑   a. 2
    ❑   b. 4
    ❑   c. 8
    ❑   d. 16

Quick Answer: **56**
Detailed Answer: **73**

13. RAID 0 is also known as _____.

    ❑   a. Duplexing
    ❑   b. Mirroring
    ❑   c. Striped Disk Array
    ❑   d. Parity

Quick Answer: **56**
Detailed Answer: **73**

14. On an ATX system board that integrates the EIDE interface
    connection into the board, how many devices can be attached
    to each interface connection?

    ❑   a. 2
    ❑   b. 1
    ❑   c. 3
    ❑   d. 4

Quick Answer: **56**
Detailed Answer: **73**

Objective 1.7: Identify proper procedures for installing and configuring common SCSI devices.

Choose the appropriate installation or configuration sequences in
given scenarios. Recognize the associated cables.

1. If a 2-pin jumper block on an adapter card is used to represent
   a binary digit, how many numbers can be represented by a
   3-jumper block combination?

   ❑   a. 3
   ❑   b. 5
   ❑   c. 8
   ❑   d. 10

Quick Answer: **56**
Detailed Answer: **73**

2. Which of the following connectors is adopted in SCSI for 32-bit transfers?

   ❑ a. 25-pin DB

   ❑ b. 15-pin Centronics

   ❑ c. 50-pin Centronics

   ❑ d. 68-pin Centronics

Quick Answer: **56**
Detailed Answer: **73**

3. What are the priority assignments given to Wide SCSI devices?

   ❑ a. 0=highest priority, 15=lowest priority

   ❑ b. 0=lowest priority, 15=highest priority

   ❑ c. 1=lowest priority, 14=highest priority

   ❑ d. 1=highest priority, 14=lowest priority

Quick Answer: **56**
Detailed Answer: **73**

4. What is the major difference between internal and external SCSI devices?

   ❑ a. External devices use BERG connectors, whereas internal devices use A and B cable connectors.

   ❑ b. External devices use SCSI IDs above 7, whereas internal SCSI devices use IDs between 0 and 7.

   ❑ c. External devices require additional power supplies, whereas internal devices use the computer's options power connectors.

   ❑ d. External devices must be configured manually, but internal devices can be configured through the system's PnP process.

Quick Answer: **56**
Detailed Answer: **73**

5. What are the SCSI ID numbers that can be specified by a 3-position, 2-pin jumper block?

   ❑ a. 0–8

   ❑ b. 1–9

   ❑ c. 1–8

   ❑ d. 0–7

Quick Answer: **56**
Detailed Answer: **73**

6. What is the maximum number of devices that can be supported by a Wide Fast SCSI controller?

   ❑ a. 7

   ❑ b. 8

   ❑ c. 12

   ❑ d. 15

Quick Answer: **56**
Detailed Answer: **74**

7. A SCSI chain must be terminated at _____.

   ❑ a. the last device in the chain

   ❑ b. the SCSI adapter

   ❑ c. either end

   ❑ d. both ends

Quick Answer: **56**
Detailed Answer: **74**

8. The maximum recommended cable length of a complete SCSI chain is _____ feet.

- ❑ a. 50
- ❑ b. 30
- ❑ c. 20
- ❑ d. 10

9. The maximum number of devices that can be connected on a standard SCSI-1 host adapter is _____.

- ❑ a. 10
- ❑ b. 8
- ❑ c. 15
- ❑ d. 16

10. Fast SCSI-2 ports use _____.

- ❑ a. a 34-pin connector
- ❑ b. a 40-pin connector
- ❑ c. a 50-pin connector
- ❑ d. a 68-pin connector

11. SCSI-2 ports use _____.

- ❑ a. a 34-pin external interface
- ❑ b. a 40-pin external interface
- ❑ c. a 50-pin internal interface
- ❑ d. a 68-pin internal interface

12. Which option is not true concerning SCSI controller identifiers?

- ❑ a. ID #1 is reserved for the controller.
- ❑ b. ID #0 is reserved for the first (primary) hard drive.
- ❑ c. It is possible to have eight SCSI devices including the controller connected together.
- ❑ d. It is possible to have six external SCSI devices connected together.

13. If a single standard SCSI interface can support up to seven SCSI devices, how many SCSI devices can be installed using two SCSI cards?

- ❑ a. 14
- ❑ b. 7
- ❑ c. Zero, because two SCSI interfaces cannot exist in the same system
- ❑ d. 49

14. When two external SCSI drives are added to a unit, _____.

   ❑   a.   the second drive is connected to the HDD connection of the first drive

   ❑   b.   the first drive is connected to the SCSI connection of the second drive

   ❑   c.   the second drive is connected to the SCSI connection of the first drive

   ❑   d.   the first drive is connected to the HDD connection of the second drive

Quick Answer: **56**
Detailed Answer: **74**

15. What is the maximum permissible length for a Fast SCSI daisy chain?

   ❑   a.   10 feet
   ❑   b.   15 feet
   ❑   c.   20 feet
   ❑   d.   25 feet

Quick Answer: **56**
Detailed Answer: **74**

16. How many SCSI devices can be attached to a Wide SCSI host adapter?

   ❑   a.   16
   ❑   b.   8
   ❑   c.   7
   ❑   d.   15

Quick Answer: **56**
Detailed Answer: **74**

17. What is the permissible length for a standard SCSI cable segment?

   ❑   a.   6 feet
   ❑   b.   3 feet
   ❑   c.   9 feet
   ❑   d.   12 feet

Quick Answer: **56**
Detailed Answer: **74**

18. What is the maximum permissible length for a standard SCSI chain including the internal cable?

   ❑   a.   20 feet
   ❑   b.   15 feet
   ❑   c.   10 feet
   ❑   d.   25 feet

Quick Answer: **56**
Detailed Answer: **74**

19. When installing SCSI devices in a system, which device or devices should be terminated?

   ❑   a.   Only the last SCSI device.
   ❑   b.   All SCSI devices.
   ❑   c.   The first and last SCSI devices.
   ❑   d.   SCSI devices do not require termination.

Quick Answer: **56**
Detailed Answer: **74**

20. What is the maximum length for an external standard SCSI daisy-chain?

   ❑ a. 20 feet
   ❑ b. 10 feet
   ❑ c. 3 feet
   ❑ d. 15 feet

Quick Answer: **56**
Detailed Answer: **75**

21. Which form of SCSI termination provides the best form of termination for a single-ended SCSI bus?

   ❑ a. Passive termination
   ❑ b. Active termination
   ❑ c. Forced-perfect termination
   ❑ d. Manual termination

Quick Answer: **56**
Detailed Answer: **75**

22. After installing a scanner to the end of a SCSI daisy-chain, you discover that both the scanner and your SCSI CD-ROM drive have stopped working. What is likely to be the problem?

   ❑ a. The scanner is using an incompatible protocol.
   ❑ b. Both devices are using the same ID number.
   ❑ c. Both devices are set to slave.
   ❑ d. The ribbon cable is bad.

Quick Answer: **56**
Detailed Answer: **75**

23. Which of the following are features of LVD SCSI interfaces and cables? (Select all that apply.)

   ❑ a. 3-volt (V) operation
   ❑ b. Lower power consumption
   ❑ c. Higher speed
   ❑ d. Greater transmission distances

Quick Answer: **56**
Detailed Answer: **75**

24. Which SCSI ID is typically used for the system's SCSI adapter?

   ❑ a. SCSI-7
   ❑ b. SCSI-6
   ❑ c. SCSI-0
   ❑ d. SCSI-8

Quick Answer: **56**
Detailed Answer: **75**

25. Which SCSI ID is typically used for the system's internal hard disk drive?

   ❑ a. SCSI-1
   ❑ b. SCSI-0
   ❑ c. SCSI-7
   ❑ d. SCSI-8

Quick Answer: **56**
Detailed Answer: **75**

26. Which of these standard SCSI devices has the highest priority?

   ❏ a. SCSI-6
   ❏ b. SCSI-1
   ❏ c. SCSI-7
   ❏ d. SCSI-0

Quick Answer: **56**
Detailed Answer: **75**

27. How are SCSI devices identified and differentiated from each other?

   ❏ a. Jumpers that determine master/slave/single status
   ❏ b. ID number assigned to the device
   ❏ c. Order in which they are connected on the cable
   ❏ d. Drive letter assigned to the device

Quick Answer: **56**
Detailed Answer: **75**

28. How many devices can be daisy-chained on a single standard SCSI controller?

   ❏ a. 15
   ❏ b. 2
   ❏ c. 8
   ❏ d. 7

Quick Answer: **56**
Detailed Answer: **75**

29. Which of the following is not a valid SCSI connector?

   ❏ a. 68-pin Centronics
   ❏ b. 25-pin DB
   ❏ c. 50-pin Centronics
   ❏ d. 34-pin Centronics

Quick Answer: **56**
Detailed Answer: **75**

30. Which of the following connectors is used for an internal SCSI ribbon cable?

   ❏ a. 25-pin
   ❏ b. 48-pin
   ❏ c. 50-pin
   ❏ d. 68-pin

Quick Answer: **56**
Detailed Answer: **75**

31. Which of the following interfaces uses a 50-pin cable?

   ❏ a. An EIDE interface
   ❏ b. An internal SCSI interface
   ❏ c. A VESA bus
   ❏ d. An LPT port

Quick Answer: **56**
Detailed Answer: **76**

32. Which of the following types of SCSI signal specification uses a core voltage of 3.3V?

- ❑ a. Single-edged
- ❑ b. HVD
- ❑ c. Ultra Wide
- ❑ d. LVD

Objective 1.8: Identify proper procedures for installing and configuring common peripheral devices.

1. What are the default color depth and refresh rate of a VGA adapter?

- ❑ a. 8-bit, 30Hz
- ❑ b. 16-bit, 60Hz
- ❑ c. 24-bit, 80Hz
- ❑ d. 32-bit, 90Hz

2. What is the standard resolution of a VGA card?

- ❑ a. 640×480
- ❑ b. 800×600
- ❑ c. 1,024×768
- ❑ d. 1,280×1,024

3. What is the function of an Infrared Monitor?

- ❑ a. It controls the functions of the device that is communicating via the IrDA port.
- ❑ b. It identifies the type of device that is communicating via the IrDA port.
- ❑ c. It is a standard video monitor attached to the computer via an IrDA port.
- ❑ d. It alerts you when an infrared device is within range.

4. Where are IrDA operations first enabled?

- ❑ a. Infrared Monitor
- ❑ b. CMOS Setup
- ❑ c. Windows Control Panel
- ❑ d. On the system board

5. How do you install an IrDA device that is not PnP capable?

   ❑ a. Right-click the desktop and select Enable Wireless Link in the pop-up menu.

   ❑ b. Use the Infrared icon in the Control Panel.

   ❑ c. Use the Add New Hardware Wizard in the Control Panel.

   ❑ d. Right-click the Infrared icon in the Taskbar and select Enable Wireless Link from the pop-up menu.

Quick Answer: **56**
Detailed Answer: **76**

6. How does the Windows operating system alert the user that an infrared device is within range to communicate with the host computer?

   ❑ a. An Infrared device window pops up.

   ❑ b. An Infrared device icon appears in My Computer.

   ❑ c. An Infrared device icon appears in the Control Panel.

   ❑ d. An Infrared device icon appears on the Taskbar.

Quick Answer: **56**
Detailed Answer: **76**

7. A technician is asked to purchase a digital camera for her company. Her main concern is whether the digital camera can connect to the workstation properly. Which of the following connections cannot be used to connect a digital camera to a workstation?

   ❑ a. Parallel ports

   ❑ b. PS/2 ports

   ❑ c. USB ports

   ❑ d. IEEE-1394 FireWire ports

Quick Answer: **56**
Detailed Answer: **76**

8. How does a dot-matrix printer place characters on a page?

   ❑ a. Magnetically controlled pins place dots on the paper.

   ❑ b. Magnetically charged ink particles are attracted to an ionized form on the paper.

   ❑ c. It squirts precisely controlled drops of ink onto the paper.

   ❑ d. Fully formed metal characters force ink from a ribbon onto the paper.

Quick Answer: **56**
Detailed Answer: **76**

9. You are installing a scanner for a friend. The installation instructions call for you to connect the parallel printer to the scanner, which in turn connects to the parallel port of the host computer. However, there is no signal cable in the scanner box and your friend says he has not seen it. You reinstall the old printer cable that was originally used with just the printer and the scanner will not work. What should you do?

   ❑ a. Obtain an IEEE-1284–compliant cable

   ❑ b. Return the scanner

   ❑ c. Obtain an RS-232C–compliant cable

   ❑ d. Obtain an IEEE-1394–compliant cable

Quick Answer: **56**
Detailed Answer: **76**

10. What additional piece of hardware is typically required to install an external modem that is not associated with installing an internal modem?

   ❑   a. An IEEE-1394–compliant signal cable

   ❑   b. An IEEE-1284–compliant signal cable

   ❑   c. An RJ-45 telephone cable

   ❑   d. An AC power supply adapter

Quick Answer: **56**
Detailed Answer: **76**

11. Which of the following modem types is not considered a high-speed broadband communications device?

   ❑   a. A DSL modem

   ❑   b. An ISDN modem

   ❑   c. An analog modem

   ❑   d. A cable modem

Quick Answer: **56**
Detailed Answer: **77**

12. The default value for VGA/PCI-compliant video adapters is _____.

   ❑   a. 800×600 using 16 colors

   ❑   b. 640×480 using 16 colors

   ❑   c. 1,024×768 using 256 colors

   ❑   d. 600×800 using 256 colors

Quick Answer: **56**
Detailed Answer: **77**

13. What type of device would you expect to find in an AGP slot?

   ❑   a. SCSI card

   ❑   b. AMR card

   ❑   c. Network card

   ❑   d. Video card

Quick Answer: **56**
Detailed Answer: **77**

Objective 1.9: Identify procedures to optimize PC operations in specific situations.

1. You are installing an OEM processor upgrade that calls for you to install a faster Pentium III processor in an existing system. While OEM processors do not include a fan and heat-sink unit, you suspect that you need to upgrade the system's cooling capabilities to accommodate the faster processor. However, you are not sure which fan and heat-sink module needs to be installed. What should you do to ensure proper cooling for this processor?

   ❑ a. Flash the BIOS to upgrade it for the new processor. The Flash program contains updated fan control information for the new processor.

   ❑ b. Because both processors are Pentium IIIs, there is no need to change the fan unit. The BIOS will adapt to the new processor automatically.

   ❑ c. Install the fastest compatible fan unit available. The BIOS will automatically adjust the fan speed to compensate for any additional heat and you will have ensured that enough cooling capability is available.

   ❑ d. You must research and locate a proper cooling system for this processor by matching its operating temperature specification to the fan unit.

   Quick Answer: **56**
   Detailed Answer: **77**

2. After upgrading a multiple-processor system board by installing an additional processor, the system automatically enters the CMOS Setup utility upon bootup. What is the most likely cause for this?

   ❑ a. The terminating resistor pack should have been removed from the vacant processor socket before installing the new processor.

   ❑ b. This is a typical response to restarting the system with additional microprocessors installed.

   ❑ c. The additional processor is most likely outside the acceptable stepping range of the original processor, creating an error condition that needs additional system configuration.

   ❑ d. When this action occurs, it indicates that the BIOS has not been updated to accommodate the new processor. Therefore, the system opens the CMOS Setup utility on startup.

   Quick Answer: **56**
   Detailed Answer: **77**

. . . .

3. You have been asked to upgrade a system board in a network server by installing additional processors on the board. There are two empty processor sockets on the system board. What do you need to do to perform this upgrade? (Select two.)

Quick Answer: **56**
Detailed Answer: **77**

- ❑ a. You should check the production run number (stepping level) of the processor to ensure that it is within one production run of its companion processors.
- ❑ b. You should install terminators in the vacant sockets to prepare them for the new processors.
- ❑ c. Perform a BIOS upgrade.
- ❑ d. Run the SNMP utility to verify the operation of the multiple processor arrangement.

4. You replace an ATA-33 drive with a new ATA-100 drive. What is the maximum data throughput when connecting an ATA-100 hard disk drive with the current 40-wire IDE cable?

Quick Answer: **56**
Detailed Answer: **77**

- ❑ a. 33Mbps
- ❑ b. 10Mbps
- ❑ c. 66Mbps
- ❑ d. Will not work together

5. An IDE hard drive interface that does not contain an enhanced BIOS has a maximum disk partition size of _____.

Quick Answer: **56**
Detailed Answer: **77**

- ❑ a. 504MB
- ❑ b. 1GB
- ❑ c. 2GB
- ❑ d. 32MB

6. Which of the following is the best way to optimize your cooling system?

Quick Answer: **57**
Detailed Answer: **78**

- ❑ a. Use fewer devices.
- ❑ b. Drill holes in the side panels.
- ❑ c. Remove the side panels.
- ❑ d. Add additional case fans to increase airflow through the computer.

7. Which of the following can be done to reduce the risk of thermal failure caused by the accumulation of dust particles? (Select two correct answers.)

Quick Answer: **57**
Detailed Answer: **78**

- ❑ a. Remove the side panels from the chassis.
- ❑ b. Optimize the speed of the fan.
- ❑ c. Replace the fans with foam filters.
- ❑ d. Install foam filters at chassis openings.

8. How can adding additional processors optimize the overall system use?

Quick Answer: **57**
Detailed Answer: **78**

- ❑ a. By lowering the temperature of the hard drive
- ❑ b. By distributing the processing load
- ❑ c. By increasing bus speeds
- ❑ d. By increasing CD-ROM speeds

9. Which of the following will improve the performance of a newly installed adapter card?

Quick Answer: **57**
Detailed Answer: **78**

- ❑ a. Setting the IRQ to 7
- ❑ b. Increasing the voltage by 5
- ❑ c. Obtaining the latest drivers
- ❑ d. Configuring it to COM1

10. What can you do to enhance the speed of a video card that runs slow when used for a long period of time?

Quick Answer: **57**
Detailed Answer: **78**

- ❑ a. Increase the voltage level.
- ❑ b. Remove one of the chassis fans.
- ❑ c. Add an additional fan to the video card or the system board.
- ❑ d. Remove the heat sinks.

Objective 1.10: Determine the issues that must be considered when upgrading a PC.

In a given scenario, determine when and how to upgrade system components.

1. What is the first thing that should be done prior to flashing a BIOS?

Quick Answer: **57**
Detailed Answer: **78**

- ❑ a. Write down bus frequency.
- ❑ b. Back up the hard drive.
- ❑ c. Make a backup of the BIOS on a floppy disk.
- ❑ d. Reboot the computer.

2. How can you upgrade an older computer system that uses a nonremovable, non-Flash ROM BIOS?

Quick Answer: **57**
Detailed Answer: **78**

- ❑ a. Replace the motherboard.
- ❑ b. Install more RAM.
- ❑ c. Replace the CPU.
- ❑ d. Install a larger hard drive.

. . . .

3. When upgrading the BIOS, which of the following is an important consideration?

Quick Answer: **57**
Detailed Answer: **78**

❏   a. Writing the new ROM BIOS
❏   b. Getting the latest version
❏   c. Getting the same version
❏   d. Erasing the existing ROM BIOS

4. What is the most important step to be taken before upgrading the BIOS in a system?

Quick Answer: **57**
Detailed Answer: **78**

❏   a. Install all updates to your operating system.
❏   b. Get the latest version of the BIOS from the manufacturer.
❏   c. Remove the BIOS IC from the motherboard.
❏   d. Make a backup copy of your BIOS data on a floppy disk and record all the CMOS configuration settings.

5. If your BIOS does not have the capability to be altered electronically (flashed), how can you upgrade the system's microprocessor to a newer, faster version?

Quick Answer: **57**
Detailed Answer: **78**

❏   a. Set the core voltage, bus frequency, and bus ration manually using the jumpers.
❏   b. Download an appropriate patch to the operating system from the manufacturer's Web site.
❏   c. Replace the ROM BIOS IC with an upgraded one from the manufacturer.
❏   d. Use ultraviolet light to erase the ROM BIOS IC.

6. A Flash BIOS is used for _____.

Quick Answer: **57**
Detailed Answer: **79**

❏   a. resetting the default BIOS settings
❏   b. upgrading the BIOS without additional hardware
❏   c. inputting temporary BIOS settings for troubleshooting purposes
❏   d. making newer motherboards backward compatible

7. Under what conditions would you normally expect to upgrade the system's BIOS?

Quick Answer: **57**
Detailed Answer: **79**

❏   a. When you forget the CMOS password
❏   b. When power comes on but the screen stays blank
❏   c. When you upgrade the microprocessor
❏   d. When the battery goes dead

8. To upgrade the BIOS in a computer that uses a socketed, non-reprogrammable ROM BIOS, you must _____.
   - ❏ a. upgrade the CPU
   - ❏ b. install faster RAM
   - ❏ c. buy a larger monitor
   - ❏ d. change the ROM BIOS IC

Quick Answer: **57**
Detailed Answer: **79**

9. Which PCMCIA slot supports a removable hard drive?
   - ❏ a. Type I
   - ❏ b. Type II
   - ❏ c. Type III
   - ❏ d. Type II and Type III

Quick Answer: **57**
Detailed Answer: **79**

10. A Type III PCMCIA card is _____ thick.
    - ❏ a. 3.3mm
    - ❏ b. 5.0mm
    - ❏ c. 7.5mm
    - ❏ d. 10.5mm

Quick Answer: **57**
Detailed Answer: **79**

11. A Type II PCMCIA card is _____ thick.
    - ❏ a. 3.3mm
    - ❏ b. 5.0mm
    - ❏ c. 7.5mm
    - ❏ d. 10.5mm

Quick Answer: **57**
Detailed Answer: **79**

12. A Type I PCMCIA card is _____ thick.
    - ❏ a. 7.5mm
    - ❏ b. 5.0mm
    - ❏ c. 3.3mm
    - ❏ d. 10.5mm

Quick Answer: **57**
Detailed Answer: **79**

13. A _____PCMCIA card is 5mm thick.
    - ❏ a. Type IV
    - ❏ b. Type I
    - ❏ c. Type III
    - ❏ d. Type II

Quick Answer: **57**
Detailed Answer: **79**

14. How many Type II PC Cards can normally be installed in a typical portable computer?
    - ❏ a. 1
    - ❏ b. 2
    - ❏ c. 3
    - ❏ d. 4

Quick Answer: **57**
Detailed Answer: **79**

. . . .

15. A _____ PCMCIA card is 10.5mm thick.

   ❑   a.   Type II
   ❑   b.   Type I
   ❑   c.   Type III
   ❑   d.   Type IV

Quick Answer: **57**
Detailed Answer: **79**

16. Which type of PC Card would normally be used for a PCMCIA modem?

   ❑   a.   Type IV
   ❑   b.   Type I
   ❑   c.   Type III
   ❑   d.   Type II

Quick Answer: **57**
Detailed Answer: **79**

17. You have three PCMCIA cards: a Flash memory card, a modem, and a PC Card hard drive. Which of these cards can fit in the slots of a notebook computer that includes two standard Type II slots?

   ❑   a.   Flash memory, hard drive
   ❑   b.   Modem, hard drive
   ❑   c.   Flash memory, modem
   ❑   d.   Only the modem

Quick Answer: **57**
Detailed Answer: **79**

18. _____ are power-generating devices that use electrochemical reactions between hydrogen and oxygen to produce electrical power.

   ❑   a.   Fuel cells
   ❑   b.   Anhydrous batteries
   ❑   c.   Ni-MH batteries
   ❑   d.   Li-ion batteries

Quick Answer: **57**
Detailed Answer: **79**

19. Which of the following power sources uses electrochemical reactions between hydrogen and oxygen to produce electrical power?

   ❑   a.   Lithium batteries
   ❑   b.   Fuel cells
   ❑   c.   NiCad batteries
   ❑   d.   Solar power batteries

Quick Answer: **57**
Detailed Answer: **80**

20. Which PCMCIA card specification is intended primarily for use with removable hard drives?

   ❑   a.   Cardbus cards
   ❑   b.   Type I cards
   ❑   c.   Type II cards
   ❑   d.   Type III cards

Quick Answer: **57**
Detailed Answer: **80**

21. You want to upgrade your existing computer to play exotic games. In particular, you want to install a dual processor system board, additional high-speed RAM, a high-end video display card, and a Windows XP Professional operating system. Your current system is using a 200W power supply, a Pentium II microprocessor, 128MB of SD-RAM, a 30GB EIDE drive, and a 52X CD-ROM drive. What other equipment needs to be upgraded to reach the desired function for this system?

 - ❑ a. A faster HDD unit is needed.
 - ❑ b. A larger power supply is needed.
 - ❑ c. A larger HDD unit is needed.
 - ❑ d. A DVD drive should be installed to replace the CD-ROM drive.

22. What specification must you observe when upgrading a power supply?

 - ❑ a. Current
 - ❑ b. Wattage
 - ❑ c. Voltage
 - ❑ d. Resistance

Quick Check Answer Key

Objective 1.1

1. a
2. a
3. b
4. b
5. d
6. a
7. b
8. a
9. c
10. c
11. b
12. a
13. d
14. c
15. d
16. a
17. b
18. c
19. d
20. d
21. c
22. b
23. a
24. c
25. d
26. b

27. b, c
28. d
29. b
30. a, b
31. c
32. a
33. d
34. d
35. b
36. c
37. b
38. c
39. b
40. b
41. b
42. c

Objective 1.2

1. b
2. d
3. a
4. b
5. c
6. b
7. b
8. a
9. c
10. b

11. d
12. c
13. b
14. b
15. d
16. a
17. c
18. c
19. d
20. d
21. d
22. a
23. c
24. c
25. c
26. a
27. d
28. b
29. a
30. b
31. b

Objective 1.3

1. b
2. a, d
3. a
4. b
5. d

6. c

7. a

8. d

9. b

10. d

11. b

12. c

13. d

14. a

15. b

16. c

17. a, b

18. d

19. c

20. b

21. c

22. a

23. b, d

24. d

25. b

26. a, c, d

27. a

28. d

Objective 1.4

1. a

2. d

3. b

4. c

5. a

6. d

7. a

8. a

9. d

10. b

11. a

12. c

13. d

14. b

15. d

16. a

17. c

18. a

19. b

20. a

21. d

22. b

23. c

24. c

25. b

26. d

27. a, b

28. d

29. c

30. a, b

31. a, b, d

32. c

33. d

Objective 1.5

1. b

2. c

3. a, d

4. d

5. b

6. d

7. a

8. d

9. c

10. c

11. b

12. d

13. c

14. c

15. d

16. c

17. b

18. b

19. a, d

20. d

21. b, c

22. a

23. b

24. b

25. c

26. d

27. c

28. a

29. b

30. d

31. b

32. a

33. a

Objective 1.6

1. b

2. a

3. b

4. c

5. b

6. d

7. b

8. c

9. a

10. d

11. b

12. b

13. c

14. a

Objective 1.7

1. c

2. d

3. b

4. c

5. d

6. d

7. d

8. c

9. b

10. c

11. c

12. a

13. a

14. c

15. a

16. d

17. b

18. a

19. c

20. d

21. c

22. b

23. a, b, c

24. a

25. b

26. c

27. b

28. d

29. d

30. c

31. b

32. d

Objective 1.8

1. b

2. a

3. d

4. b

5. c

6. d

7. b

8. a

9. a

10. d

11. c

12. b

13. d

Objective 1.9

1. d

2. b

3. a, c

4. a

5. a

6. d

7. b, d

8. b

9. c

10. c

17. c

18. a

19. b

20. d

21. b

22. b

Objective 1.10

1. c

2. a

3. b

4. d

5. c

6. b

7. c

8. d

9. c

10. d

11. b

12. c

13. d

14. b

15. c

16. d

Answers and Explanations

Objective 1.1

1. **a.** The monitor's signal cable connects to a 3-row, 15-pin female D-shell connector at the back of the system unit.

2. **a.** In a PC-compatible system, each sector holds 512 bytes of data.

3. **b.** Standard VGA resolution is defined as 720×400 pixels using 16 colors in text mode, and 640×480 pixels using 16 onscreen colors in graphics mode.

4. **b.** The system is reset at startup to a predetermined condition. From this state, it carries out software instructions from its BIOS program. This program is permanently stored in the ROM memory ICs located on the system board.

5. **d.** The Basic Input/Output System (BIOS) program contains the basic instructions for communications between the microprocessor and the various input and output devices in the system. The MBR is a special program used by BIOS to load control programs into RAM.

6. **a.** The ATX system board connector is a 20-pin connector that contains a signal line that the system board can use to turn off the power supply. This power-saving feature is referred to as a soft switch.

7. **b.** In Microsoft systems, each sector holds 512 bytes of data.

8. **a.** Each track on the surface of a magnetic disk is divided into an equal number of equal-sized blocks called sectors. The number of sectors on a track can range from 8 to more than 60, depending on the disk and drive type, and the operating system software used to format it.

9. **c.** The video output connector is a 3-row DB-15 female connector used with analog VGA displays.

10. **c.** PC-AT compatibles featured a rechargeable battery to the system board to maintain the information stored in CMOS when the system was turned off.

11. **b.** The configuration storage area known as CMOS RAM integrates the advanced software configuration function to their chipsets along with the system's Real-Time Clock (RTC) function. The RTC keeps track of time and date information for the system.

12. **a.** Cache memory is a fast RAM system used to hold information that the microprocessor is likely to use.

13. **d.** The system's configuration settings are the system's main method of getting information about what options are installed. They must be set to accurately reflect the actual options being used with the system.

14. **c.** When the system is turned on or reset, the PC begins carrying out software instructions from its BIOS program, which is permanently stored in the ROM BIOS memory IC located on the system board. The information stored in the IC represents all the inherent intelligence that the system has until it can load more data from another source, such as a disk drive or remote server computer.

15. **d.** When a PC is turned on, the system is reset to a starting condition and begins carrying out the software instructions from its BIOS program. First, the BIOS performs POST to verify that the system is operating correctly. Next, it places starting values in the system's programmable devices. This process is called initialization. Finally, the BIOS performs the bootstrap.

16. **a.** The BIOS software (programming) and hardware (the ROM chip) are referred to as firmware. Some I/O devices, such as video and network adapter cards, have additional firmware that act as extensions to the system's BIOS.

17. **b.** The BIOS performs a series of diagnostic tests (called POST, or Power On Self Test) on the system to verify that it is operating correctly. While performing its normal tests and boot-up functions, the BIOS displays an active RAM memory count as it is being tested.

18. **c.** The VGA/SVGA adapter on the back of the computer has a 15-pin, 3-row female D-shell connector.

19. **d.** Traditionally, most external CD-ROM drives have employed SCSI interface connectors.

20. **d.** A typical CD can hold 680MB of programs and data on a single, inexpensive, removable media.

21. **c.** In PC systems, the cable can provide for one or two floppy drives that will automatically be recognized as logical drives A and B by the system. The drive connected to the very end of the cable will be designated as drive A.

22. **b.** In a magnetic disk system, information is stored as magnetized spots arranged in concentric circles around the disk. These circles are referred to as tracks. Each disk track is divided into an equal number of equal-sized blocks called sectors. Sectors generally contain 512 bytes.

23. **a.** A VGA resolution is defined as 640×480 pixels using 16 onscreen colors in graphics mode and 720×400 pixels using 16 colors in text mode.

24. **c.** SVGA is available in the format of up to 1,280×1,024 pixels video controller capabilities. VGA is capable of up to 640×480 pixels. XGA produces up to 1,024×768 resolution. HGA provides 720×348 resolution.

25. **d.** In AT-compatible power supplies, two 6-wire bundles, typically marked P8 and P9, deliver power to the system board. The physical construction of these power connectors is identical. They are designed to plug in to the system board's P1 and P2 power plugs, respectively.

26. **b.** In AT and ATX units, the on/off switch is located on the front panel of the system unit and connected to the power supply by a cable. In the ATX design, a special soft switch line is included that enables the system to shut itself off under control of the system software.

27. **b, c.** **(b)** PCI slots are available in 32 or 64 bits; ISA slots are 16 bits. **(c)** PCI slots are designed shorter.

28. **d.** There are notches and dots on the various ICs that provide important keys when replacing a microprocessor. These notches and dots specify the location of pin 1. This pin must be lined up with the pin 1 notch of the socket.

29. **b.** The microprocessor is the major component of any system board. It can be thought of as the brains of the computer system because it reads, interprets, and executes software instructions, and also carries out arithmetic and logical operations for the system.

30. **a, b.** **(a)** System boards are sometimes referred to as motherboards. **(b)** Another name for system boards is planar boards.

31. **c.** Read-only memory (ROM) contains the computer's permanent startup programs. ROM is nonvolatile. Its contents remain with or without power being applied.

32. **a.** RAM is a volatile type of memory. Its contents disappear when power is removed from the memory.

33. **d.** Dual Inline Memory Modules (DIMMs) are larger 168-pin boards designed to work efficiently with Pentium-class microprocessors. They use special snap-in sockets that are keyed so you cannot install them backward.

34. **d.** The BIOS has three main functions: performing the POST, initializing the system, and seeking and loading an operating system to which it can transfer control.

35. **b.** A monitor with a .28 dot pitch has pixels that are located .28mm apart.

36. **c.** The term Triad is not associated with monitors in any way. A color monitor employs a combination of three color phosphors, that is, red, green, and blue (RGB), arranged in adjacent trios of dots or bars called picture elements, pixels, or PELs.

37. **b.** Resolution can be expressed as a function of how close pixels can be grouped together on the screen. The closer the pixels to one another, the sharper the image. This form of resolution is expressed in terms of dot pitch. A monitor with a .28 dot pitch has pixels that are located .28mm apart.

38. **c.** Color CRTs add a metal grid in front of the phosphor coating called a shadow mask. It ensures that an electron gun assigned to one color doesn't strike a dot of another color.

39. **b.** In most cases, the EIDE connector on the PC-compatible ATX system board is used for internal CD-ROM drives. The BIOS for these boards also provides direct CD-ROM drive support.

40. **b.** The SCSI drives employ host adapter cards that plug into the system board's expansion slots. They are referred to as host adapters because most of the interface's control circuitry is actually on the drive; therefore, calling the card a controller would be incorrect.

41. **b.** The average storage capacity of a CD-ROM disc is about 680MB.

42. **c.** The power consumption of LCD displays is very low. The screen is scanned by sequentially activating the panel's row and column electrodes. The pixels appear to be continuously lit because the scanning rate is very high. The electrodes can be controlled using very low DC voltage levels.

Objective 1.2

1. **b.** The notches and dots on the various ICs specify the location of the IC's pin 1. When inserting a microprocessor, make sure to correctly align the IC's pin 1 with the socket's pin 1 position.

2. **d.** Plugging non–hot-swappable devices, such as the keyboard, into the system while it is turned on can cause a system crash or even damage parts of the system.

3. **a.** A good rule of thumb to remember when attaching P8 and P9 connectors to the system board is that the black wires in each bundle should be next to each other in the middle.

4. **b.** In Windows 9x, an advanced CD-ROM device driver called *CDFS (CD-ROM File System)* was implemented to provide protected-mode operation of the drive.

5. **c.** The 5-pin DIN connector is one of the most common PC keyboard connectors.

6. **b.** ECC (Error-Checking and Correcting) provides additional data integrity by detecting bit-level errors and often recalculates and repairs the defective bit in the bit stream it processes.

7. **b.** Modern system boards typically provide two or more Dual Inline Memory Module (DIMM) 168-pin sockets.

8. **a.** The major difference between the AT and the ATX power supply types is in their form factors. The ATX power supply is smaller in size than the AT power supply and the hole patterns of the two specifications are different. Another point that differentiates power supplies is their power (or wattage) rating. Typical power ratings include 150, 200, and 250-watt versions.

9. **c.** In AT-compatible power supplies, two 6-wire bundles are marked P8 and P9. The physical construction of these power connectors is significantly different than that of the other bundles. P8 and P9 are designed so that they can be plugged into the system board's P1 and P2 power plugs, respectively.

10. **b.** SIMMs and DIMMs are keyed. The SIMMs used on Pentium boards are typically 72 pins, whereas the DIMM socket accepts 168-pin DIMM units; therefore, it is almost physically impossible to plug them in wrong.

11. **d.** A ZIF socket is used to enable the microprocessor to be set in the socket without force and then be clamped in place. To release the microprocessor from the socket, the lever arm must be set free from the socket to release the pressure on the microprocessor's pins.

12. **c.** A water cooler system is designed to cool processors. There are four main components in a water cooler system, which are water reservoir tank, water pump, condenser coil radiator, and CPU cooling block. The condenser coil radiator is used to cool the water and exhaust heat to the outside of the case.

13. **b.** In a refrigerant-cooled microprocessor system, the evaporator is the component that connects directly to the microprocessor and extracts heat from it.

14. **b.** In a liquid-cooled microprocessor system, the CPU cooling block is the component that connects directly to the microprocessor and extracts heat from it.

15. **d.** USB devices can be added to or removed from the system while it is powered up and fully operational. This is referred to as hot-swapping or hot plugging the device.

16. **a.** The original AT-compatible BIOS featured a 504MB capacity limit. To overcome this, newer BIOSs include enhanced modes that employ special Logical Block Addressing (LBA) techniques to utilize the larger partition sizes available through newer operating systems.

17. **c.** The first step of installing a USB device is enabling the USB resources in the CMOS Setup screen. In some cases, this involves enabling the port and reserving an IRQ resource for the device.

18. **c.** Universal Serial Bus (USB) provides a fast, flexible method of attaching up to 127 peripheral devices to the computer. The peripherals can be daisy-chained, or networked together using connection hubs that enable the bus to branch out through additional port connections.

19. **d.** IEEE-1394, also called FireWire, is capable of using the high-speed Isochronous transfer mode to support data transfer rates up to 400Mbps. This actually makes the FireWire bus superior to the low-speed USB bus but slower than the full-speed USB.

20. **d.** Wait for the operating system to recognize the device and configure it through the PnP process. Microsoft Windows 98, Windows 2000, and Windows XP operating systems detect the presence of the USB or FireWire device and start their Found New Hardware Wizard program to guide you through the installation process.

21. **d.** In an ATX system, the mouse and keyboard both use a 6-pin PS/2 mini-DIN connector. It is quite possible to plug these devices into the wrong connector if the color coding system is not followed.

22. **a.** The original version of Windows 95 set a size limit for logical drives at 2GB. The FDISK version in the upgraded OSR2 version of Windows 9x extended the maximum partition size to 8GB. Therefore, when using Windows 98, one partition would be required to utilize a 5GB hard drive.

23. **c.** The original AT-compatible BIOS featured a 504MB capacity limit. To overcome this limitation, newer BIOSs include enhanced modes that employ Logical Block Addressing (LBA) techniques to utilize the larger partition sizes available through newer operating systems. This technique, known as Enhanced Cylinder, Heads, Sectors (ECHS), effectively increases the number of R/W heads the system can recognize from 16 to 256.

24. **c.** Logic drives are dependent on the extended partition. If there are logical drives defined within an extended partition, the extended partition cannot be deleted. The only way to delete an extended partition is to delete its logical drives first.

25. **c.** To prepare a new SCSI hard drive for use by the system, the CMOS configuration needs to be verified for the drive, and the drive needs to be partitioned and high-level formatted.

26. **a.** The Microsoft CD Extension (MSCDEX) driver was used to provide access to the system's CD-ROM drives. The MSCDEX lines can be found in the AUTOEXEC.BAT file.

27. **d.** The original version of Windows 95 set a size limit for logical drives at 2GB.

28. **b.** In a FAT-based system, the extended partition may be subdivided into 23 logical drives from drive E to drive Z.

29. **a.** The floppy disk drive connected to the 34-pin header at the end of the cable will be assigned the drive A designation by the system. A floppy drive connected to the edge connector in the middle of the cable will be designated as the B drive.

30. **b.** When the system checks the MBR of the physical disk during the boot process, it also checks to see which partition on the disk has been marked as active. It then jumps to that location, reads the information in that partition boot record, and boots to the operating system in that logical drive.

31. **b.** When the primary partition is created on a hard disk, a special table called the *partition table* is created in its master boot sector. This table is used to store information about the partitions and logical drives on the disk. It includes information about where each partition and logical drive begins and ends on the physical drive.

Objective 1.3

1. **b.** USB devices are rated as full-speed and low-speed devices based on their communication specification. Under the USB 1.1 specification, low-speed USB devices run at 12Mbps. On the other hand, full-speed USB devices operate under the USB 2.0 specification (also referred to as high-speed USB) and support data rates up to 480Mbps.

2. **a, d.** Historically, most external CD-ROM drives employed SCSI interface connectors. Newer SCSI CD-ROM's employ USB connection.

3. **a.** If the type of RAM device being added to expand the existing banks of memory is incorrect, the system might not recognize this additional RAM. The problem will show up in the form of a short memory count during the POST routines.

4. **b.** When installing an external CD-ROM drive, verify that the power switch, or power supply, is turned off before connecting the CD-ROM's power supply to the external drive unit.

5. **d.** The proper procedure for removing a PC Card from the computer begins with clicking the PC Card status indicator on the Taskbar. Then, select the command to stop the operation of the PC Card you want to remove. When the operating system prompts you, physically remove the PC Card from the system.

6. **c.** When the notebook is in the docking station, its normal I/O devices (keyboard, display, and pointing device) are disabled and the docking station's peripherals take over.

7. **a.** Older portables included one FDD and one HDD as standard equipment. Newer models tend to include a CD-ROM drive and an HDD as standard internal units.

8. **d.** Although the system's PC Card software driver can be executed directly on the card, instead of moving it into RAM for execution, the PC Card enablers must be loaded before the card can be activated.

9. **b.** When an LCD panel fails, the most common repair is to replace the entire display panel/housing assembly.

10. **d.** The external power supply used with portable systems basically converts AC voltage into a DC voltage that the system can use to power its internal components and recharge its batteries.

11. **b.** A docking station is a specialized structure that extends a notebook computer's expansion bus so that it can be used with a collection of desktop devices, such as an AC power source, a full-sized keyboard and CRT monitor, as well as modems, mice, and standard PC port connectors. Port replicators do not provide additional expansion slots for use.

12. **c.** Many of the Pentium chipsets provide a standby mode that turns off selected components, such as the hard drive and display, until a system event, such as a keyboard entry or a mouse movement, occurs.

13. **d.** Notebook computers are natural selections for use as wireless networking clients. Because they are portable, they can be used anywhere within any wireless Access Point's hot spot. Many enterprises are creating hot spots to enable traveling computer users to access the Internet through their Access Point (for a fee).

14. **a.** Many wireless configuration applications include a built-in power meter program that shows the relative signal strength being received from the Access Point. When you're positioning a computer that has a wireless network card, you should use this tool to maximize the location of the computer. Likewise, if you are operating in a multiple Access Point environment, you can use this tool to identify the best Access Point to use in a given location.

15. **b.** Concentrator is used to connect computers to a network system. LAN adapter, docking station, and port replicator enable file printing from a notebook.

. . . .

16. **c.** Type 802.11b cards have a limited range of operation (about 500 feet). This estimation relies on a clear line-of-sight pathway existing between the card and the Access Point. The signals used under this wireless specification do not travel well through objects.

17. **a, b.** The installation process for a PC Card wireless network adapter involves inserting the wireless card in the PCMCIA slot and loading the OEM drivers from the manufacturer's CD. The wireless PC Card adapter should be auto-detected by the system.

18. **d.** The proper procedure for removing a PC Card from the computer begins with clicking on the PC Card status indicator on the Taskbar. Then, select the command to stop the operation of the PC Card you want to remove. When the operating system prompts you, physically remove the PC Card from the system.

19. **c.** To install the PC Card Wizard on a Windows 9x system, you must navigate the Start/Settings/Control Panel path and access the Add/Remove Programs applet. Click the Windows Setup tab, select a category, and then click on the Details tab. If you don't see the component listed in the Add/Remove Programs dialog box, it might be one that is only present on the Windows 9x distribution CD.

20. **b.** At different times, you might want to stop a PC Card driver from being loaded. To turn off support for a PC Card, access the Device Manager tab and expand the PC Card slot node. Then, double-click the PC Card controller and in the Device usage area, check the Disable in This Hardware Profile check box option.

21. **c.** Windows 2000 does not supply a PC Card Installation Wizard.

22. **a.** Because PCMCIA cards are hot-swappable, the operating system's socket service must update the system when a new card is installed or an existing card is removed. If not, the system would lose track of its actual resources. The card service portion delivers the correct device driver for the installed PC Card. (That is, when a PC Card modem is removed and replaced with a LAN card, the operating system must automatically update its capability of controlling and using the new card.)

23. **b, d.** The operating system must support the PCMCIA slots at two levels—at the socket level (universal support for all PCMCIA devices) and at the card level (specific drivers to handle the function of the particular card installed).

24. **d.** Cardbus is a redefined and enhanced 32-bit version of the PC Card standard. The main purpose of this new specification is to extend the PCMCIA bus to higher speeds with more powerful devices, and to provide support of 32-bit I/O and memory data paths.

25. **b.** In 1989, the PCMCIA bus standard was introduced primarily to accommodate the notebook and sub-notebook computer markets. A small form-factor expansion-card format, referred to as the PC Card standard, was also adopted for use. This format was derived from earlier proprietary laptop/notebook memory card designs.

26. **a, c, d.** Portable computers have two ideal characteristics: They are compact and lightweight. Portable computer designers work constantly to decrease the size and power consumption of all the computer's components.

27. **a.** System boards for portable computers are not designed to fit a standardized form factor. Instead, they are designed to fit around all of the components that must be installed in the system. Therefore, system boards used in portable computers tend to be proprietary to the model they are designed for. Mounting hole positions are determined by where they will best suit the placement of the other system components.

28. **d.** The power consumption of LCD displays is very low because no current passes through the display to light the pixels. The screen is scanned by sequentially activating the panel's row and column electrodes. The electrodes can be controlled (turned on and off) using very low DC voltage levels.

Objective 1.4

1. **a.** A VGA or SVGA BIOS is assigned to use I/O address C0000 to C7FFF.

2. **d.** Typical Pentium-based system boards include two enhanced IDE controllers to handle their hard disk drive/CD-ROM hosting function. Each controller can handle up to two IDE drives. To add the third IDE device in a system containing a single IDE controller, you will have to add the second IDE controller card to the system.

3. **b.** The floppy disk drive controller is assigned to use the interrupt channel IRQ6 in PC-compatible systems.

4. **c.** The primary IDE drive controller responds to I/O addresses between 1F0h and 1F7h.

5. **a.** Interrupt channel 8 (IRQ8) is assigned to internal Real-Time Clock interrupt.

6. **d.** COM1 is assigned as port address hex 3F8 and uses IRQ channel 4.

7. **a.** During a program's execution, the microprocessor frequently reads from or writes to I/O devices. Regardless of how the peripheral is connected to the system (serial or parallel), polling is used as one of four methods to initiate data transfer between the system and the peripheral. Polling is where the microprocessor examines the status of the peripheral under program control.

8. **a.** The first IDE controller, also called Primary IDE controller, is assigned IRQ14, whereas the Secondary controller uses IRQ15 to interrupt the system.

9. **d.** I/O devices generally have the capability to interrupt the microprocessor while it is executing a program. The I/O device does this by issuing an Interrupt Request (IRQ) input signal to the microprocessor.

10. **b.** The IRQ1 is the reserved internal interrupt for the keyboard controller used to indicate the keyboard buffer is full. It is not available for other devices, even on systems without a keyboard.

11. **a.** For most PCs, COM1 is assigned as port address hex 3F8 and uses IRQ channel 4. The COM2 port is typically assigned port address hex 2F8 and IRQ3. Because a serial mouse is using COM1 for input, the modem should be configured for addresses 2F8, IRQ3, and COM2.

12. **c.** IRQ channel 8 (IRQ8) is designated and internally connected for Real-Time Clock.

13. **d.** The first serial port uses I/O port address 3F8, which means that the bit pattern 1111111000 appearing on the address bus would activate the first serial port.

14. **b.** The primary IDE drive controller responds to I/O addresses between 1F0h and 1F7h, whereas the second IDE drive controller answers to addresses between 170h and 177h.

15. **d.** The first IDE drive controller responds to I/O addresses between 1F0h and 1F7h, whereas the second IDE drive controller answers to addresses between 170h and 177h.

16. **a.** DMA generally involves a high-speed I/O device (for example, FDD), taking over the system's buses to perform read and write operations with the primary memory, without the intervention of the system microprocessor.

17. **c.** There are two DMA controllers of four channels each. One of these channels (DMA4) is a cascade channel and is not available for designation. Therefore, although there are eight DMA channels total, only seven are actually available.

18. **a.** The COM2 port is typically assigned to port address 2F8h and IRQ3.

19. **b.** COM1 is assigned as port address hex 3F8 and uses IRQ4.

20. **a.** The floppy disk drive controller is assigned to use the I/O port address hex 3F0 and the IRQ6 in PC-compatible systems.

21. **d.** COM1 is assigned as port address hex 3F8 and uses IRQ4.

22. **b.** IRQ9 cascades to IRQ2 in INTC1.

23. **c.** The IRQ0 is used for the Timer/Counter interrupt. It is an internal IRQ and cannot be used for other devices.

24. **c.** The typical Floppy-disk Drive Controller divides the floppy disk into 80 tracks per side, with 9 or 18 512-byte sectors per side. This provides the system with a 720kB (double-density) or 1.44MB (high-density) of storage on each disk.

25. **b.** Of the possible 15 interrupt channels available (IRQ0 through IRQ15), IRQ02, 8, and 13 are reserved for use inside the PC. The other IRQ inputs are available to the system for user-definable interrupt functions.

26. **d.** While executing a program, I/O devices generally have the capability to request immediate service by issuing an Interrupt Request (IRQ) input signal to the microprocessor. In a PC-compatible system, each device capable of interrupting the microprocessor must be assigned a unique IRQ number. The system uses this number to identify which device is in need of service.

27. **a, b.** The occurrence of a Parity Check (PCK) error in the DRAM memory will cause an NMI signal to be sent to the microprocessor. The system then will shut down without storing any of the potentially bad data. An NMI type of interrupt in the system will occur without saving any of the potentially bad data when an active IO Channel Check (IOCHCK) input is received from an adapter card located in one of the board's expansion slots.

28. **d.** The floppy disk drive controller is assigned the IRQ-6 channel in PC-compatible systems.

29. **c.** Older ISA adapter cards typically had no PnP function and had to be configured manually. In these situations, the system has no way to reconfigure the card, so you must tell it which resources are required for it. This function is performed through the PnP and PCI Setup screens in the CMOS Setup routine and reserves certain resources so that they are available for the legacy device.

30. **a, b.** When discussing the standard PC I/O ports, also referred to as legacy ports, it is common to differentiate between traditional standard ports (Centronic parallel ports and RS-232C serial ports) and newer standard ports (PS/2 mouse and keyboard ports and infrared ports).

31. **a, b, d.** Network adapter cards use the Interrupt Request (IRQ) setting to communicate with the system and exchange information with the system using the I/O port address. The base memory address provides the network adapter cards a starting point in memory for DMA transfers.

32. **c.** It is necessary to disable the COM2 port on older systems because the system checks available COM ports when booting up. By disabling this setting,

possible interrupt conflict problems are avoided. In addition, some communication software will assign a COM port to an empty serial port. By disabling the port, it will not be available for service and, therefore, no conflict will occur.

33. **d.** Older ISA LAN cards typically had no PnP function and had to be configured manually. When configuring a non-PnP ISA LAN card, you must be aware of which system resources it needs and what settings it can work with. This information can typically be found in the device's installation guide.

Objective 1.5

1. **b.** The master I/O block on the ATX back panel contains two DB-9M COM-port connectors for use with serial devices and a DB-25F parallel-port connector for SPP, EPP, and ECP parallel devices.

2. **c.** Older AT-class systems use a 5-pin DIN connector for the keyboard.

3. **a, d.** The COM2 port is typically assigned port address 2F8h and IRQ3. COM4 also uses IRQ3 but usually resides at 2E8h. COM1 is mostly assigned as port address 3F8h and uses IRQ channel 4. COM3 uses IRQ4 too with an I/O address of 3E8h.

4. **d.** Normal interrupt settings for printer ports in a PC-compatible system are IRQ5 or IRQ7. IRQ7 is normally assigned to the LPT1 printer port, whereas IRQ5 typically serves the LPT2 port, if installed.

5. **b.** IRQ7 is normally assigned to the LPT1 printer port, whereas IRQ5 typically serves the LPT2 port, if installed.

6. **d.** The DB-15F connector is the standard for the PC game port and is used to attach joysticks and other game-playing devices to the system.

7. **a.** COM4 usually resides at 2E8 and uses IRQ3.

8. **d.** COM1 is assigned to use port address 3F8h and IRQ channel 4.

9. **c.** The COM2 port is typically assigned port address 2F8h and IRQ3.

10. **c.** Since the advent of the PC AT, a system's first serial port has typically been implemented in a 9-pin D-shell male connector on the computer.

11. **b.** An IrLPT is used with character printers to provide a wireless interface between the computer and the printer.

12. **d.** The standard infrared protocol is used to provide a standard serial port interface with transfer rates up to 115Kbps.

13. **c.** IrDA protocols specify communication ranges up to 2 meters (6 feet) but most specifications usually state 1 meter as the maximum range.

14. **c.** USB peripherals obtain their power supply primarily from the interface. They are also permitted to have their own power sources if necessary.

15. **d.** When two serial ports are located close enough together, a null modem connection can be implemented. A null modem connection employs a crossover wiring technique for the TXD/RXD lines and permits two serial ports to communicate directly without using modems.

16. **c.** The COM2 port is typically assigned port address 2F8h and uses IRQ3.

17. **b.** COM1 uses IRQ4 and is assigned an I/O address of 3F8h for the first serial port.

18. **b.** IRQ7 is normally assigned to the LPT1 parallel printer port and is located at 378h.

19. **a, d.** (a) The IBM version of the interface, which became known as the Standard Parallel Port (SPP) specification for printers, reduced the pin count to 25 at the computer end of the connection. (d) At the printer end of the SPP cable, it employs a standard 36-pin Centronics connector. 36-pin mini Centronic connectors can often be found at the printer ends of newer printer cable, too.

20. **d.** The cable length used for the parallel printer should be kept to less than 10 feet. If longer lengths are needed, the cable should have a low-capacitance value. The cable should also be shielded to minimize Electromagnetic Field Interference (EFI).

21. **b, c.** In an ATX system, the mouse usually plugs in to a 6-pin PS/2 mini-DIN connector on the back of the system unit. This connector is identical to the keyboard connector and can easily be confused with it.

22. **a.** Item B in the ATX back panel is a DB-25F connector, which is used by the LPT port for printers.

23. **b.** Item C is a Centronics 50-pin connector, which is used by the SCSI port.

24. **b.** The graphic shows an ATX back panel. In an ATX system, the VGA port employs a 3-row DB-15F connector, which is indicated by A.

25. **c.** The game and VGA ports in a PC both use 15-pin D-shell connectors. However, the VGA port organizes the pins into three rows, whereas the game port uses only two rows. Therefore, unlike the keyboard and mouse ports on an ATX system, these ports cannot be confused.

26. **d.** RS-232 serial printer cable is recommended no longer than 50 feet. However, some references use 100 feet as the acceptable length of an RS-232C serial cable. Serial connections are tricky enough without problems generated by the cable being too long. Make the cable as short as possible.

27. **c.** Normal IRQ settings for printer ports in a PC-compatible system are IRQ5 or IRQ7. IRQ7 is normally assigned to the LPT1 printer port, whereas IRQ5 typically serves the LPT2 port, if installed.

28. **a.** IRQ7 is an external interrupt used by the LPT1 printer port.

29. **b.** The microphone (audio-in) and speakers (audio-out) are plugged into the appropriate RCA jacks on the back of the sound card.

30. **d.** Audio-in and audio-out ports can be found as RCA jacks on the back of the sound card.

31. **b.** In an ATX system, the mouse and keyboard both use a 6-pin PS/2 mini-DIN connector. It is quite possible to plug these devices into the wrong connector if the color coding system is not followed.

32. **a.** The mouse connectors used in an ATX and an AT system are different. In an ATX system, the mouse plugs in to a 6-pin PS/2 mini-DIN connector. In AT-class systems, the mouse is plugged in to a 9-pin serial port. When choosing a new mouse for an upgrade or a replacement, the type of mouse connector used on the system unit is an important consideration.

33. **a.** A single IEEE-1394 connection can be used to connect up to 63 devices to a single port with the maximum segment length of 4.5 meters (14 feet).

Objective 1.6

1. **b.** ATA-33 specification boosts throughput between the IDE device and the system to 33.3MBps. This standard employs the 40-pin IDE signal cable. ATA-66 provides higher data throughput by doubling the number of conductors in the IDE signal cable to 80.

2. **a.** IDE bus driver support is built into the BIOS of system boards that have integrated IDE host adapters.

3. **b.** The ATAPI interface can be used to control drive units such as a tape or CD-ROM providing maximum throughput of 16.7MBps through the 40-pin IDE signal cable.

4. **c.** ATAPI specification provides EIDE drivers for use with CD-ROM drives and new data transfer methods.

5. **b.** If a second IDE drive is added as a slave drive with two additional logical drives, MS-DOS will reassign the partitions on the first drive to be logical drives C and E, while the partitions on the slave drive will be D and F.

6. **d.** An IDE drive can be set as the Master drive in a multidrive system, or the Slave drive in the same multidrive system. It can also be set up for Cable Select (CS) operation where the system determines its configuration setting.

7. **b.** The IDE controller structure is an integrated portion of most PC system boards. This structure includes BIOS and chipset support for the IDE version the board will support, as well as the IDE host connector.

8. **c.** Ultra ATA-66 supports 33.3MBps data rates when used with a standard 40-pin/40-conductor (80 wires in total) IDE signal cable.

9. **a.** In the Microsoft operating system environment, each logical drive is assigned a different drive letter (such as C, D, E, and so on) to identify it to the system.

10. **d.** RAID5 is an Array of Independent Data Disks with distributed parity blocks (or striped with parity disks).

11. **b.** In an older Pentium system, an IDE drive may be configured by the manufacturer as a single drive and partitioned into two logical drives. To support more storage devices, an additional IDE adapter card may be added to the system. In this case, the first IDE drive will be configured as the master drive, and the second IDE drive becomes the slave drive.

12. **b.** Any system board supporting EIDE technology can support up to four devices—two (Master and Slave) on the Primary channel and two (Master and Slave) on the Secondary channel.

13. **c.** RAID 0 is also known as Striped Disk Array without Fault Tolerance, which uses the drives in a parallel array.

14. **a.** Under the Enhanced IDE (EIDE) specification, the host supplies two IDE interfaces that can each handle a master and a slave device in a daisy-chained configuration.

Objective 1.7

1. **c.** Three 2-pin jumpers in an adapter card will create eight possible locations in binary, which are 000, 001, 011, 100, 101, 110, and 111.

2. **d.** In PC systems, 50-pin shielded cables with Centronics connectors are used for external SCSI connections. A 68-pin Q-cable version was also adopted in SCSI for 32-bit transfers. The Apple Macintosh employs a variation of the SCSI standard that features a proprietary miniature 25-pin D-shell connector.

3. **b.** Wide SCSI can support up to 16 devices including the controller, which is referred to as SCSI-15 with the highest priority. SCSI-0 is assigned to the internal hard disk drive with the lowest priority.

4. **c.** External SCSI devices require an additional external power source.

5. **d.** A 3-position, 2-pin jumper block can create 8 SCSI ID numbers (0 through 7), or in binary (000, 001, 010, 011, 100, 101, 110, and 111).

6. **d.** Wide Fast SCSI-2 doubles the bus size to 16 bits and employs the faster transfer methods to provide a maximum bus speed of 20MBps (2 bytes× 10MHz=20MBps), supporting a chain of up to 15 devices.

7. **d.** The SCSI daisy-chain must be terminated with a resistor network pack at both ends. Single-connector SCSI devices are normally terminated internally.

8. **c.** The maximum recommended length for a complete standard SCSI chain is 20 feet (6 meters) including three feet of internal cable.

9. **b.** The original SCSI-1 specification established a data bus width of 8 bits and permitted up to 8 devices to be connected to the bus (including the controller).

10. **c.** A Fast SCSI-2 system uses 50-pin connectors with an improved data transfer rate of 10Mbps but has the maximum usable cable length reduced in half from 6 meters to 3 meters.

11. **c.** A 50-conductor alternative cable using 50-pin D-shell connectors has been added to the A-cable specification for SCSI-2 devices.

12. **a.** The SCSI specification refers to the SCSI controller as SCSI-7 (by default), and then classifies the first internal hard drive as SCSI-0.

13. **a.** It is possible to use multiple SCSI host adapters within a single system to increase the number of devices that can be used. The system's first SCSI controller can handle up to 7 devices, whereas the additional SCSI controller can boost the system to support up to 14 SCSI devices.

14. **c.** Additional SCSI devices are added to the system by daisy-chaining them together so that the SCSI input of the second device is attached to the SCSI output of the first device, and so forth.

15. **a.** As the speed of the Fast SCSI-2 bus was increased, it caused crosstalk to occur earlier, which cut the maximum usable cable length in half (from 6 meters to 3 meters, or about 10 feet).

16. **d.** Wide SCSI bus can assign up to 16 possible ID numbers with SCSI-15 being the default ID number for the controller.

17. **b.** To prevent data corruption caused by induced noise, a maximum single SCSI segment of less than 3 feet (1 meter) is recommended.

18. **a.** The maximum recommended length for a complete standard SCSI chain is 20 feet (6 meters).

19. **c.** The SCSI daisy-chain must be terminated with a resistor network pack at both ends. If not, a SCSI terminator cable (containing a built-in resistor pack) must be installed at the end of the chain. Single-connector SCSI devices are normally terminated internally.

20. **d.** A maximum single SCSI segment of less than 3 feet (1 meter) is recommended. For 6 possible external devices, the total length of the cable is 18 feet. You can realistically count on about 3 feet of internal cable. Therefore, the maximum total length of the chain is reduced to about 15 feet (4.5 meters).

21. **c.** FPT is a more advanced form of active termination in which the diode clamps are added to the circuitry to force the termination to the correct voltage. This virtually eliminates any signal reflections or other problems and provides for the best form of termination of a single-ended SCSI bus.

22. **b.** Each SCSI device in a chain must have a unique ID number assigned to it. If two devices are set to the same ID number, one or both of them will appear invisible to the system.

23. **a, b, c.** The SCSI LVD interface runs faster and consumes less power than traditional SCSI HVD interfaces. LVD interfaces also operate on 3V logic levels instead of the older, TTL-compatible 5V levels.

24. **a.** The SCSI specification refers to the SCSI controller as SCSI-7 (by default), and then classifies the first internal hard drive as SCSI-0.

25. **b.** Even though there are a total of eight possible SCSI ID numbers for each controller, only six are available for use with external devices. The SCSI specification refers to the SCSI controller as SCSI-7 (by default), and then classifies the first internal hard drive as SCSI-0. External devices can use the remaining SCSI ID numbers, SCSI-1 to SCSI-6.

26. **c.** The SCSI specification refers to the SCSI controller as SCSI-7 with the highest priority, and then classifies the first internal hard drive as SCSI-0.

27. **b.** Each SCSI device in a chain must have a unique ID number assigned to it. Even though there are a total of eight possible SCSI ID numbers for each controller, only six are available for use with external devices.

28. **d.** It is possible to use multiple SCSI host adapters within a single system to increase the number of devices that can be used. The system's first SCSI controller can handle up to 7 devices, while the additional SCSI controller can boost the system to support up to 14 SCSI devices.

29. **d.** In PC systems, 50-pin shielded cables with Centronics connectors are used for external SCSI connections. A 68-pin Q-cable version was also adopted in SCSI for 32-bit transfers. The Apple Macintosh employs a variation of the SCSI standard that features a proprietary miniature 25-pin D-shell connector.

30. **c.** In PC-compatible systems, the SCSI interface uses a 50-pin signal cable arrangement. The 50-pin SCSI connections are referred to as A-cables.

31. **b.** In PC-compatible systems, the SCSI interface uses a 50-pin signal cable arrangement. Internally, the cable is a 50-pin flat ribbon cable.

32. **d.** LVD interfaces operate on 3-volt logic levels instead of the older TTL-compatible 5-volt levels to make them run faster and consume less power.

Objective 1.8

1. **b.** The default values for VGA/PCI-compatible adapters include a standard 640×480 pixel screen resolution at 16 colors, with a refresh rate of 60Hz.

2. **a.** Standard VGA resolution is defined as 720×400 pixels using 16 colors in text mode, and 640×480 pixels using 16 onscreen colors in graphics mode.

3. **d.** Windows provides an Infrared Monitor utility that can be used to track the computer's activity. When this utility is running, it will alert you when infrared devices are within range of your computer by placing the Infrared icon on the Taskbar.

4. **b.** Infrared port operations must first be enabled through the CMOS Setup utility.

5. **c.** If you are not sure whether the device you are installing is Plug-and-Play capable, check its users guide. If it is not a Plug-and-Play device, install its drivers by accessing the Add New Hardware icon in the Control Panel.

6. **d.** When another IrDA device comes within range of the host port, the Infrared icon will appear on the Windows desktop and in the Taskbar.

7. **b.** Digital cameras are mobile devices that are mostly plugged in to the computer simply to download pictures. Therefore, most digital cameras feature the capability of being connected to parallel ports, serial ports, and USB ports. Some cameras can also communicate through IEEE-1394 FireWire ports.

8. **a.** The printhead is a collection of print wires set in an electromagnetic head unit. Dots are created on the paper by energizing selected electromagnets, which extend the desired print wires from the printhead. The print wires impact an ink ribbon, which impacts the paper.

9. **a.** Scanners are bidirectional devices (they have to be told how much area to scan and they must send the graphical data back to the computer). Therefore, they require an IEEE-1284 bidirectional parallel cable if they are to be installed between the parallel port and the printer.

10. **d.** External modems make use of external power supply packs. The cable types listed do not apply to modem connections.

11. **c.** Analog modems are used for dial-up networking through the traditional telephone lines. Their maximum transmission speed tops out at 56Kbps. Also, they do not use broadband transmission techniques. The other modems are all high-speed broadband devices.

12. **b.** Under the basic VGA specification, the resolution is a relatively low 640×480 dots and uses only 16 colors.

13. **d.** The video adapter card typically plugs into one of the system's expansion slots. Most newer video adapter cards are designed for use with AGP slots.

Objective 1.9

1. **d.** For Pentium III and Pentium 4 processors, the recommended operating temperature is 35°C. You must find a fan that is rated to work with that processor's temperature/speed specification.

2. **b.** You should not interpret an automatic entry into the CMOS Setup utility as an error when the system is initially booted after adding an additional processor. This is the process that systems often use to recognize new processors. You can use the system's CMOS Setup utility (or its administrative tools package) to ensure that the system board is recognizing all the installed processors, and that they are working properly.

3. **a, c.** (a) You should check the production run number of the processor to ensure that it is within one production run of its companion processors. In the case of Intel processors, this is referred to as a *stepping level*. (If you have a Pentium III 750MHz processor with stepping level 4, you should install additional processors that are defined as stepping 3, 4, or 5.) (**c**) For major upgrades, such as installing additional or newer/faster processors, the system BIOS might need to be upgraded.

4. **a.** When upgrading an IDE hard drive, make sure that the system board supports the type of IDE drive you are installing. Also verify that the correct cabling is being used to connect the new drive to the system. Installing a new ATA-100 drive in a system using the old IDE cable will cause the drive's operation to be diminished to the level of the old drive. Without the new cables, communications with the drives will be limited to the lesser standard determined by the 40-conductor signal cable.

5. **a.** The original AT-compatible BIOS featured a 504MB capacity limit. To overcome this, newer BIOSs include enhanced modes that employ special Logical Block Addressing (LBA) techniques to utilize the larger partition sizes available through newer operating systems.

6. **d.** Additional case fans can be installed to increase or redirect the airflow through the chassis.

7. **b, d.** (**b**) Optimizing the speed of the fan lowers the relative dust accumulation that can lead to thermal failure. (**d**) The risk of thermal failure can also be reduced by installing foam filters at the chassis openings to filter the incoming air.

8. **b.** One way to optimize the overall system use is to add additional processors to distribute the processing load.

9. **c.** To improve the performance of a newly installed adapter card, you will need to obtain the latest drivers from the manufacturer's Web site.

10. **c.** The operating speeds of the video cards have increased causing more heat and requiring active cooling methods. Adding a fan to the video card or to the system board will keep the card from becoming too hot and slowing the speed of the card.

Objective 1.10

1. **c.** Before flashing the BIOS, it is a good idea to make a backup copy of the original BIOS program. In case the process fails, you can use the backup to restore the settings back to their original form.

2. **a.** If the BIOS does not possess the Flash option and does not support the new microprocessor, a new BIOS chip that does support it must be obtained. If not, the entire system board will typically need to be upgraded.

3. **b.** Often, later BIOS versions are developed by the system board's manufacturer to permit installation of faster processors as they come on the market. Therefore, you should always check the manufacturer's Internet support site to determine whether the system board can support the processor type and speed you intend to upgrade to.

4. **d.** Before upgrading the system BIOS, record the CMOS settings and back up the original BIOS program. In case the process fails, you can use the original BIOS program to attempt to restore the settings back to their original form.

5. **c.** When the microprocessor is upgraded, the BIOS should also be flashed with the latest compatibility firmware. If the BIOS does not possess the Flash option and does not support the new microprocessor, a new BIOS chip that does support it must be obtained. If not, the entire system board will typically need to be upgraded.

6. **b.** When the microprocessor is upgraded, the BIOS should also be flashed with the latest compatibility firmware. If the BIOS does not possess the Flash option and does not support the new microprocessor, a new BIOS chip that does support it must be obtained.

7. **c.** When upgrading the microprocessor, verify that the existing BIOS can be upgraded to support the new microprocessor specifications. Often, later BIOS versions are developed by the system board's manufacturer to permit installation of faster processors as they come on the market.

8. **d.** When upgrading the microprocessor, the ROM BIOS should also be flashed with the latest compatible firmware. If a non-reprogrammable (non-flashable) BIOS is being used, you must replace the BIOS IC with a new IC. If the BIOS IC is not socketed (removable), or a compatible BIOS chip cannot be obtained, the entire system board will need to be upgraded.

9. **c.** PCMCIA Type III cards are 10.5mm thick and are intended primarily for use with removable hard drives.

10. **d.** PCMCIA Type III cards are 10.5mm thick and are intended primarily for use with removable hard drives.

11. **b.** The PCMCIA Type II cards are 5mm thick and support virtually any traditional expansion function except removable hard drive units.

12. **c.** The PCMCIA Type I cards, introduced in 1990, are 3.3mm thick and work as memory expansion units.

13. **d.** The PCMCIA Type II cards are 5mm thick and support virtually any traditional expansion function, except removable hard drive units.

14. **b.** Most notebooks provide two PCMCIA slots that can accept a wide variety of I/O device types.

15. **c.** Type III cards are 10.5mm thick and are intended primarily for use with removable hard drives.

16. **d.** Modems slide into Type II PCMCIA slots and connect to the telephone jack through a special phone cable. The cable plugs into a small slot on the card and into the phone jack using a standard RJ-11 connector.

17. **c.** Two standard Type II slots can physically accommodate two Type I cards, two Type II cards, one Type I card and one Type II card, or a single Type III card. Therefore, either a PC Card hard drive or both a Flash memory card and a modem can be installed in the slots.

18. **a.** Fuel cells are power-generating technologies that use electrochemical reactions between hydrogen and oxygen to produce electrical power.

19. **b.** Fuel cells are power-generating technologies that use electrochemical reactions between oxygen and hydrogen, which can be either extracted from methanol or pure hydrogen to produce electrical power. The reaction between the hydrogen and oxygen produces water vapor and heat with any form of combustion taking place.

20. **d.** Currently, PCMCIA Type III cards are being produced. These cards are 10.5mm thick and are intended primarily for use with removable hard drives.

21. **b.** Each time a new device is added to the system, more electrical power is required. For example, upgrading the processor can easily increase the power consumption by more than 20 watts (W). Replacing RAM with faster RAM devices increases power consumptions as well. Simply, increasing the installed memory from 128MB to 256MB will almost double the power consumption of the system's memory (that is, from 6W to 12W). Adding high-end video adapters used for games may consume up to 100W. A typical hard disk drive can require up to 20 or 30W each.

22. **b.** When upgrading a power supply, one thing to take into account is its wattage rating requirements. The wattage rating is a measurement of the total power the supply can deliver to the system. More heavily equipped systems (that is, more disk drives and peripherals) require power supplies with higher wattage ratings.

Hardware Domain 2.0: Diagnosing and Troubleshooting

Objective 2.1: Recognize common problems associated with each module and their symptoms, and identify steps to isolate and troubleshoot the problems.

1. When can you safely disconnect a keyboard from a computer?
   - ❏ a. While the computer is booting
   - ❏ b. Anytime while the computer is running
   - ❏ c. When the computer is turned off
   - ❏ d. While the operating system is in Safe Mode

Quick Answer: **102**
Detailed Answer: **104**

2. If the mouse attached to your portable computer does not work but the TouchPad unit does, what step should you take to get the mouse working correctly?
   - ❏ a. Switch the mouse to the other USB slot to access the enabled USB port connection.
   - ❏ b. Switch the mouse to the other serial port connector to access the correct COM port.
   - ❏ c. Switch the mouse to the other PS/2 mini-DIN connector because it must be plugged into the connector for the full-size keyboard.
   - ❏ d. Check the computer's documentation for an Fn key combination requirement for the mouse.

Quick Answer: **102**
Detailed Answer: **104**

Quick Check

3. You have a Windows XP–based portable system and you want to use different I/O equipment when the system is in its docking station than when you are using it on the road. You don't want to have to reconfigure the computer each time you leave the office and return. What Windows XP feature can you use to avoid this situation?

Quick Answer: **102**
Detailed Answer: **104**

- ❏ a. Manually configure the computer with both hardware profiles you want to use. Select the desired profile from the Start menu after startup.
- ❏ b. If the system is PnP compliant, different hardware profiles are created by the Windows XP operating system when the computer is docked and undocked. So, simply turn on the system in both configurations and accept the profiles generated.
- ❏ c. Allow the Windows operating system to detect the notebook configuration when it is out of the docking station. Then manually configure a hardware profile for when the docking station is connected. Select the desired profile from the Start menu after startup.
- ❏ d. Allow the Windows operating system to detect the notebook configuration when it is in the docking station. Then manually configure a hardware profile for when it is not connected to the docking station. Select the desired profile from the Start menu after startup.

4. You notice that the length of time that your portable computer can run on the battery before it shuts down is significantly shorter than it used to be. What can you do to restore some additional usage to the battery?

Quick Answer: **102**
Detailed Answer: **104**

- ❏ a. Place the battery in a commercial battery charger overnight to build the level of charge in the battery backup.
- ❏ b. Keep the external AC power adapter plugged into the notebook whenever possible to increase the amount of charge in the battery.
- ❏ c. You must fully discharge the battery and then recharge it over repeated cycles.
- ❏ d. Take the battery out of the computer and warm it in an oven on low heat for an hour.

5. What conditions could cause the Device Manager utility to display an exclamation point on a yellow background next to a PC Card adapter?

- ❑ a. The PC Card device might be faulty.
- ❑ b.   The PC Card controller in the notebook might be faulty.
- ❑ c. The operating system does not support the installed PC Card device.
- ❑ d. The enabling for PC Card slots has been disabled in the CMOS.

6. If the Windows Device Manager displays the PCMCIA socket but no name for the card, this indicates that there is a problem with the PCMCIA socket installation. What steps should be taken to correct a PCMCIA socket installation problem?

- ❑ a. Disable the PCMCIA socket listing in the Device Manager and reboot the computer without it.
- ❑ b. Remove the PCMCIA socket listing in the Device Manager, reboot the computer, and allow the Windows PnP process to detect the socket and install the appropriate driver for it.
- ❑ c. In the PCMCIA socket's Properties page, select the Repair option on the Hardware tab.
- ❑ d. In the PCMCIA socket's Properties page, verify its resource allocations on the Resources tab.

7. What is the fastest way to verify that a PC Card is being recognized by the system and that it is working correctly?

- ❑ a. Access the Windows Event Viewer in the MMC and verify that the PC Card is functioning.
- ❑ b. Access the Hardware Profile tab under the Control Panel's System icon and check the status of the PC Card.
- ❑ c. Access the Add New Hardware Wizard in the Control Panel and check the status of the PC Card.
- ❑ d. Access the Device Manager under the Control Panel's System icon and check the status of the PC Card.

8. In a portable PC system, which part of the system provides control of the power management function?

- ❑ a. The Applied Power Management application software
- ❑ b. The operating system
- ❑ c. The system board chip set
- ❑ d. CMOS

. . . .

9. One of the biggest problems for portable computers is _____.

Quick Answer: **102**
Detailed Answer: **105**

   ❏ a. heat buildup inside the case
   ❏ b. lack of full-sized keys on their keyboards
   ❏ c. lack of expandability due to a limited number of I/O ports
   ❏ d. lack of disk drive capacity

10. If a PC will not maintain the time and date after replacing the system board battery, what should be considered next?

Quick Answer: **102**
Detailed Answer: **105**

   ❏ a. The power supply
   ❏ b. The system board
   ❏ c. The front panel connections
   ❏ d. The battery contacts

11. If the CD-ROM and hard drive both stop working after you install a CD-RW drive, what is the likely cause?

Quick Answer: **102**
Detailed Answer: **105**

   ❏ a. The cable was installed backward on the CD-ROM drive.
   ❏ b. The CD-ROM drive was not enabled in the CMOS utility.
   ❏ c. The drivers were configured incorrectly.
   ❏ d. The Master/Slave selection jumper isn't set correctly on the CD-RW drive.

12. A 601 error code represents what type of problem?

Quick Answer: **102**
Detailed Answer: **105**

   ❏ a. I/O error
   ❏ b. Hard disk drive failure
   ❏ c. Floppy disk drive failure
   ❏ d. Parity error

13. If you turn the sound volume in Windows 2000 entirely to the right channel and the sound comes out the speaker marked "Left," what is wrong?

Quick Answer: **102**
Detailed Answer: **105**

   ❏ a. The software for the CD player needs to be reinstalled.
   ❏ b. The audio cable is bad.
   ❏ c. The right speaker is bad.
   ❏ d. The speakers are sitting on the wrong sides.

14. What should be done following the replacement of a system board battery?

Quick Answer: **102**
Detailed Answer: **105**

   ❏ a. Run CMOS Setup utility to reconfigure the system.
   ❏ b. Reinstall Windows.
   ❏ c. Run Disk Defragmenter.
   ❏ d. Disable the L2 cache.

15. Which of the following components would you take on site to repair a system that, as you have been informed by the customer, has lights on when the computer turns on but nothing shows up on the display?

❑ a. CD-ROM

❑ b. Video card

❑ c. Power supply

❑ d. UPS

Quick Answer: **102**
Detailed Answer: **105**

16. What is the first thing you should check when a customer complains of a machine that was working yesterday and is completely dead today?

❑ a. AC outlet for power

❑ b. Power supply

❑ c. Motherboard

❑ d. Power switch

Quick Answer: **102**
Detailed Answer: **105**

17. If your tape backup stops responding every time you print, what could be the problem?

❑ a. There is probably an IRQ conflict.

❑ b. The tape drive needs an updated driver.

❑ c. The tape drive needs to be reinstalled.

❑ d. The printer is bad and needs to be replaced.

Quick Answer: **102**
Detailed Answer: **105**

18. You build your first PC at home. When you turn on your computer, the floppy drive fails to work. Also, you notice that the floppy drive operating light is on continuously. What is the problem?

❑ a. The floppy drive is bad and needs to be replaced.

❑ b. The motherboard BIOS needs to be upgraded.

❑ c. The floppy drive cable has been connected backward.

❑ d. The power supply connection to the floppy drive is bad.

Quick Answer: **102**
Detailed Answer: **105**

19. What is wrong if the light on the floppy disk drive stays on?

❑ a. The cable is reversed.

❑ b. The computer is locked up.

❑ c. The system keeps looking for a floppy disk.

❑ d. Nothing—it's a power light.

Quick Answer: **102**
Detailed Answer: **105**

. . . .

20. What happens if you mix PC100 and PC66 RAM?

   ❏   a. The system will run at the speed of the faster RAM.

   ❏   b. Only part of the RAM will be recognized by the system.

   ❏   c. The system will simply adapt to the installed memory types and no effect will be seen.

   ❏   d. The system will crash and a hard memory failure will occur.

Quick Answer: **102**
Detailed Answer: **106**

21. What is a "201" error code?

   ❏   a. BIOS failure

   ❏   b. RAM failure

   ❏   c. HDD failure

   ❏   d. VGA failure

Quick Answer: **102**
Detailed Answer: **106**

22. Which of the following would cause a keyboard error at boot-up? (Select all that apply.)

   ❏   a. Stuck keys.

   ❏   b. The keyboard is unplugged.

   ❏   c. The typematic rate is set too high in CMOS.

   ❏   d. The keyboard has been disabled in CMOS.

Quick Answer: **102**
Detailed Answer: **106**

23. How do you open a malfunctioning CD-ROM drive?

   ❏   a. Push the tip of a paper clip in the tray-release access hole on the front face of the drive.

   ❏   b. Pull on the carriage.

   ❏   c. Flip a switch on the back of the CD-ROM.

   ❏   d. You can't open a malfunctioning CD-ROM drive.

Quick Answer: **102**
Detailed Answer: **106**

24. When discharging a monitor, which of the following tools should you never use?

   ❏   a. Leather insulated shoes

   ❏   b. High-voltage regulator

   ❏   c. Ground strap

   ❏   d. Surge suppressor

Quick Answer: **102**
Detailed Answer: **106**

25. You've installed one IDE hard drive and it is working fine. You install a second IDE hard drive and neither hard drive works. What could be the problem?

    Quick Answer: **102**
    Detailed Answer: **106**

    ❏ a. The hard drives are connected in the wrong order on the IDE cable.
    ❏ b. The second hard drive is on the secondary IDE port with its jumper set in the Slave position.
    ❏ c. Both hard drives are connected to the Primary IDE port and the jumpers on both drives are set as Masters.
    ❏ d. One drive is connected as Primary Master and the other as Secondary Master, but the power connector isn't connected to the Secondary Master.

26. You install a 12GB SCSI drive as the system's primary drive but the system cannot see it. What should you do?

    Quick Answer: **102**
    Detailed Answer: **106**

    ❏ a. Try a different SCSI drive.
    ❏ b. Enable large drives in the SCSI BIOS.
    ❏ c. Use an IDE drive.
    ❏ d. Exchange the SCSI signal cable for the correct type.

27. In a PC-compatible system, IRQ4 is normally assigned to _____.

    Quick Answer: **102**
    Detailed Answer: **106**

    ❏ a. the device connected to the COM1 port
    ❏ b. the device connected to the LPT1 port
    ❏ c. the device connected to the COM2 port
    ❏ d. the device connected to the LPT2 port

28. A Windows 9x system was working fine yesterday, but today you get a Boot Record Not Found message. What is the first thing you should do?

    Quick Answer: **102**
    Detailed Answer: **106**

    ❏ a. Run the FDISK program and reformat the hard drive.
    ❏ b. Replace the hard drive with a known-good unit.
    ❏ c. Create an emergency boot disk.
    ❏ d. Run the FDISK program using the /MBR switch.

29. What is the problem if a computer continually locks up after being on for 5 minutes?

    Quick Answer: **102**
    Detailed Answer: **106**

    ❏ a. The power supply is bad.
    ❏ b. There is an IRQ conflict.
    ❏ c. The keyboard is defective.
    ❏ d. The CPU fan may not be working.

. . . .

30. _____ switches to low-power mode if there is no signal change for a given period of time. (Select the best answer.)

- ❏ a. An LCD device
- ❏ b. An RGB monitor
- ❏ c. A CRT monitor
- ❏ d. An Energy Star–compliant monitor

31. When opening the cover of a CRT, you should be careful because _____.

- ❏ a. the CRT can implode if dropped
- ❏ b. the CRT can store voltages in excess of 25,000 volts
- ❏ c. excess radiation can damage your eyes
- ❏ d. the monitor case might not fit back together

32. A newly installed sound card works properly except during printing. What is the problem?

- ❏ a. The LPT printer cable is bad.
- ❏ b. There is an IRQ conflict between the printer and sound card.
- ❏ c. The printer is out of toner.
- ❏ d. The motherboard is bad.

33. After you install a new Local Area Network card and attach it to the local hub, you cannot access or see any other computers on the network. What item should you most likely check first?

- ❏ a. The cabling between the NIC and the hub
- ❏ b. The hub
- ❏ c. The NIC card
- ❏ d. The network drivers

34. What type of tool is used to discharge the built-up voltage from a CRT?

- ❏ a. Grounding wire
- ❏ b. Heavy-duty screwdriver
- ❏ c. Tweezers
- ❏ d. Wrist strap

35. If the computer is turned on, plugged in, and no display is present, what action should be taken first?

- ❏ a. Check the video controller card.
- ❏ b. Check the interior of the monitor for blackened areas.
- ❏ c. Check the video cable for continuity.
- ❏ d. Check the monitor's On/Off switch.

36. A 601 error code during bootup most likely indicates a
_____.

  ❑   a. problem with the hard drive
  ❑   b. problem with the floppy drive
  ❑   c. problem with the I/O controller card
  ❑   d. CMOS setup error

Quick Answer: **102**
Detailed Answer: **107**

37. In an IBM-compatible BIOS, a memory error is signified by a
_____.

  ❑   a. 100 error code
  ❑   b. 301 error code
  ❑   c. 201 error code
  ❑   d. 601 error code

Quick Answer: **102**
Detailed Answer: **107**

38. What command-line utility should be run if an Invalid Media
Type message is encountered after replacing a hard drive?

  ❑   a. DEFRAG
  ❑   b. SCANDISK
  ❑   c. CHKDSK
  ❑   d. FDISK

Quick Answer: **102**
Detailed Answer: **107**

39. A 301 error code during bootup indicates _____.

  ❑   a. a floppy drive failure
  ❑   b. a keyboard failure
  ❑   c. a hard drive failure
  ❑   d. a video display adapter failure

Quick Answer: **102**
Detailed Answer: **107**

40. How can a balance problem that occurs with add-on stereo
speakers be corrected?

  ❑   a. Swap the speaker positions.
  ❑   b. Replace the sound card.
  ❑   c. Adjust the sound balance in the operating system.
  ❑   d. Replace the speakers.

Quick Answer: **102**
Detailed Answer: **107**

41. What AT command is used to reset a modem?

  ❑   a. ATM
  ❑   b. ATZ
  ❑   c. ATW
  ❑   d. ATT

Quick Answer: **102**
Detailed Answer: **107**

. . . .

42. What must you do first if you want to troubleshoot a USB problem on a Windows 2000 system?

- ❑ a. Open Device Manager.
- ❑ b. Log on as a member of the Administrators group.
- ❑ c. Select the USB driver and click the Properties button.
- ❑ d. Restart the system.

43. What can be done to repair system boards with defective onboard IDE controllers and to upgrade older IDE systems?

- ❑ a. Replace the system board.
- ❑ b. Replace the ROM BIOS.
- ❑ c. Install an IDE host adapter.
- ❑ d. Replace the IDE controller.

44. How can a CD be retrieved from a disabled CD-ROM drive?

- ❑ a. Insert a straightened paper clip into the tray-release access hole in the front panel.
- ❑ b. Press the Open/Close button.
- ❑ c. Eject the disk using the operating system.
- ❑ d. Use a thin knife to gently pry open the door.

45. What command is used to restore the DOS operating system files to the hard disk drive?

- ❑ a. FORMAT C:
- ❑ b. MBR /RENEW
- ❑ c. FDISK /MBR
- ❑ d. SYS C:

46. What command is used to restore a drive's master boot record and partition information?

- ❑ a. MBR /RENEW
- ❑ b. FDISK /MBR
- ❑ c. SYS C:
- ❑ d. FORMAT C:

47. In newer systems, where are the SCSI drive support and large drive support enabled?

- ❑ a. In the CONFIG.SYS file
- ❑ b. In Device Manager
- ❑ c. In the CMOS Setup utility
- ❑ d. In the Registry

48. What happens when you mix different IDE drive types on a single signal cable?
   - ❏ a. Only the master device is disabled.
   - ❏ b. Only the slave device is disabled.
   - ❏ c. Both master and slave devices are disabled.
   - ❏ d. The system works normally.

Quick Answer: 102
Detailed Answer: 108

49. How many master drive selections are there for each IDE channel?
   - ❏ a. four
   - ❏ b. two
   - ❏ c. three
   - ❏ d. one

Quick Answer: 102
Detailed Answer: 108

50. What condition is indicated by the Invalid Media Type error messages?
   - ❏ a. The MBR is missing or corrupt.
   - ❏ b. The drive is not formatted.
   - ❏ c. Operating system files are missing or corrupt.
   - ❏ d. The HDD cable is not attached.

Quick Answer: 102
Detailed Answer: 108

51. What condition is indicated by the Hard Drive Boot Failure error messages?
   - ❏ a. The MBR is missing or corrupt.
   - ❏ b. The drive is not formatted.
   - ❏ c. Operating system files are missing or corrupt.
   - ❏ d. The HDD cable is not attached.

Quick Answer: 102
Detailed Answer: 108

52. What condition is indicated by the Missing Operating System error messages?
   - ❏ a. The drive is not formatted.
   - ❏ b. The MBR is missing or corrupt.
   - ❏ c. Operating system files are missing or corrupt.
   - ❏ d. The HDD cable is not attached.

Quick Answer: 102
Detailed Answer: 108

53. What action can be taken when you encounter an Invalid Drive or Drive Specification error message? (Select the best answer.)
   - ❏ a. Repartition the drive.
   - ❏ b. Reformat the drive.
   - ❏ c. Repartition and reformat the drive.
   - ❏ d. Reinstall the operating system.

Quick Answer: 102
Detailed Answer: 108

. . . .

54. What are the consequences of installing the FDD cable in
    reverse?

    ❑ a. The FDD will still work normally.

    ❑ b. The FDD doesn't spin.

    ❑ c. The FDD light flashes and the drive reads the disk but can-
         not write to it.

    ❑ d. The FDD light stays on constantly and the boot record on
         the disk will be erased.

Quick Answer: **102**
Detailed Answer: **108**

55. What does a 601 error code indicate?

    ❑ a. RAM failure

    ❑ b. Invalid switch memory error

    ❑ c. CMOS checksum test error

    ❑ d. FDD error

Quick Answer: **102**
Detailed Answer: **108**

56. What action should be taken to clear up fuzzy characters on a
    CRT display?

    ❑ a. Reinstall the video driver.

    ❑ b. Replace the video card.

    ❑ c. Degauss the CRT.

    ❑ d. Reinstall the operating system.

Quick Answer: **102**
Detailed Answer: **108**

57. An Energy Star–compliant monitor _____.

    ❑ a. switches to low-power mode when no signal change occurs
         for a given period of time

    ❑ b. shuts off automatically when no signal change occurs for a
         given period of time

    ❑ c. adjusts for room lighting automatically

    ❑ d. uses more energy than non-ESC monitors

Quick Answer: **102**
Detailed Answer: **108**

58. Booting to Windows results in a distorted image that prevents
    you from manipulating the operating system. What can you do
    to correct this problem?

    ❑ a. Boot to Safe Mode and reinstall/configure the driver.

    ❑ b. Reboot the system to the command line.

    ❑ c. Replace the video card.

    ❑ d. Replace the monitor.

Quick Answer: **102**
Detailed Answer: **108**

59. When you move the cursor across the screen, it randomly
    jumps and freezes. What should you do to correct this?

    ❑ a. Unplug the mouse and then plug it back in.

    ❑ b. Clean the dirt from inside the mouse.

    ❑ c. Reinstall the mouse driver.

    ❑ d. Replace the mouse.

Quick Answer: **102**
Detailed Answer: **108**

60. What is a common condition that will produce a keyboard error message?

- ❑ a. The OS keyboard settings are incorrect.
- ❑ b. A key is stuck down.
- ❑ c. A key is stuck open.
- ❑ d. The keyboard is locked.

Quick Answer: **102**
Detailed Answer: **109**

61. A defective _____ can cause the system to continually lose track of time.

- ❑ a. battery
- ❑ b. microprocessor
- ❑ c. RAM module
- ❑ d. BIOS ROM

Quick Answer: **102**
Detailed Answer: **109**

62. What are the effects on the system of heat buildup and micro-processor fan failures?

- ❑ a. The system slows down.
- ❑ b. The system shuts down.
- ❑ c. The system restarts.
- ❑ d. The system locks up.

Quick Answer: **102**
Detailed Answer: **109**

63. How can you correct hard-memory errors?

- ❑ a. Replace all RAM modules.
- ❑ b. Remove all RAM modules.
- ❑ c. Replace the microprocessor.
- ❑ d. Restart the computer.

Quick Answer: **102**
Detailed Answer: **109**

64. What are the consequences of mixing RAM types and speeds within a system? (Select all that apply.)

- ❑ a. It will cause the system to lock up.
- ❑ b. The system will run slower.
- ❑ c. Hard-memory errors will occur.
- ❑ d. There is no effect.

Quick Answer: **102**
Detailed Answer: **109**

65. How can you correct soft-memory errors?

- ❑ a. Replace all RAM modules.
- ❑ b. Remove all RAM modules.
- ❑ c. Restart the computer.
- ❑ d. Replace the microprocessor.

Quick Answer: **102**
Detailed Answer: **109**

66. What type of failures are hard-memory errors?

❑ a. RAM failures that generate NMI errors
❑ b. Infrequent errors in the OS and applications
❑ c. Errors in the storage and retrieval of data to the hard drive
❑ d. Errors caused by a physical jolt to the system

Quick Answer: **102**
Detailed Answer: **109**

67. What does a 201 error code indicate?

❑ a. Invalid switch memory error
❑ b. DMA controller error
❑ c. CMOS checksum test error
❑ d. RAM failure

Quick Answer: **102**
Detailed Answer: **109**

68. When should a BIOS chip be replaced?

❑ a. When upgrading hard drives
❑ b. When upgrading to newer hardware that the existing BIOS does not support
❑ c. When upgrading video cards
❑ d. When it's been flashed too many times

Quick Answer: **102**
Detailed Answer: **109**

69. A non-PnP internal modem can only use the standard COM2 port. What should be done before setting up its software?

❑ a. Put the modem on COM1, IRQ5.
❑ b. Put the modem on COM1, IRQ12.
❑ c. Disable COM2 in CMOS.
❑ d. Plug in the phone cord.

Quick Answer: **102**
Detailed Answer: **109**

70. If you install an ISA modem that only has jumper settings for COM1 and COM2, what action do you need to take to make sure that it receives the proper resources in a PnP system?

❑ a. Disable the COM port in CMOS.
❑ b. Set the COM port in CMOS to auto.
❑ c. Enable the COM port in CMOS.
❑ d. Set the modem to COM2 in CMOS.

Quick Answer: **102**
Detailed Answer: **109**

71. One of your customers is having problems with a new CD-RW drive he has installed on his system. The system contains a single EIDE HDD and a 52x CD-ROM drive. When he attempts to make copies of a disc between the CD-ROM drives, he receives buffer underrun errors. What suggestions can you give him to improve his copy operations? (Select all that apply.)

Quick Answer: **102**
Detailed Answer: **110**

   ❑   a. Place the CD-ROM or DVD writer on an IDE channel of its own. This keeps the drive from competing with other drives for the channel's available bandwidth.
   ❑   b. Conduct the write operation on the same drive as the read operation and use reduced write speed options.
   ❑   c. Locate a Flash program for the drive's BIOS to upgrade it so that it provides better support for the write function.
   ❑   d. Switch the Master/Slave settings on the HDD and CD-RW drive so that the CD-RW drive has first position for the primary controller.

72. If you put a boot disk into drive A and the computer boots to drive C instead, what is the cause of this?

Quick Answer: **102**
Detailed Answer: **110**

   ❑   a. You must first press Esc to be able to boot to the floppy drive.
   ❑   b. The floppy drive is configured as a slave drive.
   ❑   c. The boot sequence isn't set to boot to drive A first in the BIOS.
   ❑   d. The disk doesn't have the correct version of DOS.

73. Which network utilities can be used to identify the IP address of a known remote location?

Quick Answer: **102**
Detailed Answer: **110**

   ❑   a. NetSTAT and NET VIEW
   ❑   b. PING and TRACERT
   ❑   c. ARP and NET VIEW
   ❑   d. IPCONFIG and WINIPCFG

74. What type of device is commonly used to make checks on a LAN cable?

Quick Answer: **102**
Detailed Answer: **110**

   ❑   a. OTDR
   ❑   b. Multimeter
   ❑   c. Voltmeter
   ❑   d. Line (Cable) tester

75. What is the number-one reason for LAN installation failures?

- ❏ a. Excessive traffic
- ❏ b. NOS failures
- ❏ c. Cabling faults
- ❏ d. Incorrect protocol

Quick Answer: **102**
Detailed Answer: **110**

76. What is the first step in checking out a monitor that appears dead?

- ❏ a. Check to see that the power cord is plugged in.
- ❏ b. Check the motherboard battery.
- ❏ c. Check the power supply connection to the motherboard.
- ❏ d. Check to see that the power light is on.

Quick Answer: **102**
Detailed Answer: **110**

Objective 2.2: Identify basic trouble-shooting procedures and tools, and how to elicit problem symptoms from customers.

1. To check a fuse with a multimeter, you would use the _____ setting.

- ❏ a. voltage (volts)
- ❏ b. current (amps)
- ❏ c. resistance (ohms)
- ❏ d. inductance (henries)

Quick Answer: **103**
Detailed Answer: **110**

2. Which of the following questions would be helpful to ask computer operators when they present a problem to you?

- ❏ a. Are you still under warranty?
- ❏ b. What were you doing when it happened and when did it occur?
- ❏ c. How long have you been operating a computer?
- ❏ d. Where are you located?

Quick Answer: **103**
Detailed Answer: **110**

3. If a system produces an error message before the single beep during bootup, what type of problem is normally indicated?

- ❏ a. Configuration
- ❏ b. Hardware
- ❏ c. Operating system
- ❏ d. Bootup

Quick Answer: **103**
Detailed Answer: **110**

4. When checking for a good 2-amp fuse, the VOM should read
_____.

Quick Answer: **103**
Detailed Answer: **111**

- ❏ a. 30 ohms
- ❏ b. 15 ohms
- ❏ c. 2 ohms
- ❏ d. 0.0 ohms

5. When measuring voltage, it is a good idea to first set the
DMM to _____.

Quick Answer: **103**
Detailed Answer: **111**

- ❏ a. the lowest possible voltage setting
- ❏ b. a midrange setting
- ❏ c. the highest possible voltage setting
- ❏ d. ohms

6. Speakers are checked using the _____ setting of a
multimeter.

Quick Answer: **103**
Detailed Answer: **111**

- ❏ a. volt
- ❏ b. amp
- ❏ c. capacitance
- ❏ d. ohm

7. When a Press F1 to Continue message appears during bootup,
what type of action is indicated?

Quick Answer: **103**
Detailed Answer: **111**

- ❏ a. A floppy disk is needed in drive A.
- ❏ b. The system needs to be reconfigured.
- ❏ c. The operating system is missing from the hard drive and
needs to be reloaded.
- ❏ d. The keyboard is disconnected.

8. What reading should be obtained when using an ohmmeter to
check a speaker?

Quick Answer: **103**
Detailed Answer: **111**

- ❏ a. 8 ohms
- ❏ b. 6 ohms
- ❏ c. 30 ohms
- ❏ d. 0 ohms

9. When checking a 1-amp fuse with an ohmmeter, the value
reading for a good fuse should be _____.

Quick Answer: **103**
Detailed Answer: **111**

- ❏ a. infinite
- ❏ b. 1 amp
- ❏ c. 1 Kohms
- ❏ d. 0 ohms

. . . .

10. When checking the power supply unit with a digital multi-meter, it should be set to _____.

    ❑   a. DC current
    ❑   b. DC voltage
    ❑   c. AC current
    ❑   d. AC voltage

11. When using the ohmmeter function of a DMM to perform tests, you must always _____.

    ❑   a. connect the meter in series with the device being tested
    ❑   b. connect the meter in parallel with the device being tested
    ❑   c. remove the device being tested from the circuit board
    ❑   d. open the circuit that contains the device being tested

12. To measure voltage, a multimeter should be connected _____.

    ❑   a. in series with the item being checked
    ❑   b. in line with the item being checked
    ❑   c. in parallel with the item being checked
    ❑   d. in place of the item being checked

13. Which of the following items would not be considered a field-replaceable unit (FRU)?

    ❑   a. CPU
    ❑   b. Hard disk drive
    ❑   c. Chassis
    ❑   d. Video card

14. What type of computer component can you usually replace in the field?

    ❑   a. ERU
    ❑   b. FSU
    ❑   c. FRU
    ❑   d. FRC

15. After the system has successfully completed POSTs, you see an error message Bad or Missing Command File. What type of problem is this?

    ❑   a. Operating system problem
    ❑   b. Configuration problem
    ❑   c. Hardware problem
    ❑   d. Bootup problem

16. What is the most common type of malfunction observed after the installation of a new hardware or software component?

   ❑   a.   Operating system problem
   ❑   b.   Configuration problem
   ❑   c.   Hardware problem
   ❑   d.   Corrupted or missing files

Quick Answer: **103**
Detailed Answer: **112**

17. What is the most commonly used repair technique?

   ❑   a.   Using a multimeter to test the signals from each component
   ❑   b.   Testing each component on a test rig
   ❑   c.   Substituting known-good parts for suspected bad components
   ❑   d.   Replacing all possible FRUs

Quick Answer: **103**
Detailed Answer: **112**

18. What type of problem causes a Press F1 to Continue error message to be displayed?

   ❑   a.   The video display is defective.
   ❑   b.   The operating system is missing from the hard drive.
   ❑   c.   An FDD is defective.
   ❑   d.   The configuration information is wrong.

Quick Answer: **103**
Detailed Answer: **112**

19. During the bootup procedure, what usually occurs after the memory test counts up on the screen?

   ❑   a.   The BIOS message appears on the screen.
   ❑   b.   The system begins searching for a boot record.
   ❑   c.   The hard disk drive light comes on briefly.
   ❑   d.   The POST is completed and the system beeps.

Quick Answer: **103**
Detailed Answer: **112**

20. What event marks the transition from basic hardware problems to bootup problems?

   ❑   a.   The power light comes on.
   ❑   b.   The operating system bootup screen appears.
   ❑   c.   A single beep sound occurs.
   ❑   d.   The operating system bootup is completed.

Quick Answer: **103**
Detailed Answer: **112**

21. What questions should you ask the user when you are first examining a defective unit? (Select all that apply.)

   ❑   a.   What were you doing when the problem occurred?
   ❑   b.   Is the unit new? Did it ever work?
   ❑   c.   Was there an error message? What did it say?
   ❑   d.   How much experience do you have with this type of computer?

Quick Answer: **103**
Detailed Answer: **112**

. . . .

22. What is the most important factor to consider when assessing the situation at a new troubleshooting call?

   ❑   a.   The operating system
   ❑   b.   The user
   ❑   c.   The power supply
   ❑   d.   The system configuration

Quick Answer: **103**
Detailed Answer: **112**

23. What are the voltages that should be expected when testing a PC?

   ❑   a.   –1.2V DC, +1.2V DC, –0.5V DC, +0.5V DC
   ❑   b.   –1.2V AC, +1.2V AC, –0.5V AC, +0.5V AC
   ❑   c.   –3.3V DC, +3.3V DC, –1.5V DC, +1.5V DC
   ❑   d.   –12V DC, +12V DC, –5V DC, +5V DC

Quick Answer: **103**
Detailed Answer: **112**

24. What meter reading would you expect from an open speaker?

   ❑   a.   4 ohms
   ❑   b.   Infinite (or a blank display)
   ❑   c.   8 ohms
   ❑   d.   0 ohms

Quick Answer: **103**
Detailed Answer: **112**

25. Which multimeter reading should you expect from measuring a good speaker?

   ❑   a.   8 ohms
   ❑   b.   0 ohms
   ❑   c.   4 ohms
   ❑   d.   Infinity

Quick Answer: **103**
Detailed Answer: **112**

26. What multimeter reading would you expect to receive from measuring a good 2-amp fuse?

   ❑   a.   15 ohms
   ❑   b.   2 ohms
   ❑   c.   0 ohms
   ❑   d.   30 ohms

Quick Answer: **103**
Detailed Answer: **113**

27. Which of the following is not a software tool commonly used by a repair technician?

   ❑   a.   Antivirus utility
   ❑   b.   Emergency boot disk
   ❑   c.   Hardware diagnostic utility
   ❑   d.   Software diagnostic utility

Quick Answer: **103**
Detailed Answer: **113**

28. During the bootup procedure, a single beep indicates that the
_____.

- ❏ a. operating system has been loaded
- ❏ b. speaker is malfunctioning
- ❏ c. power is low
- ❏ d. POST has been completed

Quick Answer: **103**
Detailed Answer: **113**

Quick Check Answer Key

Objective 2.1

1. c	26. b	52. b
2. d	27. a	53. c
3. b	28. d	54. d
4. c	29. d	55. d
5. a	30. d	56. c
6. b	31. b	57. a
7. d	32. b	58. a
8. d	33. a	59. b
9. a	34. b	60. b
10. d	35. d	61. a
11. d	36. b	62. d
12. c	37. c	63. a
13. d	38. d	64. a, c
14. a	39. b	65. c
15. b	40. a	66. a
16. a	41. b	67. d
17. a	42. b	68. b
18. c	43. c	69. c
19. a	44. a	70. a
20. d	45. d	71. a, b, c
21. b	46. b	72. c
22. a, b	47. c	73. b
23. a	48. c	74. d
24. c	49. d	75. c
25. c	50. b	76. a
	51. a	

Objective 2.2

1. c
2. b
3. b
4. d
5. c
6. d
7. b
8. a
9. d
10. b
11. d
12. c
13. c
14. c
15. d
16. b
17. c
18. d
19. c
20. c
21. a, b, c
22. b
23. d
24. b
25. a
26. c
27. d
28. d

Answers and Explanations

Objective 2.1

1. **c.** Many newer peripheral devices can safely be unplugged and reattached to the system while power is applied; this is not so with the standard keyboard. Disconnecting or plugging the keyboard into the system while power is applied can cause the operating system or even the system board to fail due to the power surge and Electrostatic Discharge (ESD).

2. **d.** If the portable's TouchPad works but the external mouse does not, check the documentation for an Fn key combination requirement for the mouse.

3. **b.** The Windows XP Professional operating system uses hardware profiles to determine which drivers to load when the system hardware changes (docked or undocked). It uses the Docked Profile to load drivers when the portable computer is docked and the Undocked Profile when the computer starts up without the docking station. These hardware profiles are created by the Windows XP operating system when the computer is docked and undocked if the system is PnP compliant.

4. **c.** To correct battery memory problems, you must start the portable computer using only the battery and allow it to run until it completely discharges the battery and quits. Then recharge the battery for at least 12 hours. Repeat this process several times watching for consistently increasing operating times.

5. **a.** If the adapter's icon shows an exclamation mark on a yellow background, the card is not functioning properly. Turn off the system and reinsert the device in a different PCMCIA slot. If the same problem appears, there are three possible sources of problems: The card might be faulty, the PC Card controller in the PC might be faulty, or the operating system might not support the device in question.

6. **b.** To correct a PCMCIA socket installation problem, remove the PCMCIA socket listing in the Device Manager, reboot the computer, and allow the Windows PnP process to detect the socket and install the appropriate driver for it. If the names of the PCMCIA cards do not appear after the restart, then the reinstallation process was not successful. Therefore, the PCMCIA socket you are using is not supported by the operating system version.

7. **d.** To verify that the PC Card device is working, access the Device Manager under the Windows Control Panel's System applet. If there is a problem with the PC Card device, it will appear in the Device Manager. If the adapter's icon shows an exclamation mark on a yellow background, the card is not functioning properly.

8. **d.** In a portable PC system, control of the power management system is provided through the BIOS CMOS Setup utility.

9. **a.** One of the biggest problems for portable computers is heat buildup inside the case. Because conventional power supplies (and their fans) are not included in portable units, separate fans must be designed into portables to carry heat out of the unit. The closeness of the portable's components and the small amount of free air space inside its case also adds to heat-related design problems.

10. **d.** If a PC will not maintain the time and date after replacing the system board battery, check the contacts of the battery holder for corrosion.

11. **d.** If the CD-ROM and hard drive both stop working after you install a CD-RW drive, verify their Master/Slave jumper settings to make sure that they are set correctly. When three or four IDE devices are installed in a system, you must determine which devices can share the channels most effectively.

12. **c.** During bootup, an IBM-compatible 601 error code is associated with FDD failures.

13. **d.** When placing the speakers on the wrong sides, increasing the volume on the right speaker will instead increase the output of the left speaker. The obvious cure for this problem is to physically switch the positions of the speakers.

14. **a.** If a battery fails, or if it has been changed, the contents of the CMOS configuration will be lost. After replacing the battery, it is always necessary to run the CMOS Setup utility to reconfigure the system.

15. **b.** In the case of hardware problems, the components associated with video problems include the video adapter card, the monitor and, to a lesser degree, the system board.

16. **a.** When the system exhibits no signs of life, the first thing to do is confirm that the power supply cord is plugged into a functioning outlet.

17. **a.** In most PC systems, two COM ports share the same IRQ line. If two devices are connected to the same IRQ line, a conflict occurs because it is not likely that the interrupt handler software can service both devices. Therefore, check whether the tape drive and the printer share the same IRQ line if the tape backup stops responding every time you print.

18. **c.** Reversed FDD signal cable will cause the FDD activity light to stay on constantly.

19. **a.** If the FDD activity light stays on constantly, the FDD signal cable is reversed.

20. **d.** Mixing RAM types and speeds can cause the system to lock up and produce hard-memory errors.

21. **b.** A 201 error code indicates a RAM failure.

22. **a, b.** (a) The keys of the keyboard can wear out over time. This might result in keys maintaining electrical contact (sticking) even when pressure is removed. The stuck key will produce an error message when the system detects it during bootup. (b) An unplugged keyboard, or one with a bad signal cable, will produce a keyboard error message during startup.

23. **a.** If the drive is inoperable and there is a CD or DVD locked inside, you should insert a straightened paper clip into the tray-release access hole that is usually located beside the ejection button. This will release the spring-loaded tray and pop out the disc.

24. **c.** Always discharge the anode of the picture tube to the receiver chassis before handling the CRT tube. But due to the high voltage levels, you should never wear antistatic grounding straps when working inside the monitor.

25. **c.** If a working IDE hard drive fails because a second IDE hard drive has been installed, it is probably because they are connected to the same IDE port and both drives are set as Master. On IDE drives, there can only be one master drive selection on each IDE channel.

26. **b.** Check the CMOS Setup utility to make sure that SCSI support has been enabled along with large SCSI drive support if the computer cannot see a large SCSI drive installed on the system.

27. **a.** The IRQ4 line is assigned for both COM1 and COM3 ports.

28. **d.** If the clean boot disk has a copy of the FDISK program on it, you can attempt to restore the drive's master boot record (including its partition information) by typing the FDISK /MBR command at the A: prompt.

29. **d.** If the system consistently locks up after being on for a few minutes, this is a good indication that the microprocessor's fan is not running or that some other heat buildup problem is occurring.

30. **d.** Monitors that possess this power-saving feature revert to a low-power mode when they do not receive a signal change for a given period of time.

31. **b.** The voltage levels present during operation are lethal. Electrical potentials as high as 25,000V are present inside the unit when it is operating.

32. **b.** If the sound card operates correctly except when a printing operation is in progress, an IRQ conflict probably exists between the sound card and the printer port if they are assigned to two COM ports that share the same IRQ line.

33. **a.** Cabling is the single largest cause of networking problems. Because this is a new installation, the cabling and connections are particularly suspect.

34. **b.** The built-up charge on the anode inside a CRT must be shorted to ground so that the monitor can be handled safely. This operation is typically performed with a large, long-handled screwdriver and a shorting clip.

35. **d.** If you suspect a video display hardware problem, the first task is to check the monitor's On/Off switch to see that it is in the On position.

36. **b.** A 601 error code during bootup most likely indicates an FDD failure.

37. **c.** In an IBM-compatible BIOS, a RAM failure is signified by a 201 error code.

38. **d.** If an invalid media type message appears, indicating that the controller cannot find a recognizable track/sector pattern on the drive, use the FDISK utility to partition the drive.

39. **b.** An IBM-compatible error code for a keyboard is 301.

40. **a.** It is possible to place the speakers on the wrong sides. This will produce a problem when you try to adjust the balance between them. The obvious cure for this problem is to physically switch the positions of the speakers.

41. **b.** The AT command ATZ is entered at the command line to reset the modem and enter the Command mode. You should receive a 0, or OK response, if the command was processed.

42. **b.** To use the Windows 2000 Device Manager utility to troubleshoot USB problems, you must be logged on as an administrator, or as a member of the Administrators group.

43. **c.** If the onboard IDE controller becomes defective, it is possible to install an IDE host adapter card in an expansion slot and use it without replacing the system board. This action can also be used to upgrade IDE systems to EIDE systems for additional IDE devices. The onboard IDE controller might need to be disabled before the system can address the new host adapter version.

44. **a.** If the drive is inoperable and there is a CD or DVD locked inside, you should insert a straightened paper clip into the tray-release access hole that's usually located beside the ejection button. This will release the spring-loaded tray and pop out the disc.

45. **d.** SYS C: copies the IO.SYS, MSDOS.SYS, and COMMAND.COM system files from the boot disk to the hard disk drive.

46. **b.** If the clean boot disk has a copy of the FDISK program on it, you may attempt to restore the drive's master boot record (including its partition information) by typing the command FDISK /MBR.

47. **c.** In newer systems, SCSI drive support and large drive support are both enabled in the BIOS.

48. **c.** Mixing device types will create a situation in which the system cannot provide the different types of control information each device needs. The drives are incompatible and you might not be able to access either device.

49. **d.** When troubleshooting the HDD, make sure that there is only one master drive selection on each IDE channel.

50. **b.** An Invalid Media Type message appears when the controller cannot find a recognizable track/sector pattern on the drive. It indicates that the drive is not properly formatted.

51. **a.** A Hard Drive Boot Failure message indicates that the disk's Master Boot Record is missing or has become corrupt.

52. **b.** A Missing Operating System message indicates that the disk's Master Boot Record is missing or has become corrupt.

53. **c.** If the system cannot see a hard drive after booting from the floppy disk, an Invalid Drive… or Invalid Drive Specification error message will be returned in response to any attempt to access the drive. You must examine the complete HDD system. Repartition the drive first. Next, reformat the drive to make the disk bootable.

54. **d.** Reversing the signal cable causes the FDD activity light to stay on continuously. The reversed signal cable will also erase the Master Boot Record from the disk, making it nonbootable.

55. **d.** A 601 error code indicates that a floppy disk drive error has been detected during bootup.

56. **c.** If a display has fuzzy characters, you might need to remove built-up electromagnetic fields from the screen through a process called *degaussing*.

57. **a.** Energy Star–compliant monitors have a power-saving feature of reverting to a low-power mode when they do not receive a signal change for a given period of time.

58. **a.** If the Windows video problem prevents you from being able to work with the display, restart the system, press the F8 function key when the Starting Windows message appears, and select the Safe Mode option. This should load Windows with the standard VGA driver and should furnish a starting point for installing the correct driver for the monitor being used.

59. **b.** When a trackball mouse is moved across the table, the trackball picks up dirt or lint, which can hinder its movement, typically evident by the cursor periodically freezing and jumping onscreen.

60. **b.** The stuck key will produce an error message when the system detects it.

61. **a.** If a system refuses to maintain time and date information, the CMOS back-up battery, or its recharging circuitry, the system is normally faulty.

62. **d.** If the system consistently locks up after being on for a few minutes, this is a good indication that the microprocessor's fan is not running or that some other heat-buildup problem is occurring.

63. **a.** These errors are caused by permanent physical failures that generate NMI errors in the system and require that the memory units be checked by substitution.

64. **a, c.** Mixing RAM types and speeds in a system can cause the system to lock up and produce hard-memory errors.

65. **c.** RAM failures basically fall into two major categories and create two different types of failures, which are soft-memory errors and hard-memory errors. Soft-memory errors are caused by infrequent and random glitches in the operation of applications and the system. You can clear these events just by restarting the system.

66. **a.** RAM failures basically fall into two major categories and create two different types of failures, which are soft-memory errors and hard-memory errors. Hard-memory errors are caused by permanent physical failures that generate NMI errors in the system and require that the memory units be checked by substitution.

67. **d.** A 201 error code is a symptom associated with system board hardware failures indicating a RAM failure.

68. **b.** In situations in which new devices, such as microprocessors, RAM devices, and hard drives, have been added to the system, the original BIOS might not be able to support them. As a result, the system might not function and the BIOS might need to be upgraded. Always check the Web sites of the device and the system board manufacturers to obtain the latest BIOS upgrade and support information.

69. **c.** To install a non-PnP device on a specific COM port (for example, COM2), you must first disable that port in the system's CMOS settings in order to avoid a device conflict.

70. **a.** To install a non-PnP device on a specific COM port (for example, COM2), you must first disable that port in the system's CMOS settings in order to avoid a device conflict. If not, the system might try to allocate that resource to some other device because it has no way of knowing that the non-PNP device requires it.

71. **a, b, c.** (a) To minimize buffer underruns, place the CD-ROM or DVD writer on an IDE channel of its own. This keeps the drive from competing with other drives for the channel's available bandwidth. (b) Conducting the write operation on the same drive as the read operation and using reduced write speed options in the R/W application software can minimize data flow problems. (c) Because the drive has already been purchased and installed, check the drive's documentation for suggestions and check the drive manufacturer's Web site for newer R/W applications and driver versions. You might also be able to locate a Flash program for the drive's BIOS to upgrade it so that it provides better support for the write function.

72. **c.** If the system does not boot to the floppy A: drive first, examine the advanced CMOS Setup to check the system's boot order.

73. **b.** Both PING and TRACERT can be used to identify the IP address of a known network address.

74. **d.** The most efficient way to test network cable is to use a line tester to check its functionality.

75. **c.** Cabling is one of the biggest problems encountered in a network installation. The most efficient way to test network cable is to use a line tester to check its functionality.

76. **a.** If you suspect a video display hardware problem, first examine the power cord to see that it is plugged in and check to see that the monitor's power switch is in the On position.

Objective 2.2

1. **c.** One of the main uses of the resistance function is to test fuses. You should disconnect at least one end of the fuse from the system and set the meter on the 1-Kohm resistance setting.

2. **b.** The user is one of the most common sources of PC problems. In most situations, your first troubleshooting step should be to talk to the user. Gather information from the user regarding the environment the system is being used in, any symptoms or error codes produced by the system, and the situations that existed when the failure occurred.

3. **b.** Errors that occur, or are displayed, before the single beep during the bootup process indicate that a hardware problem of some type exists.

4. **d.** One of the main uses of the resistance function is to test fuses. You must disconnect at least one end of the fuse from the system and set the meter on the 1-Kohm resistance setting. If the fuse is good, the meter should read about 0 ohms, regardless of the fuse's ampere value.

5. **c.** It is normal practice to first set the meter to its highest voltage range to make certain that the voltage level being measured does not damage the meter.

6. **d.** To check the speaker, just disconnect the speaker from the system, select the resistance (ohms) function, and connect a meter lead to each end. If the speaker is good, the meter should read about 8 ohms. If the speaker is defective, the resistance reading should be 0 ohms for an electrical short or infinite for an open circuit.

7. **b.** The Press F1 to Continue configuration error message means that the system detects invalid configuration information and needs to be reconfigured.

8. **a.** When using an ohmmeter to check a speaker, the meter should read about 8 ohms if the speaker is good, although a smaller speaker might be 4 ohms.

9. **d.** One of the main uses of the resistance function is to test fuses. You must disconnect at least one end of the fuse from the system. You should set the meter on the 1-Kohm resistance setting. If the fuse is good, the meter should read about 0 ohms.

10. **b.** In computer and peripheral troubleshooting, fully 99% of the tests made are DC voltage readings. These measurements most often involve checking the DC side of the power supply unit.

11. **d.** Resistance checks require that you electrically isolate the component being tested from the system. For most circuit components, this means desoldering at least one end from the board.

12. **c.** The DC voltage function is used to take measurements in live DC circuits. It should be connected in parallel with the device being checked.

13. **c.** A chassis cannot be simply exchanged in the field as a hard disk drive, CPU, or video card can; therefore, the chassis is not an FRU.

14. **c.** A field-replaceable unit (FRU) is the portion of the system that you can conveniently replace in the field. FRU devices include the keyboard, video display, video adapter card, I/O adapter card, and so forth.

15. **d.** The system produces a single beep indicating that it has completed its POST and initialization process. After the beep tone has been produced in the startup sequence, the system shifts over to the process of booting up and begins looking for and loading the operating system. If the command file is missing or corrupted, the system cannot be booted up.

16. **b.** Configuration or setup problems tend to occur whenever a new hardware option is added to the system, or when the system is used for the very first time. These problems result from mismatches between the system's programmed configuration held in CMOS memory and the actual equipment installed in the system.

17. **c.** If a problem is not caused by a configuration error, it likely is a defective component. The most widely used repair method involves substituting known-good components for suspected bad components.

18. **d.** The Press F1 to Continue configuration error message is caused by invalid configuration information; therefore, the system needs to be reconfigured.

19. **b.** If enabled in the CMOS boot sequence, the floppy disk drive access light comes on briefly after the memory test counts up. However, in most systems, the next action is a check of the hard drive.

20. **c.** You can use the single beep that most PCs produce between the end of the POST and the beginning of the bootup process as a key to separate hardware problems from software problems.

21. **a, b, c.** (a) Ask the user to demonstrate the procedures that led to the malfunction in a step-by-step manner. This communication can help you narrow down a problem to a particular section of the computer. (b) Determine if the unit ever works. If the unit has been working, take note of the environment in which the equipment is being used and how heavy its usage is. If the unit has never been used, the problem might have occurred during the installation and configuration. (c) Most PCs have reasonably good built-in self tests that are run each time the computer is powered up. These tests can prove very beneficial in detecting hardware-oriented problems within the system. A numerically coded error message or written description of the error is issued for a self-test failure or setup mismatch.

22. **b.** The user is one of the most common sources of PC problems. In most situations, your first troubleshooting step should be to talk to the user.

23. **d.** The DC voltages that can normally be expected in a PC-compatible system are +12V, +5V, –5V, and –12V. The actual values for these readings may vary by 5% in either direction.

24. **b.** If the speaker is defective, the resistance reading should be 0 for an electrical short or infinite for an open circuit.

25. **a.** When testing a speaker using a multimeter, the meter should read about 8 ohms if the speaker is good. If the speaker is defective, the resistance reading should be 0 ohms for an electrical short or infinite for an open circuit.

26. **c.** You should set the meter on the 1-Kohm resistance setting. If the fuse is good, the meter should read about 0 ohms.

27. **d.** In addition to hardware tools, a computer repair technician should have a collection of software tools at his disposal. Typical software tools used by computer technicians include emergency boot/start disks to get broken systems started, antivirus utilities, and hardware diagnostic utility packages. A software diagnostics utility is not commonly used.

28. **d.** The single beep indicates that the system has completed its POST and initialization process. After this point, the operation of the machine has shifted to looking for and loading an operating system.

Hardware Domain 3.0: PC Preventive Maintenance, Safety, and Environmental Issues

Objective 3.1: Identify the various types of preventive maintenance measures, products, and procedures and when and how to use them.

1. When an external modem uses the COM2 port, no other device should use the _____ port.
   - ❏ a. COM1
   - ❏ b. LPT1
   - ❏ c. COM4
   - ❏ d. LPT2

Quick Answer: **128**
Detailed Answer: **129**

2. The best protection against data loss caused by power failure is _____.
   - ❏ a. a surge suppressor
   - ❏ b. a tape backup
   - ❏ c. a UPS
   - ❏ d. a RAID system

Quick Answer: **128**
Detailed Answer: **129**

3. Which of the following is not a function of an uninterruptible power supply?
   - ❏ a. Providing a high level of protection from sags and spikes
   - ❏ b. Long-term battery backup
   - ❏ c. Monitoring the power input line and switching to the output of the batteries whenever a loss in power is detected
   - ❏ d. Keeping the batteries online so that there is no switching done when the power drops

Quick Answer: **128**
Detailed Answer: **129**

4. The electric power goes out in your town. What kind of device do you need to have installed in order to protect your system from spike damage when the power comes back on?

- ❏ a. Power strip
- ❏ b. Power suppressor
- ❏ c. Switchable power supply
- ❏ d. UPS

Quick Answer: **128**
Detailed Answer: **129**

5. Which of the following devices should not be plugged directly into a UPS?

- ❏ a. A modem
- ❏ b. A monitor
- ❏ c. A dot-matrix printer
- ❏ d. A laser printer

Quick Answer: **128**
Detailed Answer: **129**

6. A voltage surge is measured in _____.

- ❏ a. seconds
- ❏ b. nanoseconds
- ❏ c. microseconds
- ❏ d. milliseconds

Quick Answer: **128**
Detailed Answer: **129**

7. A short overvoltage occurrence (nanoseconds) is called a _____.

- ❏ a. spike
- ❏ b. surge
- ❏ c. brownout
- ❏ d. sag

Quick Answer: **128**
Detailed Answer: **129**

8. When a slight power line interruption occurs, which device will help the most?

- ❏ a. A UPS
- ❏ b. A surge suppressor
- ❏ c. A separate AC outlet for the monitor
- ❏ d. A shorter power cable

Quick Answer: **128**
Detailed Answer: **129**

9. Cooling fans should be mounted on all ICs operating at clock speeds above _____.

- ❏ a. 33MHz
- ❏ b. 66MHz
- ❏ c. 100MHz
- ❏ d. 400MHz

Quick Answer: **128**
Detailed Answer: **129**

. . . .

10. A _____ is used to protect computer equipment from power-line variations or power outages.

Quick Answer: **128**
Detailed Answer: **129**

- ❏ a. preliminary ESD
- ❏ b. surge protector
- ❏ c. USPS
- ❏ d. UPS

11. A _____ is used to protect computer equipment from very small overvoltage occurrences.

Quick Answer: **128**
Detailed Answer: **129**

- ❏ a. USPS
- ❏ b. UPS
- ❏ c. surge suppressor
- ❏ d. preliminary ESD

12. A _____ is an undervoltage condition that lasts for a very short period of time.

Quick Answer: **128**
Detailed Answer: **130**

- ❏ a. spike
- ❏ b. sag
- ❏ c. surge
- ❏ d. brownout

13. A _____ is an undervoltage condition that lasts for an extended period of time.

Quick Answer: **128**
Detailed Answer: **130**

- ❏ a. brownout
- ❏ b. voltage sag
- ❏ c. surge
- ❏ d. spike

14. How can you prevent images from being burned into the screen of a video display monitor if it is not set up to blank itself after a period of no activity?

Quick Answer: **128**
Detailed Answer: **130**

- ❏ a. Set the Auto off feature under the Display icon in the Control Panel.
- ❏ b. Use the Device Manager utility to set up a turn-off time for the display.
- ❏ c. Install a screensaver that will continuously change the display on the screen.
- ❏ d. Access the CMOS Setup utility and set the monitor to sleep after a given amount of inactive time.

15. What is the best method of recovering quickly from operator errors and hard disk drive failures?

Quick Answer: **128**
Detailed Answer: **130**

     ❑   a.   Install a RAID disk system.
     ❑   b.   Periodically back up the hard drive on another media.
     ❑   c.   Install a tape drive to hold the system's important data.
     ❑   d.   Place all important data on rewritable CD-ROMs or DVDs.

16. For security purposes in a client/server network, where should backup copies be stored? (Select all that apply.)

Quick Answer: **128**
Detailed Answer: **130**

     ❑   a.   In a locked file cabinet next to the server
     ❑   b.   In a safe outside of the building
     ❑   c.   In a drawer near the server
     ❑   d.   On a shelf in the server closet

17. What is the first thing you should do if your trackball mouse responds erratically when you move it across the screen?

Quick Answer: **128**
Detailed Answer: **130**

     ❑   a.   Replace the mouse.
     ❑   b.   Check for IRQ conflicts.
     ❑   c.   Clean the mouse.
     ❑   d.   Plug the mouse in on another COM port.

18. Which of the following storage media would not be adversely affected by RFI interference leaking from an old monitor?

Quick Answer: **128**
Detailed Answer: **130**

     ❑   a.   A floppy disk
     ❑   b.   A removable hard disk drive
     ❑   c.   A backup DAT tape
     ❑   d.   A CD-ROM disc

19. Which of the following is an acceptable method of cleaning oxide buildups from adapter board contacts?

Quick Answer: **128**
Detailed Answer: **130**

     ❑   a.   A wet rag
     ❑   b.   Warm soapy water
     ❑   c.   Electrical contact cleaner spray
     ❑   d.   A nylon cloth

20. A problem that can occur in areas of high humidity is _____.

Quick Answer: **128**
Detailed Answer: **130**

     ❑   a.   leaks around PCB chips
     ❑   b.   loose chips on the motherboard
     ❑   c.   electrostatic discharge between components
     ❑   d.   an overheated CPU

21. Which solution can be used for antistatic cleaning?

    ❑ a. A water and fabric softener solution

    ❑ b. A water and ammonia solution

    ❑ c. A water and bleach solution

    ❑ d. A hydrogen tetrachloride solution

Quick Answer: **128**
Detailed Answer: **130**

22. Which item is best suited for general cleaning of monitors?

    ❑ a. An antistatic spray

    ❑ b. A common flower mister

    ❑ c. A glass cleaner

    ❑ d. A damp cloth

Quick Answer: **128**
Detailed Answer: **131**

23. How should you clean a trackball mouse?

    ❑ a. Use a damp cloth to clean buildup from the rollers.

    ❑ b. Use a cotton swab to clean buildup from the rollers.

    ❑ c. Use an X-Acto knife to clean buildup from the rollers.

    ❑ d. Use a pencil eraser to clean buildup from the rollers.

Quick Answer: **128**
Detailed Answer: **131**

24. Which peripheral item is most subject to problems created by environmental dust?

    ❑ a. Printer

    ❑ b. Floppy disk drive

    ❑ c. Mouse

    ❑ d. Keyboard

Quick Answer: **128**
Detailed Answer: **131**

25. What product is recommended for manual cleaning of floppy disk drives and tape drive R/W heads?

    ❑ a. Soft cloths

    ❑ b. Cotton swabs

    ❑ c. A pencil eraser

    ❑ d. Foam swabs

Quick Answer: **128**
Detailed Answer: **131**

26. Which of the following are common sources of heat buildup that can be found around a PC installation? (Select all that apply.)

    ❑ a. Direct sunlight

    ❑ b. Location of heaters

    ❑ c. Excess body heat

    ❑ d. Papers piled on equipment

Quick Answer: **128**
Detailed Answer: **131**

27. What precautions should be taken when storing backup copies of the system's disk drives?

    ❑   a. All personnel should have access to the backups.
    ❑   b. Only the network administrator should have access to the backups.
    ❑   c. All backups should be cleaned regularly.
    ❑   d. All backups should be tested regularly.

Quick Answer: **128**
Detailed Answer: **131**

28. Which of the following can lead to problems with excess heat buildup?

    ❑   a. Open HVAC ducts
    ❑   b. Closed computer cases
    ❑   c. Closed window shades
    ❑   d. High humidity

Quick Answer: **128**
Detailed Answer: **131**

29. At what point does heat buildup become a problem for most PCs?

    ❑   a. Room temperatures above 85°F
    ❑   b. Room temperatures above 90°F
    ❑   c. Room temperatures above 95°F
    ❑   d. Room temperatures above 100°F

Quick Answer: **128**
Detailed Answer: **131**

30. What is the main reason to use a static-free vacuum?

    ❑   a. It is small and portable and enables you to get in between the keyboard keys and other small spaces.
    ❑   b. It generates less ESD than a normal vacuum.
    ❑   c. It is grounded so ESD does not occur.
    ❑   d. It has a spinning brush to pick up all the lint.

Quick Answer: **128**
Detailed Answer: **131**

31. What two effects do leaving off expansion slot covers after an upgrade have on the operation of the system?

    ❑   a. It permits dust to accumulate in the system unit.
    ❑   b. It disrupts airflow patterns inside the case.
    ❑   c. It diminishes the ground potential of the system.
    ❑   d. It has no discernible effect on the system.

Quick Answer: **128**
Detailed Answer: **131**

32. _____ is/are unlikely to lead to equipment failure.

    ❑   a. Dust buildup
    ❑   b. Periodic system upgrades
    ❑   c. Temperature extremes
    ❑   d. Rough handling

Quick Answer: **128**
Detailed Answer: **131**

33. What should you do if you suspect corrosion might cause a problem with an adapter card?
   - ❏ a. Apply a fabric softener and water solution to the contacts.
   - ❏ b. Brush its contacts with a small paintbrush.
   - ❏ c. Wipe its contacts gently with a damp cloth.
   - ❏ d. Rub its contacts very gently with a soft pencil eraser.

Quick Answer: **128**
Detailed Answer: **131**

34. How can you remove dust from the inside of the case?
   - ❏ a. Apply a fabric softener and water solution.
   - ❏ b. Rub gently with a dry towel.
   - ❏ c. Wipe gently with a damp cloth.
   - ❏ d. Use a small paintbrush.

Quick Answer: **128**
Detailed Answer: **132**

35. What should be done after cleaning the exterior of computer components?
   - ❏ a. Apply a fabric softener and water solution to their exteriors.
   - ❏ b. Rub them with a dry towel.
   - ❏ c. Wipe them with a damp cloth.
   - ❏ d. Use a small paintbrush to remove dust from their interiors.

Quick Answer: **128**
Detailed Answer: **132**

36. What type of cleaning solution should be used on the exterior of computer components?
   - ❏ a. Window cleaner
   - ❏ b. Soap and water
   - ❏ c. Bleach and water
   - ❏ d. Do not clean them

Quick Answer: **128**
Detailed Answer: **132**

37. What is the best type of cleaning tool for use on the exterior of computer components?
   - ❏ a. Damp cloth
   - ❏ b. Vacuum cleaner
   - ❏ c. Brush
   - ❏ d. Antistatic spray

Quick Answer: **128**
Detailed Answer: **132**

Objective 3.2: Identify various safety measures and procedures and when and how to use them.

1. What is the cause of chip creep?
   - ❏ a. Cyclic variations in temperature
   - ❏ b. Excess humidity
   - ❏ c. Repeated power surge
   - ❏ d. Electromagnetic interference

Quick Answer: **128**
Detailed Answer: **132**

2. When working around electrical equipment including computers, what type of fire extinguisher should be on hand?
- ❑ a. Class A
- ❑ b. Class B
- ❑ c. Class C
- ❑ d. Class D

Quick Answer: **128**
Detailed Answer: **132**

3. What surge-suppressor rating describes how quickly its protective circuitry can react to changes in the incoming line and limit the amount of change that passes through?
- ❑ a. Clamping voltage
- ❑ b. Clamping speed
- ❑ c. Filter value
- ❑ d. Surge limiting

Quick Answer: **128**
Detailed Answer: **132**

4. The best method of limiting EMI in a PC system is to _____.
- ❑ a. wear a wrist strap to protect the system from EMI discharges
- ❑ b. properly ground the system using a three-wire power cable
- ❑ c. route signal cables and power cables together to cancel induced electrical noise
- ❑ d. remove any unused back-panel slot covers to permit EMI to vent from the system unit

Quick Answer: **128**
Detailed Answer: **132**

5. Damaging Electrostatic Discharge is most likely to occur when _____.
- ❑ a. working around rubber mats
- ❑ b. using test instruments on a system
- ❑ c. the humidity is low
- ❑ d. you accidentally get too close to the power supply unit while it is operating

Quick Answer: **128**
Detailed Answer: **132**

6. The most effective grounding system for a microcomputer is _____.
- ❑ a. an ESD wrist or ankle strap
- ❑ b. the safety ground plug at a commercial AC receptacle
- ❑ c. the ground plane of the system board
- ❑ d. the chassis ground provided by the brass standoff(s)

Quick Answer: **128**
Detailed Answer: **132**

7. When would it be inappropriate to use an ESD wrist strap?
- ❑ a. While working on hard disk drives
- ❑ b. While working on system boards
- ❑ c. While working on CRT video monitors
- ❑ d. While working on printers

Quick Answer: **128**
Detailed Answer: **132**

8. In terms of maintenance issues, how are the effects of ESD and EMI different?

   ❑ a. EMI is not destructive, whereas ESD can be very destructive.

   ❑ b. ESD is not destructive, whereas EMI can be very destructive.

   ❑ c. EMI improves system efficiency, whereas ESD can be very destructive.

   ❑ d. ESD improves system efficiency, whereas EMI can be very destructive.

Quick Answer: **128**
Detailed Answer: **132**

9. What type of equipment should be used to minimize the chances of ESD during normal computer maintenance work?

   ❑ a. Surge protector

   ❑ b. Terrycloth towel

   ❑ c. Wrist strap

   ❑ d. Screwdriver

Quick Answer: **128**
Detailed Answer: **133**

10. _____ is the gradual deterioration of the electrical connection between the pins of an IC and its socket.

   ❑ a. Degradation

   ❑ b. Chip creep

   ❑ c. Rust

   ❑ d. Tarnish

Quick Answer: **128**
Detailed Answer: **133**

11. In addition to wearing a wrist grounding strap, what other precaution can you take to prevent ESD discharges?

   ❑ a. Remove dust from the equipment and workplace using compressed air.

   ❑ b. Install a dehumidifier.

   ❑ c. Use Styrofoam sheets on the workbench surface.

   ❑ d. Install static-free carpet in the work area.

Quick Answer: **128**
Detailed Answer: **133**

12. ESD is most likely to occur when _____.

   ❑ a. you unplug a power supply unit

   ❑ b. the relative humidity is above 50%

   ❑ c. the relative humidity is below 50%

   ❑ d. you touch the power supply unit while it is operating

Quick Answer: **128**
Detailed Answer: **133**

13. Which voltage level is more dangerous—110V AC at 5 amps, or 25,000V DC at 5 microamperes?

   ❑ a. 25,000V is much more dangerous than 110V.

   ❑ b. Neither is particularly dangerous.

   ❑ c. Both are extremely dangerous.

   ❑ d. 5 amps is much more dangerous than 5 microamperes.

Quick Answer: **128**
Detailed Answer: **133**

14. Which UPS rating describes how long it can supply power to a given load?

- ❏ a. Volt-ampere rating
- ❏ b. Wattage rating
- ❏ c. Ampere-hour rating
- ❏ d. Clamping-voltage rating

Quick Answer: **128**
Detailed Answer: **133**

15. What are the voltage levels commonly found in a CRT?

- ❏ a. 250,000V
- ❏ b. 250V
- ❏ c. 25,000V
- ❏ d. 25V

Quick Answer: **128**
Detailed Answer: **133**

16. The local weather report indicates that an electrical storm with severe winds is likely to occur in your area overnight. What reasonable precautions should you take to protect your computers?

- ❏ a. Monitor the computers until the storm passes.
- ❏ b. Plug the computers into a surge protector.
- ❏ c. Turn off the computers.
- ❏ d. Unplug the computers.

Quick Answer: **128**
Detailed Answer: **133**

17. What is the best device for transporting computer equipment?

- ❏ a. A server rack
- ❏ b. The original packaging
- ❏ c. A sturdy carton filled with Styrofoam peanuts
- ❏ d. An antistatic bag

Quick Answer: **128**
Detailed Answer: **133**

18. Why is it important that the UPS notifies the host system that a power failure has occurred? (Choose all that apply.)

- ❏ a. So that the host computer's operating system can conduct an orderly shutdown of the system
- ❏ b. So that the host computer can tell the operator how much time is available before he must shut down the system
- ❏ c. So that the host computer's management software can notify an administrator that a problem has occurred
- ❏ d. So that the host computer can shift into hibernate mode to conserve power

Quick Answer: **128**
Detailed Answer: **133**

19. What is the best tool for releasing the charge on a CRT anode?

Quick Answer: **128**
Detailed Answer: **134**

- ❑ a. Terrycloth towel
- ❑ b. Screwdriver
- ❑ c. Wrist strap
- ❑ d. Your finger

Objective 3.3: Identify environmental protection measures and procedures and when and how to use them.

1. Which of the following are legitimate ways of disposing of chemical solvents and cans?

Quick Answer: **128**
Detailed Answer: **134**

- ❑ a. If they are not listed on the MSDS sheets, dispose of them in your normal trash-disposal system.
- ❑ b. Open the containers and allow the liquids to evaporate so they can be buried.
- ❑ c. If your local code calls for it, dispose of the items in a Subtitle D dump site.
- ❑ d. Burn them in an acceptable disposal oven.

2. _____ are those substances that can pass through a standard paint filter.

Quick Answer: **128**
Detailed Answer: **134**

- ❑ a. Color liquids
- ❑ b. Acoustic liquids
- ❑ c. Free liquids
- ❑ d. Geomantic liquids

3. What are all hazardous materials required to have that accompany them when they change hands?

Quick Answer: **128**
Detailed Answer: **134**

- ❑ a. Disposal bags
- ❑ b. Material Safety Data Sheet (MSDS)
- ❑ c. Red flags
- ❑ d. Mr. Yuk stickers

4. Which of the following types of information are contained in MSDSs? (Select two correct answers.)

Quick Answer: **128**
Detailed Answer: **134**

- ❑ a. Physical properties of the listed material
- ❑ b. The retail price
- ❑ c. Fire and explosion data
- ❑ d. Local emergency hotline number

5. Which of the following is a nonhazardous, solid-waste dump site that can be used for dumping hardware?

- ❑ a. Subtitle A
- ❑ b. Subtitle B
- ❑ c. Subtitle C
- ❑ d. Subtitle D

Quick Answer: **128**
Detailed Answer: **134**

6. How should you dispose of a toner cartridge?

- ❑ a. You should obtain the proper toner material, refill the cartridge, and reuse it.
- ❑ b. It should be recycled through the manufacturer.
- ❑ c. It should be incinerated.
- ❑ d. It should be wrapped in plastic and disposed of in a normal garbage receptacle.

Quick Answer: **128**
Detailed Answer: **134**

7. When disposing of a CRT, you should first _____.

- ❑ a. pack it in its original container and dispose of it in the normal garbage
- ❑ b. discharge the HV anode and dispose of it in the normal garbage pickup
- ❑ c. check applicable local ordinances and dispose of it in accordance with local regulations
- ❑ d. smash the CRT's glass envelope with a hammer and dispose of it in a Subtitle D dump site

Quick Answer: **128**
Detailed Answer: **134**

8. The correct method to use for disposing of batteries is to _____.

- ❑ a. recycle them
- ❑ b. place them in a designated garbage receptacle
- ❑ c. burn them in an incinerator
- ❑ d. crush them and have them recycled

Quick Answer: **128**
Detailed Answer: **134**

9. If you purchase a spare battery for a new notebook computer, how should you store the second battery?

- ❑ a. Store it fully charged in a refrigerator.
- ❑ b. Fully charge it and store it at room temperature.
- ❑ c. Fully discharge it and store it at room temperature.
- ❑ d. Fully discharge it and then store it in the refrigerator.

Quick Answer: **128**
Detailed Answer: **134**

10. What is the recommended method for storing computer equipment?

Quick Answer: **128**
Detailed Answer: **134**

   ❑   a.   Place it in a nonstatic cardboard box.
   ❑   b.   Wrap it in aluminum foil.
   ❑   c.   Place it in an antistatic bag.
   ❑   d.   Wrap it in protective Styrofoam.

11. What technique is used to minimize the effects of EMI in a personal computer system?

Quick Answer: **128**
Detailed Answer: **135**

   ❑   a.   Line filtering
   ❑   b.   Grounding
   ❑   c.   Using protective wrist straps
   ❑   d.   Adding humidity to the environment

Quick Check Answer Key

Objective 3.1

1. c
2. c
3. b
4. d
5. d
6. d
7. a
8. b
9. a
10. d
11. c
12. b
13. a
14. c
15. b
16. a, b
17. c
18. d
19. c
20. d
21. a
22. d
23. b
24. d
25. d
26. a, b, d
27. b
28. d
29. a
30. c
31. a, b
32. b
33. d
34. d
35. a
36. b
37. a

Objective 3.2

1. a
2. c
3. b
4. b
5. c
6. b
7. c
8. a
9. c
10. b
11. d
12. c
13. d
14. c
15. c
16. d
17. b
18. a, b, c
19. b

Objective 3.3

1. c
2. c
3. b
4. a, c
5. d
6. b
7. c
8. a
9. c
10. c
11. b

Answers and Explanations

Objective 3.1

1. **c.** If two devices are connected to the same IRQ line, a conflict occurs because it is not likely that the interrupt handler software can service both devices. The IRQ3 line works for both COM2 and COM4. When an external modem uses the COM2 port, no other device should use the COM4 port.

2. **c.** In the case of a complete shutdown, or a significant sag, the best protection from losing programs and data is an uninterruptible power supply (UPS). A UPS is a battery-based system that monitors the incoming power and kicks in when unacceptable variations occur in the power source.

3. **b.** The primary mission of the UPS is to keep the system running when a power failure occurs. Because it's battery based, it cannot keep the system running infinitely. For this reason, you should not connect nonessential, power-hungry peripheral devices such as a laser printer to the UPS supply.

4. **d.** An uninterruptible power supply is an extremely good power-conditioning system. Because it always sits between the commercial power and the computer, it can supply a constant power supply to the system to protect it from spike damage.

5. **d.** If a UPS is being used to keep a critical system in operation during the power outage, the high current drain of the laser printer would severely reduce the length of time that the UPS could keep the system running.

6. **d.** Overvoltage conditions are classified as surges when their duration is measured in milliseconds or longer.

7. **a.** Overvoltage conditions are classified as spikes when their duration is measured in nanoseconds or less.

8. **b.** A surge suppressor protects the system from damages caused by minor power line interruptions. It passively filters the incoming power signal to smooth out variations.

9. **a.** A cooling fan should be placed on any IC operating at clock speeds above 33MHz.

10. **d.** Uninterruptible power supplies are battery-based systems that monitor the incoming power and kick in when unacceptable variations or outages occur in the power source.

11. **c.** A surge suppressor is used to protect computer equipment from very small overvoltage occurrences by passively filtering the incoming power signal to smooth out variations.

12. **b.** Sags, an undervoltage condition, can include voltage sags and brownouts. A voltage sag typically lasts only a few milliseconds, but a brownout can last for a protracted period of time. Sags can cause the system to suddenly reboot because it thinks the power has been turned off.

13. **a.** A brownout is an undervoltage condition and can last for a protracted period of time, which makes it easy to spot.

14. **c.** If a monitor is to be left on for an extended period of time with the same image on it, this can cause the image to become permanently "burned" into the phosphorous coating. To prevent this from occurring, install a screensaver package to constantly refresh the contents of the display.

15. **b.** To recover from hardware failures, operator mistakes, and acts of nature, you should make system backups of the hard drive.

16. **a, b.** (a) Copies of the system backup should be stored in a convenient but secure place. In the case of secure system backups, such as client/server networks, the backup copies should be stored where the network administrators can have access to them, but not the general public (for example, a locked file cabinet). (b) Many companies maintain a copy of their backup away from the main site. This is done for protection in case of disasters such as fire.

17. **c.** If your trackball mouse responds erratically when you move it across the screen, the first thing you should do is clean the mouse. Use a lint-free swab to clean the X and Y trackball rollers inside the mouse.

18. **d.** Because the CD-ROM stores data in the form of spots burned into an optical media, the RFI escaping from the monitor would not affect it. However, all of the other storage devices rely on magnetic storage that is susceptible to damage from RFI and other magnetic-field disturbances.

19. **c.** The oxidation buildup occurring on electrical connectors and contacts reduces the flow of electricity through the connection. Even with proper handling, some corrosion can occur over time. This oxidation can be sanded off with emery cloth, rubbed off with a common pencil eraser or special solvent wipe, or dissolved with an electrical contact cleaner spray. The only acceptable answer offered in this question is the use of contact cleaner.

20. **d.** High humidity can lead to heat-related problems and failures.

21. **a.** The application of an antistatic spray or antistatic solution prevents the buildup of static charges on the components of the system. A solution composed of 10 parts water and 1 part common household fabric softener makes an effective and economical antistatic solution.

22. **d.** A damp cloth is the best general-purpose cleaning tool for use with computer equipment, such as a monitor.

23. **b.** With a trackball mouse, the trackball should be removed and cleaned periodically. Use a lint-free swab to clean the X and Y trackball rollers inside the mouse.

24. **d.** Unlike the floppy disk drive, the mouse, and the printer, the keyboard's electronic circuitry is open to the atmosphere and should be vacuumed regularly. Dust buildup on the keyboard circuitry can cause its ICs to fail due to overheating.

25. **d.** Manual cleaning of read/write (R/W) heads should be performed with isopropyl alcohol using a foam swab. Cotton swabs can shed fibers that can contaminate the drive and damage portions of its R/W head.

26. **a, b, d.** Sources of heat buildup around the computer and its peripherals include direct sunlight from an outside window, locations of portable heaters in the winter, and papers and books piled up around the equipment.

27. **b.** Copies of the system backup should be stored in a convenient but secure place. In the case of secure system backups, such as client/server networks, the backup copies should be stored where the network administrators can have access to them, but not the general public (for example, a locked file cabinet).

28. **d.** High humidity can lead to heat-related problems.

29. **a.** Microcomputers are designed to run at normal room temperatures. If the ambient temperature rises above about 85°F, heat buildup can become a problem.

30. **c.** A static-free vacuum can be used to remove dust from inside cases and keyboards. Be sure to use a static-free vacuum because normal vacuums are, by their nature, static generators. The static-free vacuum has special grounding to remove the static buildup it generates.

31. **a, b.** (a) The missing cover permits dust to accumulate in the system, forming the insulating blanket that traps heat next to active devices and can cause component overheating. (b) The missing slot cover interrupts the designed airflow patterns inside the case, causing components to overheat due to missing or inadequate airflow.

32. **b.** As with any electronic device, computers are susceptible to failures caused by dust buildup, rough handling, and extremes in temperature.

33. **d.** Oxidation can be removed from adapter card contacts with emery cloth, rubbed off with a common pencil eraser or special solvent wipe, or dissolved with an electrical-contact cleaner spray.

34. **d.** To remove dust from the inside of computer cases, a small paintbrush is handy.

35. **a.** The outer-surface cleaning should be followed by the application of an anti-static spray or antistatic solution to prevent the buildup of static charges on the components of the system.

36. **b.** Outer-surface cleaning can be accomplished with a simple soap-and-water solution, followed by a clear water rinse. Care should be taken to make sure that none of the liquid splashes, or drips, into the inner parts of the system.

37. **a.** Outer-surface cleaning can be accomplished with a simple soap-and-water solution, followed by a clear water rinse. Care should be taken to make sure that none of the liquid splashes, or drips, into the inner parts of the system. A damp cloth is easily the best general-purpose cleaning tool for use with computer equipment.

Objective 3.2

1. **a.** Normal operating vibrations and temperature cycling can degrade the electrical connections between ICs and sockets over time. This gradual deterioration of electrical contact between chips and sockets is referred to as chip creep.

2. **c.** A Class C fire extinguisher specified for use around electrical equipment should be on hand around computers.

3. **b.** The surge suppressor's clamping speed rating describes how quickly it can react to changes in the incoming power level and act to minimize it.

4. **b.** Proper grounding is the best defense against the disruptive effects of EMI.

5. **c.** ESD is most likely to occur during periods of low humidity. If the relative humidity is below 50%, static charges can accumulate easily. ESD generally does not occur when the humidity is above 50%.

6. **b.** To avoid damaging static-sensitive computer devices, ground yourself by touching the power supply housing with your finger before touching any components inside the system. This technique will only work safely if the power cord is attached to a grounded power outlet. The ground plug on a standard power cable is the best tool for overcoming ESD problems.

7. **c.** Antistatic straps should never be worn while working on higher-voltage components, such as monitors and power supply units.

8. **a.** Unlike ESD, which is the most damaging form of electrical interference associated with digital equipment and is destructive, the effects of EMI can be corrected without damage.

9. **c.** Professional service technicians use grounding straps to minimize the chances of ESD during normal computer maintenance work involving MOS devices. These antistatic devices can be placed around the wrists or ankles to ground the technician to the system being worked on. These straps release any static present on the technician's body, and pass it harmlessly to ground potential.

10. **b.** Normal operating vibrations and temperature cycling can degrade the electrical connections between ICs and sockets over time. This gradual deterioration of electrical contact between chips and sockets is referred to as chip creep. It is a good practice to reseat any socket-mounted devices when handling a printed circuit board.

11. **d.** Of the possible choices provided, installing antistatic carpet is the only option that will help to minimize ESD.

12. **c.** ESD is most likely to occur during periods of low humidity. If the relative humidity is below 50%, static charges can accumulate easily. Anytime the charge reaches about 10,000V, it is likely to discharge to grounded metal parts.

13. **d.** 110V AC at 5 amps is much more dangerous than 25,000V DC at 5 microamperes according to the current-delivering capabilities (5 amps versus 5 microamperes) they create.

14. **c.** The ampere-hour rating of the UPS describes how long it can supply power to a given size electrical load after a failure has occurred.

15. **c.** Extremely high voltage levels (in excess of 25,000V) may be present inside the CRT housing, even up to a year after electrical power has been removed from the unit.

16. **d.** Remove all power cords associated with the computer, and its peripherals, from the power outlet during thunder or lightning storms.

17. **b.** Computer devices should be stored or transported in their original boxes using their original packing foam and protective storage bag because the contours in the packing foam of these devices are not compatible from model to model, or device to device. If the original boxes and packing materials are not available, make sure to use sturdy cartons and cushion the equipment well on all sides before shipping.

18. **a, b, c.** When a disruption occurs, the UPS notifies the host computer so that its operating system can conduct an orderly shutdown of the system without losing data. The management software can also be configured to notify the system users to save and shut down, as well as to email or page an administrator to alert him to the failure.

19. **b.** While touching only the insulated handle of the screwdriver, slide the blade of the screwdriver under the rubber cup of the anode and make contact with its metal connection. This should bleed off the high voltage charge to ground.

Objective 3.3

1. **c.** Check your local waste management agency before disposing of them. Some landfills will not accept chemical solvents and cans. In this case, these items must be disposed of in a Subtitle-D dump site.

2. **c.** Free liquids are those substances that can pass through a standard paint filter. If the liquid passes through the filter, it is free liquid and cannot be disposed of in the landfill.

3. **b.** All hazardous materials are required to have Material Safety Data Sheets (MSDSs) that accompany them when they change hands. They are also required to be on hand in areas where hazardous materials are stored and commonly used.

4. **a, c.** The MSDS contains information about what the material is, its hazardous ingredients, its physical properties, fire and explosion data, reactive data, spill or leak procedures, and any special protection or precaution information.

5. **d.** Subtitle D dump sites are nonhazardous, solid-waste dump sites that can handle hardware components.

6. **b.** Toner cartridges can be refilled and recycled. They can be very messy to refill and often do not function as well as new cartridges do. In many cases, the manufacturer of the product will have a policy of accepting spent cartridges.

7. **c.** Local regulations concerning acceptable disposal methods for computer-related components should always be checked before disposing of any electronic equipment, such as a CRT.

8. **a.** The desired method of battery disposal is recycling. It should not be too difficult to find a drop site that will handle recycling batteries and other hazardous materials.

9. **c.** If the battery is expected to be stored for more than 30 days (as you would expect the replacement for a new computer to be) then you should fully discharge the battery and store it at normal room temperature.

10. **c.** The best place to store computer equipment is in its original shipping box, surrounded by an antistatic bag wrapped in protective foam. The only correct version of this scenario in this question is the antistatic bag. Without this item, the other options are potentially harmful for digital equipment.

11. **b.** Grounding is an important aspect of limiting electromagnetic interference (not to be confused with destructive ESD). Proper grounding routes induced EMI signals away from logic circuitry and toward ground potential where it is absorbed.

Hardware Domain 4.0: Motherboard/Processors/Memory

Objective 4.1: Distinguish between the popular CPU chips in terms of their basic characteristics.

1. What would cause the BIOS to see a Pentium III 500MHz processor as only a 400MHz processor?
   - ❏ a. The CPU is only inserted half into the socket.
   - ❏ b. The chip settings are incorrect.
   - ❏ c. The BIOS only supports processor speeds up to 400MHz.
   - ❏ d. Lack of processor speed information in the BIOS code.

Quick Answer: **172**
Detailed Answer: **174**

2. What type of processor can be put in Slot A?
   - ❏ a. Pentium II
   - ❏ b. Pentium III
   - ❏ c. Cyrux
   - ❏ d. AMD Athlon

Quick Answer: **172**
Detailed Answer: **174**

3. What is the main difference between a Pentium II and a Pentium III processor?
   - ❏ a. Slot pin configuration
   - ❏ b. The size of the processor
   - ❏ c. The Pentium III needs special fans to stay cool
   - ❏ d. L2 cache size

Quick Answer: **172**
Detailed Answer: **174**

4. Pentium II processors moved to a _____ external clock and front side bus.
   - ❏ a. 200MHz
   - ❏ b. 100MHz
   - ❏ c. 60MHz
   - ❏ d. 50MHz

Quick Answer: **172**
Detailed Answer: **174**

5. The various levels of cache available with a Pentium Pro are
   _____.

   ❑   a.   L2 and L3
   ❑   b.   L1 and L2
   ❑   c.   L1, L2, and L3
   ❑   d.   L1, L2, L3, and L4

Quick Answer: **172**
Detailed Answer: **174**

6. How much cache memory is provided for use with Pentium II
   systems?

   ❑   a.   128KB/256KB
   ❑   b.   256KB
   ❑   c.   512KB
   ❑   d.   1MB

Quick Answer: **172**
Detailed Answer: **174**

7. What are the typical sizes of the L2 cache for Pentium MMX
   processors?

   ❑   a.   128KB and 256KB
   ❑   b.   256KB and 512KB
   ❑   c.   512KB and 1MB
   ❑   d.   128KB and 512KB

Quick Answer: **172**
Detailed Answer: **174**

8. If you upgrade a 600MHz processor to a 1GHz version and
   the system still shows a 600MHz processor during the POST,
   what type of problem is indicated?

   ❑   a.   Incompatible motherboard BIOS
   ❑   b.   Incompatible operating system
   ❑   c.   Insufficient RAM
   ❑   d.   Defective microprocessor

Quick Answer: **172**
Detailed Answer: **174**

9. Explain how an older Socket 7 system knows what type of
   processor is installed in the system.

   ❑   a.   Interrogation of the microprocessor
   ❑   b.   Jumpers on the motherboard
   ❑   c.   Orientation of the microprocessor
   ❑   d.   CMOS setup utility

Quick Answer: **172**
Detailed Answer: **174**

10. What is the appropriate socket for the Duron microprocessor?

   ❑   a.   Socket 423
   ❑   b.   Super Socket 7
   ❑   c.   Socket 370
   ❑   d.   Socket A

Quick Answer: **172**
Detailed Answer: **174**

11. Which processors can be used in a Slot A system board?

- ❏ a. Duron/600
- ❏ b. Athlon K7/550
- ❏ c. Celeron/266
- ❏ d. Pentium II/233

Quick Answer: **172**
Detailed Answer: **174**

12. What is the appropriate socket for the Pentium 4 microprocessor?

- ❏ a. Socket 370
- ❏ b. Super Socket 7
- ❏ c. Socket 423
- ❏ d. Slot A

Quick Answer: **172**
Detailed Answer: **175**

13. What is the appropriate socket for the original Celeron microprocessor?

- ❏ a. Super Socket 7
- ❏ b. Slot 1
- ❏ c. Socket 370
- ❏ d. Slot A

Quick Answer: **172**
Detailed Answer: **175**

14. Which microprocessor can use a Slot 1 connection?

- ❏ a. Celeron/66
- ❏ b. Duron/600
- ❏ c. Athlon K7/550
- ❏ d. Pentium Pro

Quick Answer: **172**
Detailed Answer: **175**

15. What is the major improvement of Pentium III microprocessors compared to Pentium II?

- ❏ a. L2 cache is enlarged to 512KB
- ❏ b. Improved microprocessor die
- ❏ c. Improved to 128-bit system bus
- ❏ d. Lower voltage requirement

Quick Answer: **172**
Detailed Answer: **175**

16. Which type of system board sockets can accept a Pentium III microprocessor? (Select two.)

- ❏ a. Super Socket 7
- ❏ b. Socket 370
- ❏ c. Slot 1
- ❏ d. Socket A

Quick Answer: **172**
Detailed Answer: **175**

17. Which processors can be used in a Socket 370 system?

   ❑ a. Celeron, Duron
   ❑ b. Pentium MMX, Celeron
   ❑ c. Pentium III, Pentium 4
   ❑ d. Celeron, Pentium III

Quick Answer: **172**
Detailed Answer: **175**

18. What is the appropriate socket for the Pentium II micro-processor?

   ❑ a. Super Socket 7
   ❑ b. Slot 1
   ❑ c. Socket 370
   ❑ d. Slot A

Quick Answer: **172**
Detailed Answer: **175**

19. Which of the following is not a component of a Pentium II SEC cartridge?

   ❑ a. Tag RAM
   ❑ b. 262-contact socket interface
   ❑ c. Processor core
   ❑ d. L2 burst SRAM

Quick Answer: **172**
Detailed Answer: **175**

20. Which microprocessor has cache memory that operates at half the core bus speed of the other microprocessor sections?

   ❑ a. Pentium III
   ❑ b. Pentium Pro
   ❑ c. Pentium II
   ❑ d. Celeron

Quick Answer: **172**
Detailed Answer: **175**

21. What is the appropriate socket for the Pentium Pro microprocessor?

   ❑ a. Super Socket 7
   ❑ b. Socket 8
   ❑ c. Socket 7
   ❑ d. Socket 370

Quick Answer: **172**
Detailed Answer: **175**

22. What is the appropriate socket for the Pentium MMX microprocessor?

   ❑ a. Super Socket 7
   ❑ b. Socket 7
   ❑ c. Socket 8
   ❑ d. Socket 370

Quick Answer: **172**
Detailed Answer: **175**

23. Which microprocessor works with a 66MHz front side bus?

    ☐   a. PIII/450
    ☐   b. P75
    ☐   c. Celeron
    ☐   d. Duron/600

Quick Answer: **172**
Detailed Answer: **175**

24. Pentium III processors can be used in _____. (Select two correct answers.)

    ☐   a. Slot 1
    ☐   b. Socket 370
    ☐   c. Slot A
    ☐   d. Socket 7

Quick Answer: **172**
Detailed Answer: **175**

25. Which of the following processors use Slot 1 to be installed into a system board? (Select all that apply.)

    ☐   a. Pentium 233
    ☐   b. Pentium II
    ☐   c. Pentium III
    ☐   d. Celeron

Quick Answer: **172**
Detailed Answer: **175**

26. What would cause the system to show the presence of a 600MHz Pentium III processor after you have just completed an upgrade to a 933MHz Pentium III processor? (Select all that apply.)

    ☐   a. Motherboard BIOS version does not support the new processor
    ☐   b. Microprocessor is not aligned with pin 1
    ☐   c. Incorrect Core Voltage, Bus Frequency, or Bus Ratio settings
    ☐   d. Incompatible RAM type

Quick Answer: **172**
Detailed Answer: **176**

27. Which of the following types of device is used with microprocessors to supply special voltage levels for different types of microprocessors that might be installed?

    ☐   a. Voltmeter
    ☐   b. RAM
    ☐   c. Voltage module regulator
    ☐   d. Voltage regulator module

Quick Answer: **172**
Detailed Answer: **176**

28. If the core voltage level configuration on a system board is set too low for the microprocessor that is actually installed, what will happen?

   ❑   a. The BIOS will detect this during the PnP process and correct the voltage level.
   ❑   b. The microprocessor will refuse to start.
   ❑   c. The microprocessor will either overheat slowly or burn out, depending on the level of overvoltage applied.
   ❑   d. The system will speed up the cooling fan and display an error message on the screen.

29. If the core voltage level configuration on a system board is set too high for the microprocessor that is actually installed, what will happen?

   ❑   a. The microprocessor will refuse to start.
   ❑   b. The BIOS will detect this during the PnP process and correct the voltage level.
   ❑   c. The microprocessor will either overheat slowly or burn out, depending on the level of overvoltage applied.
   ❑   d. The system will speed up the cooling fan and display an error message on the screen.

30. Which portion of the PC system is responsible for controlling the operating temperature of the microprocessor?

   ❑   a. The Health Management portion of the PCI chipset
   ❑   b. The Health Management portion of the microprocessor
   ❑   c. The Health Management portion of the operating system
   ❑   d. The Health Management portion of the BIOS

Objective 4.2: Identify the types of RAM (random access memory), form factors, and operational characteristics.

1. How many total bits need to be stored in RAM to provide parity for a 64-bit data bus?

   ❑   a. None
   ❑   b. 64
   ❑   c. 72
   ❑   d. 128

2. What does ECC RAM do?

- ❑ a. ECC RAM stores system configuration settings.
- ❑ b. ECC RAM detects memory errors and corrects them.
- ❑ c. ECC RAM stores cached data.
- ❑ d. ECC RAM runs at twice the bus speed.

Quick Answer: **172**
Detailed Answer: **176**

3. Which components use WRAM?

- ❑ a. Sound cards
- ❑ b. Video cards
- ❑ c. Network interface cards
- ❑ d. Modems

Quick Answer: **172**
Detailed Answer: **176**

4. What is the difference between EDO DRAM and Fast Page Mode DRAM? (Select two correct answers.)

- ❑ a. EDO DRAM is an advanced version of Fast Page Mode DRAM.
- ❑ b. Fast Page Mode DRAM is an advanced version of EDO DRAM.
- ❑ c. The memory access of EDO DRAM is accomplished in two cycles rather than three.
- ❑ d. The memory access of Fast Page Mode DRAM is accomplished in one cycle rather than two.

Quick Answer: **172**
Detailed Answer: **176**

5. What is the purpose of Parity?

- ❑ a. Detecting OS problems
- ❑ b. Removing bad sectors
- ❑ c. Deleting files
- ❑ d. Detecting memory errors

Quick Answer: **172**
Detailed Answer: **176**

6. Parity error messages are a sign of _____.

- ❑ a. damaged port connectors
- ❑ b. a bad CMOS battery
- ❑ c. faulty RAM
- ❑ d. missing cache memory

Quick Answer: **172**
Detailed Answer: **177**

7. What are the effects of mixing RAM modules with different speed ratings?

- ❑ a. The system will run normally.
- ❑ b. The system might not run, or will crash periodically.
- ❑ c. The system will run at the speed of the memory bus.
- ❑ d. The system will run at the speed of the slowest RAM stick.

Quick Answer: **172**
Detailed Answer: **177**

8. How many 32-bit SIMMs would be required to operate a Pentium MMX system board?

Quick Answer: **172**
Detailed Answer: **177**

  ❑ a. 2
  ❑ b. 1
  ❑ c. 3
  ❑ d. 44

9. How big is the data bus in a non-parity 72-pin RAM module?

Quick Answer: **172**
Detailed Answer: **177**

  ❑ a. 8-bit
  ❑ b. 16-bit
  ❑ c. 32-bit
  ❑ d. 64-bit

10. Where is the L1 cache located in a Pentium system?

Quick Answer: **172**
Detailed Answer: **177**

  ❑ a. On the motherboard
  ❑ b. In the Pentium core
  ❑ c. On the microprocessor PCB
  ❑ d. In the RAM

11. What is the term used to describe the method of checking memory for errors by adding an additional status bit to each byte?

Quick Answer: **172**
Detailed Answer: **177**

  ❑ a. Refreshing
  ❑ b. CAS
  ❑ c. ECC
  ❑ d. Parity

12. What method is used to correct single bit errors in RAM?

Quick Answer: **172**
Detailed Answer: **177**

  ❑ a. Refreshing
  ❑ b. Parity
  ❑ c. ECC
  ❑ d. Latency

13. What type of error will a memory parity error create?

Quick Answer: **172**
Detailed Answer: **177**

  ❑ a. Fatal exception error
  ❑ b. NMI error
  ❑ c. Corrupt Windows operation system file
  ❑ d. GPF error

14. Which type of RAM is faster, EDO RAM or Fast Page Mode RAM?

   ❑   a. They are both the same.
   ❑   b. Fast Page Mode RAM is faster.
   ❑   c. EDO RAM is faster.
   ❑   d. There is no such thing as Fast Page Mode RAM.

Quick Answer: **172**
Detailed Answer: **177**

15. What is WRAM typically used for?

   ❑   a. Video
   ❑   b. RAM
   ❑   c. Cache
   ❑   d. CMOS

Quick Answer: **172**
Detailed Answer: **177**

16. What does it mean when referring to RAM memory as being volatile?

   ❑   a. The component is a potential fire hazard.
   ❑   b. Data will not disappear if the power goes off.
   ❑   c. Data is rewritable.
   ❑   d. Data disappears if the power goes off.

Quick Answer: **172**
Detailed Answer: **177**

17. What is the process of recharging a DRAM's memory bits called?

   ❑   a. Survey
   ❑   b. Latency
   ❑   c. Strobe
   ❑   d. Refresh

Quick Answer: **172**
Detailed Answer: **178**

18. Which types of memory are considered volatile?

   ❑   a. ROM BIOS
   ❑   b. Magnetic memory
   ❑   c. RAM
   ❑   d. CD-ROM disks

Quick Answer: **172**
Detailed Answer: **178**

19. _____ mismatches can cause problems that range from preventing bootup to creating operating system or application failures.

   ❑   a. BIOS
   ❑   b. RAM
   ❑   c. Microprocessor
   ❑   d. Disk drive

Quick Answer: **172**
Detailed Answer: **178**

. . . .

20. What type of error checking is associated with parity operations?

Quick Answer: **172**
Detailed Answer: **178**

   ❑ a. 8-bit

   ❑ b. XOR

   ❑ c. Parity checking

   ❑ d. ECC

21. A purchasing manager is confused by the different types of RAM that can be purchased. He is specifically looking for RAM that is only used for a laptop. Which of the following types of RAM should he purchase?

Quick Answer: **172**
Detailed Answer: **178**

   ❑ a. MicroDIMM

   ❑ b. DDR RAM

   ❑ c. SODIMM

   ❑ d. RDRAM

22. How many pins does a MicroDIMM possess?

Quick Answer: **172**
Detailed Answer: **178**

   ❑ a. 233

   ❑ b. 144

   ❑ c. 321

   ❑ d. 387

23. Which portable computer memory technology is nearly square, 144-pin, and has 32 million×64-bit plug-in modules that are available with either SDRAM or DDR SDRAM components onboard?

Quick Answer: **172**
Detailed Answer: **178**

   ❑ a. Mobile DDR modules

   ❑ b. SODIMM modules

   ❑ c. FlashRAM modules

   ❑ d. MicroDIMM modules

24. If the RAM count presented during the POST does not equal the amount of RAM actually installed in the system, what types of problems might the system be having? (Select all that apply.)

Quick Answer: **172**
Detailed Answer: **178**

   ❑ a. Bad RAM module

   ❑ b. The system is using split-bank RAM arrangement and only two slots have been populated

   ❑ c. Wrong type of RAM module

   ❑ d. Bad voltage regulation from the power supply

Objective 4.3: Identify the most popular types of motherboards, their components, and their architecture (bus structures).

1. What is true about PCI slots?

   ❑   a. They are longer than ISA slots.
   ❑   b. They are 32-bit slots.
   ❑   c. They operate at 16MHz.
   ❑   d. They are 16-bit slots.

Quick Answer: **172**
Detailed Answer: **178**

2. What type of system bus expansion slot connector has two separate slots?

   ❑   a. VESA
   ❑   b. ISA
   ❑   c. PC bus
   ❑   d. PCI

Quick Answer: **172**
Detailed Answer: **178**

3. What is the speed of the ISA bus?

   ❑   a. 16MHz
   ❑   b. 33MHz
   ❑   c. 8.33MHz
   ❑   d. 4.77MHz

Quick Answer: **172**
Detailed Answer: **179**

4. When a new card is installed in the system, what does the PnP function do?

   ❑   a. It checks to see which resources are needed and what is available and assigns system resources as required.
   ❑   b. It assigns the next available IRQ and I/O address.
   ❑   c. It assigns a DMA interrupt to the device.
   ❑   d. It handles interrupt requests from the device.

Quick Answer: **172**
Detailed Answer: **179**

5. What is the major advantage of ATX system boards over the older AT specification?

   ❑   a. 200MHz PCI bus
   ❑   b. Closer board components
   ❑   c. Soft power switch
   ❑   d. More RAM slots

Quick Answer: **172**
Detailed Answer: **179**

6. When installing a ribbon cable, the red stripe should point to
_____.
- ❑ a. pin 2
- ❑ b. pin 34
- ❑ c. pin 40
- ❑ d. pin 1

7. What types of expansion slots might be used for a SCSI host
adapter card? (Select two.)
- ❑ a. PCI
- ❑ b. ISA
- ❑ c. AGP
- ❑ d. AMR

8. What is the maximum data throughput when connecting an
Ultra ATA 66 hard disk drive with a 40-pin/40-conductor IDE
cable?
- ❑ a. 66MBps
- ❑ b. 10MBps
- ❑ c. 33MBps
- ❑ d. Will not work together

9. If you connect four two-partition IDE drives to a system
board, what will the drive designation be for the primary partition on the master drive of the secondary IDE controller?
- ❑ a. F:
- ❑ b. D:
- ❑ c. C:
- ❑ d. E:

10. Which of the following is not part of the typical ATX motherboard?
- ❑ a. 5-pin DIN
- ❑ b. Parallel printer port
- ❑ c. Game port
- ❑ d. 6-pin DIN

11. Locate the printer port from the figure depicting an ATX back panel.

Quick Answer: **172**
Detailed Answer: **179**

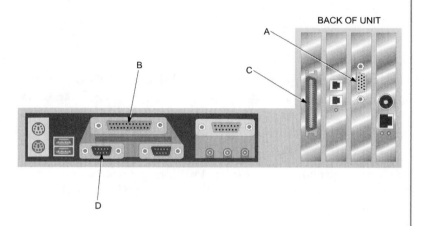

- ❏ a. A
- ❏ b. B
- ❏ c. C
- ❏ d. D

12. Locate the serial port connector on the diagram of an ATX back panel.

Quick Answer: **172**
Detailed Answer: **179**

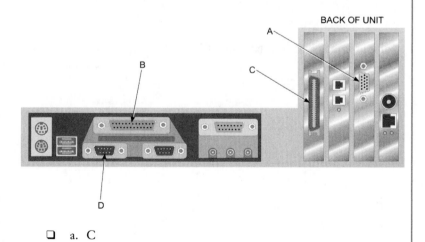

- ❏ a. C
- ❏ b. B
- ❏ c. D
- ❏ d. A

13. Which two of the following expansion slots can be used for an ISA card?

Quick Answer: **172**
Detailed Answer: **179**

- ❏ a. PCI
- ❏ b. EISA
- ❏ c. PC bus
- ❏ d. VESA

14. What type of expansion card is plugged into an AGP slot?

Quick Answer: **172**
Detailed Answer: **179**

- ❏ a. Sound
- ❏ b. Modem
- ❏ c. Network
- ❏ d. Graphics

15. Which IRQ resources are allocated first in the PnP configuration process?

Quick Answer: **172**
Detailed Answer: **179**

- ❏ a. Legacy devices
- ❏ b. ISA devices
- ❏ c. PCI devices
- ❏ d. Motherboard devices

16. What type of expansion bus is the most common found on new motherboards?

Quick Answer: **172**
Detailed Answer: **179**

- ❏ a. ISA
- ❏ b. PCI
- ❏ c. VESA
- ❏ d. PC bus

17. Which of the following has a 32-bit data bus? (Select all that apply.)

Quick Answer: **172**
Detailed Answer: **180**

- ❏ a. ISA
- ❏ b. AGP
- ❏ c. PCI
- ❏ d. PC bus

18. Which of the following has an 8-bit data bus?

    ❑   a. AGP

    ❑   b. ISA

    ❑   c. PC bus

    ❑   d. PCI

Quick Answer: **172**
Detailed Answer: **180**

19. What size is the data bus in an ISA slot?

    ❑   a. 16-bit

    ❑   b. 8-bit

    ❑   c. 32-bit

    ❑   d. 64-bit

Quick Answer: **172**
Detailed Answer: **180**

20. At what speed does the ISA slot run?

    ❑   a. 8MHz

    ❑   b. 33MHz

    ❑   c. 66MHz

    ❑   d. 133MHz

Quick Answer: **172**
Detailed Answer: **180**

21. Locate the power supply connector from the figure depicting an AT motherboard.

Quick Answer: **172**

Detailed Answer: **180**

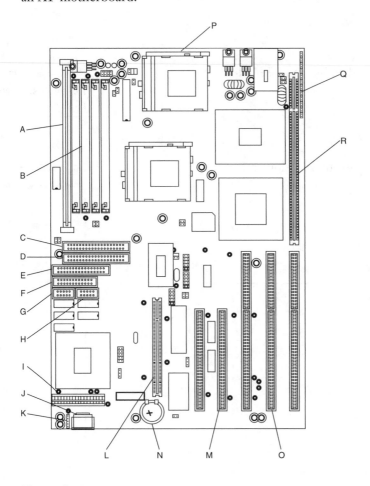

□   a. J
□   b. I
□   c. P
□   d. R

22. From the figure depicting an AT motherboard, identify the front panel connector.

Quick Answer: **172**
Detailed Answer: **180**

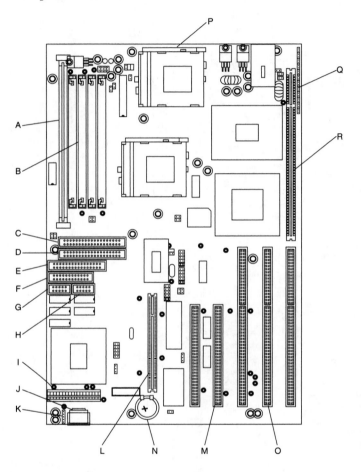

❏   a. I
❏   b. J
❏   c. K
❏   d. Q

23. From the figure depicting an AT motherboard, identify the keyboard connector.

Quick Answer: **172**
Detailed Answer: **180**

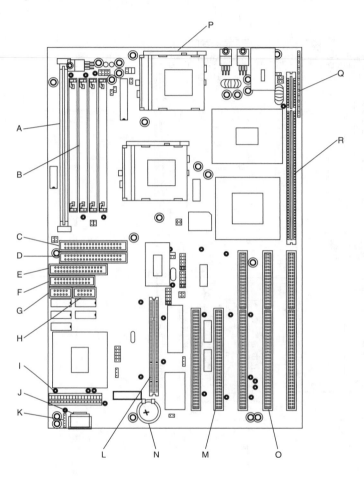

- ❑ a. I
- ❑ b. J
- ❑ c. K
- ❑ d. Q

24. From the figure depicting an AT motherboard, identify the FDD connector.

Quick Answer: **172**
Detailed Answer: **180**

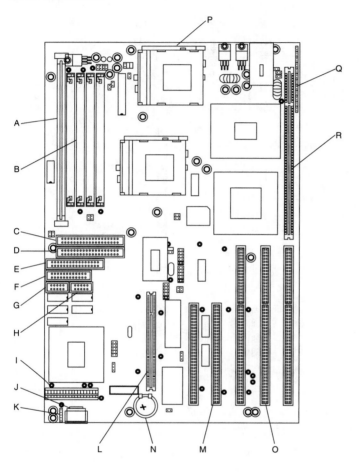

- ❏ a. G
- ❏ b. C
- ❏ c. F
- ❏ d. E

. . . .

Quick Check

25. From the figure depicting an AT motherboard, identify the SIMM slots.

Quick Answer: **173**
Detailed Answer: **180**

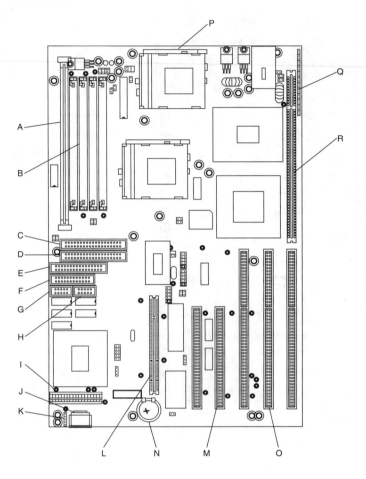

- ❏   a.   A
- ❏   b.   B
- ❏   c.   M
- ❏   d.   O

26. From the figure depicting an AT motherboard, identify the COM port connections.

Quick Answer: **173**
Detailed Answer: **180**

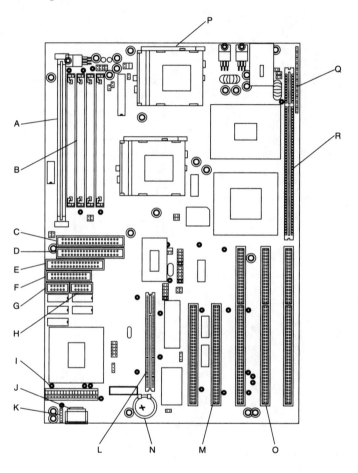

- ❏ a. A
- ❏ b. C
- ❏ c. G
- ❏ d. L

27. From the figure depicting an AT motherboard, identify the VESA expansion slot.

Quick Answer: **173**
Detailed Answer: **180**

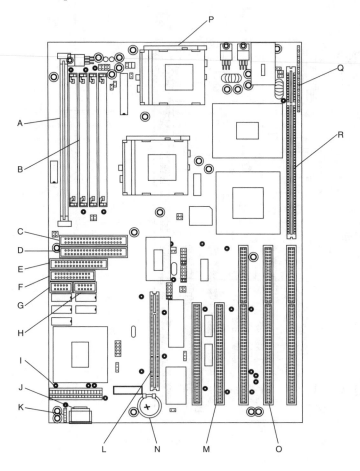

- ❑ a. O
- ❑ b. M
- ❑ c. R
- ❑ d. L

28. What type of system board can use a software-controlled power-off switch?

Quick Answer: **173**
Detailed Answer: **180**

- ❑ a. ATX
- ❑ b. AT
- ❑ c. XT
- ❑ d. NTX

29. From the figure depicting an ATX motherboard, identify the DIMM slots.

Quick Answer: **173**
Detailed Answer: **180**

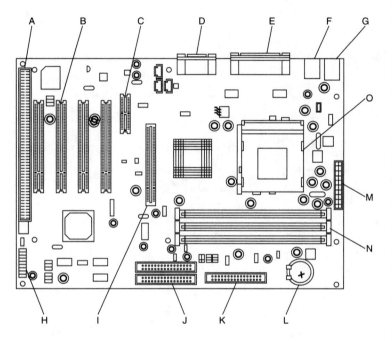

- ❑ a. I
- ❑ b. N
- ❑ c. H
- ❑ d. B

30. From the figure depicting an ATX motherboard, identify the battery.

Quick Answer: **173**
Detailed Answer: **180**

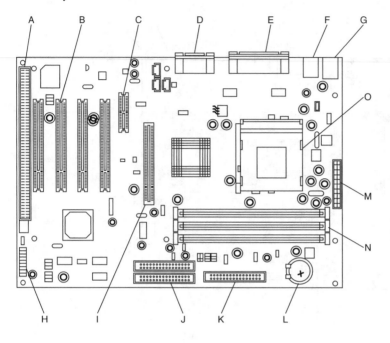

- ❏ a. O
- ❏ b. H
- ❏ c. G
- ❏ d. L

Quick Check

Quick Answer: **173**
Detailed Answer: **180**

31. From the figure depicting an ATX motherboard, identify the IDE connectors.

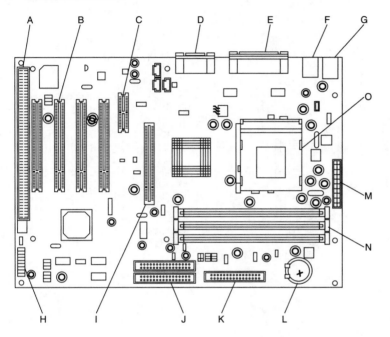

- ❏ a. J
- ❏ b. C
- ❏ c. K
- ❏ d. M

32. From the figure depicting an ATX motherboard, identify the AGP expansion slot.

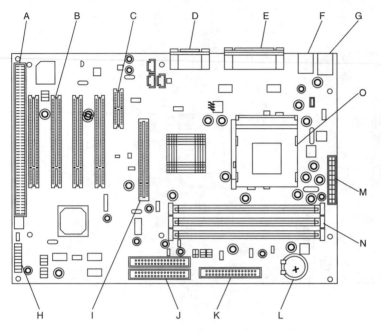

❏   a. I
❏   b. B
❏   c. A
❏   d. N

33. From the figure depicting an ATX motherboard, identify the ISA expansion slot.

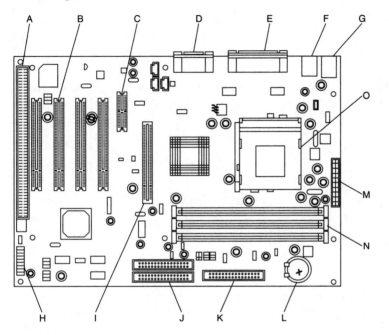

- ❑ a. C
- ❑ b. B
- ❑ c. A
- ❑ d. D

34. What type of device would you expect to find in an AGP slot?

- ❑ a. SCSI card
- ❑ b. Video card
- ❑ c. AMR card
- ❑ d. Network card

35. In a PCI 2.3 bus, what size is the Data bus?

- ❑ a. 16 bits
- ❑ b. 32 bits
- ❑ c. 8 bits
- ❑ d. 64 bits

36. In a Pentium computer, a 34-pin ribbon cable is used to interface a _____ to the system.

   ❏ a. hard drive

   ❏ b. floppy drive

   ❏ c. monitor

   ❏ d. scanner

Quick Answer: **173**
Detailed Answer: **181**

37. An internal SCSI-2 ribbon cable is outfitted with a _____ connector.

   ❏ a. 15-pin

   ❏ b. 40-pin

   ❏ c. 50-pin

   ❏ d. 80-pin

Quick Answer: **173**
Detailed Answer: **181**

38. Which of the following interfaces employs a 50-pin cable?

   ❏ a. An internal SCSI interface

   ❏ b. An EIDE interface

   ❏ c. A VESA bus

   ❏ d. An LPT port

Quick Answer: **173**
Detailed Answer: **181**

39. What is the maximum data throughput of a Video card that is AGP 8x compliant that is used in a motherboard with an AGP slot that is AGP 8x?

   ❏ a. 5.33GBps

   ❏ b. 1.07GBps

   ❏ c. 2.1GBps

   ❏ d. 7.33GBps

Quick Answer: **173**
Detailed Answer: **181**

40. Which of the following describes the difference between the PCI 32-bit local bus and the PCI 64-bit local bus?

   ❏ a. The data transfer performance of the PCI local bus is 132MBps using a 32-bit bus and 264MBps using a 64-bit bus.

   ❏ b. The PCI 32-bit bus operates at the 3.3V DC power supply level; 64-bit bus operates with a 5V DC power supply voltage.

   ❏ c. The PCI 32-bit bus has a maximum clock frequency of 66MHz and the PCI 64-bit bus operates at 132MHz.

   ❏ d. The PCI 32-bit bus includes two internal interrupt lines and the PCI 64-bit bus has four internal interrupt lines.

Quick Answer: **173**
Detailed Answer: **181**

41. What action should be taken when upgrading an AGP card or system board containing an AGP slot?

Quick Answer: **173**
Detailed Answer: **181**

 ❑ a. Set the CMOS setting for the AGP function to Autodetect so that the system will automatically establish compatibility between the slot and the card.

 ❑ b. Always install Universal AGP cards so that you can always be sure the slot and card will be compatible.

 ❑ c. Consult the system board and AGP adapter card's documentation to verify their compatibility with the other component.

 ❑ d. Obtain the correct BIOS Flash routine for the new AGP device so that you can upgrade the BIOS to work with the adapter.

42. Which interface standard was developed as a variation of the PCI bus design to handle the intense data throughput associated with three-dimensional graphics?

Quick Answer: **173**
Detailed Answer: **181**

 ❑ a. The USB port

 ❑ b. The AGP slot

 ❑ c. The IEEE-1394 FireWire port

 ❑ d. The AMR slot

43. On a PCI-based Pentium chipset system board, the _____ connects the system's microprocessor to the North Bridge memory controller.

Quick Answer: **173**
Detailed Answer: **181**

 ❑ a. Back side bus

 ❑ b. Front side bus

 ❑ c. PCI bus

 ❑ d. L2 access bus

44. _____ is a configuration in which the microprocessor's clock is set at a higher speed than the IC manufacturer suggests in an effort to get extra performance from the system.

Quick Answer: **173**
Detailed Answer: **181**

 ❑ a. Double-clocking

 ❑ b. Microprocessor optimization

 ❑ c. Turbo-clocking

 ❑ d. Over-clocking

45. What is the maximum length of a low-speed USB cable?

Quick Answer: **173**
Detailed Answer: **181**

 ❑ a. 5 meters

 ❑ b. 1 meter

 ❑ c. 3 meters

 ❑ d. 10 meters

. . . .

46. What is the maximum length of a high-speed USB segment?

❑   a.   5 meters

❑   b.   3 meters

❑   c.   10 meters

❑   d.   15 meters

47. Between two low-speed USB devices, what is the maximum segment length of a USB cable?

❑   a.   2 meters

❑   b.   3 meters

❑   c.   4 meters

❑   d.   5 meters

48. Between two full-speed USB devices, what is the maximum segment length of a USB cable?

❑   a.   2 meters

❑   b.   3 meters

❑   c.   4 meters

❑   d.   5 meters

49. What is the main difference between USB and IEEE-1394 ports?

❑   a.   Hot-swap capability

❑   b.   Transmission speed

❑   c.   Cable size

❑   d.   Daisy-chained devices

50. Which of the following is the fastest bus type?

❑   a.   FireWire

❑   b.   Full-speed USB

❑   c.   IrDA

❑   d.   EIDE

51. Which PCI slot specifications provide true 64-bit data bus capabilities to work efficiently with Pentium microprocessors? (Select all that apply.)

❑   a.   PCI 2.3

❑   b.   PCI 2.2

❑   c.   PCI 2.1

❑   d.   PCI 1.3

52. What type of expansion bus uses a 124-pin slot?

Quick Answer: **173**
Detailed Answer: **182**

- ❏ a. AGP
- ❏ b. PC bus
- ❏ c. PCI
- ❏ d. ISA

Objective 4.4: Identify the purpose of CMOS (Complementary Metal-Oxide Semiconductor) memory, what it contains, and how and when to change its parameters.

1. Where is the PnP information stored in the BIOS?

Quick Answer: **173**
Detailed Answer: **182**

- ❏ a. ESCD
- ❏ b. RTC
- ❏ c. PnP Registry
- ❏ d. Device Manager

2. During which portion of the startup process does the BIOS communicate with the system's PnP devices?

Quick Answer: **173**
Detailed Answer: **182**

- ❏ a. The CMOS configuration process
- ❏ b. The POST
- ❏ c. The OS bootstrap operation
- ❏ d. The initialization phase

3. The system's time and date information is stored in the _____.

Quick Answer: **173**
Detailed Answer: **182**

- ❏ a. System RAM
- ❏ b. ROM BIOS
- ❏ c. Real-Time Clock Registers
- ❏ d. CMOS Setup

4. The system's time and date information can be found in the _____.

Quick Answer: **173**
Detailed Answer: **183**

- ❏ a. CMOS
- ❏ b. ROM
- ❏ c. RAM
- ❏ d. ROM BIOS

5. What should be done if the CMOS contains a password you don't know?

- ❏ a. Enter the CMOS program and replace or erase the password.
- ❏ b. Install the CMOS shorting jumper to erase the CMOS data; then re-enter the configuration information.
- ❏ c. Keep trying different passwords until you find one that works.
- ❏ d. Find a machine that does not use password protection.

6. During the startup of the system, the BIOS collects information about all the intelligent (programmable) devices in the system. Where does this information get stored?

- ❏ a. In a special section of the CMOS RAM known as the Extended System Configuration Data (ESCD) area
- ❏ b. In the Flash portion of the system BIOS
- ❏ c. In the Flash portion of the BIOS extension (BIOSE)
- ❏ d. In the Registry of the operating system

7. What item in your CMOS settings can prevent you from upgrading your operating system?

- ❏ a. Hard disk drive type
- ❏ b. USB support
- ❏ c. Virus Warning function
- ❏ d. Autodetect Hard Drive function

8. Which of the following is a valid CMOS printer configuration?

- ❏ a. PnP
- ❏ b. ESD
- ❏ c. PPP
- ❏ d. ECP

9. What action must be taken to restore the system if the CMOS password is forgotten in an ATX system?

- ❏ a. Unplug the computer from the wall and remove the battery.
- ❏ b. Remove the battery.
- ❏ c. Short the CMOS-enabling jumper and remove the battery.
- ❏ d. Change the Password Enable setting in CMOS.

10. What are the effects of forgetting a CMOS password?

- ❏ a. You cannot start the computer.
- ❏ b. You cannot boot to the operating system.
- ❏ c. You cannot log in to the computer.
- ❏ d. You cannot shut down the computer.

11. What type of devices can be used with a half-duplex/ bidirectional parallel printer cable? (Select two.)

- ❏ a. EPP devices
- ❏ b. ECP devices
- ❏ c. USB devices
- ❏ d. SPP devices

Quick Answer: **173**
Detailed Answer: **183**

12. Which utility must be used to enable the ECP and EPP modes for the parallel port?

- ❏ a. BIOS
- ❏ b. DMA
- ❏ c. FDISK
- ❏ d. CMOS

Quick Answer: **173**
Detailed Answer: **183**

13. If you place a bootable floppy in drive A and the system boots to drive C, what action should you take to correct this?

- ❏ a. Reconfigure the Drive Seek Sequence in the CMOS Setup utility.
- ❏ b. Reconfigure the Drive Seek Sequence in the operating system Control Panel.
- ❏ c. Disconnect the IDE cable to the drive to force the system to boot off the floppy drive.
- ❏ d. Reconfigure the floppy jumpers to make it a bootable drive.

Quick Answer: **173**
Detailed Answer: **183**

14. When your computer boots up, you want it to search for a boot sector on a floppy, then a CD-ROM drive, and then the hard disk drive. What boot sequence should you set in CMOS?

- ❏ a. CD-ROM, A, C
- ❏ b. A, C, CD-ROM
- ❏ c. A, CD-ROM, C
- ❏ d. A, C, SCSI

Quick Answer: **173**
Detailed Answer: **184**

15. Which functions should be disabled when performing an operating system upgrade?

- ❏ a. PnP resource allocation
- ❏ b. BIOS virus-detection functions
- ❏ c. EPP and ECP
- ❏ d. RAM memory checks

Quick Answer: **173**
Detailed Answer: **184**

. . . .

16. What can happen when you change the translation mode setting for an existing IDE drive?

Quick Answer: **173**
Detailed Answer: **184**

- ❏ a. Incorrect rotational speed for drive's geometry
- ❏ b. Access limited to the first 528MB of the drive
- ❏ c. Slower drive access time
- ❏ d. Loss of all data on the drive

17. What must be enabled in the CMOS to support hard drive sizes over 504MB, and to allow the IDE controller to convert the sector/head/cylinder addresses into a physical block address that improves data throughput?

Quick Answer: **173**
Detailed Answer: **184**

- ❏ a. Normal
- ❏ b. Auto
- ❏ c. LBA
- ❏ d. Large

18. What section of the CMOS setup utility enables you to specify time intervals between notices to backup to pop up periodically when the system is booted?

Quick Answer: **173**
Detailed Answer: **184**

- ❏ a. The Chipset Features screen
- ❏ b. The Security subsystem
- ❏ c. The PnP/PCI Configuration screen
- ❏ d. Power Management functions

19. What does the Suspend mode actually do?

Quick Answer: **173**
Detailed Answer: **184**

- ❏ a. Suspend mode causes everything in the system except the microprocessor to shut down.
- ❏ b. Suspend mode causes the microprocessor clock to shut down after a defined period of inactivity.
- ❏ c. Suspend mode causes the microprocessor clock to slow down after a defined period of inactivity.
- ❏ d. Suspend mode causes the system to stop its system clock until F5 is pressed.

20. Which interface type is *not* capable of Full Duplex operation?

Quick Answer: **173**
Detailed Answer: **184**

- ❏ a. USB port
- ❏ b. A parallel port
- ❏ c. Serial port
- ❏ d. IEEE-1394 port

21. Which parallel port type has the highest throughput?

   ❑ a. ECP
   ❑ b. EPP
   ❑ c. SPP
   ❑ d. UPP

Quick Answer: **173**
Detailed Answer: **184**

22. What type of communication is possible with an IEEE-1284 parallel cable?

   ❑ a. Selectable half- or full-duplex
   ❑ b. Bidirectional, full-duplex
   ❑ c. Simplex
   ❑ d. Bidirectional, half-duplex

Quick Answer: **173**
Detailed Answer: **184**

23. What is the major difference between EPP and ECP operation of the parallel port?

   ❑ a. Serial
   ❑ b. Bidirectional
   ❑ c. 16-bit
   ❑ d. DMA mode

Quick Answer: **173**
Detailed Answer: **184**

24. Which specification employs DMA operations to provide the highest data throughput for a parallel port?

   ❑ a. EPP
   ❑ b. SPP
   ❑ c. ECP
   ❑ d. PPP

Quick Answer: **173**
Detailed Answer: **184**

25. What should you do first if the system clock fails to keep proper time?

   ❑ a. Clean the battery contacts.
   ❑ b. Replace the battery.
   ❑ c. Reload the operating system.
   ❑ d. Replace the motherboard.

Quick Answer: **173**
Detailed Answer: **184**

Quick Check Answer Key

Objective 4.1

1. c
2. d
3. d
4. b
5. b
6. c
7. b
8. a
9. b
10. d
11. b
12. c
13. b
14. a
15. a
16. b, c
17. d
18. b
19. b
20. c
21. b
22. b
23. c
24. a, b
25. b, c, d
26. a, c
27. d
28. b
29. c
30. d

Objective 4.2

1. c
2. b
3. b
4. a, c
5. d
6. c
7. b
8. a
9. c
10. b
11. d
12. c
13. b
14. c
15. a
16. d
17. d
18. c
19. b
20. c
21. c
22. b
23. d
24. a, b, c

Objective 4.3

1. b
2. a
3. c
4. a
5. c
6. d
7. a, b
8. c
9. d
10. a
11. b
12. c
13. b, d
14. d
15. a
16. b
17. b, c
18. c
19. a
20. a
21. b
22. d
23. b
24. d

25. b

26. c

27. c

28. a

29. b

30. d

31. a

32. a

33. c

34. b

35. d

36. b

37. c

38. a

39. c

40. a

41. c

42. b

43. b

44. d

45. c

46. a

47. b

48. d

49. b

50. b

51. a, b

52. c

Objective 4.4

1. a

2. d

3. c

4. a

5. b

6. a

7. c

8. d

9. a

10. b

11. a, b

12. d

13. a

14. c

15. b

16. d

17. c

18. b

19. a

20. b

21. a

22. d

23. d

24. c

25. a

Answers and Explanations

Objective 4.1

1. **c.** The BIOS version must support the parameters of the microprocessor. If a 500MHz Pentium III processor were installed in a system whose BIOS only supports processor speeds up to 400MHz, the BIOS will only report a processor speed of 400MHz during the POST portion of the startup.

2. **d.** The Athlon is a Pentium III clone processor that is available in a Slot 1 cartridge clone, called the Slot A specification.

3. **d.** The original Pentium III processor was designed around the Pentium II core, but increased the L2 cache size to 512KB.

4. **b.** Prior to Pentium II, all Pentium processors used 50, 60, and 66MHz external clock frequencies to generate their internal operating frequencies. The Pentium II processor moved to a 100MHz external clock and front side bus.

5. **b.** The Pentium Pro 512KB L2 cache complements the 16KB L1 cache in the Pentium Pro core. The L2 onboard cache stores the most frequently used data not found in the processor's internal L1 cache, as close to the processor core as it can be without being integrated directly into the IC.

6. **c.** The Pentium II includes all of the multimedia enhancements from the MMX processor, and retains the power of the Pentium Pro's Dynamic execution and 512KB L2 cache features.

7. **b.** The typical L2 cache used with the Pentium MMX was 256KB or 512KB.

8. **a.** The BIOS version must support the parameters of the new 1GHz microprocessor. If the BIOS code does not fully support the new processor, the BIOS will only report a processor speed of 600MHz during the POST portion of the startup.

9. **b.** Older Socket 7 systems enable system boards to be configured for different types of microprocessors with different operating speeds by using the external clock frequencies to generate their internal operating frequencies. The value of the internal multiplier was controlled by external hardware jumper settings on the system board.

10. **d.** Duron is a Celeron clone processor that conforms to the AMD Socket A specifications and uses 0.18-micron IC manufacturing technology.

11. **b.** The Athlon is a Pentium III clone processor that uses Slot A. The K7 version ran between 500MHz and 700MHz, providing a 128KB L1 cache as well as a 512KB L2 cache, and employed a 100MHz system bus.

12. **c.** Pentium 4 employs a modified Socket 370 PGA design that uses 423 pins and boasts operating speeds above 2GHz.

13. **b.** The Pentium Celeron version featured a 66MHz bus speed and only 128KB of L2 cache. Initially, the Celeron was packaged in the Slot 1 SEC cartridge.

14. **a.** Intel followed the Pentium II processor with an improved, low-cost design called the Pentium Celeron. The Celeron version featured a 66MHz front side bus speed and only 128KB of L2 cache. Initially, the Celeron was packaged in the Slot 1 SEC cartridge.

15. **a.** The original Pentium III was designed around the Pentium II core, but increased the L2 cache size to 512KB.

16. **b, c.** Later versions of the Pentium III processor were developed for the Intel Socket 370 specification. The original Pentium III processor was designed around the Pentium II core with a new Slot 1–compatible design.

17. **d.** Later versions of the Pentium III and Celeron processors were developed for the Intel Socket 370 specification.

18. **b.** The Pentium II processor is housed in an SEC cartridge. Its proprietary 242-contact socket design is referred to as the Slot 1 specification and was designed to enable the microprocessor to operate at bus speeds in excess of 300MHz.

19. **b.** The components of a Pentium II SEC cartridge are the Pentium II processor core, a tag RAM, and an L2 burst SRAM.

20. **c.** The Pentium II adopts the Pentium Pro's 512KB L2 cache feature but only operates at half the bus speed.

21. **b.** The specification for Socket 8 is developed for the Pentium Pro processor.

22. **b.** The Pentium MMX processor was available in 166, 200, and 233MHz versions and used a 321-pin, SPGA Socket 7 format.

23. **c.** Intel followed the Pentium III design with a less expensive version that it named the Pentium Celeron. Unlike the original Pentium III, the Celeron version featured a 66MHz front side bus speed and only 128KB of L2 cache.

24. **a, b.** Intel quickly followed the Celeron release with a new Slot 1–compatible design called the Pentium III. Later versions of the Pentium III and Celeron processors were developed for the Intel Socket 370 specification. This design returned to a 370-pin, ZIF socket/SPGA package arrangement.

25. **b, c, d.** Although the Intel Slot 1 design was originally developed for the Pentium II, it also serves its Celeron and Pentium III processor designs. Like Socket 7, the Slot 1 specification provides for variable processor core voltages (2.8 to 3.3) that permit faster operation and reduced power consumption.

26. **a, c.** (a) The BIOS version must support the parameters of the microprocessor. If a microprocessor upgrade is performed and the BIOS code does not fully support the new processor, it will not operate at the correct speed intended for the processor installed. (c) Incorrect core voltage, bus frequency, or bus ratio settings will result in incorrect system speed, random lockups, and startup failure.

27. **d.** The microprocessor's supply voltage is controlled by a voltage regulator module on the system board.

28. **b.** If the core voltage level is set too high for the actual microprocessor installed in the system, the microprocessor will probably overheat slowly, or burn out, depending on the amount of voltage applied. Conversely, if the voltage level is configured too low for the installed processor, the system will most likely refuse to start.

29. **c.** If the core voltage level is set too high for the actual microprocessor installed in the system, the microprocessor will probably overheat slowly, or burn out, depending on the amount of voltage applied. Conversely, if the voltage level is configured too low for the installed processor, the system will most likely refuse to start.

30. **d.** The BIOS controls the cooling system through its Health Management system. This includes monitoring the actual temperature of the microprocessor and manipulating the cooling system to maintain a designated temperature level.

Objective 4.2

1. **c.** Because each byte of storage needs a parity-checking bit, 8 parity bits are added to a 64-bit data bus to become a 72-bit module.

2. **b.** The ECC RAM detects and corrects errors in the information it processes.

3. **b.** Windows RAM (WRAM), a special version of Video RAM (VRAM), is designed to optimize video memory–related activities by transferring blocks of data at a time.

4. **a, c.** (a) EDO is an advanced type of Fast Page Mode DRAM, also referred to as Hyper Page Mode DRAM. (c) The advantage of EDO DRAM is encountered when multiple sequential memory accesses are performed. By not turning off the data pin, each successive access after the first access is accomplished in two clock cycles rather than three.

5. **d.** Parity checking is a simple self test used to detect RAM read-back errors.

6. **c.** With bits constantly moving in and out of RAM, it is crucial that all of the bits be transferred correctly or you will have faulty RAM. When a parity error occurs, the BIOS executes its NMI handler routine, which will normally place a parity error message on the screen, along with an option to shut down the system, or continue.

7. **b.** It is important to install RAM that is compatible with the bus speed the system is running. Normally, installing RAM that is rated faster than the bus speed will not cause problems. However, installing slower RAM, or mixing RAM speed ratings in a system, will cause the system to not start or to periodically lock up.

8. **a.** A Pentium MMX system board requires two 32-bit SIMMs to make a bank for the 64-bit processor.

9. **c.** SIMMs typically come in 30-pin/8-bit or 72-pin/32-bit non-parity data-storage configurations.

10. **b.** The original built-in first-level cache, L1 cache, is used in Pentium systems for both instructions and data. Control of L1 cache is handled directly by the microprocessor.

11. **d.** Parity checking is a simple self test used to detect RAM read-back errors. When a data byte is being stored in memory, the parity generator/checker chip produces a parity bit that is added to the data byte. Whenever the data word is read back from the memory, the parity bit is reapplied to the parity generator and recalculated.

12. **c.** Some types of advanced RAM include Error Checking and Correcting (ECC) capabilities to detect and correct single-bit errors or to detect errors in two bits in the information they process.

13. **b.** When a parity error occurs, a Non-Maskable Interrupt (NMI) signal is cogenerated in the system, causing the BIOS to execute its NMI handler routine. This routine will normally place a parity error message on the screen, along with an option to shut down the system, or continue.

14. **c.** EDO RAM increases the speed at which RAM operations are conducted by cutting out the 10-nanosecond wait time normally required between issuing memory addresses.

15. **a.** WRAM is a special version of video RAM. It operates at speeds of up to 150% of typical VRAM and costs up to 20% less by transferring blocks of data at a time.

16. **d.** Any data stored in RAM will be lost if power to the computer is disrupted for any reason.

17. **d.** DRAM stores data bits on rows and columns of IC capacitors, which lose their charge over time. It is necessary to recharge a DRAM's memory bits periodically even if power is applied to the chip. The process of recharging a DRAM's memory bits to maintain data is called *refresh*.

18. **c.** Whether the RAM is made up of static or dynamic RAM devices, all RAM systems have the disadvantage of being volatile.

19. **b.** Normally, installing RAM that is rated faster than the bus speed will not cause problems. However, installing slower RAM, or mixing RAM speed ratings in a system, will cause the system to not start or to periodically lock up.

20. **c.** The most popular form of error detection in PC compatibles is parity checking. In this methodology, an extra bit is added to each word in RAM and checked each time it is used.

21. **c.** The Small Outline DIMM (SODIMM) has been developed for use in notebook computers. The basic difference between SODIMMs and regular DIMMs is that the SODIMM is significantly smaller than the standard DIMM so that it takes up less space in notebook computers.

22. **b.** MicroDIMMs are nearly square, 144-pin, 32 million×64-bit plug-in modules.

23. **d.** MicroDIMM modules are nearly square, 144-pin, 32 million×64-bit plug-in modules that are available with either SDRAM or DDR SDRAM components onboard. They are 1.54 inches (38mm) by approximately 1 inch (25.4mm) high and, unlike SODIMMs, do not have any notches along their edge connector contacts. The height of MicroDIMM modules varies between different manufacturers.

24. **a, b, c.** (a) A bad RAM module will cause incorrect memory count. (b) Split-bank arrangements use a different specification for DIMM Slot 1 than they do for Slots 2 and 3. Slot 1 is usually organized into one bank, whereas the other two slots combine to form the second bank. If you are not careful when populating these slots, you might create a situation in which the system's memory controller cannot access all the installed RAM. (c) Mixing memory device types can cause assorted memory errors, including complete system failures, random lockups, and miscounted RAM.

Objective 4.3

1. **b.** A PCI slot is a 32-bit expansion slot. It is typically included on 80486- and Pentium-based computers along with traditional ISA slots.

2. **a.** A VESA expansion slot connector consists of an ISA slot and an additional VESA connector.

3. **c.** Although the ISA bus ran at microprocessor-compatible speeds up to 10 or 12MHz, incompatibility with slower I/O cards caused manufacturers to settle for running the bus at 8 or 8.33MHz in newer designs.

4. **a.** If the BIOS detects the presence of a new device during the detection phase, it disables the resource settings for its existing cards, checks to see what resources are required and available, and then reallocates the system's resources as necessary.

5. **c.** The ATX system board uses a software-activated power switch. The PS-ON and 5VSB (5V Standby) signals can be controlled by the operating system to perform automatic system shutdowns.

6. **d.** When connecting a ribbon cable to the system board, pin 1 of the connector must line up with the signal cable's red indicator stripe.

7. **a, b.** SCSI host adapters are typically available for use with ISA, EISA, and PCI bus interfaces.

8. **c.** When connecting an Ultra ATA 66 hard disk drive with a 40-pin/40-conductor IDE cable, the Ultra ATA 66 hard disk drive will operate at speeds compatible with the older IDE standard, which has the maximum data throughput of 33MBps.

9. **d.** The hierarchy of assigning logical drive designations in the IDE interface calls for primary partitions to be assigned sequentially from ID1 master, ID1 slave, ID2 master, to ID2 slave with logical drive letters starting with C. This is followed by assigning extended partitions for each drive in the same order.

10. **a.** The ATX system board uses a 6-pin mini-DIN keyboard connector, not a 5-pin DIN connector.

11. **b.** B is the printer connector; D is the COM1 connector, which is the serial port connector; A and C are PCI expansion slots.

12. **c.** D is the COM1 connector, which is the serial port connector; B is the printer connector; A and C are PCI expansion slots.

13. **b, d.** Both the EISA and VESA slots can accommodate ISA cards.

14. **d.** Newer Pentium systems include an advanced Accelerated Graphics Port (AGP) interface for video graphics.

15. **a.** As the PnP process has no method for reconfiguring legacy devices during the resource assignment phase, the process begins by assigning preconfigured resources, such as IRQ assignments, to these devices before servicing the system's PnP devices.

16. **b.** Currently, most Pentium system boards include a combination of PCI, AGP, and might include a single ISA connector for compatibility purposes (or none at all).

17. **b** and **c.** The 32-bit expansion buses include the MCA bus, the EISA bus, the VESA bus, and the PCI bus. The AGP slot is a special version of the PCI.

18. **c.** The ISA slot is the consummate 16-bit expansion bus.

19. **a.** The PC bus slot is the most famous example of an 8-bit expansion slot.

20. **a.** Although the PCI bus speed has improved, the operating speed of the ISA bus has remained constant at 8MHz.

21. **b.** I is the power connector; J is the keyboard connector; P is the microprocessor socket; R is the VESA slot.

22. **d.** Q is the front panel connectors; I is the power connector; J is the keyboard connector; K is the mouse connector.

23. **b.** J is the keyboard connector; Q is the front panel connectors; I is the power connector; K is the mouse connector.

24. **d.** E is the FDD connector; C is the IDE2 connector; F is the PRT1 connector; G is the COM1 connector.

25. **b.** B is the SIMM slots; A is the DIMM slot; M is the PC bus slots; O is the ISA slots.

26. **c.** G is the COM1 connector; C is the IDE2 connector; A is the DIMM slot; L is the PCI slot.

27. **c.** R is the VESA slot; M is the PC bus slots; O is the ISA slots; L is the PCI slot.

28. **a.** The ATX system board uses a software-activated power switch. The PS-ON and 5VSB (5V Standby) signals can be controlled by the operating system to perform automatic system shutdowns.

29. **b.** N identifies DIMM slots; B is the PCI expansion slots; I is the AGP expansion slot; H is the front panel connections.

30. **d.** L is the battery; H is the front panel connections; G is the block where the keyboard connector and the mouse connector are located; O is the microprocessor.

31. **a.** J indicates the IDE connectors, which control hard drives and CD-ROM drives. C is an AMR/CNR expansion slot; M is the power connector; K is the FDD connector.

32. **a.** I points to the AGP expansion slot; B identifies a PCI expansion slot; A is the ISA expansion slot; N is the DIMM slots.

33. **c.** A is the ISA expansion slot; B is the PCI expansion slots; C is the AMR/CNR slot; D is the speaker connector.

34. **b.** Newer Pentium systems include an advanced Accelerated Graphics Port (AGP) interface for video graphics.

35. **d.** The PCI 2.3 bus specification features a true 64-bit data bus.

36. **b.** Along with the I/O port connections, Pentium system boards moved the hard- and floppy-disk drive controller functions and interface connections to the system board. The FDC portion of the chipset can control two floppy-disk drives whose signal cable connects to the system board at the 34-pin BERG block.

37. **c.** The built-in SCSI-2 connector on a system board is made through a 50-pin BERG header.

38. **a.** An internal SCSI device must be capable of connecting to the type of SCSI cable being used. In a PC, this is most often a 50-pin ribbon cable.

39. **c.** The AGP specification was introduced by Intel to provide a 32-bit video channel that runs at 66MHz in basic 1X video mode. The standard also supports three high-speed modes that include 2X (5.33MBps), 4X (1.07GBps), and 8X (2.1GBps) mode.

40. **a.** The Peripheral Component Interconnect (PCI) local bus is designed to incorporate a low-cost, high-performance local bus, the Plug-and-Play function, and the capability to expand with the introduction of new microprocessors and peripherals. The data transfer rate of the PCI local bus is 132MBps using a 32-bit bus and 264MBps using a 64-bit bus.

41. **c.** When upgrading an AGP card or system board containing an AGP slot, you should always consult the system board and AGP adapter card's documentation to verify their compatibility with each other.

42. **b.** The AGP interface is a variation of the PCI bus design that has been modified to handle the intense data throughput associated with three-dimensional graphics.

43. **b.** The buses between the microprocessor and the North Bridge are referred to as the front side bus (FSB).

44. **d.** In some configurations, the microprocessor clock is set at a higher speed than the IC manufacturer suggests. This is referred to as *over-clocking the processor*. Because the basic microprocessor is running faster than designed, both the front side bus and the PCI bus run faster than their stated values by a factor directly proportional to the amount that the microprocessor is over-clocked.

45. **c.** USB devices are rated as full-speed and low-speed devices based on their communication specification. Under the USB 1.1 specification, low-speed USB devices run at 12Mbps. The length limit for cables serving low-speed devices is 9 feet 10 inches (3 meters).

46. **a.** Full-speed USB devices operate under the USB 2.0 specification (also referred to as *high-speed USB*) and support data rates up to 480Mbps. The maximum cable length for full-speed USB communication is 16 feet 5 inches (5 meters).

47. **b.** USB devices are rated as full-speed and low-speed devices based on their communication specification. Under the USB 1.1 specification, low-speed USB devices run at 12Mbps. The length limit for cables serving low-speed devices is 9 feet 10 inches (3 meters).

48. **d.** Full-speed USB devices operate under the USB 2.0 specification (also referred to as high-speed USB) and support data rates up to 480Mbps. The maximum cable length for full-speed USB communication is 16 feet 5 inches (5 meters).

49. **b.** Low-speed USB devices run at 12Mbps. FireWire is capable of supporting data transfer rates up to 400Mbps. Full-speed USB devices operating under the USB 2.0 specification support data rates up to 480Mbps.

50. **b.** Full-speed USB devices operate under the USB 2.0 specification (also referred to as high-speed USB) and support data rates up to 480Mbps. FireWire is capable of using the high-speed Isochronous transfer mode to support data transfer rates up to 400Mbps.

51. **a, b.** The PCI 2.2 and PCI 2.3 versions of the bus implemented two new slot structures to provide a true 64-bit data bus. The new PCI specification runs at 66MHz to provide a 264Mbps data throughput.

52. **c.** The PCI bus specification uses multiplexed address and data lines to conserve the pins of the basic 124-pin PCI connector.

Objective 4.4

1. **a.** The BIOS stores the PnP information it collects from the devices in a special section of the CMOS RAM known as the Extended System Configuration Data (ESCD) area. This information is stored in the same manner as standard BIOS settings are stored.

2. **d.** The BIOS communicates with the PnP devices during the initialization phase of the startup process to determine what types of hardware devices are installed, where they are located in the system, and what resources they require.

3. **c.** PC chipsets include a Real-Time Clock (RTC) function that keeps track of time and date information for the system.

4. **a.** PC chipsets include a Real-Time Clock (RTC) function that keeps track of time and date information for the system. During the startup process, the operating system acquires the time and date information from the CMOS RTC module.

5. **b.** The password setting prevents users without the password from accessing the system. If the system has an unknown password, it will be necessary to clear the CMOS. Most system boards have a jumper that can be shorted to reset the CMOS to its default settings. If this option is used, you must reenter the original configuration information.

6. **a.** The BIOS stores the PnP information it collects from the devices in a special section of the CMOS RAM known as the ESCD area.

7. **c.** The BIOS built-in virus warning utility should be turned off when conducting an upgrade to the operating system. This built-in utility checks the drive's boot sector for changes. The changes that the new operating system will attempt to make to the boot sector will be interpreted as a virus and the utility will act to prevent the upgrade from occurring.

8. **d.** The Extended Capabilities Port (ECP) is an option of the parallel printer port configuration for fast, buffered bidirectional operation.

9. **a.** In ATX systems, it will be necessary to unplug the power from the commercial outlet to reduce the voltage to the CMOS registers before removing the backup battery for resetting the contents of the CMOS RAM.

10. **b.** Because the CMOS password controls access to all parts of the system, even before the bootup process occurs, there is some danger that the user will forget his password. When this occurs, it will be impossible to gain access to the system without completely resetting the contents of the CMOS RAM.

11. **a, b.** The UARTs can be configured to support half-duplex transmission modes. Therefore, the bidirectional EPP and ECP devices can be used with a half-duplex/bidirectional parallel printer cable.

12. **d.** In most Pentium-based systems, the standard I/O functions of the Multi I/O card have been integrated into the system board. In these systems, the CMOS Integrated Peripherals screen provides configuration and enabling settings for the system board's onboard parallel port. Options of the parallel printer port are normal SPP, EPP, ECP, or ECP+EPP.

13. **a.** The Features Setup screen is used to configure different bootup options. These options include establishing the system's bootup sequence. The sequence can be set so that the system checks the floppy drive for a boot sector first, or so that it checks the hard drive without checking the floppy drive.

14. **c.** The Features Setup screen can be used to configure the system's bootup sequence. If you want it to search for a boot sector on a floppy, then a CD-ROM drive, and then the hard disk drive, the boot sequence should be set as A, CD-ROM, and C.

15. **b.** The BIOS built-in virus warning utility should be turned off when conducting an upgrade to the operating system. This built-in utility checks the drive's boot sector for changes. The changes that the new operating system will attempt to make to the boot sector will be interpreted as a virus and the utility will act to prevent the upgrade from occurring.

16. **d.** When changing the translation mode setting for an existing IDE drive, it is possible to lose all data on the drive if care is not taken.

17. **c.** For larger drives (more than 504MB), the Large and LBA modes are used. The LBA mode should be selected if drives support LBA mode. In this mode, the IDE controller converts the sector/head/cylinder address into a physical block address that improves data throughput.

18. **b.** Newer BIOSs offer a variety of security options that can be set through the CMOS setup utility. Typically, these options include items such as setting passwords and supervisory passwords to control access. The Security configuration screen might also include options for setting virus check and backup reminders that will pop up periodically when the system is booted.

19. **a.** The Power Management fields enable the user to select from three power-saving modes: Doze, Standby, and Suspend. These are green, PC-compatible, power-saving modes that cause the system to incrementally step down from maximum power usage. At the Suspend mode, everything in the system except the microprocessor shuts down.

20. **b.** The Parallel Printer port operates bidirectional, half-duplex transfers.

21. **a.** The Extended Capabilities Port (ECP) supports high-throughput DMA operations for both forward- and reverse-direction transfers.

22. **d.** An IEEE-1284 parallel cable is used for bidirectional, half-duplex communication.

23. **d.** Unlike EPP, ECP supports DMA operations.

24. **c.** ECP supports high-throughput DMA operations for both forward- and reverse-direction transfers.

25. **a.** If the system continually fails to keep good time, you should start by checking for corrosion on the battery contacts. Clean the contacts with a pencil eraser and retry the battery.

Hardware Domain 5.0: Printers

Objective 5.1: Identify printer technologies, interfaces, and options and upgrades.

1. What type of port uses a DB-25F connector?

   - ❏ a. Printer port
   - ❏ b. Game port
   - ❏ c. VGA port
   - ❏ d. COM2 port

   Quick Answer: **199**
   Detailed Answer: **200**

2. In a laser printer, a thermal fuse is used to prevent _____.

   - ❏ a. heat-sink failure
   - ❏ b. a fuser from overheating
   - ❏ c. a high-voltage power supply from overheating
   - ❏ d. a low-voltage power supply from overheating

   Quick Answer: **199**
   Detailed Answer: **200**

3. What does the fuser unit do in a laser printer?

   - ❏ a. It transfers the image from the drum to the paper.
   - ❏ b. It melts toner to the paper.
   - ❏ c. It transfers images to the drum.
   - ❏ d. It cleans the drum.

   Quick Answer: **199**
   Detailed Answer: **200**

4. What type of paper-handling mechanism is required for printing multipart forms?

   - ❏ a. Friction feed
   - ❏ b. Single-sheet feed
   - ❏ c. Double-sheet feed
   - ❏ d. Tractor feed

   Quick Answer: **199**
   Detailed Answer: **200**

5. What is the order of operation of a laser printer?

  ❑ a. Conditioning, cleaning, writing, developing, fusing, transferring

  ❑ b. Cleaning, conditioning, writing, developing, transferring, fusing

  ❑ c. Writing, conditioning, cleaning, developing, transferring, fusing

  ❑ d. Conditioning, cleaning, writing, developing, transferring, fusing

Quick Answer: **199**
Detailed Answer: **200**

6. A _____ font is defined as a mathematical function.

  ❑ a. true

  ❑ b. vector-based

  ❑ c. bitmapped

  ❑ d. raster

Quick Answer: **199**
Detailed Answer: **200**

7. The advantages of vector-based fonts over bitmapped fonts are that _____. (Select two.)

  ❑ a. vector-based fonts require less storage space than bitmapped fonts

  ❑ b. vector-based fonts can be scaled and rotated, whereas bitmapped fonts cannot

  ❑ c. vector-based fonts load from the hard drive much faster than bitmapped fonts

  ❑ d. vector-based fonts load into the printer much quicker than bitmapped fonts

Quick Answer: **199**
Detailed Answer: **200**

8. In a laser printer, a positive charge on the transfer corona wire causes _____.

  ❑ a. the positive image to appear on the print drum

  ❑ b. the toner to be transferred from the drum to the paper

  ❑ c. the excess toner to be dislodged from the drum after printing

  ❑ d. the negative image to appear on the print drum

Quick Answer: **199**
Detailed Answer: **200**

9. What type of printer delivers ink to the page by applying power to an electromagnet, which in turn forces a wire to strike an inked ribbon?

  ❑ a. A laser printer

  ❑ b. A drum printer

  ❑ c. An inkjet printer

  ❑ d. A dot-matrix printer

Quick Answer: **199**
Detailed Answer: **200**

10. Which component of a laser printer transfers toner to the paper?

Quick Answer: **199**
Detailed Answer: **201**

- ❏ a. The drum
- ❏ b. The fuser assembly
- ❏ c. The transfer corona wire
- ❏ d. The platen

11. The primary corona wire (conditioning roller) of a laser printer _____.

Quick Answer: **199**
Detailed Answer: **201**

- ❏ a. transfers toner to the paper
- ❏ b. applies a uniform negative charge to the drum
- ❏ c. presses toner into the paper
- ❏ d. transfers characters to the paper

12. Which is not a common pin configuration for a dot-matrix printhead?

Quick Answer: **199**
Detailed Answer: **201**

- ❏ a. 9-pin
- ❏ b. 12-pin
- ❏ c. 18-pin
- ❏ d. 24-pin

13. Which two of the following indicate the presence of a network-ready printer?

Quick Answer: **199**
Detailed Answer: **201**

- ❏ a. Network cable connected to the printer
- ❏ b. RJ-45 jacks on the back of the printer
- ❏ c. RS-232 port on the back of the printer
- ❏ d. RJ-11 jacks on the back of the printer

14. What is the recommended clear distance and the maximum angle specified for IrDA printer connections?

Quick Answer: **199**
Detailed Answer: **201**

- ❏ a. 3 meters, 45°
- ❏ b. 2 meters, 30°
- ❏ c. 1 meter, 15°
- ❏ d. 4 meters, 60°

15. What is the recommended maximum length of a standard parallel printer cable?

Quick Answer: **199**
Detailed Answer: **201**

- ❏ a. 10 feet (3 meters)
- ❏ b. 3 feet (1 meter)
- ❏ c. 30 feet (9 meters)
- ❏ d. 50 feet (15 meters)

16. What is the recommended maximum length of an RS-232 cable?

Quick Answer: **199**
Detailed Answer: **201**

- ❏ a. 100 feet (30 meters)
- ❏ b. 30 feet (9 meters)
- ❏ c. 10 feet (3 meters)
- ❏ d. 50 feet (15 meters)

17. What problem can be created by using a noncompliant parallel cable with an IEEE-1284 bidirectional parallel device?

Quick Answer: **199**
Detailed Answer: **201**

- ❏ a. The printer doesn't work.
- ❏ b. The printer output is jumbled.
- ❏ c. All characters print on the same line.
- ❏ d. Characters print but not graphics.

18. You purchase 24 pounds of 24lb bond paper. How many sheets are involved, and what size are they?

Quick Answer: **199**
Detailed Answer: **201**

- ❏ a. 1,000 sheets, 17"×22"
- ❏ b. 500 sheets, 8.5"×11"
- ❏ c. 1,000 sheets, 8.5"×11"
- ❏ d. 500 sheets, 17"×22"

19. What are the components found in a typical electrophotographic cartridge? (Select all that apply.)

Quick Answer: **199**
Detailed Answer: **201**

- ❏ a. Conditioning wire
- ❏ b. Drum assembly
- ❏ c. Corona wire
- ❏ d. Developing roller

20. What is the HP laser printer cartridge called?

Quick Answer: **199**
Detailed Answer: **201**

- ❏ a. Cartridge assembly
- ❏ b. HP cartridge
- ❏ c. Electrophotographic cartridge
- ❏ d. Cartridge unit

21. What is the function of the fuser unit in a laser printer?

Quick Answer: **199**
Detailed Answer: **202**

- ❏ a. It cleans the excess toner off of the drum assembly.
- ❏ b. It melts the toner onto the paper.
- ❏ c. It transfers toner to the paper.
- ❏ d. It squirts the ink onto the paper.

22. What is the purpose of the thermal fuse in laser printers?

Quick Answer: **199**
Detailed Answer: **202**

   ❑ a. It heats the fusing unit.

   ❑ b. It protects the paper from burning.

   ❑ c. It fuses the toner image to the paper.

   ❑ d. It monitors the temperature of the unit.

23. What are the two functions of the two corona wires in a laser printer?

Quick Answer: **199**
Detailed Answer: **202**

   ❑ a. They transfer toner from the drum to the paper.

   ❑ b. They fuse the toner to the paper.

   ❑ c. They condition the drum to be written on.

   ❑ d. They clean the drum.

24. You should never expose the drum of a laser printer to _____.

Quick Answer: **199**
Detailed Answer: **202**

   ❑ a. cold

   ❑ b. a strong light source

   ❑ c. air

   ❑ d. toner

25. What are the operational stages of a typical laser printer?

Quick Answer: **199**
Detailed Answer: **202**

   ❑ a. Conditioning, writing, developing, transferring, fusing, cleaning

   ❑ b. Conditioning, writing, transferring, developing, fusing, cleaning

   ❑ c. Cleaning, conditioning, writing, transferring, developing, fusing

   ❑ d. Cleaning, conditioning, writing, developing, transferring, fusing

26. What two techniques are used to form the ink drops in an inkjet printer?

Quick Answer: **199**
Detailed Answer: **202**

   ❑ a. Mechanical vibration

   ❑ b. Thermal shock

   ❑ c. Air pressure

   ❑ d. Electromagnetic acceleration

27. What printer type produces print by squirting ink at the page?

Quick Answer: **199**
Detailed Answer: **202**

   ❑ a. Laser

   ❑ b. Thermal

   ❑ c. Inkjet

   ❑ d. Dot-matrix

Quick Check

28. What types of connectors are often used at the computer and the printer ends, respectively, of a parallel-printer cable?
    - ❑ a. DB-9 and DB-25
    - ❑ b. 36-pin Centronics and DB-25
    - ❑ c. DB-25 and DB-9
    - ❑ d. DB-25 and 36-pin Centronics

Quick Answer: **199**
Detailed Answer: **202**

29. Which of the following is not a type of interface connection commonly used with printers?
    - ❑ a. USB
    - ❑ b. SCSI
    - ❑ c. IDE
    - ❑ d. IrDA

Quick Answer: **199**
Detailed Answer: **202**

30. What is the main circuit board in a dot-matrix printer called?
    - ❑ a. Main control board
    - ❑ b. Printhead board
    - ❑ c. Control panel
    - ❑ d. Sensor board

Quick Answer: **199**
Detailed Answer: **202**

31. How many print wires are in a typical dot-matrix printhead?
    - ❑ a. 6, 12, or 14
    - ❑ b. 9, 18, or 24
    - ❑ c. 9, 12, or 18
    - ❑ d. 6, 10, or 12

Quick Answer: **199**
Detailed Answer: **203**

32. What is the major purpose of a tractor-feed mechanism and where is it most commonly used?
    - ❑ a. It is used on color printers that print continuous forms.
    - ❑ b. It is used on inkjet printers that print continuous forms.
    - ❑ c. It is used on laser printers that print continuous forms.
    - ❑ d. It is used on dot-matrix printers that print continuous forms.

Quick Answer: **199**
Detailed Answer: **203**

33. Which font types are generated by establishing starting points and then calculating mathematical formulas?
    - ❑ a. Vector-based fonts
    - ❑ b. Raster-scanned fonts
    - ❑ c. Bitmapped fonts
    - ❑ d. TrueType outline fonts

Quick Answer: **199**
Detailed Answer: **203**

. . . .

34. What are the benefits and drawbacks of bitmapped characters? (Select all that apply.)

Quick Answer: **199**
Detailed Answer: **203**

- ❏ a. Bitmapped fonts store dot patterns for all the possible size and style variations of the characters in the set.
- ❏ b. Bitmapped fonts typically cannot be scaled and rotated.
- ❏ c. Bitmapped characters can be printed out directly and quickly.
- ❏ d. Each character is composed of a set of reference points in bitmapped fonts.

35. Which of the following printers can produce photographic quality, continuous-tone images?

Quick Answer: **199**
Detailed Answer: **203**

- ❏ a. Dot-matrix printer
- ❏ b. Dye-sublimation printer
- ❏ c. Direct thermal printer
- ❏ d. Thermal wax transfer printer

36. Which of the following statements is correct regarding direct thermal printers and thermal wax transfer printers?

Quick Answer: **199**
Detailed Answer: **203**

- ❏ a. Thermal wax transfer printers require special thermal paper on which to print.
- ❏ b. In the thermal printer, the printhead moves across the page.
- ❏ c. The early fax machine technology was based on direct thermal printing.
- ❏ d. Both direct thermal printers and thermal wax transfer printers are available in monochrome version only.

37. What types of connectors are often used at the computer and the printer ends of an RS-232 serial printer cable, respectively?

Quick Answer: **199**
Detailed Answer: **203**

- ❏ a. DB-9 and DB-25
- ❏ b. DB-25 and 36-pin Centronics
- ❏ c. DB-25 and DB-9
- ❏ d. 36-pin Centronics and DB-25

Objective 5.2: Recognize common printer problems and techniques used to resolve them.

1. If you have cleared a paper jam from a laser printer, but the printer still indicates that a jam is present, what action should be taken first?

   □   a. Remove the paper tray from the printer.

   □   b. Open the top cover to clear any interlock errors.

   □   c. Open the unit to check for additional bits of paper that might have been left behind.

   □   d. Press the Clear button to reset the machine.

   Quick Answer: **199**
   Detailed Answer: **204**

2. What will cause an inkjet printer to produce wavy graphics? (Select two correct answers.)

   □   a. Bad paper-feed rollers

   □   b. Low ink

   □   c. Improper paper thickness setting

   □   d. Mismatched ink cartridge

   Quick Answer: **199**
   Detailed Answer: **204**

3. How do you increase the density of a printout from an inkjet printer?

   □   a. Make everything on the page in boldface when typing it.

   □   b. Print the page twice.

   □   c. Use darker ink.

   □   d. Adjust it in the printing software.

   Quick Answer: **199**
   Detailed Answer: **204**

4. What causes the printout from a dot-matrix printer to get lighter from left to right?

   □   a. Wrong spacing between the platen and the printhead carriage rod

   □   b. Bad printhead

   □   c. Bad ribbon

   □   d. Bad toner cartridge

   Quick Answer: **199**
   Detailed Answer: **204**

5. You receive a page from your laser printer that is completely black. Which of the following components is most likely to be involved in this type of problem?

   □   a. The drum is bad.

   □   b. The fuser's compression roller is always on.

   □   c. The primary corona wire has failed.

   □   d. The transfer corona wire is bad.

   Quick Answer: **199**
   Detailed Answer: **204**

6. What type of failure would cause your laser printer to start up in an offline condition?

   ❏ a. The offline button has been pressed.

   ❏ b. The printer interface cable might be defective.

   ❏ c. The printer driver is incorrect.

   ❏ d. The toner cartridge is empty.

Quick Answer: **199**
Detailed Answer: **204**

7. If a standalone printer passes the self test and the user still cannot print, what else could be the cause of the problem?

   ❏ a. Fuse error

   ❏ b. Laser error

   ❏ c. Pickup roller

   ❏ d. Printer interface

Quick Answer: **199**
Detailed Answer: **204**

8. Typically, the first test to perform when a printer won't print is the _____.

   ❏ a. cable check

   ❏ b. self test

   ❏ c. loopback test

   ❏ d. configuration check

Quick Answer: **199**
Detailed Answer: **204**

9. In a dot-matrix printer, touching the _____ can result in a burn.

   ❏ a. platen

   ❏ b. printer cable

   ❏ c. ribbon

   ❏ d. printhead

Quick Answer: **199**
Detailed Answer: **204**

10. If a system already has a laser printer connected to LPT1, and you wish to add an additional color inkjet printer, what is the next best I/O option?

   ❏ a. Connect the color printer to LPT2.

   ❏ b. Connect the color printer to COM1.

   ❏ c. Connect the color printer to COM2 so that the mouse can remain on COM1.

   ❏ d. Install a printer switch box so that both printers can use LPT1.

Quick Answer: **199**
Detailed Answer: **204**

11. What is the most likely problem indicated by light printout of a dot-matrix type of printer?

   ❏ a. Printhead misalignment

   ❏ b. Worn platen

   ❏ c. Spent ribbon

   ❏ d. Incorrect printer setup

Quick Answer: **199**
Detailed Answer: **205**

12. The best way to ensure good print resolution when using an inkjet printer is to _____.

    ❑ a. use the best-quality paper available

    ❑ b. use fresh ink cartridges

    ❑ c. use only the black color function to print

    ❑ d. use high-resolution cartridges

Quick Answer: **199**
Detailed Answer: **205**

13. Which of the following is true about laser printers?

    ❑ a. Laser printers should not be used as local printers.

    ❑ b. Laser printers should not be used as network printers.

    ❑ c. Laser printers should not be used with a print-sharing device, such as a printer switch box.

    ❑ d. Laser printers should not be used as graphics printers.

Quick Answer: **199**
Detailed Answer: **205**

14. After a jammed paper has been removed, what might need to be done to clear the paper jam?

    ❑ a. Disconnect the interface cable.

    ❑ b. Open the printer's access door.

    ❑ c. Set the printer to the Online mode.

    ❑ d. Use the Form Feed button.

Quick Answer: **199**
Detailed Answer: **205**

15. What are two consequences of incorrectly setting the paper tray switches in a laser printer?

    ❑ a. Paper will not feed.

    ❑ b. Pages are sized incorrectly for the actual paper size.

    ❑ c. Pages are smudged.

    ❑ d. Pages are all white.

Quick Answer: **199**
Detailed Answer: **205**

16. What type of problem will produce smudged pages from a laser printer?

    ❑ a. Failure in the fusing section

    ❑ b. Bad or misaligned laser-scanning module

    ❑ c. Low contrast setting

    ❑ d. Broken, contaminated, or corroded corona wire

Quick Answer: **199**
Detailed Answer: **205**

17. What type of problem will produce blank pages from a laser printer? (Select two.)

    ❑ a. Bad or misaligned laser-scanning module

    ❑ b. Failure in the fusing section

    ❑ c. Contrast is set too low

    ❑ d. Corona wire is broken, contaminated, or corroded

Quick Answer: **199**
Detailed Answer: **205**

18. Which type of printer is not a good candidate for use with print-sharing devices?

Quick Answer: **199**
Detailed Answer: **205**

❑   a. Daisy-wheel
❑   b. Dot-matrix
❑   c. Inkjet
❑   d. Laser

19. Which type of printer can be a source of electrocution, eye damage, and burns?

Quick Answer: **199**
Detailed Answer: **205**

❑   a. Laser
❑   b. Dot-matrix
❑   c. Inkjet
❑   d. Daisy-wheel

20. Paper jams in a laser printer can be caused by _____. (Select all that apply.)

Quick Answer: **199**
Detailed Answer: **206**

❑   a. using paper that is too thick
❑   b. incorrect paper settings
❑   c. using coated paper
❑   d. using colored paper

21. Where are paper jams likely to occur in a laser printer? (Select all that apply.)

Quick Answer: **199**
Detailed Answer: **206**

❑   a. Pickup area
❑   b. Registration area
❑   c. Fusing area
❑   d. Control area

22. What types of problems can cause smudged or disfigured print in an inkjet printer? (Select two.)

Quick Answer: **199**
Detailed Answer: **206**

❑   a. Misaligned platen
❑   b. Worn-out paper-feed rollers
❑   c. Improperly set paper-thickness selector
❑   d. Worn-out ribbon

23. Which inkjet printer setting can adversely affect troubleshooting procedures?

Quick Answer: **199**
Detailed Answer: **206**

❑   a. Maintenance Mode
❑   b. Page Feed
❑   c. Self Test
❑   d. Tray Selector

Quick Check

24. What are the consequences of using a solvent to unclog an inkjet nozzle?
    - ❏ a. Clogged inkjets
    - ❏ b. Improper drop placement
    - ❏ c. Discolored ink
    - ❏ d. Ink running into the printer

Quick Answer: **199**
Detailed Answer: **206**

25. What are two symptoms of an inkjet printer cartridge going dry?
    - ❏ a. Print becomes noticeably faint.
    - ❏ b. Resolution becomes unacceptable.
    - ❏ c. One dark line crosses the page.
    - ❏ d. Black streaks run down the page.

Quick Answer: **199**
Detailed Answer: **206**

26. You receive a document from your laser printer that has random sections of missing print. What component is typically associated with this type of symptom?
    - ❏ a. The laser-scanning module
    - ❏ b. The drum
    - ❏ c. The transfer corona wire
    - ❏ d. The fuser's compression roller

Quick Answer: **199**
Detailed Answer: **206**

27. What type of output will be generated by a dot-matrix printer when the paper advance does not work?
    - ❏ a. A black page
    - ❏ b. One or more dark lines running down the page
    - ❏ c. One dark line across the page
    - ❏ d. A blank page

Quick Answer: **199**
Detailed Answer: **206**

28. The _____ of a dot-matrix printer generates a great deal of heat and can be a burn hazard when working on these units.
    - ❏ a. paper tray
    - ❏ b. platen
    - ❏ c. ribbon
    - ❏ d. printhead

Quick Answer: **199**
Detailed Answer: **206**

29. When you retrieve a copy of a document from the office laser printer, your touch smears the type on the page. What type of problem is indicated by this symptom?
    - ❏ a. The drum is going bad.
    - ❏ b. An incorrect type of replacement toner has been used.
    - ❏ c. The transfer corona wire has failed.
    - ❏ d. The fusing roller has failed.

Quick Answer: **199**
Detailed Answer: **207**

30. Which two ways would correct the problem in which the tops of characters are missing from a dot-matrix printer?

Quick Answer: **199**
Detailed Answer: **207**

- ❏ a. The carriage assembly might need to be adjusted to the proper height and angle.
- ❏ b. Reseat the printhead in the printhead cartridge.
- ❏ c. Reseat the platen.
- ❏ d. Replace the ribbon.

31. When you receive your copy of a document from the office laser printer, you notice that there are small white spots that occur at regular intervals along the length of the page. Which laser printer component is normally associated with a symptom such as this?

Quick Answer: **199**
Detailed Answer: **207**

- ❏ a. The primary corona has a flat spot on it.
- ❏ b. The drum has been contaminated.
- ❏ c. The transfer corona wire is dirty.
- ❏ d. The laser circuitry is failing.

32. Your laser printer has started to produce documents that have long white stripes down the length of the page. What type of problem is indicated by this symptom?

Quick Answer: **199**
Detailed Answer: **207**

- ❏ a. The drum is failing.
- ❏ b. The fuser is not heating evenly.
- ❏ c. The conditioning roller has a spot on it.
- ❏ d. The toner cartridge is not evenly distributing toner.

33. What is the most likely cause of uneven or faded print in a dot-matrix printer?

Quick Answer: **199**
Detailed Answer: **207**

- ❏ a. Worn-out ribbon
- ❏ b. Misaligned platen
- ❏ c. Misaligned printhead
- ❏ d. Worn-out printhead

34. What item in a dot-matrix printer requires the most attention?

Quick Answer: **199**
Detailed Answer: **207**

- ❏ a. Ribbon cartridge
- ❏ b. Printhead
- ❏ c. Tension knob
- ❏ d. Control panel

35. What does it mean if the printer produces a satisfactory self-test printout but will not print from the computer?

   ❏ a. The printer is the problem.
   ❏ b. The printer is not the problem.
   ❏ c. The cabling is the problem.
   ❏ d. The computer is the problem.

Quick Answer: **199**
Detailed Answer: **207**

36. What prevents ink from leaking out of an inkjet when it is not printing?

   ❏ a. Electrical current
   ❏ b. Closed valve
   ❏ c. Hydraulic pressure
   ❏ d. Surface tension

Quick Answer: **199**
Detailed Answer: **207**

37. If you wanted to add a color inkjet printer to a system with a secondary printer port that already had a laser printer attached to LPT1, how could you configure it?

   ❏ a. Connect the color printer to LPT2.
   ❏ b. Connect the color printer to COM1.
   ❏ c. Connect the color printer to COM2, so that the mouse can remain on COM1.
   ❏ d. Install a printer switch box, so that both printers can use LPT1.

Quick Answer: **199**
Detailed Answer: **207**

38. The best method of cleaning stray toner from the inside of a laser printer is to _____.

   ❏ a. spray it out with compressed air
   ❏ b. wash it out with a water/fabric softener solution
   ❏ c. wipe it out with a damp cloth
   ❏ d. vacuum it out

Quick Answer: **199**
Detailed Answer: **207**

39. You begin to notice stray specks and stains on the documents produced by your laser printer. What actions should you take to clear up this problem? (Select all that apply.)

   ❏ a. Change the cartridge so that a new primary corona wire is installed.
   ❏ b. Change the fuser assembly.
   ❏ c. Change the laser-scanning module.
   ❏ d. Change the cleaning pad.

Quick Answer: **199**
Detailed Answer: **207**

Quick Check Answer Key

Objective 5.1

1. a
2. b
3. b
4. d
5. b
6. b
7. a, b
8. b
9. d
10. c
11. b
12. b
13. a, b
14. c
15. a
16. c
17. a
18. d
19. b, c, d
20. c
21. b
22. d
23. a, c
24. b
25. d
26. a, b
27. c
28. d
29. c
30. a
31. b
32. d
33. a
34. a, b, c
35. b
36. c
37. a

Objective 5.2

1. b
2. a, c
3. d
4. a
5. c
6. b
7. d
8. b
9. d
10. a
11. c
12. b
13. c
14. b
15. a, b
16. a
17. a, d
18. d
19. a
20. a, b, c
21. a, b, c
22. b, c
23. a
24. d
25. a, b
26. a
27. c
28. d
29. d
30. a, b
31. b
32. d
33. a
34. a
35. b
36. d
37. a
38. d
39. a, d

Answers and Explanations

Objective 5.1

1. **a.** Parallel I/O devices, such as printers, are connected to a 25-pin female D-shell connector at the rear of the system.

2. **b.** A thermal fuse protects the fuser assembly from overheating. If the temperature of the fuser is not controlled correctly, it can cause severe damage to the printer, as well as present a potential fire hazard.

3. **b.** After the image has been transferred to the paper, a pair of compression rollers in the fusing unit melts and presses the toner particles into the paper.

4. **d.** Tractor feeds are used with very heavy forms, such as multiple-part continuous forms.

5. **b.** Before the laser writes, the drum is cleaned and conditioned. Through the laser, a charged image is written on the drum and attracts toner that is expelled by the developer roller. After being transferred from the drum to the paper, the toner is then pressed and fused on the paper.

6. **b.** Vector-based fonts store the outlines of different styles as sets of starting points and mathematical formulas for each character.

7. **a, b.** (a) Vector-based fonts store the outlines of different styles as sets of starting points and mathematical formulas for each character, while bitmapped fonts store dot patterns for all of the possible size and style variations of each character. Therefore, the vector-based approach requires much less storage space. (b) Because a vector-based font is defined as a mathematical function, it can be scaled and rotated by mathematical calculation. A bit-mapped character, on the other hand, is defined as a set of pixel settings. It is very difficult to change the size, shape, or resolution of a bitmapped character without reducing the quality of the image.

8. **b.** The toner is transferred to the paper from the drum because of the highly positive charge the transfer corona wire applies to the paper. The positive charge attracts the more negative toner particles away from the drum, and onto the page.

9. **d.** The printhead in a dot-matrix printer is a vertical column of print wires that are controlled by electromagnets. Dots are created on the paper by energizing selected electromagnets, which extend the desired print wires from the printhead. The print wires impact an ink ribbon, which impacts the paper.

10. **c.** The transfer corona wire (transfer roller) is responsible for transferring the toner from the drum to the paper. The toner is transferred to the paper because of the highly positive charge the transfer corona wire applies to the paper.

11. **b.** A high voltage, applied to the primary corona wire, creates a highly charged negative field that conditions the drum to be written on by applying a uniform negative charge (-600V) to it.

12. **b.** A typical printhead might contain 9, 18, or 24 print wires. The number of print wires used in the printhead is a major determining factor when discussing a printer's character quality.

13. **a, b.** (a) It is relatively easy to determine whether a printer is networked by the presence of a coaxial or a twisted-pair network signal cable connected directly to the printer. (b) The presence of the RJ-45 jacks on the back of the printer also indicate that the printer is network capable, even if it is not being used in that manner.

14. **c.** As with all IrDA connections, the distance and angle of transfer are limited. The recommended clear distance between the two devices is 1 meter and the maximum angle between the transmitters and receivers is 15°.

15. **a.** The recommended maximum length of a standard parallel printer cable is 10 feet (3 meters), although some equipment manufacturers specify 6 feet (1.8 meters) maximums for their cables. You should believe these recommendations when you see them.

16. **c.** The recommended maximum length of an RS-232 cable is 50 feet (15 meters). However, some references use 100 feet as the acceptable length of an RS-232C serial cable. Serial connections are tricky enough without problems generated by the cable being too long. Make the cable as short as possible.

17. **a.** Using an older, noncompliant unidirectional cable with a bidirectional parallel device will prevent the device from communicating properly with the system and might prevent it from operating. Some failures will produce error messages, such as Printer Not Ready.

18. **d.** Paper is specified in terms of its weight per 500 sheets at 17"×22" (that is, 500 sheets of 17"×22", 21lb bond paper weighs 21lbs).

19. **b, c, d.** In Hewlett-Packard printers, the main portion of the printing system is contained in the electrophotographic cartridge. This cartridge contains the toner supply, the corona wire, the drum assembly, and the developing roller.

20. **c.** In Hewlett-Packard printers, the main portion of the printing system is contained in the electrophotographic cartridge.

21. **b.** After the image has been transferred to the paper, a pair of compression rollers in the fusing unit melts and presses the toner particles onto the paper.

22. **d.** It protects the fuser assembly from overheating. If the temperature of the fuser is not controlled correctly, it can cause severe damage to the printer, as well as present a potential fire hazard.

23. **a, c.** (a) The transfer corona wire (transfer roller) is responsible for transferring the toner from the drum to the paper. The toner is transferred to the paper because of the highly positive charge the transfer corona wire applies to the paper. (c) A high voltage, applied to the primary corona wire, creates a highly charged negative field that conditions the drum to be written on by applying a uniform negative charge (-600V) to it.

24. **b.** Great care should be taken when installing a new drum unit. Exposing the drum to light for more than a few minutes can damage it.

25. **d.** Before the laser writes, the drum is cleaned and conditioned. Through the laser, a charged image is written on the drum and attracts toner that is expelled by the developer roller. After being transferred from the drum to the paper, the toner is then pressed and fused on the paper.

26. **a, b.** (a) Mechanical vibration uses vibrations from a piezoelectric crystal to force ink through a nozzle. (b) Thermal shock heats the ink in a capillary tube, just behind the nozzle. This increases the pressure of the ink in the tube and causes it to explode through the opening.

27. **c.** Inkjet printers produce characters by squirting a precisely controlled stream of ink drops onto the paper. The drops must be controlled very precisely in terms of their aerodynamics, size, and shape, or the drop placement on the page becomes inexact, and the print quality falters.

28. **d.** At the printer end of a Centronics parallel port, a 36-pin connector is used. Of course, the computer end of the cable should have a DB-25M connector to plug into the system's DB-25F LPT port.

29. **c.** Printers can be installed using USB buses, SCSI buses, or infrared ports, but not the IDE bus. An IDE interface is a systems-level interface that is the standard PC disk drive interface.

30. **a.** The primary component of a dot-matrix printer is a main control board. It contains the logic circuitry required to convert the signals, received from the computer's adapter card, into character patterns, as well as to generate the control signals to position the printhead properly on the page.

31. **b.** A typical printhead might contain 9, 18, or 24 print wires. The number of print wires used in the printhead is a major determining factor when discussing a printer's character quality.

32. **d.** Tractor feeds are used with very heavy forms, such as multiple-part continuous forms, and are most commonly found on dot-matrix printers.

33. **a.** Vector-based fonts store the outlines of the character styles as sets of starting points and mathematical formulas. When a particular character is needed, the character generator sets the starting point for the character in the print cell and generates its outline from the formula. These types of fonts can be scaled up and down to achieve various sizes.

34. **a, b, c.** (a) Bitmapped fonts store dot patterns for all of the possible size and style variations of the characters in the set. Because a complete set of dots must be stored for each character and size that might be needed, this type of font tends to take up large amounts of memory. (b) Each bitmapped character is handled as a rectangular grid of pixels. The bitmap for each character specifies what color each pixel should be and represents the character at a particular size and resolution. It is very difficult to change the size, shape, or resolution of a bitmapped character without sacrificing the quality of the image. (c) Because a complete set of dots must be stored for each character at particular size, shape, and resolution that might be needed, bitmapped characters can be printed out directly and quickly without any mathematical calculation.

35. **b.** In the dye-sublimation printer, a heating element strip is used to transfer the color substance on a plastic film to the paper. The heating element contains thousands of small heat points, which creates fine patterns of color dots. Different temperatures can be applied to the element to produce different shades.

36. **c.** The print wires are heated in the direct thermal printer so that they can burn dot patterns into special thermal paper. Early facsimile (fax) machine technology was based on this type of thermal printing. Even now, thermal printers are widely used for barcode printing, battery-powered hand-held printing devices, and credit card receipt printers.

37. **a.** A typical RS-232 printer serial cable will have a DB-9F connector that connects to the PC's COM port, and a DB-25M connector that plugs into the printer.

Objective 5.2

1. **b.** Many times, a paper-jam error will remain even after the paper has been removed from the laser printer. This is typically caused by an interlock error. Simply opening the printer's main access door should clear the error.

2. **a, c.** (a) Bad paper-feed rollers will cause an inkjet printer to produce wavy graphics. If the paper thickness settings are correct but the print output is disfigured, you will need to replace the paper-feed rollers. (**c**) If an inkjet printer's paper thickness selector is set improperly, the paper can slip as it moves through the printer and cause wavy graphics to be produced. Check the printer's paper thickness settings. If they are correct and the print output is disfigured, you will need to replace the paper-feed rollers.

3. **d.** The density of the printout from an inkjet printer can be adjusted through its printing software. However, when the print becomes noticeably faint, or the resolution becomes unacceptable, the cartridge will need to be replaced.

4. **a.** If the output of the printer gets lighter as it moves from left to right across the page, it might become necessary to adjust the spacing between the platen and the printhead carriage rod to obtain proper printing.

5. **c.** A bad primary corona can cause black pages to be produced. When this occurs, no uniform charge is placed on the drum to repel toner.

6. **b.** When the printer starts up in an offline condition, there is probably some type of problem with the printer/computer interface that will not allow them to communicate. Disconnect the interface cable to see if the printer will start up in a Ready state.

7. **d.** If the printer runs the self test, and prints clean pages, then most of the printer has been eliminated as a possible cause of problems. The problem could be in the computer, the cabling, or the interface portion of the printer.

8. **b.** Nearly every printer is equipped with a built-in self test. The easiest way to determine whether a printer is at fault is to run its self test. If the self test runs and prints clean pages, most of the printer has been eliminated as a possible source of problems.

9. **d.** To exchange the printhead assembly, make sure that the printhead assembly is cool enough to be handled. These units can get hot enough to cause a serious burn.

10. **a.** To install two printers to a system, the best arrangement is to use an LPT2 port to attach the additional printer to the system. Beyond two printers, it would be better to network the printers to the system.

11. **c.** As the ribbon wears out, the printing will become faint and uneven. When the print becomes noticeably faint, the cartridge should be replaced.

12. **b.** The best way to ensure good print resolution when using an inkjet printer is to use fresh ink cartridges. When the print becomes noticeably faint, or the resolution becomes unacceptable, the cartridge will need to be replaced.

13. **c.** It is not a good idea to use laser printers with a printer switch box. A better arrangement is to use an LPT2 port to attach an additional printer to the system. Beyond two printers, it would be better to network the printers to the system.

14. **b.** Many times, a paper-jam error will remain even after the paper has been removed from the laser printer. This is typically caused by an interlock error. Simply opening the printer's main access door should clear the error.

15. **a, b.** (a) If the paper does not feed at all, the place to begin checking is the paper-tray area. The paper trays have a complex set of sensors and pickup mechanisms that must all be functioning properly to begin the paper handling. (b) A mechanical arm and photo detector are used to sense the presence of paper in the tray. If these switches are set incorrectly, the printer could print a page that was sized incorrectly for the actual paper size.

16. **a.** When the heating element or lamp in the fusing area does not receive adequate AC power from the power supply, the toner will not affix to the page as it should. This condition will result in smudged output.

17. **a, d.** (a) A white page indicates that no information is being written on the drum. This condition basically involves the laser-scanning module, the control board, and the power supply. (d) White page fault can occur when the corona wire becomes broken, contaminated, or corroded, so that the attracting charge between the drum and paper is severely reduced.

18. **d.** When troubleshooting a laser printer, check to see if the printer is connected to the system through a print-sharing device. If so, connect the printer directly to the system and try it. It is not a good idea to use laser printers with these types of devices.

19. **a.** Unlike other printer types, the laser printer tends to have several high-voltage, high-temperature, and vision hazards inside it. To get the laser printer into a position where you can observe its operation, you might need to place yourself in potential contact with those areas. Be aware that laser printers can be a source of electrocution, eye damage (from the laser), and burns (from the fuser assembly).

20. **a, b, c.** (a) Using paper that is too heavy or too thick can result in jams, as can overloading paper trays. (b) Using the wrong type of paper can defeat the separation pad and allow multiple pages to be drawn into the printer. In this case, the multiple sheets might move through the printer together, or they might result in a jam. (c) Using coated paper stock can be hazardous because the coating might melt, which can cause a paper jam or fire.

21. **a, b, c.** Due to the extreme complexity of the laser printer's paper-handling system, paper jams are a common problem. This problem tends to increase in frequency as the printer's components wear from use. Basically, paper jams occur in all three main sections of the printer. These sections are the pickup area, the registration area, and the fusing area.

22. **b, c.** (b) Bad paper-feed rollers will cause an inkjet printer to produce wavy graphics. If the paper thickness settings are correct but the print output is disfigured, you will need to replace the paper-feed rollers. (c) If an inkjet printer's paper thickness selector is set improperly, the paper can slip as it moves through the printer and cause wavy graphics to be produced. Check the printer's paper thickness settings. If they are correct and the print output is disfigured, you will need to replace the paper-feed rollers.

23. **a.** During the troubleshooting process, if the printhead assembly does not move at any time, check to see if the printer is in maintenance mode. In this mode, the printer typically keeps the printhead assembly in the home position. If no mode problems are present, the printhead positioning motor should be replaced.

24. **d.** Using solvents to clear blockages in the jets can dilute the ink and allow it to flow uncontrollably through the jet.

25. **a, b.** The single item in an inkjet printer that requires the most attention is the ink cartridge (or cartridges). As the ink cartridge empties, the printing will eventually become faint and uneven, and the resolution of the print on the page will diminish.

26. **a.** Missing print in a laser printer is normally attributed to the laser-scanning module. If the laser printer is not correctly installed or positioned, it cannot deliver lines of print to the page.

27. **c.** When the paper does not advance, the output will usually be a thick, dark line across the page.

28. **d.** To exchange the printhead assembly, make sure that the printhead assembly is cool enough to be handled. These units can get hot enough to cause a serious burn.

29. **d.** If the output of the printer smudges when you touch it, the fuser has failed to bond the toner to the paper. The heating lamp in the fuser is broken or not receiving sufficient power to melt the toner.

30. **a, b.** If the tops of characters are missing, the printhead is misaligned with the platen. It might need to be reseated in the printhead carriage, or the carriage assembly might need to be adjusted to the proper height and angle.

31. **b.** When problems occur at cyclic intervals on a printer page from a laser printer, the problem is normally associated with one of the rotating parts (the drum, the fuser rollers, the developing roller, and so on). In this case, the drum might have been touched, or exposed to a light source so that it has a spot on it that does not hold toner.

32. **d.** White lines that run along the length of the page from a laser printer are normally a sign of poorly distributed toner. Remove the toner cartridge and shake it to distribute the toner more evenly. If this does not work, replace the toner cartridge with a new one.

33. **a.** As the ribbon wears out, the printing will become faint and uneven. When the print becomes noticeably faint, the cartridge should be replaced.

34. **a.** The single item in a dot-matrix printer that requires the most attention is the ribbon cartridge. It is considered a consumable part of the printer and must be changed often.

35. **b.** If the printer runs the self test and prints clean pages, then most of the printer has been eliminated as a possible cause of problems. The problem could be in the computer, the cabling, or the interface portion of the printer.

36. **d.** The inkjet nozzle is designed to provide the proper shape and trajectory for the ink drops so that they can be directed precisely toward the page. The nozzles are also designed so that the surface tension of the ink keeps it from running out of the nozzle uncontrollably.

37. **a.** When connecting two printers to a system, a better arrangement is to simply use an LPT2 port to attach the second printer to the system. Beyond two printers, it would be better to network the printers to the system.

38. **d.** Use a special laser toner vacuum cleaner and toner cloth to remove dust buildup and excess toner from the interior of the laser printer. Care should be taken to remove all excess toner from the unit.

39. **a, d.** Specks and stains on a page are typically caused by a worn cleaning pad or a defective primary corona wire. A worn cleaning pad will not pick up excess toner left over from the fusing process. Likewise, if the corona wire does not regulate the charge level on the drum, dark spots will appear in the print.

Hardware Domain 6.0: Basic Networking

Quick Check ✓

Objective 6.1: Identify the common types of network cables, their characteristics, and connectors.

1. What type of cable is used for 10BASE-2?

   ❏ a. Thicknet coaxial
   ❏ b. Fiber-optic cable
   ❏ c. Twisted pair
   ❏ d. Thinnet coaxial cable

   Quick Answer: **224**
   Detailed Answer: **225**

2. What is the maximum segment length of 100BASE-T connections?

   ❏ a. 50 meters
   ❏ b. 1,000 meters
   ❏ c. 100 meters
   ❏ d. 2,000 meters

   Quick Answer: **224**
   Detailed Answer: **225**

3. What type of cable is specified for 100BASE-TX?

   ❏ a. CAT6
   ❏ b. CAT5
   ❏ c. CAT3
   ❏ d. CAT2

   Quick Answer: **224**
   Detailed Answer: **225**

4. A 10BASE-T NIC connects to the network with _____.

   ❏ a. an RJ-45 connector
   ❏ b. a BERG connector
   ❏ c. a 15-pin D-shell connector
   ❏ d. a 40-pin SCSI connector

   Quick Answer: **224**
   Detailed Answer: **225**

5. A non-PnP Network Interface Card (NIC) has a 10/100 rating. This means the card is _____.

   ❑ a. capable of data transfer rates of 10 or 100Mbps

   ❑ b. designed for use on networks of between 10 and 100 computers

   ❑ c. capable of data transfer rates of 10 or 100MBps

   ❑ d. designed for use on networks separated by a distance between 10 and 100 miles

Quick Answer: **224**
Detailed Answer: **225**

6. The maximum segment length of a 10BASE-5 network connection is _____.

   ❑ a. 15 meters

   ❑ b. 185 meters

   ❑ c. 500 meters

   ❑ d. 1,000 meters

Quick Answer: **224**
Detailed Answer: **225**

7. An RJ-45 connector is most commonly used with _____.

   ❑ a. disk drive units

   ❑ b. fiber-optic cabling

   ❑ c. coaxial cabling

   ❑ d. unshielded twisted-pair cabling

Quick Answer: **224**
Detailed Answer: **225**

8. Which specification can be classified as a BUS topology?

   ❑ a. Token Ring

   ❑ b. ARCnet

   ❑ c. Ethernet

   ❑ d. Fiber Link

Quick Answer: **224**
Detailed Answer: **225**

9. What does the activity from the light on the network adapter's back plate mean?

   ❑ a. Data is being uploaded.

   ❑ b. The connection is alive.

   ❑ c. Data is being downloaded.

   ❑ d. Data is being encrypted.

Quick Answer: **224**
Detailed Answer: **225**

10. Which type of cabling is used to support the 100BASE-FX IEEE standard?

   ❑ a. UTP

   ❑ b. Fiber-optic

   ❑ c. STP

   ❑ d. Thick coaxial

Quick Answer: **224**
Detailed Answer: **225**

11. Which network types have full duplex capabilities? (Select all that apply.)

Quick Answer: **224**
Detailed Answer: **225**

   ❏   a.   Ethernet
   ❏   b.   Token Ring
   ❏   c.   Fiber-optic
   ❏   d.   ARCnet

12. What is the maximum cable segment length for a 10BASE-T network?

Quick Answer: **224**
Detailed Answer: **225**

   ❏   a.   5,000 meters
   ❏   b.   500 meters
   ❏   c.   250 meters
   ❏   d.   100 meters

13. What type of cable does 10BASE-T and 100BASE-T use?

Quick Answer: **224**
Detailed Answer: **225**

   ❏   a.   UTP
   ❏   b.   STP
   ❏   c.   Fiber-optic
   ❏   d.   RG-58

14. What type of Ethernet network uses RG-58 cable?

Quick Answer: **224**
Detailed Answer: **226**

   ❏   a.   10BASE-T
   ❏   b.   10BASE-5
   ❏   c.   10BASE-2
   ❏   d.   100BASE-FX

15. What is the maximum segment length associated with the 10BASE-2 networking standard?

Quick Answer: **224**
Detailed Answer: **226**

   ❏   a.   500 meters
   ❏   b.   100 meters
   ❏   c.   200 meters
   ❏   d.   185 meters

16. What is the maximum segment length associated with the 10BASE-5 LAN networking standard?

Quick Answer: **224**
Detailed Answer: **226**

   ❏   a.   185 meters
   ❏   b.   500 meters
   ❏   c.   200 meters
   ❏   d.   100 meters

17. What type of network employs SC connectors?

Quick Answer: **224**
Detailed Answer: **226**

   ❏   a.   Client-server UTP
   ❏   b.   Peer-to-peer UTP
   ❏   c.   Ethernet fiber-optic
   ❏   d.   Token Ring fiber-optic

18. What type of cabling is involved in the CAT5 cable rating?

   ❑ a. UTP

   ❑ b. Thin coaxial

   ❑ c. STP

   ❑ d. Thick coaxial

Quick Answer: **224**

Detailed Answer: **226**

19. Which connector is not used with network cables?

   ❑ a. ST

   ❑ b. RJ-45

   ❑ c. BNC

   ❑ d. SCSI

Quick Answer: **224**

Detailed Answer: **226**

20. Which of the following connections is used in conjunction with Token Ring networking?

   ❑ a. TCP/IP

   ❑ b. IDC

   ❑ c. USB

   ❑ d. UDC

Quick Answer: **224**

Detailed Answer: **226**

21. Why is it required to use plenum-rated cable in ducts?

   ❑ a. To prevent toxic gases from spreading throughout the facility

   ❑ b. To avoid the heat buildup

   ❑ c. To reduce the EMI

   ❑ d. To protect the cabling from oxidation

Quick Answer: **224**

Detailed Answer: **226**

22. A fellow technician receives an order to purchase coaxial cable for your company's network system. The supplier offers RG-6, RG-58, and RG-59 coaxial cables. The technician is unable to tell the difference between them. Which of the following statements describes them correctly?

   ❑ a. RG-6 coaxial cable is the preferred type of coaxial cable for residential structured wiring.

   ❑ b. Thinnet Ethernet cabling (RG-59) is used for 10BASE-2 networks.

   ❑ c. RG-58 cable is widely used for CATV and video services.

   ❑ d. The appearances of RG-59 and RG-6 are very similar; it is very possible to employ the wrong cable just by visual examination.

Quick Answer: **224**

Detailed Answer: **226**

23. Older ISA NICs might require _____.

   ❑ a. an RS-232 cable

   ❑ b. manual configuration

   ❑ c. PnP configuration

   ❑ d. a power cord

Quick Answer: **224**

Detailed Answer: **226**

24. What effects will running applications across the network have on its performance?

❏ a. The units on the network will communicate faster.
❏ b. The unit running the application will not have access to other parts of the network.
❏ c. The units on the network might slow down.
❏ d. The units on the network might crash.

Quick Answer: **224**
Detailed Answer: **227**

25. What effects will a missing terminator or bad cable/connector have on an Ethernet network? (Select all that apply.)

❏ a. Network nodes might stop functioning
❏ b. Lost data
❏ c. Network slowdown
❏ d. Network nodes are not visible to each other

Quick Answer: **224**
Detailed Answer: **227**

26. Which of the following actions is likely to crash the local area network?

❏ a. Shutting down a workstation on a 10BASE-T LAN
❏ b. Disconnecting a workstation on a 10BASE-5 LAN
❏ c. Shutting down a workstation on a 10BASE-5 LAN
❏ d. Disconnecting a workstation on a 10BASE-T LAN

Quick Answer: **224**
Detailed Answer: **227**

Objective 6.2: Identify basic networking concepts including how a network works.

1. What protocol is required for Internet access?

❏ a. NetBEUI
❏ b. FTP
❏ c. TCP/IP
❏ d. HTTP

Quick Answer: **224**
Detailed Answer: **227**

2. In _____ network, all of the nodes have the capability to serve as both a client and a server.

❏ a. an Ethernet
❏ b. a peer-to-peer
❏ c. a client/server
❏ d. a local area

Quick Answer: **224**
Detailed Answer: **227**

3. An unshielded twisted-pair cable has _____.

❏ a. four twisted wires inside
❏ b. four pairs of twisted wires inside
❏ c. two pairs of twisted wires inside
❏ d. four sets of four twisted wires inside

Quick Answer: **224**
Detailed Answer: **227**

4. If you're connecting two computers together using CAT5 cable and RJ-45 connectors, what kind of cable must be used?

Quick Answer: **224**
Detailed Answer: **227**

- ❏ a. Crossover cable
- ❏ b. Patch cable
- ❏ c. Serial cable
- ❏ d. Parallel cable

5. When connecting two computers directly together to transfer data through their serial ports, what cable type should be used?

Quick Answer: **224**
Detailed Answer: **227**

- ❏ a. Standard serial cable
- ❏ b. Null modem cable
- ❏ c. Standard parallel cable
- ❏ d. SCSI cable

6. A workstation can share its printer with other nodes on the network. What type of networking is this?

Quick Answer: **224**
Detailed Answer: **227**

- ❏ a. Client/server network
- ❏ b. Peer-to-peer network
- ❏ c. Star network
- ❏ d. Ring network

7. What are the advantages of having a client/server network? (Select two correct answers.)

Quick Answer: **224**
Detailed Answer: **228**

- ❏ a. Centralized administration
- ❏ b. Unlimited access to all files in the network for connected nodes
- ❏ c. Data and resource security
- ❏ d. Shared printers

8. What is true of peer-to-peer networking?

Quick Answer: **224**
Detailed Answer: **228**

- ❏ a. Nodes act only as clients.
- ❏ b. Nodes act only as servers.
- ❏ c. Nodes act as both clients and servers.
- ❏ d. Nodes act as either clients or servers.

9. A cable that has a single conductor with a braided copper shield around it is called a(n) _____.

- ❏ a. UTP cable
- ❏ b. Ethernet cable
- ❏ c. Token Ring cable
- ❏ d. Coaxial cable

Quick Answer: **224**
Detailed Answer: **228**

10. In a client/server network, _____.

- ❏ a. at least one unit depends on the other units for its information
- ❏ b. at least one unit is reserved just to serve the other units
- ❏ c. each unit has its own information, and can serve as either client or server
- ❏ d. each unit handles some information for the network

Quick Answer: **224**
Detailed Answer: **228**

11. What are the major advantages of client/server over peer-to-peer networks? (Select two.)

- ❏ a. Centralized administration
- ❏ b. Data and resource security
- ❏ c. Less cable to maintain
- ❏ d. Low cost

Quick Answer: **224**
Detailed Answer: **228**

12. Nodes in _____ networks can serve as both clients and servers for different functions.

- ❏ a. Token Ring
- ❏ b. client/server
- ❏ c. peer-to-peer
- ❏ d. nondifferentiated

Quick Answer: **224**
Detailed Answer: **228**

· ·

Quick Check ✓

Quick Answer: **224**
Detailed Answer: **228**

13. From the network topologies figure, identify the mesh topology.

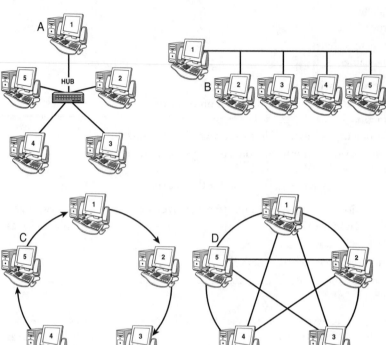

☐ a. B
☐ b. D
☐ c. C
☐ d. A

14. From the network topologies figure, identify the star topology.

Quick Answer: **224**
Detailed Answer: **228**

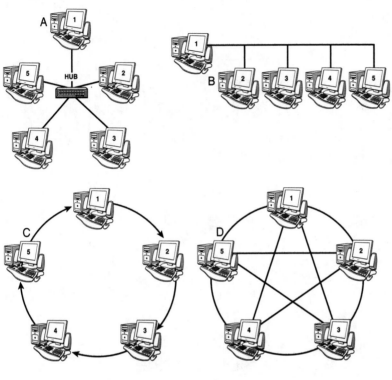

❑　a. A
❑　b. B
❑　c. C
❑　d. D

. . . .

15. From the network topologies figure, identify the ring
topology.

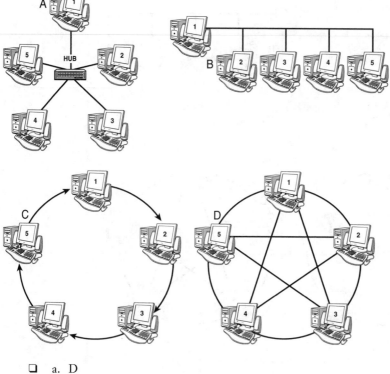

❑   a. D
❑   b. B
❑   c. A
❑   d. C

16. From the network topologies figure, identify the bus topology.

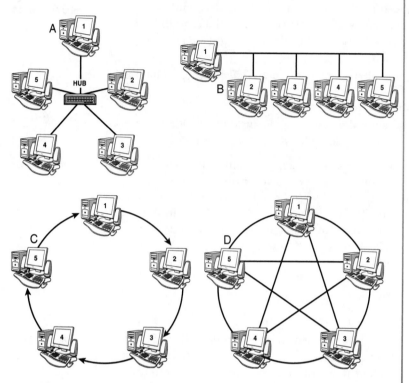

- ❑ a. C
- ❑ b. A
- ❑ c. B
- ❑ d. D

17. Which of the following networking protocols is also the same protocol that the Internet uses?

- ❑ a. IPX/SPX
- ❑ b. AppleTalk
- ❑ c. TCP/IP
- ❑ d. NetBEUI

18. You install a new wireless network for a client. However, your client has been reading about network security, and asks you to increase the security of the network while maintaining the wireless nature of the network. What do you suggest to accomplish this?

    ❑   a. Connect all workstations to the Wireless Access Point using CAT5.
    ❑   b. Turn on Wired Equivalent Privacy.
    ❑   c. Install more Wireless Access Points throughout the network.
    ❑   d. Change Encryption from 40-bit keys to 16-bit keys.

Quick Answer: **224**
Detailed Answer: **229**

19. Your network consists of PCs and a number of older Macintosh computers that are used for digital editing purposes. The users would like to be able to have the PCs and Macintosh computers networked together; however, the Macintosh computers are unable to use the TCP/IP protocol. What protocol should you attempt to try next?

    ❑   a. AppleTalk
    ❑   b. NWLink
    ❑   c. IPX/SPX
    ❑   d. NetBEUI

Quick Answer: **224**
Detailed Answer: **229**

20. You join a new division as part of the technical staff of a large company. This new division integrates Windows XP workstations with an older network that uses Netware 4.0 and older software. Due to software incompatibility, TCP/IP is not a viable option. Which of the following networking protocols should the network be using?

    ❑   a. NetBEUI
    ❑   b. IPX/SPX
    ❑   c. NWLink
    ❑   d. AppleTalk

Quick Answer: **224**
Detailed Answer: **229**

21. Under CompTIA's definition, a LAN can exist with as few as _____ computers.

    ❑   a. Five
    ❑   b. Three
    ❑   c. Four
    ❑   d. Two

Quick Answer: **224**
Detailed Answer: **229**

Objective 6.3: Identify common technologies available for establishing Internet connectivity and their characteristics.

1. A user complains that he is unable to find a cord or plug to connect his brand-new PDA to the workstation. Reading through the PDA manual, you note no mention of additional cords to interface with the PDA. All other functions of the PDA appear to be working. Which of the following conclusions is most likely correct?

   ❑   a. The PDA is defective.
   ❑   b. The PDA uses wireless connections to transfer data.
   ❑   c. The PDA is missing cabling.
   ❑   d. The PDA does not have batteries installed.

Quick Answer: **224**
Detailed Answer: **229**

2. Which device connects two network segments while directing data toward the appropriate IP address?

   ❑   a. NIC
   ❑   b. Bridge
   ❑   c. Brouter
   ❑   d. Router

Quick Answer: **224**
Detailed Answer: **229**

3. What services do all ISPs provide their Internet customers? (Select all that apply.)

   ❑   a. DNS routing
   ❑   b. Internet identity through IP addresses
   ❑   c. Spam filtering
   ❑   d. Email services

Quick Answer: **224**
Detailed Answer: **230**

4. An external modem connects to the computer through a _____ port.

   ❑   a. parallel
   ❑   b. serial
   ❑   c. SCSI
   ❑   d. joystick

Quick Answer: **224**
Detailed Answer: **230**

5. The CIO of your company asks you for technical assistance about choosing an Internet service provider for your company. Due to cost cutting, she is interested in choosing a satellite Internet access solution, but is unfamiliar with how uplinked versus downlinked satellites operate. Which of the following statements is correct regarding satellite Internet access?

- ❑ a. Data are uplinked when received by a satellite dish from a satellite in orbit.
- ❑ b. Satellite downlink has a maximum download speed of 1.5Mbps.
- ❑ c. Satellite downlink operation means that a satellite in orbit receives television signals from a satellite transceiver dish.
- ❑ d. In most satellite Internet access systems, the satellite dish uses a transceiver to uplink data to the Web.

Quick Answer: **224**
Detailed Answer: **230**

6. The main responsibility of a modem is to _____.

- ❑ a. carry on an electronic conversation with another modem
- ❑ b. initiate a communication session
- ❑ c. convert between digital and analog signal formats
- ❑ d. force a remote system to match its speed capabilities

Quick Answer: **224**
Detailed Answer: **230**

7. In a full-duplex data circuit, the direction of travel is _____.

- ❑ a. both directions, but not simultaneously
- ❑ b. both directions, simultaneously
- ❑ c. both directions, sequentially
- ❑ d. one direction only

Quick Answer: **224**
Detailed Answer: **230**

8. A modem that conducts communications in only one direction at a time is called _____.

- ❑ a. a simplex modem
- ❑ b. a full-duplex modem
- ❑ c. a half-duplex modem
- ❑ d. a full-simplex modem

Quick Answer: **224**
Detailed Answer: **230**

9. When two devices can send signals to each other at the same time over the same wire, this is called _____ communications.

- ❑ a. full-duplex
- ❑ b. half-duplex
- ❑ c. simplex
- ❑ d. multi-quadraplex

Quick Answer: **224**
Detailed Answer: **230**

10. Your company moves to a new location. Because your company is very small, you use a DSL connection to connect all users to the Internet. When setting up the network, you connect the DSL modem using an RJ-11 connector to the phone outlet, connect the DSL modem to a router using a CAT5 cable, and plug the DSL modem into a power source. You connect all the workstations to the router using CAT5 cable, and put line filters on all phone lines and the phone line used for the DSL modem. When testing the system, no users can connect to the Internet. However, after you unplug the DSL modem and remove all the line filters, the phone line is still operational. What is the most likely solution to this situation?

Quick Answer: **224**
Detailed Answer: **230**

- ❏ a. Replace the DSL modem.
- ❏ b. Remove the line filter for the phone line for the DSL modem.
- ❏ c. Connect the DSL modem using an RJ-45 connector to the phone outlet instead.
- ❏ d. Replace the CAT5 cable with coaxial cable.

11. A client complains that after replacing his DSL modem, his home DSL connection isn't working. When you inspect his computer, you notice that none of the lights on the DSL modem are on, and the only two cables that plug into the DSL modem connect via the RJ-11 and RJ-45 connectors. You are able to ping port 127.0.0.1. What is the most likely problem with the DSL?

Quick Answer: **224**
Detailed Answer: **230**

- ❏ a. The NIC card is improperly set up.
- ❏ b. The phone line is not plugged into the DSL modem.
- ❏ c. The Ethernet cable is not plugged into the DSL modem.
- ❏ d. The power cord is not plugged into the DSL modem.

12. A client complains that his Internet isn't working. When you go to his office, you note that he's using DSL as his method of accessing the Internet. The user mentions that the Ethernet cable that plugs into the DSL modem does not plug properly into the computer's 56K modem, and that he had to force the Ethernet cable into the modem to get it to properly fit. What should you do to solve the problem?

Quick Answer: **224**
Detailed Answer: **230**

- ❏ a. Change the modem settings using the Control Panel Wizards to enable DSL.
- ❏ b. Replace the Ethernet cable with phone line.
- ❏ c. Plug the DSL modem into a workstation via a network interface card.
- ❏ d. Add a DSL line filter to the phone outlet that the DSL modem plugs into.

. . . .

Quick Check Answer Key

Objective 6.1	Objective 6.2	Objective 6.3
1. d	1. c	1. b
2. c	2. b	2. d
3. b	3. b	3. a, b, d
4. a	4. a	4. b
5. a	5. b	5. c
6. c	6. b	6. c
7. d	7. a, c	7. b
8. c	8. c	8. c
9. b	9. d	9. a
10. b	10. b	10. b
11. a, b, c	11. a, b	11. d
12. d	12. c	12. c
13. a	13. b	
14. c	14. a	
15. d	15. d	
16. b	16. c	
17. c	17. c	
18. a	18. b	
19. d	19. a	
20. d	20. c	
21. a	21. d	
22. a		
23. b		
24. c		
25. b, c, d		
26. b		

Answers and Explanations

Objective 6.1

1. **d.** Thinnet Ethernet cabling is used for 10BASE-2 networks.

2. **c.** The recommended maximum length of a 10/100BASE-T segment is 100 meters.

3. **b.** The cables used with the TX version of Fast Ethernet can be CAT5 UTP or STP.

4. **a.** The original UTP LAN (10BASE-T LAN) connections are made through modular RJ-45 registered jacks and plugs.

5. **a.** Network cards capable of supporting transmission rates of both 10Mbps and 100Mbps (not MBps) are classified as 10/100 Ethernet cards.

6. **c.** The maximum length specified for Ethernet is 1.55 miles (2.5Km), with a maximum segment length between nodes of 500 meters. This type of LAN is referred to as a 10BASE-5 LAN by the IEEE organization.

7. **d.** UTP LAN cable connects a computer and a hub using RJ-45 connectors.

8. **c.** Ethernet is classified as a bus topology that has been implemented across several different network media, including coaxial cable, twisted-pair copper cable, fiber-optic cable, and wireless.

9. **b.** The lights on the network adapter's back plate play a very important part in diagnosing problems with the LAN connection. If the lights are active, the connection is alive. Refer to the card's user manual for definitions of its activity lights.

10. **b.** 100BASE-FX Fast Ethernet designation indicates the network is using fiber-optic cabling with a data rate of 100Mbps.

11. **a, b, c.** (a) When operating in full-duplex mode, the Ethernet (802.3) transfer rate of 10Mbps is boosted to 20Mbps. (b) Token Ring (802.5) can operate in a high-speed, full-duplex mode (two-way simultaneous communication) to raise the transfer rate to 32Mbps. (c) FDDI fiber-optic networks can also be set up for full duplex operations.

12. **d.** The recommended maximum length of a 10BASE-T segment is 100 meters (actually, the maximum segment length of the T version of any Ethernet connection is 100 meters).

13. **a.** Unshielded twisted-pair (UTP) cable is used in the 10BASE-T and 100BASE-T LAN.

14. **c.** Thinnet Ethernet cabling used for 10BASE-2 networks employs thinner, industry-standard RG-58 coaxial cable and BNC or T connectors.

15. **d.** The 10BASE-2 Ethernet LAN uses RG-58 coaxial cable, and has a maximum segment length of 185 meters.

16. **b.** The maximum length specified for Ethernet is 1.55 miles (2.5Km), with a maximum segment length between nodes of 500 meters. This type of LAN is referred to as a 10BASE-5 LAN by the IEEE organization.

17. **c.** The SC connector is the dominant connector for fiber-optic Ethernet networks. The connector is designed so that it correctly aligns the end of the fiber cable with the receiver.

18. **a.** Unshielded twisted pair (UTP) is categorized in different ratings for different networking applications. CAT5 cabling is currently the most widely used specification for data communication wiring.

19. **d.** An RJ-45 connector terminates UTP cable. Coaxial cable is connected to equipment through BNC connectors. The ST connector is used in the fiber-optic Ethernet networks. SCSI connectors are not used with network cables.

20. **d.** Some Token Ring networks employ special connectors called Universal Data Connectors (UDCs) to interconnect their 4-wire STP (Type-1A) cables in very noisy electronic environments. The UDC device was developed as a part of IBM's Token Ring networking standard to provide highly dependable connections even under adverse conditions.

21. **a.** Plenum-rated cables are cables that are suitable for use in ducts, plenums, and other spaces used for environmental air because of their fire-resistant and low smoke-producing characteristics. If catching fire, the cables located in a plenum area give off toxic gases, which will spread throughout the facility as part of the air circulation system.

22. **a.** RG-6 coaxial cable is the preferred type of coaxial cable for residential structured wiring. It is widely used for video distribution and also for connecting satellite-receiving antenna systems to standard, digital, and high-definition television (HDTV) receivers.

23. **b.** An improperly configured network adapter card can prevent the system from gaining access to the network. With non-PnP network cards, such as most ISA NIC cards, it is necessary to configure the card manually through hardware jumpers, or through logical configuration switches in BIOS Extension EPROM.

24. **c.** Diagnostic efforts and tests run across the network can use a lot of the network's bandwidth. This reduced bandwidth causes the operation of all the units on the network to slow down. This is due simply to the added usage of the network.

25. **b, c, d.** (**b**) Data moving through the network can be lost when there is an open connection on an Ethernet network. (**c**) A general slowdown of data movement across the network can occur due to reduced bandwidth caused by an open connection on an Ethernet network. (**d**) Nodes may not be able to see, or connect to, each other if a terminator is missing or a cable/connector turns bad on an Ethernet network.

26. **b.** Disconnecting a unit from a network that uses coaxial cable creates an unterminated condition in the network that can cause several different types of problems such as data loss, network slowdown, and network failure.

Objective 6.2

1. **c.** TCP/IP is the most widely used network protocol today due mainly to the Internet. No matter what type of computer platform or software is being used, the information must move across the Internet in the form of TCP/IP packets.

2. **b.** A common definition of a peer-to-peer network is that all of the nodes can act as both clients and servers of the other nodes under different conditions.

3. **b.** Unshielded twisted-pair (UTP) networking cable contains four pairs of individually insulated wires. The wires are color coded and terminated in an RJ-45 connector.

4. **a.** When connecting two computers together using CAT5 cable and RJ-45 connectors, the cable would be referred to as a crossover cable instead of a null modem.

5. **b.** If only two units are connected, point-to-point communications software and a simple null modem can be employed. A null modem cable connects the two units together and provides direct communication between the computers without using modems.

6. **b.** In a typical peer-to-peer network arrangement, the users connected to the network can share access to different network resources, such as hard drives and printers.

7. **a, c.** (a) The server in a client/server LAN configuration typically holds programs and data for its client computers. (**c**) The server of a client/server network provides security and network policy enforcement by controlling the access to data and resources it holds for its clients. In some client/server LAN design, the client machine, called a *diskless workstation*, doesn't even store any data.

8. **c.** In a peer-to-peer network, nodes connected to the network share access to different network resources. The node that controls a resource acts as a server of the other nodes, but it also acts as a client of other nodes that share resources with others.

9. **d.** Coaxial cable (often referred to simply as coax) is familiar to most people as the conductor that carries cable TV into their homes. Coaxial cable is constructed with an insulated solid or stranded wire core surrounded by a dielectric insulating layer and a solid or braided metallic shield.

10. **b.** In a client/server network, dependent workstations (clients) operate in conjunction with a dedicated master computer (server). The network control tends to be very centralized. The server typically holds the programs and data for its client computers. It also provides security and network policy enforcement.

11. **a, b.** (a) The server in a client/server LAN configuration typically holds programs and data for its client computers. In some client/server LAN designs, the client machine, called a diskless workstation, doesn't even store any data. (**b**) It provides security and network policy enforcement by controlling the access to data and resources it holds for its clients.

12. **c.** In a peer-to-peer arrangement, users connected to the network can share access to different network resources and act as both clients and servers of the other users.

13. **b.** The mesh design offers the most basic network connection scheme. In this design, each node has a direct physical connection to all the other nodes in the network. While the overhead for connecting a mesh network in a LAN environment is prohibitive, this topology is employed in two very large network environments: the public telephone system and the Internet.

14. **a.** The logical layout of the star network resembles the branches of a tree. All the nodes are connected in branches that eventually lead back to a central unit. Nodes communicate with each other through the central unit. The central station coordinates the network's activity by polling the nodes, one by one, to determine whether they have any information to transfer.

15. **d.** In a ring network configuration, the communication bus is formed into a closed loop. Each node inspects the information on the LAN as it passes by. A repeater, built into each ring LAN card, regenerates every message not directed to it and sends it to the next appointed node. The originating node eventually receives the message back and removes it from the ring.

16. **c.** In the bus topology, the nodes, or stations, of the network connect to a central communication link. Each node has a unique address along the bus that differentiates it from the other users on the network.

17. **c.** Transmission Control Protocol/Internet Protocol (TCP/IP) is the most popular network protocol currently in use due largely to the fact that the Internet is based on it. TCP/IP has also become the protocol of choice for corporate networks because most operating systems support this protocol.

18. **b.** In order to minimize the risk of security compromise on a wireless LAN, the IEEE-802.11b standard provides a security feature called Wired Equivalent Privacy (WEP). WEP provides a method for encrypting data transmissions and authenticating each computer on the network.

19. **a.** AppleTalk is required for Windows computers to communicate with Apple Macs running older Apple operating systems in the network. Newer Macs should be using the TCP/IP protocol for networking.

20. **c.** NWLink is Microsoft's version of the Internetwork Packet Exchange/Sequenced Packet Exchange (IPX/SPX) network protocol used in Novell NetWare environments.

21. **d.** In concept, a minimum of three stations must be connected to have a true LAN. If only two units are connected, point-to-point communications software and a simple null modem can be employed.

Objective 6.3

1. **b.** Because all other functions of the PDA appear to be working, and the PDA is brand new, the PDA being defective or missing batteries is not likely. The manual does not mention additional cords to interface with the PDA; it shouldn't need an external cable. The conclusion is that the PDA uses wireless connections to transfer data between the PDA and the workstation.

2. **d.** Each network segment has a protective gateway to act as an entry and exit point for the segment. In most cases, the gateway is a device called a *router*. A router is an intelligent device that connects network segments as well as receives data and directs it toward a designated IP address.

3. **a, b, d.** Services that most ISPs deliver to their customers include Internet identity through IP addresses, email services through POP3 and SMTP servers, Internet news service through USENET archive servers, and Internet routing through DNS servers.

4. **b.** The external modem is usually a box that resides outside the system unit and is connected to one of the computer's serial ports by an RS-232 serial cable.

5. **c.** Signals are uplinked to a satellite in orbit around the Earth and then down-linked to satellite receiver dishes. In most systems, the satellite dish has no uplink capabilities; so, to retrieve information from the Web, they send data through the telephone connection. Download speeds are very good (up to 1.5Mbps) but upload speeds are limited to the 56Kbps speed of the dial-up modem.

6. **c.** A modem consists of two major blocks: a modulator and a demodulator. The modulator is a transmitter that converts the parallel/digital computer data into a serial/analog format for transmission. The demodulator is the receiver that accepts the serial/analog transmission format and converts it into a parallel/digital format usable by the computer, or peripheral.

7. **b.** Full-duplex mode multiplexes the send and receive signal frequencies, which enables both modems to send and receive data simultaneously.

8. **c.** In half-duplex mode, modems exchange data, but only in one direction at a time.

9. **a.** When a modem is used to send signals in only one direction, it is operating in simplex mode. Modems capable of both transmitting and receiving data are divided into two groups, based on their mode of operation. In half-duplex mode, modems exchange data, but only in one direction at a time. Multiplexing or full-duplex modems send and receive signal frequencies that will enable both modems to send and receive data simultaneously.

10. **b.** If a filter is put on the DSL connection, the Internet connection might not work correctly.

11. **d.** DSL modems require an external power source to function.

12. **c.** DSL modems plug into a workstation via a network interface card, which uses an RJ-45 connector. A 56K modem connects directly into a phone line, and does not interact with a DSL modem in any fashion.

PART II
Operating Systems

Operating System Domain 1.0: Operating System Fundamentals

Quick Check

Objective 1.1: Identify the major desktop components and interfaces and their functions.

Differentiate the characteristics of Windows 9x/Me, Windows NT 4.0 Workstation, Windows 2000 Professional, and Windows XP.

1. When a Windows 98 system runs out of available RAM, what action does the operating system take?

   ❑ a. It moves data from RAM to virtual memory.
   ❑ b. It moves disk memory to RAM.
   ❑ c. It moves virtual memory to RAM.
   ❑ d. It dumps virtual memory.

Quick Answer: **266**
Detailed Answer: **269**

2. Virtual memory is _____.

   ❑ a. a section of floppy drive space that works like RAM
   ❑ b. a section of RAM that works like hard drive space
   ❑ c. an area of programmable RAM that retains its programming after the power is turned off
   ❑ d. a section of hard drive space that works like RAM

Quick Answer: **266**
Detailed Answer: **269**

3. What is the safest method of changing Registry entries in Windows 2000?

   ❑ a. Use Device Manager.
   ❑ b. Use a file editor.
   ❑ c. Use REGEDIT.
   ❑ d. Use REGEDT32.

Quick Answer: **266**
Detailed Answer: **269**

4. Windows Explorer doesn't show the system files under the Windows directory. What could be the problem?

Quick Answer: **266**
Detailed Answer: **269**

- ❑ a. Windows needs to be reinstalled.
- ❑ b. By default, Windows doesn't show system files.
- ❑ c. The files are not necessary for Windows.
- ❑ d. The files are corrupted.

5. How do you rename a file in Windows?

Quick Answer: **266**
Detailed Answer: **269**

- ❑ a. Right-click the file and then select Rename from the pop-up menu.
- ❑ b. Double-click on the file and enter the new name.
- ❑ c. Click on the file and enter the new name.
- ❑ d. Click on the file and then select Rename from the pop-up menu.

6. How do you create a new folder using Windows Explorer?

Quick Answer: **266**
Detailed Answer: **269**

- ❑ a. Select a parent directory, click the Edit menu, select New, and then Folder.
- ❑ b. Select a parent directory, click the Edit menu, and then select New Folder.
- ❑ c. Select a parent directory, click the File menu, select New, and then click Folder.
- ❑ d. Select a parent directory, click the File menu, and then select New Folder.

7. Which method is used to change file attributes from the Windows Explorer?

Quick Answer: **266**
Detailed Answer: **269**

- ❑ a. Edit the appropriate Registry entry with RegEdt32.
- ❑ b. Right-click on the file and select Properties.
- ❑ c. Highlight the file and choose the Select Options entry in the System Tools menu.
- ❑ d. Highlight the file and choose the Select Options entry in the View menu.

8. Which two of the following file types are normally not shown in Windows Explorer?

Quick Answer: **266**
Detailed Answer: **269**

- ❑ a. .INI
- ❑ b. .DAT
- ❑ c. .BMP
- ❑ d. .PCX

Quick Check

9. How do you navigate to various parts of Windows 9x through the Windows Explorer?

   ❑ a. Expand a folder contents listing by clicking on the backslash (\) to expand it, and repeat until you locate the target file/folder.

   ❑ b. Expand a folder contents listing by clicking on the minus sign (–) to expand it, and repeat until you locate the target file/folder.

   ❑ c. Expand a folder contents listing by clicking on the asterisk (*) to expand it, and repeat until you locate the target file/folder.

   ❑ d. Expand a folder contents listing by clicking on the plus sign (+) to expand it, and repeat until you locate the target file/folder.

Quick Answer: **266**
Detailed Answer: **269**

10. Which key combinations can be used to toggle between items on the Taskbar? (Select two correct answers.)

   ❑ a. Shift+Tab

   ❑ b. Ctrl+Tab

   ❑ c. Alt+Tab

   ❑ d. Alt+Esc

Quick Answer: **266**
Detailed Answer: **270**

11. When a file is deleted from the Recycle Bin, what happens to the file?

   ❑ a. It goes to the trash.

   ❑ b. It may be recovered.

   ❑ c. It is restored.

   ❑ d. It is converted to another file system.

Quick Answer: **266**
Detailed Answer: **270**

12. To shift between open applications in Windows, press _____. (Select two correct answers.)

   ❑ a. Alt+Tab

   ❑ b. Ctrl+Alt+Del

   ❑ c. Esc

   ❑ d. Alt+Esc

Quick Answer: **266**
Detailed Answer: **270**

13. Which function in Device Manager will enable you to manage and configure a device driver?

   ❑ a. Properties

   ❑ b. Resources

   ❑ c. Settings

   ❑ d. Options

Quick Answer: **266**
Detailed Answer: **270**

. . . .

14. Which path can be used to access the Device Manager Windows 9x?

Quick Answer: **266**
Detailed Answer: **270**

- ❑ a. Start/Settings/Control Panel and then double-click on Device Manager
- ❑ b. Start/Settings/Control Panel/System and then click on the Device Manager tab
- ❑ c. Start/Settings/Control Panel/System, click on the Hardware tab, and then click on Device Manager
- ❑ d. Start/Programs/Accessories/System Tools and then select Device Manager

15. How is a Startup disk created in Windows 9x?

Quick Answer: **266**
Detailed Answer: **270**

- ❑ a. Start/Settings/Control Panel/System and then click the Startup tab
- ❑ b. Start/Programs/Accessories/System Tools and then click the System Information tab
- ❑ c. Start/Settings/Control Panel/Add-Remove Programs and then click the Startup Disk tab
- ❑ d. Start/Programs/Accessories/System Tools and then select Backup

16. What action is required to install a hardware device not directly supported by Windows 9x?

Quick Answer: **266**
Detailed Answer: **270**

- ❑ a. It cannot be installed.
- ❑ b. Install a driver for a similar device from the same manufacturer.
- ❑ c. It must be installed manually.
- ❑ d. The system must be rebooted.

17. How do you navigate to the System Tools in Windows 9x?

Quick Answer: **266**
Detailed Answer: **270**

- ❑ a. Start/Settings/Control Panel/System Tools
- ❑ b. Start/Programs/Accessories/Administrative Tools/System Tools
- ❑ c. Start/Settings/Control Panel/Administrative Tools/System Tools
- ❑ d. Start/Programs/Accessories/System Tools

18. How can you move around the desktop, Start menu, and Taskbar by just using the keyboard?

Quick Answer: **266**
Detailed Answer: **270**

- ❑ a. Esc
- ❑ b. Tab
- ❑ c. The arrow keys
- ❑ d. Ctrl

19. Which two ways can the Recycle Bin's icon be replaced in a Windows 9x system?

    ❑ a. Establish a new shortcut to the Recycle Bin.
    ❑ b. Reinstall Windows 9x.
    ❑ c. Copy and paste the icon.
    ❑ d. Create a new folder and rename it Recycle Bin.

Quick Answer: **266**
Detailed Answer: **270**

20. What happens to information that was deleted from a removable media?

    ❑ a. It is archived and held for later deletion.
    ❑ b. It is moved into the Recycle Bin.
    ❑ c. It is relocated to the System Backup directory.
    ❑ d. It is deleted from the file system.

Quick Answer: **266**
Detailed Answer: **271**

21. What happens to files moved into the Recycle Bin?

    ❑ a. The file is archived and held for later deletion.
    ❑ b. The file is deleted.
    ❑ c. The filename is changed to make it invisible to the system.
    ❑ d. The file is overwritten.

Quick Answer: **266**
Detailed Answer: **271**

22. What do the dots in a Windows pop-up or drop-down menu indicate about the option associated with it?

    ❑ a. The item needs to be installed.
    ❑ b. The option is currently selected.
    ❑ c. The item is currently in use.
    ❑ d. The option is not available.

Quick Answer: **266**
Detailed Answer: **271**

23. What do the check marks in a Windows pop-up or drop-down menu indicate about the option associated with it?

    ❑ a. The option is currently selected.
    ❑ b. The item is currently in use.
    ❑ c. The item needs to be installed.
    ❑ d. The option was previously deleted.

Quick Answer: **266**
Detailed Answer: **271**

24. What is the primary method of creating a new folder in Windows?

    ❑ a. Select a parent directory, click the File menu, select New, and then Folder.
    ❑ b. Select a parent directory, click the Edit menu, and then select New Folder.
    ❑ c. Select a parent directory, click the Edit menu, select New, and then Folder.
    ❑ d. Select a parent directory, click the File menu, and then select New Folder.

Quick Answer: **266**
Detailed Answer: **271**

25. What is indicated when menu options are grayed?

    ❑ a. Options are not applicable to the current window.

    ❑ b. Options are applicable to the current window.

    ❑ c. Options are currently in use.

    ❑ d. Options are not installed.

Quick Answer: **266**
Detailed Answer: **271**

26. What type of information is provided by the General tab of the System Properties page? (Select two.)

    ❑ a. Microprocessor type and RAM capacity

    ❑ b. Operating system version

    ❑ c. Registered owner

    ❑ d. Date of operating system installation

Quick Answer: **266**
Detailed Answer: **271**

27. What desktop's shortcut key combination enables the user to cycle through open application windows?

    ❑ a. Alt+Esc

    ❑ b. Ctrl+Esc

    ❑ c. Shift+Tab

    ❑ d. Alt+Tab

Quick Answer: **266**
Detailed Answer: **271**

28. What type of file is the Windows Me Registry file?

    ❑ a. Text file

    ❑ b. Hierarchical database file

    ❑ c. Application file

    ❑ d. Nonexistent file

Quick Answer: **266**
Detailed Answer: **271**

29. What is the purpose of the Registry in Windows 95?

    ❑ a. It provides a storage location for graphics files.

    ❑ b. It stores user system and application configuration information.

    ❑ c. It updates the SYSTEM.INI and WIN.INI files.

    ❑ d. It stores a copy of the CMOS data.

Quick Answer: **266**
Detailed Answer: **271**

30. OSR2 is an upgrade for _____.

    ❑ a. Windows 3.11

    ❑ b. Windows 3.1

    ❑ c. Windows 95

    ❑ d. DOS 6.22

Quick Answer: **266**
Detailed Answer: **271**

31. _____ is a core component of the Windows 9x structure.

    ❑ a. GDI.EXE

    ❑ b. SYSTEM.INI

    ❑ c. CONTROL.INI

    ❑ d. PROGMAN.INI

Quick Answer: **266**
Detailed Answer: **272**

32. What utility is used to directly edit Registry entries in
    Windows 9x?

    ❑ a. REGEDT32
    ❑ b. SYSEDIT
    ❑ c. EDIT
    ❑ d. REGEDIT

Quick Answer: **266**
Detailed Answer: **272**

33. What is the basic function of the
    HKEY_CURRENT_CONFIG Registry key?

    ❑ a. User logon data
    ❑ b. Current information about devices
    ❑ c. PnP dynamic status data
    ❑ d. User-specific configuration

Quick Answer: **266**
Detailed Answer: **272**

34. What is the basic function of the HKEY_DYN_DATA
    Registry key?

    ❑ a. PnP dynamic status data
    ❑ b. User logon data
    ❑ c. User-specific configuration
    ❑ d. Current information about devices

Quick Answer: **266**
Detailed Answer: **272**

35. What is the basic function of the HKEY_USERS
    Registry key?

    ❑ a. PnP status data
    ❑ b. User-specific configuration
    ❑ c. User logon data
    ❑ d. Current information about devices

Quick Answer: **266**
Detailed Answer: **272**

36. What is the basic function of the HKEY_CURRENT_USER
    Registry key?

    ❑ a. User logon data
    ❑ b. User-specific configuration
    ❑ c. PnP status data
    ❑ d. Current information about devices

Quick Answer: **266**
Detailed Answer: **272**

37. What is the basic function of the HKEY_CLASSES_ROOT
    Registry key?

    ❑ a. User-specific configuration
    ❑ b. Associates icons with files
    ❑ c. PnP status data
    ❑ d. Current information about devices

Quick Answer: **266**
Detailed Answer: **272**

38. What file is used to load the Windows environment?

   ❏ a. WIN.COM

   ❏ b. IO.SYS

   ❏ c. START.EXE

   ❏ d. AUTOEXEC.BAT

Quick Answer: **266**
Detailed Answer: **272**

39. How can hidden and system files be shown in the Windows 9x system?

   ❏ a. Double-click on My Computer, click on Edit and select Folder Options from the menu, click the View tab, and then click on the Show Hidden Files button.

   ❏ b. Double-click on My Computer, click on Tools and select Folder Options from the menu, click the View tab, and then click on the Show Hidden Files and Folders button.

   ❏ c. Double-click on My Computer, click on File and select Properties from the menu, click the View tab, and then click on the Show Hidden Files button.

   ❏ d. Double-click on My Computer, click on View and select Folder Options from the menu, click the View tab, and then click on the Show Hidden Files button.

Quick Answer: **266**
Detailed Answer: **272**

40. Which file system is native to Windows 2000?

   ❏ a. FAT32

   ❏ b. FAT16

   ❏ c. NTFS5

   ❏ d. NTFS

Quick Answer: **266**
Detailed Answer: **272**

41. Which file system is native to Windows NT?

   ❏ a. NTFS

   ❏ b. NTFS5

   ❏ c. FAT32

   ❏ d. FAT16

Quick Answer: **266**
Detailed Answer: **272**

42. An intranet is _____ network, typically established by an organization for the purpose of running an exclusive site not open to the public.

   ❏ a. a local area

   ❏ b. an extranet

   ❏ c. a wide area

   ❏ d. a Web-based

Quick Answer: **266**
Detailed Answer: **273**

43. How do you access the command prompt in Windows NT?

- ❏ a. Click on the MS-DOS icon on the desktop.
- ❏ b. Click on the MS-DOS icon in the Control Panel.
- ❏ c. Type `CMD` in the Start/Run dialog box.
- ❏ d. Type `command` in the Start/Run dialog box.

Quick Answer: **266**
Detailed Answer: **273**

44. In the Windows 2000 environment, where do you go to access the system's administrative tools from a centralized location?

- ❏ a. Start/Settings/Control Panel/Administrative Tools/Computer Management
- ❏ b. Start/Programs/System Tools
- ❏ c. Start/Settings/Control Panel/System/Administration
- ❏ d. Start/Run/Administrative Tools

Quick Answer: **266**
Detailed Answer: **273**

45. Which Windows 2000 hive contains the Last Known Good Configuration information?

- ❏ a. Software
- ❏ b. System
- ❏ c. Security
- ❏ d. Default

Quick Answer: **266**
Detailed Answer: **273**

46. How many symmetrical processors can the Datacenter Server edition of Windows 2000 Server support?

- ❏ a. 32
- ❏ b. 8
- ❏ c. 4
- ❏ d. 16

Quick Answer: **266**
Detailed Answer: **273**

47. How many symmetrical processors can the Advanced Server edition of Windows 2000 Server support?

- ❏ a. 8
- ❏ b. 2
- ❏ c. 4
- ❏ d. 16

Quick Answer: **266**
Detailed Answer: **273**

48. Windows 2000 Professional is the _____ side of the Windows 2000 operating systems.

- ❏ a. primary domain controller
- ❏ b. workstation
- ❏ c. backup domain controller
- ❏ d. member server

Quick Answer: **266**
Detailed Answer: **273**

49. A _____ is used to block unauthorized outside users from accessing an intranet site.

- ❏ a. hub
- ❏ b. router
- ❏ c. gateway
- ❏ d. firewall

Quick Answer: **266**
Detailed Answer: **273**

50. _____ are those networks designed to facilitate business-to-business or business-to-customer operations.

- ❏ a. Local area networks
- ❏ b. Wide area networks
- ❏ c. Enterprise networks
- ❏ d. Client/server networks

Quick Answer: **266**
Detailed Answer: **273**

51. What feature do all members of a domain share?

- ❏ a. A security database
- ❏ b. Client licenses
- ❏ c. A printer
- ❏ d. Applications

Quick Answer: **266**
Detailed Answer: **273**

52. What makes Windows 98 and Windows NT/2000 incompatible?

- ❏ a. Their file systems
- ❏ b. Their Registry structures
- ❏ c. Their graphical interfaces
- ❏ d. Their partition types

Quick Answer: **266**
Detailed Answer: **273**

53. Which utility can safely be used to make changes to the Registry in Windows 2000?

- ❏ a. ScanReg
- ❏ b. RegEdit
- ❏ c. Device Manager
- ❏ d. Component Services

Quick Answer: **266**
Detailed Answer: **274**

Objective 1.2: Identify the names, locations, purposes, and contents of major system files.

1. Which Windows NT 4.0 command can be used to create a backup copy of the Registry from the command line?

   - ❑ a. Rdisk
   - ❑ b. Mkdsk
   - ❑ c. Regedit/copy
   - ❑ d. Start

Quick Answer: **266**
Detailed Answer: **274**

2. An application has a corresponding .INI file. What is the .INI file used for?

   - ❑ a. It holds the application configuration information.
   - ❑ b. It holds database information.
   - ❑ c. Applications don't use .INI files.
   - ❑ d. Only Windows applications use .INI files.

Quick Answer: **266**
Detailed Answer: **274**

3. Which system file must maintain a size of at least 1KB?

   - ❑ a. CONFIG.SYS
   - ❑ b. MSDOS.SYS
   - ❑ c. USER.DAT
   - ❑ d. WIN.INI

Quick Answer: **266**
Detailed Answer: **274**

4. Which tool is recommended for making changes to the Registry in Windows 2000?

   - ❑ a. RegEdit
   - ❑ b. Control Panel Wizards
   - ❑ c. RegEdt32
   - ❑ d. Device Manager

Quick Answer: **266**
Detailed Answer: **274**

5. What is the correct sequence of events when a DOS system is started?

   - ❑ a. It loads AUTOEXEC.BAT, CONFIG.SYS, and COMMAND.COM in order.
   - ❑ b. It loads CONFIG.SYS, COMMAND.COM, and AUTOEXEC.BAT in order.
   - ❑ c. It loads COMMAND.COM, AUTOEXEC.BAT, and CONFIG.SYS in order.
   - ❑ d. It loads COMMAND.COM, CONFIG.SYS, and AUTOEXEC.BAT in order.

Quick Answer: **266**
Detailed Answer: **274**

6. Which of the following is the virtual-memory swap file used in Windows 2000?

Quick Answer: **266**
Detailed Answer: **274**

- ❏ a. TEMP.SWP
- ❏ b. WIN.SWP
- ❏ c. WIN386.SWP
- ❏ d. PAGEFILE.SYS

7. What virtual-memory swap file is used in Windows 9x?

Quick Answer: **266**
Detailed Answer: **274**

- ❏ a. WIN.SWP
- ❏ b. WIN386.SWP
- ❏ c. TEMP.SWP
- ❏ d. PAGEFILE.SYS

8. How did the Windows versions before Windows 95 organize and monitor the system's configuration information?

Quick Answer: **266**
Detailed Answer: **274**

- ❏ a. .DAT files
- ❏ b. .CFG files
- ❏ c. .INI files
- ❏ d. .LOG files

9. Which of the following commands are normally located in a typical AUTOEXEC.BAT file? (Select all that apply.)

Quick Answer: **266**
Detailed Answer: **274**

- ❏ a. `PROMPT=$P$G`
- ❏ b. `SET TEMP=C:\TEMP`
- ❏ c. `SMARTDRV`
- ❏ d. `DOS=HIGH,UMB`

10. Which driver assigns logical drive letters to the system's floppy drives?

Quick Answer: **266**
Detailed Answer: **275**

- ❏ a. ANSI.SYS
- ❏ b. DISPLAY.SYS
- ❏ c. DRIVER.SYS
- ❏ d. KEYBOARD.SYS

11. What is the purpose of the HIMEM.SYS file?

Quick Answer: **266**
Detailed Answer: **275**

- ❏ a. Extended memory management
- ❏ b. BIOS extension management
- ❏ c. OS configuration management
- ❏ d. Creating the UMA

12. Which of these statements is normally located in the CONFIG.SYS file? (Select all that apply.)

   ❑ a. `PATH=C:\,C:\DOS,C:\MOUSE,C:\PROGRAMS`
   ❑ b. `DEVICE=C:\DOS\EMM386.EXE 1024 RAM`
   ❑ c. `DOS=HIGH,UMB`
   ❑ d. `FILES=30`

Quick Answer: **266**
Detailed Answer: **275**

13. What is the minimum file size specification associated with the MSDOS.SYS file?

   ❑ a. 1KB
   ❑ b. 16 bits
   ❑ c. 2KB
   ❑ d. 4KB

Quick Answer: **266**
Detailed Answer: **275**

14. Which two files make up the Windows 9x Registry?

   ❑ a. USER.DAT
   ❑ b. REG.DAT
   ❑ c. HIVE.DAT
   ❑ d. SYSTEM.DAT

Quick Answer: **266**
Detailed Answer: **275**

15. Which file loads the Windows 9x operating system into the system?

   ❑ a. START.EXE
   ❑ b. IO.SYS
   ❑ c. WIN.COM
   ❑ d. AUTOEXEC.BAT

Quick Answer: **266**
Detailed Answer: **275**

16. Where is USER.DAT stored in Windows 98?

   ❑ a. `C:\windows\system`
   ❑ b. `C:\windows\system32`
   ❑ c. `C:\Windows`
   ❑ d. `C:\`

Quick Answer: **266**
Detailed Answer: **275**

17. You can prevent programs in the Windows 9x Startup folder from executing on bootup by _____.

   ❑ a. holding down the Ctrl key
   ❑ b. pressing the left Shift key
   ❑ c. pressing the spacebar
   ❑ d. pressing the Enter key

Quick Answer: **266**
Detailed Answer: **275**

. . . .

18. When installing a full version of Windows 95, which of the following files are not created?

Quick Answer: **266**
Detailed Answer: **275**

  ❑ a. IO.SYS and MSDOS.SYS
  ❑ b. WIN.INI and KERNEL32.DLL
  ❑ c. CONFIG.SYS and AUTOEXEC.BAT
  ❑ d. SYSTEM.DAT and USER.DAT

19. Which file is responsible for loading Windows into memory?

Quick Answer: **266**
Detailed Answer: **275**

  ❑ a. GDI.EXE
  ❑ b. WIN.COM
  ❑ c. WIN.EXE
  ❑ d. WIN.INI

20. Where are the files that make up the Windows 95 Registry located in the system?

Quick Answer: **266**
Detailed Answer: **276**

  ❑ a. `C:\Windows`
  ❑ b. `C:\`
  ❑ c. `C:\Windows\Registry`
  ❑ d. `C:\Windows\Sysbckup`

21. Where are the Registry backup files located in Windows 98?

Quick Answer: **266**
Detailed Answer: **276**

  ❑ a. `C:\Windows`
  ❑ b. `C:\Windows\Sysbckup`
  ❑ c. `C:\Windows\Registry`
  ❑ d. `C:\`

22. What files make up the Windows 9x Registry?

Quick Answer: **266**
Detailed Answer: **276**

  ❑ a. USER.LOG, SYSTEM.LOG
  ❑ b. USER.DAT, SYSTEM.DAT
  ❑ c. USER.REG, SYSTEM.REG
  ❑ d. USER.SYS, SYSTEM.SYS

23. Which of the following is not a typical error message produced when no valid MBR is found in a system?

Quick Answer: **266**
Detailed Answer: **276**

  ❑ a. Non-System Disk Error
  ❑ b. Disk Error
  ❑ c. ROM BASIC Interpreter Not Found
  ❑ d. Missing Partition Table

24. Where is the NTUSER.DAT file stored in Windows 2000 Professional for the user Richard?

    ❑ a. In the `c:\WINDOWS` directory
    ❑ b. In the `c:\WINNT` directory
    ❑ c. In the Documents and Settings folder
    ❑ d. In the subfolder `Richard` under the `Documents_and_Settings` folder

Quick Answer: **266**
Detailed Answer: **276**

25. How are the items in the Windows 9x Startup folder prevented from running at startup?

    ❑ a. Press the left Shift key during startup.
    ❑ b. Press the left Alt key during startup.
    ❑ c. Press the left Ctrl key during startup.
    ❑ d. Press the Tab key during startup.

Quick Answer: **266**
Detailed Answer: **276**

26. The hardware detection process is carried out in Windows NT by _____.

    ❑ a. the BIOS
    ❑ b. the NTDETECT.COM file
    ❑ c. the NT kernel
    ❑ d. the AUTOCHK.EXE file

Quick Answer: **266**
Detailed Answer: **276**

27. Which of the following Windows NT files is responsible for producing the Boot Loader Menu when Windows NT/2000 starts up?

    ❑ a. NTIO.SYS
    ❑ b. BOOT.INI
    ❑ c. BOOTVID.DLL
    ❑ d. BOOTSECT.EXE

Quick Answer: **267**
Detailed Answer: **276**

28. The file that guides the Windows NT/2000 boot process is _____.

    ❑ a. NTIO.SYS
    ❑ b. NTLDR
    ❑ c. NTBOOT.SYS
    ❑ d. BOOTSECT.DOS

Quick Answer: **267**
Detailed Answer: **276**

29. Which file is needed for Windows NT 4.0 to boot?

    ❑ a. CONFIG.SYS
    ❑ b. BOOT.INI
    ❑ c. BT.INI
    ❑ d. SYSTEM.INI

Quick Answer: **267**
Detailed Answer: **276**

30. Which file is not required to boot Windows NT?
    - ❏ a. BOOT.INI
    - ❏ b. NTLDR
    - ❏ c. NTDETECT.COM
    - ❏ d. IO.SYS

Quick Answer: **267**
Detailed Answer: **276**

31. In a Windows NT/2000 system, NTBOOTDD.SYS is a _____ file.
    - ❏ a. bootup problem detection
    - ❏ b. system boot
    - ❏ c. disk drive driver
    - ❏ d. bootup disk

Quick Answer: **267**
Detailed Answer: **276**

32. What is the swap file in Windows NT/2000 called?
    - ❏ a. PAGEFILE.SYS
    - ❏ b. SWAP.SYS
    - ❏ c. WIN386.SWP
    - ❏ d. WINSWAP.SWP

Quick Answer: **267**
Detailed Answer: **276**

33. In a Windows 2000 system, where is the system information and settings for an individual user stored?
    - ❏ a. In the \Windows\System\Users folder
    - ❏ b. In the \Documents_and_Settings folder
    - ❏ c. In the \Computers_and_Users folder
    - ❏ d. In the SAM hive

Quick Answer: **267**
Detailed Answer: **277**

34. Where would you find the user configuration file in a Windows NT 4.0 system?
    - ❏ a. \WINNT\Profiles\username
    - ❏ b. \Documents_and_Settings\username
    - ❏ c. \NTUSER.DAT
    - ❏ d. \Windows\System\username

Quick Answer: **267**
Detailed Answer: **277**

Objective 1.3: Demonstrate the ability to use command-line functions and utilities to manage the operating system.

1. How do you hide a file in a folder from the command line?
    - ❏ a. Attrib -r
    - ❏ b. Attrib
    - ❏ c. Attrib +a
    - ❏ d. Attrib +h

Quick Answer: **267**
Detailed Answer: **277**

2. The command used to set the attributes of a file is _____.

Quick Answer: **267**
Detailed Answer: **277**

- ❑ a. APPEND
- ❑ b. ASSIGN
- ❑ c. ATTRIB
- ❑ d. AUTOEXEC

3. To configure the file MYFILE.TXT as read-only, use the _____ MS-DOS command.

Quick Answer: **267**
Detailed Answer: **277**

- ❑ a. ATTRIB +A MYFILE.TXT
- ❑ b. ATTRIB -A MYFILE.TXT
- ❑ c. ATTRIB +R MYFILE.TXT
- ❑ d. ATTRIB -R MYFILE.TXT

4. Which of the following characters is used as a wildcard replacement for a single character in a DOS search string?

Quick Answer: **267**
Detailed Answer: **277**

- ❑ a. ?
- ❑ b. *
- ❑ c. #
- ❑ d. %

5. Which DOS wildcard character tells the software to perform the designated command on any file found on the disk using any filename and extension?

Quick Answer: **267**
Detailed Answer: **277**

- ❑ a. +.+
- ❑ b. #.#
- ❑ c. ?.?
- ❑ d. *.*

6. Which MS-DOS file attribute is used to define whether a file can be viewed in Windows Explorer?

Quick Answer: **267**
Detailed Answer: **277**

- ❑ a. Archive
- ❑ b. Hidden
- ❑ c. System
- ❑ d. Read-only

7. Which DOS file attribute is used to define the user's ability to edit that file?

Quick Answer: **267**
Detailed Answer: **277**

- ❑ a. Archive
- ❑ b. Read-only
- ❑ c. System
- ❑ d. Hidden

. . . .

8. Which DOS file attribute is reserved for use by the operating system?

- ❑   a.   Read-only
- ❑   b.   Archive
- ❑   c.   System
- ❑   d.   Hidden

9. A remote customer calls you for assistance because his computer will not boot up to the hard drive. He has started the system with a floppy disk and tried to access the C:\ hard drive using the DIR command. However, the information scrolled off the screen and he could not read it. What does the customer need to do differently?

- ❑   a.   Use the DIR B: command.
- ❑   b.   Use the DIR /W command.
- ❑   c.   Use the DIR /P command.
- ❑   d.   Use the CHDIR command.

10. Which of these file types cannot be executed directly from the command-line prompt in Windows 2000?

- ❑   a.   .SYS
- ❑   b.   .COM
- ❑   c.   .EXE
- ❑   d.   .BAT

11. How is the MS-DOS emulator accessed in Windows 2000 and Windows XP? (Select two correct answers.)

- ❑   a.   CMD
- ❑   b.   PROMPT
- ❑   c.   COMMAND
- ❑   d.   DOS

12. If a shared file is located on another computer in your network and you need to access it, what method should you employ to specify the path to this file?

- ❑   a.   Use the UNC convention.
- ❑   b.   Use the URL entry.
- ❑   c.   Use the Path command.
- ❑   d.   Use the IE interface to connect to it.

Objective 1.4: Identify basic concepts and procedures for creating, viewing, and managing disks, directories, and files.

This includes procedures for changing file attributes and the ramifications of those changes (for example, security issues).

1. When using FDISK to look at the partition table of a hard drive with two partitions formatted by Windows 9x, what partitions will be displayed?

  ❏   a. Primary partition and secondary partition
  ❏   b. Logical partition and primary drive
  ❏   c. Primary partition and expanded partition
  ❏   d. Primary partition and extended partition

Quick Answer: **267**
Detailed Answer: **278**

2. The DOS command _____ is used to establish partitions on a hard drive.

  ❏   a. DEFRAG
  ❏   b. SCANDISK
  ❏   c. CHKDSK
  ❏   d. FDISK

Quick Answer: **267**
Detailed Answer: **278**

3. How many logical drives can be created using DOS?

  ❏   a. 8
  ❏   b. 23
  ❏   c. 38
  ❏   d. 44

Quick Answer: **267**
Detailed Answer: **278**

4. What is the maximum number of entries in the Windows 98 root directory?

  ❏   a. 128
  ❏   b. 256
  ❏   c. 512
  ❏   d. 1,024

Quick Answer: **267**
Detailed Answer: **278**

5. How many directory files or entries can be included in the MS-DOS directory?

  ❏   a. 256
  ❏   b. 512
  ❏   c. 640
  ❏   d. 1,024

Quick Answer: **267**
Detailed Answer: **278**

. . . .

6. A _____ is the disk management method of organizing files into directories and subdirectories.

- ❑ a. directory tree
- ❑ b. file allocation table
- ❑ c. source code
- ❑ d. utility

Quick Answer: 267
Detailed Answer: 278

7. A group of related sectors on an HDD is referred to as _____.

- ❑ a. a cluster
- ❑ b. a segment
- ❑ c. a cylinder
- ❑ d. a file

Quick Answer: 267
Detailed Answer: 278

8. The smallest unit of storage in a Microsoft-based disk system is called _____.

- ❑ a. an FRU
- ❑ b. a cylinder
- ❑ c. a sector
- ❑ d. a cluster

Quick Answer: 267
Detailed Answer: 278

9. What is the maximum number of items that can exist in the root directory of a FAT-based disk?

- ❑ a. 256
- ❑ b. 512
- ❑ c. 255
- ❑ d. 1,024

Quick Answer: 267
Detailed Answer: 278

10. How many items can be placed in a directory in a FAT-based system?

- ❑ a. 128
- ❑ b. 256
- ❑ c. 512
- ❑ d. 1,024

Quick Answer: 267
Detailed Answer: 279

11. What is the size of a sector in an IBM/PC-compatible disk?

- ❑ a. 8 bytes
- ❑ b. 512 bytes
- ❑ c. 16 bytes
- ❑ d. 1,024 bytes

Quick Answer: 267
Detailed Answer: 279

12. What is the smallest unit of storage on a disk that can be manipulated by the operating system?

    ❑ a. Byte
    ❑ b. Bit
    ❑ c. Pixel
    ❑ d. Cluster

Quick Answer: **267**
Detailed Answer: **279**

13. What are the primary characteristics of an extended partition? (Select two.)

    ❑ a. It can be divided into 23 logical drives.
    ❑ b. It is the first partition on the drive.
    ❑ c. It cannot be deleted if logical drives have been defined within it.
    ❑ d. It is the logical drive that the system will boot to.

Quick Answer: **267**
Detailed Answer: **279**

14. What are the primary characteristics of an active partition?

    ❑ a. It is the logical drive that the system will boot to.
    ❑ b. It can be divided into 23 logical drives.
    ❑ c. It cannot be deleted if logical drives have been defined within it.
    ❑ d. It is the first partition on the drive.

Quick Answer: **267**
Detailed Answer: **279**

15. Which two of the following characters cannot be used in a DOS filename?

    ❑ a. >
    ❑ b. ?
    ❑ c. &
    ❑ d. #

Quick Answer: **267**
Detailed Answer: **279**

16. What is the maximum number of directories or files that can be held by another directory?

    ❑ a. 256
    ❑ b. 64
    ❑ c. 512
    ❑ d. 32

Quick Answer: **267**
Detailed Answer: **279**

17. How many additional logical drives can be created in a computer using a FAT-based operating system?

    ❑ a. 23
    ❑ b. 8
    ❑ c. 1
    ❑ d. 26

Quick Answer: **267**
Detailed Answer: **279**

18. What are the possible drawbacks of converting FAT16 to FAT32? (Select two correct answers.)

Quick Answer: **267**
Detailed Answer: **279**

❑ a. Less space to save on the disk
❑ b. Possible loss of data
❑ c. Smaller partition sizes are supported
❑ d. Possible performance loss caused by slower read/write speed

19. In Windows 9x, which of the following utilities would be used to convert a FAT16 partition to FAT32?

Quick Answer: **267**
Detailed Answer: **279**

❑ a. DMADMIN.EXE
❑ b. FATCNVRT.EXE
❑ c. FSCONVRT.EXE
❑ d. CVT.EXE

20. What utility replaces the SMARTDRV utility for disk caching in Windows 9x?

Quick Answer: **267**
Detailed Answer: **279**

❑ a. VCACHE
❑ b. RAMDISK
❑ c. CACHEDISK
❑ d. RAMCACHE

21. Which command-line utility can be used to convert FAT16 partitions to FAT32 partitions?

Quick Answer: **267**
Detailed Answer: **279**

❑ a. 1CVT.EXE
❑ b. CVT.EXE
❑ c. CONVERT.EXE
❑ d. CNVRT.EXE

22. A customer cannot find the file QUESTIONPOOL.DOC while searching in a DOS environment. She should _____.

Quick Answer: **267**
Detailed Answer: **279**

❑ a. look for an abbreviated name for the file, such as QUESTION.DOC
❑ b. consider the file deleted
❑ c. look for the file in Windows 95 instead
❑ d. look for an abbreviated name for the file, such as QUESTI~1.DOC

23. What are the maximum numbers of characters that can be used for Windows 9x filenames?

Quick Answer: **267**
Detailed Answer: **280**

❑ a. 256
❑ b. 215
❑ c. 64
❑ d. 255

. . . .

24. You have a file named `Arizona's best places to see.jpg` in the folder `c:\pictures`. You can see the file in Windows Explorer, but when you view this directory in the command prompt, you can't see the file. Why?

Quick Answer: **267**
Detailed Answer: **280**

- ❑ a. The Windows command prompt deleted the file.
- ❑ b. Windows doesn't display files that have long names in the command prompt.
- ❑ c. It is displayed as `Arizon~1.jpg` in the command prompt.
- ❑ d. When viewing the file system using the command prompt, it's not in the `c:\pictures` directory.

25. Which of the following is not a dynamic volume?

Quick Answer: **267**
Detailed Answer: **280**

- ❑ a. Simple volume
- ❑ b. Basic volume
- ❑ c. Mirrored volume
- ❑ d. Striped volume

26. Under what conditions is it better to employ the FAT32 file system instead of the NTFS file system?

Quick Answer: **267**
Detailed Answer: **280**

- ❑ a. On smaller drives
- ❑ b. On larger drives
- ❑ c. On faster drives
- ❑ d. On slower drives

27. Which operating systems use the HPFS file system?

Quick Answer: **267**
Detailed Answer: **280**

- ❑ a. Windows 95/98/OSR2
- ❑ b. MS-DOS and Windows 3.x
- ❑ c. IBM OS/2
- ❑ d. Windows NT/2000

28. Which Windows 2000 utility is designed to enable administrators to configure drives and volumes located in remote computers?

Quick Answer: **267**
Detailed Answer: **280**

- ❑ a. Hierarchical Storage Manager
- ❑ b. Volume Manager
- ❑ c. FDISK.EXE
- ❑ d. Disk Management

29. What partitions can Windows 2000 use for the installation partition of a 10GB hard drive? (Select all that apply.)

Quick Answer: **267**
Detailed Answer: **280**

- ❑ a. HPFS
- ❑ b. NTFS
- ❑ c. NFS
- ❑ d. FAT32

30. Which file systems are supported in Windows 2000 Professional? (Select all that apply.)

   ❑ a. CDFS

   ❑ b. FAT16

   ❑ c. HPFS

   ❑ d. NTFS

Quick Answer: **267**
Detailed Answer: **280**

31. What file system format is used to store files on a CD-ROM?

   ❑ a. NTFS

   ❑ b. CDFS

   ❑ c. HPFS

   ❑ d. FAT

Quick Answer: **267**
Detailed Answer: **280**

32. Which of the following are advantages associated with using the NTFS file system? (Select all that apply.)

   ❑ a. Data security

   ❑ b. Support for larger drives

   ❑ c. 64-bit entries to keep track of items

   ❑ d. Handling small drives efficiently

Quick Answer: **267**
Detailed Answer: **280**

33. Which file system is the most efficient for the storage of small files?

   ❑ a. FAT

   ❑ b. VFAT

   ❑ c. FAT32

   ❑ d. NTFS

Quick Answer: **267**
Detailed Answer: **280**

34. What Windows 2000 utility can be used to prevent users other than the originator of folders and files from accessing them?

   ❑ a. File Manager

   ❑ b. Encrypted File System

   ❑ c. Microsoft Management Console

   ❑ d. Windows Explorer

Quick Answer: **267**
Detailed Answer: **281**

35. How do you identify a compressed file in Windows 2000? (Select two correct answers.)

   ❑ a. The file or folder is listed in a second color.

   ❑ b. The file or folder is listed in italic.

   ❑ c. The file or folder shows compressed/archive attribute listing in Web style.

   ❑ d. The file or folder is given a vice-clamp icon.

Quick Answer: **267**
Detailed Answer: **281**

. . . .

36. What command is used to encrypt files and folders from the Windows 2000 command line?

❑ a. Protect
❑ b. Uuencode
❑ c. Encrypt
❑ d. Cipher

Quick Answer: **267**
Detailed Answer: **281**

37. What is the maximum number of characters that can be used for Windows NT filenames?

❑ a. 264
❑ b. 215
❑ c. 255
❑ d. 256

Quick Answer: **267**
Detailed Answer: **281**

38. Which two of the following characters cannot be used in a Windows 2000 filename?

❑ a. :
❑ b. *
❑ c. &
❑ d. #

Quick Answer: **267**
Detailed Answer: **281**

39. What is the maximum number of characters that can be used for Windows 2000 filenames?

❑ a. 255
❑ b. 64
❑ c. 215
❑ d. 256

Quick Answer: **267**
Detailed Answer: **281**

40. Where are disk management tools located in Windows 2000 Professional?

❑ a. In Control Panel, the Disk Management icon
❑ b. Under Administrative Tools, the Disk Management icon
❑ c. Under System Folder, the Disk Management icon
❑ d. In Administrative Tools, the Computer Management icon

Quick Answer: **267**
Detailed Answer: **281**

41. A user wants to use his new hard drive to store sensitive company data. His computer is running Windows XP Professional. He plans on encrypting all data in his folder so only a few select users can access the data. What can you do to achieve that goal?

Quick Answer: **267**
Detailed Answer: **281**

- ❏ a. In the folder's Properties page, access the Advanced screen under the General tab and click the Encrypt Contents to Secure Data check box.
- ❏ b. Access the Security window from the Control Panel and then click the Encrypt Contents to Secure Data check box in the Advanced page.
- ❏ c. Access the Encryption window through the Start/Programs/Accessories/System Tools/Encryption path, and then select the desired folder.
- ❏ d. In the folder's Properties page, access the Advanced screen under the Security tab and click the Encrypt Contents to Secure Data check box.

42. Which file-management system is native to Windows XP?

Quick Answer: **267**
Detailed Answer: **281**

- ❏ a. FAT64
- ❏ b. NTFS6
- ❏ c. NTFS5
- ❏ d. FAT32

43. In the Windows 2000 environment, where do you go to access the system's disk drive–management tools?

Quick Answer: **267**
Detailed Answer: **281**

- ❏ a. Start/Settings/Control Panel/System/Device Manager
- ❏ b. Start/Programs/System Tools/Drives/Disk Management
- ❏ c. Start/Settings/Control Panel/Drive Management
- ❏ d. Start/Settings/Control Panel/Administrative Tools/Computer Management/Disk Management

Objective 1.5: Identify the major operating system utilities, their purpose, location, and available switches.

1. Where are the disk drive tools located in Windows 2000?

Quick Answer: **267**
Detailed Answer: **282**

- ❏ a. Computer Management
- ❏ b. System Tools
- ❏ c. Device Manager
- ❏ d. System Information

Quick Check

2. How can you kill an application in Windows 2000? (Select all that apply.)

Quick Answer: 267
Detailed Answer: 282

❑ a. Right-click the system tray, select Task Manager from the contextual menu, click the Applications tab, highlight the application, and click End Task.

❑ b. Press Ctrl+Alt+Del, click on Task Manager, click the Applications tab, highlight the application, and click End Task.

❑ c. Press Ctrl+Alt+Esc, click on Task Manager, click the Applications tab, highlight the application, and click End Task.

❑ d. Press Ctrl+Shift+Esc, click the Applications tab, highlight the application, and click End Task.

3. The _____ in Windows 2000 can be used to remove non-functioning applications from the system.

Quick Answer: 267
Detailed Answer: 282

❑ a. Computer Management tool
❑ b. Close Program tool
❑ c. Close Application tool
❑ d. Task Manager tool

4. How do you access the Windows 2000 tool that is used to restore backup copies of the Registry to the system?

Quick Answer: 267
Detailed Answer: 282

❑ a. Start/Run and then type **regback**
❑ b. Start/Programs/Accessories/System Tools/Backup and then click on Restore
❑ c. Start/Programs/Accessories/System Tools/Backup and then click on Backup
❑ d. Start/Settings/Control Panel/System, click on the Advanced tab, and then click the Startup and Recovery button

5. Which backup type will back up the entire system, and requires the least amount of time to restore the system after a failure?

Quick Answer: 267
Detailed Answer: 282

❑ a. Incremental
❑ b. Full
❑ c. Differential
❑ d. Selective

6. In Windows 9x, which utility enables you to control programs that run at startup?

Quick Answer: 267
Detailed Answer: 282

❑ a. STARTREG.EXE
❑ b. MSCONFIG.EXE
❑ c. REGEDIT.EXE
❑ d. REGEDT32.EXE

7. Where are the disk-management tools located in Windows 95?

Quick Answer: **267**
Detailed Answer: **282**

- ❑ a. Network Neighborhood
- ❑ b. Desktop
- ❑ c. System Tools
- ❑ d. Recycle Bin

8. Which utility can be used to repair lost units on the hard disk?

Quick Answer: **267**
Detailed Answer: **282**

- ❑ a. CONVERT
- ❑ b. SCANDISK /P
- ❑ c. DEFRAG
- ❑ d. CHKDSK /F

9. What utility can be used to speed up a heavily used drive?

Quick Answer: **267**
Detailed Answer: **283**

- ❑ a. Event Viewer
- ❑ b. ScanDisk
- ❑ c. Defragmenter
- ❑ d. Internet Explorer Repair Tool

10. Device Manager can show which four key resources?

Quick Answer: **267**
Detailed Answer: **283**

- ❑ a. DMA Channel, I/O Address, Card Condition, Memory Address
- ❑ b. DMA Channel, I/O Address, Memory Address, Usability
- ❑ c. IRQ Channel, DMA Channel, I/O Address, Usage History
- ❑ d. IRQ Channel, DMA Channel, I/O Address, Memory Address

11. If the backup utility is installed in Windows 95, in which directory or subdirectory is it located?

Quick Answer: **267**
Detailed Answer: **283**

- ❑ a. `C:\`
- ❑ b. `C:\PROGRAM FILES`
- ❑ c. `C:\PROGRAM FILES\ACCESSORIES`
- ❑ d. `C:\PROGRAM FILES\ACCESSORIES\SYSTEM TOOLS`

12. The Device Manager displays a red X symbol at a device's icon when _____.

Quick Answer: **267**
Detailed Answer: **283**

- ❑ a. the device is disabled due to some type of conflict
- ❑ b. the device is experiencing a direct hardware conflict with another device
- ❑ c. the selected device is not present on the system
- ❑ d. the selected device is not operating properly and requires repair

. . . .

Quick Check

13. When comparing the thorough ScanDisk operation with the standard ScanDisk operation, _____. (Select the best answer.)

Quick Answer: **267**
Detailed Answer: **283**

❏ a. the thorough operation checks the files and folders on the drive that is specified

❏ b. the standard operation checks the disk surface on the drive that is specified

❏ c. the thorough operation checks the disk surface, files, and folders on the drive that is specified

❏ d. the standard operation checks the disk surface, files, and folders on the drive that is specified

14. The DEFRAG.EXE program is used to _____.

Quick Answer: **267**
Detailed Answer: **283**

❏ a. scan the disk's surface for bad areas

❏ b. reorganize the disk's data into contiguous sectors

❏ c. spread existing data evenly over all of the blank disk space

❏ d. divide a disk's surface into various partitions

15. _____ rearranges noncontiguous files into more-efficient contiguous files.

Quick Answer: **267**
Detailed Answer: **283**

❏ a. DEFRAG

❏ b. SCANDISK

❏ c. CHKDSK

❏ d. FDISK

16. _____ is used to find and clear lost clusters on a disk.

Quick Answer: **267**
Detailed Answer: **283**

❏ a. DEFRAG

❏ b. MWSAV

❏ c. CHKDSK

❏ d. FDISK

17. Which Windows utility can be used to make changes to the Registry in Windows 2000?

Quick Answer: **268**
Detailed Answer: **283**

❏ a. REGEDIT

❏ b. SYSEDIT

❏ c. REGEDIT32

❏ d. POLEDIT

18. What does the exclamation point (!) inside a yellow circle mean when used by the Windows Device Manager?

Quick Answer: **268**
Detailed Answer: **284**

❏ a. It indicates expandable and collapsible information branches.
❏ b. The device is experiencing a direct hardware conflict with another device.
❏ c. The device has been disabled due to a user-selection conflict.
❏ d. The device is not installed properly.

19. Where would you locate information about conflicts found in Device Manager?

Quick Answer: **268**
Detailed Answer: **284**

❏ a. Open Device Manager and then click the Resources tab
❏ b. Start/Programs/Accessories/System Tools, select System Information, and then click the Resources tab
❏ c. Start/Settings/Control Panel, double-click on System, and then click the Resources tab
❏ d. Open Device Manager and double-click on the device driver's name, and then click the Resources tab

20. Which utility is used to view real-time system performance in Windows 9x?

Quick Answer: **268**
Detailed Answer: **284**

❏ a. System Monitor
❏ b. System Information
❏ c. Computer Management
❏ d. Task Manager

21. Which utility is used to ensure that only Microsoft-approved drivers are installed on the system?

Quick Answer: **268**
Detailed Answer: **284**

❏ a. SIGVERIF.EXE
❏ b. SCANREGW.EXE
❏ c. MSINFO32.EXE
❏ d. SCF.EXE

22. Which method will *not* access the Windows 2000 Defragmentation utility?

Quick Answer: **268**
Detailed Answer: **284**

❏ a. Start/Programs/Accessories and then select Disk Defragmenter
❏ b. Start/Settings/Control Panel/Administrative Tools and then double-click Computer Management
❏ c. Start/Programs/Accessories/System Tools and then select Disk Defragmenter
❏ d. Open My Computer, right-click on the drive icon and select Properties from the contextual menu, click the Tools tab, and then the Defragment Now button

23. The _____ process will provide a more efficient and faster operation of your system.

   ❏ a. ScanDisk
   ❏ b. Defragmentation
   ❏ c. CHKDSK
   ❏ d. Backup

Quick Answer: **268**
Detailed Answer: **284**

24. Which backup methodology requires the least amount of time to perform and the most amount of effort to restore the system?

   ❏ a. Incremental
   ❏ b. Differential
   ❏ c. Full
   ❏ d. Selective

Quick Answer: **268**
Detailed Answer: **284**

25. Where is the Backup and Restore function located in Windows 9x?

   ❏ a. Start/Settings/Control Panel and then double-click the Backup tool
   ❏ b. Start/Settings/Control Panel/System and then click the Backup tab
   ❏ c. Start/Programs/Accessories/System Tools and then select Backup
   ❏ d. Start/Programs/Accessories and then select Backup

Quick Answer: **268**
Detailed Answer: **284**

26. In Windows XP, where can you find a standard set of tools for managing the systems disk drives?

   ❏ a. In the Disk Manager snap-in
   ❏ b. In the Computer Management Console
   ❏ c. In the Device Manager utility
   ❏ d. In the Task Manager utility

Quick Answer: **268**
Detailed Answer: **285**

27. In Windows 2000, what event will cause ScanDisk to run automatically?

   ❏ a. ScanDisk is not set up to run automatically
   ❏ b. At the beginning of a new week
   ❏ c. When Windows is shut down incorrectly
   ❏ d. Whenever the operating system is patched or updated

Quick Answer: **268**
Detailed Answer: **285**

28. What command can be used to repair segmented files in Windows 9x?

   ❏ a. DISKSCAN /F
   ❏ b. CHECKDSK /F
   ❏ c. SCANDISK /F
   ❏ d. CHKDSK /F

Quick Answer: **268**
Detailed Answer: **285**

. . . .

29. If the backup utility is installed in Windows 2000, it is located in which directory or subdirectory?

Quick Answer: **268**
Detailed Answer: **285**

- ❑ a. `C:\PROGRAM FILES\ACCESSORIES\SYSTEM TOOLS`
- ❑ b. `C:\WINNT\SYSTEM32`
- ❑ c. `C:\WINNT\SYSTEM`
- ❑ d. `C:\PROGRAM FILES`

30. Where can you locate the three main HDD utility programs in the Windows 9x environments?

Quick Answer: **268**
Detailed Answer: **285**

- ❑ a. Start/Programs/Accessories/Computer Management
- ❑ b. Right-click on a disk drive's icon, select Properties, and then click the Tools tab
- ❑ c. Start/Programs/System Tools
- ❑ d. Right-click on a disk drive's icon and select Tools

31. What is the Close Program dialog window now referred to in Windows XP?

Quick Answer: **268**
Detailed Answer: **285**

- ❑ a. Task List
- ❑ b. End Task
- ❑ c. Task Manager
- ❑ d. Program Administration

32. A Windows XP Professional workstation has had problems during operation lately. Which of the following applications will enable you to review conflicts and problems that have occurred over time?

Quick Answer: **268**
Detailed Answer: **285**

- ❑ a. Services and Applications
- ❑ b. Autoexec.bat
- ❑ c. Config.sys
- ❑ d. Event Viewer

33. Which of the following information cannot be obtained using the Windows XP System Information utility?

Quick Answer: **268**
Detailed Answer: **285**

- ❑ a. System summary
- ❑ b. Group policy settings
- ❑ c. I/O components in the system
- ❑ d. A description of the Windows Internet Explorer

Quick Answer: **268**
Detailed Answer: **285**

34. How do you activate the Windows XP System Restore Wizard?

   ❏   a. Navigate the Start/All Programs/Accessories/System Tools path, and then select the System Restore option from the menu.

   ❏   b. Navigate the Start/Settings/Control Panel/System path, and then select the System Restore option from the Properties tab.

   ❏   c. Navigate to the Start menu's Help and Support option, select the Performance and Maintenance option from its menu, and click the Run the System Restore Wizard option.

   ❏   d. Navigate to the Start menu's Accessories menu option, select the Performance and Maintenance option from its menu, and click the Run the System Restore Wizard option.

Quick Answer: **268**
Detailed Answer: **285**

35. Which of the following is not part of the normal System State Data backup operations performed by Windows 2000 or Windows XP?

   ❏   a. The Registry

   ❏   b. The system startup files

   ❏   c. The COM+ Class registration database

   ❏   d. The System Information database

Quick Check Answer Key

Objective 1.1

1. a
2. d
3. a
4. b
5. a
6. c
7. b
8. a, b
9. d
10. c, d
11. b
12. a, d
13. a
14. b
15. c
16. c
17. b
18. b
19. a, b
20. d
21. c
22. b
23. b
24. a
25. a
26. a, b, c
27. a
28. b
29. b
30. c
31. a
32. d
33. b
34. a
35. c
36. b
37. b
38. a
39. d
40. c
41. a
42. d
43. d
44. a
45. b
46. a
47. a
48. b
49. d
50. c
51. a
52. b
53. c

Objective 1.2

1. a
2. a
3. b
4. b
5. b
6. d
7. b
8. c
9. a, b, c
10. c
11. a
12. b, c, d
13. a
14. a, d
15. c
16. c
17. b
18. c
19. b
20. a
21. b
22. b
23. d
24. d
25. a
26. b

27. b

28. b

29. b

30. d

31. c

32. a

33. b

34. a

Objective 1.3

1. d

2. c

3. c

4. a

5. d

6. b

7. b

8. c

9. c

10. a

11. a, c

12. a

Objective 1.4

1. d

2. d

3. b

4. c

5. b

6. a

7. a

8. d

9. b

10. c

11. b

12. d

13. a, c

14. a

15. a, b

16. c

17. a

18. b, d

19. d

20. a

21. b

22. d

23. d

24. c

25. b

26. a

27. c

28. d

29. b, d

30. a, b, d

31. b

32. a, b, c

33. d

34. b

35. a, c

36. d

37. c

38. a, b

39. c

40. d

41. a

42. c

43. d

Objective 1.5

1. a

2. a, b, d

3. d

4. b

5. b

6. b

7. c

8. d

9. c

10. d

11. c

12. a

13. c

14. b

15. a

16. c

17. a

18. b

19. d

20. a

21. a

22. a

23. b

24. a

25. c

26. b

27. c

28. d

29. b

30. b

31. c

32. d

33. b

34. a

35. d

Answers and Explanations

Objective 1.1

Differentiate the characteristics of Windows 9x/Me, Windows NT 4.0 Workstation, Windows 2000 Professional, and Windows XP.

1. **a.** It creates virtual memory by swapping files between RAM and the disk drive. This memory-management technique effectively creates more total memory for the system's applications to use.

2. **d.** Software creates virtual memory by swapping files between RAM and the disk drive. This memory-management technique effectively creates more total memory for the system's applications to use. However, since there is a major transfer of information that involves the hard disk drive, an overall reduction in speed is encountered with virtual-memory operations.

3. **a.** Even though entries in the Registry can be altered through the RegEdt32 and RegEdit utilities in Windows 2000, the safest method of changing hardware settings is to change their values through the Device Manager.

4. **b.** By default, Windows Explorer does not show .SYS, .INI, or .DAT files. Nothing is wrong with the system.

5. **a.** Right-clicking on a document file will produce options that enable the user to Copy, Cut, Rename, Open, or Print the document from the Windows Explorer. This menu also provides options to Create a Shortcut for the document, or to Change its Attributes.

6. **c.** To create a new folder in Explorer, select a parent directory by highlighting it in the left window. Then click the File menu button, move the cursor to the New entry, slide across to the Folder option, and click on it. A new unnamed folder icon will appear in the right Explorer window.

7. **b.** To change file attributes from the Explorer, right-click on the desired file, select the Properties option from the pop-up list, move to the General page, and click on the desired attribute boxes.

8. **a, b.** By default, Windows Explorer does not show .SYS, .INI, or .DAT files. To see hidden and system files in Windows Explorer, click the View menu option, select the Folder Options entry, click the View tab, and check the Show All Files box.

9. **d.** In Windows 9x, directories and subdirectories are referred to, and depicted as, folders and subfolders. You can expand the contents of a folder by clicking on the (+) sign beside it. Conversely, you can contract the same folder by clicking on the minus (–) sign in the same box.

10. **c, d.** (**c**) By pressing the Alt and Tab keys together, you can quickly select one of the open applications. (**d**) The Alt+Esc key combination enables the user to cycle through open application windows.

11. **b.** The Recycle Bin is a storage area for deleted files. It enables you to retrieve such files if they are deleted by mistake. If files have been thrown out of the bin but have not been overwritten, they can be recovered using a third-party software utility for recovering deleted files.

12. **a, d.** (**a**) By pressing the Alt and Tab keys together, you can quickly select one of the open applications. (**d**) The Alt+Esc key combination enables the user to cycle through open application windows.

13. **a.** Typical Device Manager Properties pages provide tabs that can be used to access General information, device Settings, device Drivers information, and device Resources requirements and usage. The information under the tabs can be used to change the properties associated with the selected device.

14. **b.** In Windows 9x, the Device Manager can be accessed through the Start/Settings/Control Panel/System path.

15. **c.** The Windows Startup Disk tab of the Add/Remove Programs applet in the Control Panel is used to create a clean Startup disk for emergency start purposes after a crash. This disk can be used to boot the system to the command prompt (not the Windows desktop) so that you can begin troubleshooting failed startups.

16. **c.** If Windows 9x does not support the device, click the Have Disk button to load drivers supplied by the device's manufacturer.

17. **b.** The Programs submenu in the Start menu has an option, Accessories, that provides access to some of the most frequently used system tools groups. These groups include the Communications utilities, the System Tools, and the Entertainment controls. The System Tools group contains many utilities that are used to maintain and optimize the system.

18. **b.** Pressing the Tab key will cycle control between the Start menu, the Quick Launch icons, the Taskbar, and the desktop icons. This key can also be helpful in navigating the system if the mouse fails.

19. **a, b.** (**a**) The Recycle Bin icon should always be present on the desktop. It can only be removed through the Registry. If its icon is missing, one alternative is to establish a shortcut to the Recycle Bin using a new icon. (**b**) Reinstalling Windows 9x will always place the Recycle Bin on the desktop.

20. **d.** In the case of removable media such as floppy disks or removable hard drives, the Recycle Bin does not retain the files deleted from the media. When a file or folder is removed from one of these devices, the file information is deleted directly from the file system.

21. **c.** The Recycle Bin is a storage area for deleted files. It enables you to retrieve such files if they are deleted by mistake. When you delete a folder or file from the Windows system, Windows removes the first three letters of the name from the drive's FAT so that it is invisible to the system. However, the system records its presence in the Recycle Bin.

22. **b.** The large dot next to the item indicates that it is the currently selected option.

23. **b.** A check mark located next to the menu option indicates that the item is currently in use.

24. **a.** To create a new folder in Explorer, select a parent directory by highlighting it in the left window. Then click the File menu button, move the cursor to the New entry, slide across to the Folder option, and click on it. A new unnamed folder icon will appear in the right Explorer window.

25. **a.** Options that apply to the current window are displayed as dark text. Options that are not applicable to the window are grayed out.

26. **a, b**, **c.** Clicking the System icon in the Control Panel produces the System Properties window that features tabs for general information, the Device Manager, hardware profiles, and system performance. The General tab shows information about the system's ownership and registration, operating system version, and microprocessor type and RAM capacity.

27. **a.** The Alt+Esc key combination enables the user to cycle through open application windows. Pressing the Ctrl+Esc keys will pop up the Start menu. The Shift+Tab combination is used to move backward through available options. By pressing the Alt and Tab keys together, you can quickly select one of the open applications.

28. **b.** The Windows Me configuration information is held in a large hierarchical database called the Registry.

29. **b.** The Registry in Windows 95 holds information about system hardware that has been identified by the enumeration or detection processes of the Plug-and-Play system.

30. **c.** Windows 95 OSR2, also known as Windows 95b, is an upgrade of the original Windows 95 package and includes patches and fixes for version 1, along with Microsoft Internet Explorer 3.0 and Personal Web Server. It also includes an enhanced file allocation table system, referred to as FAT32.

31. **a.** The Windows 9x Core consists of three components: the Kernel, the GDI, and the USER files. The GDI controls what appears on the video display and from the printer.

32. **d.** The contents of the Windows 9x Registry can be viewed and altered through the Registry Editor (REGEDIT.EXE) utility.

33. **b.** The CURRENT_CONFIG key works with the Local_Machine branch containing current information about hardware devices.

34. **a.** The DYN_DATA key works with the branch of the LOCAL_MACHINE key that holds PnP dynamic status information for various system devices including current status and problems.

35. **c.** The USERS key contains the information about the various users that have been defined to log in to the system. The information from the CURRENT_USER key is copied into this section whenever a user logs off the system, or when the system is shut down.

36. **b.** The CURRENT USER key holds the data about the user-specific configuration settings of the system, including color, keyboard, desktop, and start settings.

37. **b.** The CLASSES_ROOT key divides the system's files into two groups by file extension type and by association. This key also holds data about icons associated with the files.

38. **a.** The startup routine locates and executes WIN.COM in the \Windows folder to load the system's operating program.

39. **d.** The Folder Options' View window is used to define how the folders and files in the selected window will be displayed onscreen. This screen also determines which types of files will be displayed. To see hidden and system files, select the View tab and click on the Show Hidden Files button.

40. **c.** Windows 2000/XP features an improved NTFS referred to as NTFS5. NTFS5 enables administrators to establish user hard disk quotas limiting the amount of hard drive space to which users can have access. It also offers enhanced system security by providing an encrypted file system, protected network protocol, and authentication standards.

41. **a.** All Windows NT versions can employ two different disk management structures. In addition to the MS-DOS FAT system, Windows NT versions offer their own proprietary Windows NT File System (NTFS). The NTFS structure is designed to provide better data security and to operate more efficiently with larger hard drives than FAT systems do.

42. **d.** An intranet is a network built on the TCP/IP protocol that belongs to a single organization. It is, in essence, a private Internet. Like the Internet, intranets are designed to share information and services but they are accessible only to the organization's members, with authorization. In an intranet system, a local Web server provides Internet applications, such as email, FTP, and Web browsing for the network without using the public telephone system.

43. **d.** To access the MS-DOS emulator in Windows 9x or Windows NT 4.0, select the Run option from the Start menu and type `command` in the Run dialog box.

44. **a.** In a Windows 2000 environment, the system's administrative tools are stored in the Computer Management console, which can be accessed through the path of Start/Settings/Control Panel/Administrative Tools/Computer Management.

45. **b.** The System key contains basic information about startup information including the device drivers loaded and which services are in use. The Last Known Good Configuration settings are stored here.

46. **a.** The Datacenter Server edition of Windows 2000 Server can handle up to 64GB of RAM and 32 processors.

47. **a.** The Advanced Server edition of Windows 2000 Server can support up to 8 symmetrical processors and up to 8GB of memory.

48. **b.** The workstation side of Windows 2000 is named Windows 2000 Professional. It is designed to be a powerful desktop for the corporate computing world and easier to set up and configure than previous Windows NT platforms.

49. **d.** A hardware or software firewall is typically employed to block unauthorized, outside users from accessing the intranet site.

50. **c.** Enterprise networks facilitate business-to-business, or business-to-customer operations. LANs connect computers together in relatively close proximity. WANs connect network members from different cities or states. Client/server networks are systems in which dependent workstations, referred to as *clients*, operate in conjunction with a dedicated master computer.

51. **a.** The members of the domain share a common directory database and are organized in levels. Every domain is identified by a unique name and is administered as a single unit having common rules and procedures.

52. **b.** The Windows NT/2000 Registries are not compatible with the Windows 9x Registries. The Windows NT/2000 Registries are organized into Headkeys, Subkeys, and Values. Both Registries contain the same HKEYs, except that no HKEY_DYN_DATA key is present in the Windows NT/2000 Registry.

53. **c.** Even though entries in the Registry can be altered through the RegEdt32 and RegEdit utilities in Windows 2000, the safest method of changing hardware settings is to change their values through the Device Manager.

Objective 1.2

1. **a.** The RDISK command can be used to create a backup copy of the Registry in the \Winnt\Repair folder.

2. **a.** When a new Windows application is installed, it can install its own .INI file at that time to store its configuration information. These files can be modified to customize, or optimize, the program's execution.

3. **b.** The MSDOS.SYS file must maintain a size in excess of 1KB.

4. **b.** Most changes to the Registry should be performed through the Wizards in the Windows NT/2000/XP Control Panels.

5. **b.** The correct order of loading for these files during the startup process is CONFIG.SYS, COMMAND.COM, and AUTOEXEC.BAT.

6. **d.** Windows 2000 creates a page file named PAGEFILE.SYS when the operating system is installed. Its default size is typically set at 1.5 times the amount of RAM installed in the system. It optimizes the system's performance by distributing the swap-file space between multiple drives.

7. **b.** The Windows 9x swap file is WIN386.SWP. Windows 9x swap files do not require contiguous drive space and can be established on compressed drives that use virtual device drivers. The size of the Windows 9x swap file is variable and is dynamically assigned.

8. **c.** The Windows 3.x operating environment was added to an underlying MS-DOS structure. It included several initialization files in the \Windows directory with a file extension of .INI. The .INI files held the system's default, or current, startup settings for various Windows components.

9. **a, b, c.** (a) The PROMPT=PG command in the AUTOEXEC.BAT file causes the active drive and directory path to be displayed on the command line. (b) The SET TEMP=C:\TEMP command found in the AUTOEXEC.BAT file sets up an area for holding data temporarily in a directory named TEMP. (c) The SMARTDRV command in the AUTOEXEC.BAT file establishes a disk cache in an area of extended memory as a storage space for information read from the hard disk drive.

10. **c.** DRIVER.SYS creates the logical drive assignments for the system's floppy drives. DISPLAY.SYS supports code-page switching for the monitor type in use by the system. ANSI.SYS supports ANSI escape-code sequences used to modify the function of the system's display and keyboard. KEYBOARD.SYS is the default keyboard definition file.

11. **a.** When executed, the HIMEM.SYS file loads the DOS extended memory driver that manages the use of extended memory installed in the system.

12. **b, c, d. (b)** The `device=c:\dos\emm386.exe 1024 ram` command in the CONFIG.SYS file provides the system's microprocessor with access to the upper memory area of RAM. **(c)** The `dos=high,umb` command in the CONFIG.SYS shifts portions of DOS from conventional memory into the high memory area and the upper memory area. **(d)** The `files=30` command in the CONFIG.SYS file establishes the number of files that MS-DOS can handle at any one time at 30.

13. **a.** There is a little-known MS-DOS system requirement that the MSDOS.SYS file must maintain a size in excess of 1KB.

14. **a, d. (a)** Windows 9x creates a folder for each user who logs on to the system. Each profile contains a USER.DAT file (the second part of the Registry), which holds the Registry information for that user. **(d)** During Windows 9x startup, the system obtains hardware configuration information from the first part of the Registry, SYSTEM.DAT.

15. **c.** During the Windows 9x startup, IO.SYS loads the WIN.COM file to control the loading and testing of the Windows 9x core components. The Windows 9x program is loaded when the startup routine locates and executes WIN.COM. This file resides in the `\Windows` folder and is responsible for loading the Windows operating system.

16. **c.** USER.DAT is a Windows 98 Registry file, which is located in the `\Windows` directory.

17. **b.** Windows 9x provides a mechanism for automatically starting programs stored in the system's Startup folder whenever the operating system starts. These programs can be bypassed for troubleshooting purposes by pressing the left Shift key during startup.

18. **c.** In the Windows 9x environment, the CONFIG.SYS and AUTOEXEC.BAT files primarily exist to maintain compatibility with applications written for earlier operating systems and environments. If neither of these files is present, the system will still start and run fine.

19. **b.** WIN.COM is responsible for loading the Windows operating system into memory.

20. **a.** The contents of the Registry are located in two files stored in the \Windows directory. These are the USER.DAT and SYSTEM.DAT files.

21. **b.** The Windows 98 system makes up to five backup copies of the Registry structure each time it successfully starts Windows. The backed-up content of the Registry is stored in the \Windows\Sysbckup directory in the form of cabinet (.CAB) files, not as .DA0 files.

22. **b.** The contents of the Registry are located in two files, USER.DAT and SYSTEM.DAT, in the \Windows directory.

23. **d.** If the BIOS does not locate a valid boot record in one of the drives indicated in the CMOS Setup utility, it will most likely produce a Non-System Disk or Disk Error message, or in older machines a No ROM BASIC Interpreter Found message. The Partition Table message is not associated with the missing MBR condition.

24. **d.** In Windows 2000 and XP, the NTUSER.DAT file for the user Richard is stored in \Documents_and_Settings\Richard.

25. **a.** Windows 9x provides a mechanism for automatically starting programs stored in the system's Startup folder whenever the operating system starts. These programs can be bypassed for troubleshooting purposes by pressing the left Shift key during startup.

26. **b.** During the Windows NT startup, the NTLDR program executes a hardware detection file called NTDETECT.COM. This file is responsible for collecting information about the system's installed hardware devices and passing it to the NTLDR program. The installed hardware devices information is later used to upgrade the Windows NT Registry files.

27. **b.** When Windows NT/2000 starts up, a special hidden file named BOOT.INI is responsible for producing the Boot Loader Menu that is displayed on the screen.

28. **b.** The NT Loader program named NTLDR guides the Windows NT/2000 boot process before the Windows NT operating system takes control.

29. **b.** BOOT.INI is a special hidden boot loader menu file used in Windows NT 4.0. NTLDR uses this text file to generate the Boot Loader Menu that is displayed on the screen.

30. **d.** IO.SYS is a Windows 9x system file that is the Windows NT equivalent of NTLDR.

31. **c.** NTBOOTDD.SYS is a driver file used in a Windows NT system if the system employs a SCSI disk drive.

32. **a.** When NTOSKRNL gains control of the system from NTLDR, it establishes parameters concerning the Windows NT/2000 paging file (PAGEFILE.SYS) to hold RAM memory swap pages.

33. **b.** In a Windows 2000 system, the system information and settings for an individual user are stored in a file called NTUSER.DAT, which is maintained in the user's own subfolder under \Documents_and_Settings.

34. **a.** The user configuration file, NTUSER.DAT, in a Windows NT 4.0 system is maintained in a username subfolder under the \WINNT\Profiles directory.

Objective 1.3

1. **d.** The ATTRIB command changes file attributes such as Read Only (+R or –R), Archive (+A or –A), System (+S or –S), and Hidden (+H or –H). The + and – signs are to add or subtract the attribute from the file.

2. **c.** The ATTRIB command is used to change file attributes from the command line.

3. **c.** To change the file's attribute to Read Only, use the ATTRIB command along with the Read Only (+R or –R) switch to add the attribute from the designated file.

4. **a.** A question mark (?) can be used as a wildcard to represent a single character in a filename or extension. Multiple question marks can be used to represent multiple characters in a filename or extension.

5. **d.** The * notation is called a wildcard and enables operations to be performed with only partial source or destination information. Using the notation *.* tells the software to perform the designated command on any file found on the disk using any filename and extension.

6. **b.** The Hidden attribute is used to define whether a file can be viewed in Windows Explorer. One of the main reasons for giving a file a Hidden attribute is to prevent it from accidentally being erased.

7. **b.** The read-only attribute used with the ATTRIB command may be used to set a file as a read-only file. Read-only attributes protect the file from accidentally being overwritten.

8. **c.** The System attribute is reserved for use by the operating system and marks the file as a system file.

9. **c.** The DIR /P version of the directory command will display the directory information on the screen one page at a time.

10. **a.** Files with .COM, .EXE, or .BAT extensions can be started directly form the command-line prompt.

11. **a, c.** To access the MS-DOS emulator in Windows 2000 or XP, you must select the Run option from the Start menu and then type the command CMD (or COMMAND) into the dialog box.

12. **a.** If the file is located on another machine that you can access across a network and is shared, you need to use the Universal Naming Convention (UNC) path to access the machine, then the shared folder, and finally the desired file (for instance, \\computername\sharename\filename).

Objective 1.4

1. **d.** Basically, Microsoft Windows FAT-based operating systems provide for two types of partitions on an HDD unit. These two types of partition are called the primary partition and the extended partition.

2. **d.** The partitioning program for MS-DOS and Windows 9x is named FDISK.

3. **b.** MS-DOS, like other consumer-based Microsoft operating systems, has provided for the primary partition and the extended partition on a hard disk drive. The extended partition can be created on any unused disk space after the primary partition has been established and properly configured. The extended partition can be subdivided into 23 logical drives (the letters of the alphabet minus a, b, and c).

4. **c.** In a Windows 98 directory system, each directory and subdirectory (including the root directory) can hold up to 512 32-byte entries that describe each of the files in them.

5. **b.** In a MS-DOS directory system, each directory and subdirectory (including the root directory) can hold up to 512 32-byte entries that describe each of the files in them.

6. **a.** Every directory on a disk is a subdirectory of the root directory. All additional directories branch out from the root directory in a tree-like fashion. Therefore, a graphical representation of the disk drive's directory organization is called a *directory tree*.

7. **a.** To more effectively manage the space on larger disks, later versions of MS-DOS divided the disk into groups of logically related sectors, called *allocation units*, or *clusters*. In a FAT-based system, the cluster is the smallest piece of manageable information.

8. **d.** To more effectively manage the space on larger disks, later versions of MS-DOS divided the disk into groups of logically related sectors, called *allocation units*, or *clusters*. In a FAT-based system, the cluster is the smallest piece of manageable information.

9. **b.** On a hard disk drive, there are normally 32 sectors set aside for the root directory. Since each disk sector can hold 16 entries, the root directory for such a disk can accommodate up to 512 entries.

10. **c.** In a FAT-based system, each directory and subdirectory (including the root directory) can hold up to 512 32-byte entries that describe each of the files in them.

11. **b.** The sectors on a FAT disk hold 512 bytes each. A single file can occupy several sectors on the disk. The operating system's disk-handling routine breaks the file into sector-sized chunks and stores it in a cluster of sectors.

12. **d.** To more effectively manage the space on larger disks, later versions of MS-DOS divided the disk into groups of logically related sectors, called *allocation units*, or *clusters*. In a FAT-based system, the cluster is the smallest piece of manageable information.

13. **a, c.** After the primary partition has been established and properly configured, an additional partition, referred to as an *extended partition*, is also permitted. However, the extended partition can be subdivided into 23 logical drives. If logical drives have been defined within it, the extended partition cannot be deleted.

14. **a.** The active partition is the logical drive to which the system will boot. The system files must be located in this partition, and the partition must be set to Active for the system to boot up from the drive.

15. **a, b.** Some special characters are not allowed in MS-DOS filenames. These are: [,], :, ;, +, =, \, /, <, >, ?, and ,.

16. **c.** Microsoft directories can hold up to 512 directory or filename entries.

17. **a.** In a FAT-based system, the extended partition can be subdivided into 23 logical drives from drive E to drive Z.

18. **b, d.** (b) The main drawback of converting FAT16 to FAT32 is that there is some possibility of data corruption and loss. (d) Depending on the application of the system, the system can actually run slower with FAT32.

19. **d.** In Windows 9x, it is possible to convert partitions created on a FAT16 drive into a FAT32 file system using the CVT.EXE utility.

20. **a.** The VFAT system replaces the SMARTDRV utility in Windows 9x with a protected-mode driver named VCACHE. Under VCACHE, the size of the cache data pool is based on the amount of free memory in the system instead of a fixed amount. The program automatically allocates blocks of free memory to caching operations as needed.

21. **b.** In Windows 9x, it is possible to convert partitions created on a FAT16 drive into a FAT32 file system using the CVT.EXE utility.

22. **d.** When long filenames are displayed in DOS systems, they are truncated (shortened) to fit the 8.3 DOS character format and identified by a tilde character (-) followed by a single-digit number.

23. **d.** In Windows 9x, long filenames of up to 255 characters can be used, so that they can be more descriptive in nature.

24. **c.** In Windows 9x, long filenames of up to 255 characters can be used, so that they can be more descriptive in nature. When these filenames are displayed in DOS systems, they are truncated (shortened) to fit the 8.3 DOS character format and identified by a tilde character (-) followed by a single-digit number.

25. **b.** Dynamic disks are physical disks created through the Windows 2000 Disk Management utility to hold dynamic volumes. There are five different types of dynamic volumes, which are simple volume, spanned volume, mirrored volume, striped volume, and RAID 5 volume.

26. **a.** In most situations, the NTFS system offers better performance and features than a FAT16 or FAT32 system. The exceptions to this occur when smaller drives are being used, other file systems are being used on the same drive, or the operating system crashes.

27. **c.** IBM OS/2 employs High Performance File System (HPFS) to manage its file system. The HPFS structure retained the FAT directory structure, but featured long filenames (up to 254 characters) and volume sizes up to 8GB. Under HPFS, the unit of management was changed to physical sectors rather than clusters.

28. **d.** The Windows 2000/XP Disk Management utility contains a Dynamic Volume Management feature with a new user interface that enables administrators to configure drives and volumes located in remote computers.

29. **b, d.** The Windows 2000 operating system supports several file-management system formats including FAT, FAT16, FAT32, CDFS, and NTFS4, along with the new improved NTFS format referred to as NTFS5.

30. **a, b, d.** The Windows 2000 operating system supports several file-management system formats including FAT, FAT16, FAT32, CDFS, and NTFS4, along with the new improved NTFS format referred to as NTFS5.

31. **b.** CDFS (Compact Disk File System) is used on CD-ROM disks.

32. **a, b, c.** The NTFS system offers more efficient drive management, support for very large drives made possible by its 64-bit clustering arrangement, increased folder- and file-security capabilities, disk quotas, disk compression, file encryption, recoverable file system capabilities, and built-in RAID support.

33. **d.** The smaller cluster size of the NTFS format makes it more efficient than FAT formats for storing smaller files. It also supports larger drives (over 1GB) much more efficiently than FAT16 or FAT32 structures.

34. **b.** The Windows 2000 NTFS system provides an Encrypted File System (EFS) utility that is the basis of storing encrypted files on NTFS volumes. After a file or folder has been encrypted, only the user who encrypted it can access it. Other users cannot open or share the file (although they can delete it).

35. **a, c.** (a) Compressed files can be marked so that they are displayed in a second color for easy identification. This is accomplished through the Folder Options setting in the Control Panel. (c) The other indication that you will have concerning a compressed or encrypted file or folder is an attribute listing when the view setting is configured to display in Web style.

36. **d.** Files and folders can be encrypted from the command line using the cipher command. Files can also be encrypted through their Properties pages in the Windows Explorer.

37. **d.** Filenames in Windows NT can be a maximum of 255-characters long, including spaces.

38. **a, b.** Windows 2000/XP filenames cannot contain the following characters: /, \, :, *, ?, ", ", <, >, and I.

39. **c.** Filenames in Windows 2000 can be up to 215-characters long, including spaces.

40. **d.** In Windows 2000 Professional, disk-management tools are stored in the Storage console, which can be accessed through the path of Control Panel/Administrative Tools/Computer Management.

41. **a.** Encryption is treated as a file attribute in Windows 2000 and Windows XP. Therefore, to encrypt a file, you simply need to access its Properties page by right-clicking on it and selecting its Properties option from the pop-up menu. Move to the Advanced screen under the General tab and click the Encrypt Contents to Secure Data check box.

42. **c.** Windows 2000 and Windows XP both feature an improved NTFS referred to as NTFS5. This NTFS version enables administrators to establish user hard disk quotas, enhanced system security, an encrypted file system, and secure network protocol and authentication standards.

43. **d.** Dynamic volumes are managed through the Windows 2000/XP Disk Management snap-in tool located under the Computer Management console. To access the Disk Manager, follow the Start/Settings/Control Panel/Administrative Tools path. Double-click the Computer Management icon and click on the Disk Management entry.

Objective 1.5

1. **a.** The Windows 2000 Computer Management console can be accessed by alt-clicking the My Computer icon and selecting the Manage option from the pop-up menu. The console includes the System Tools, Storage, and Services and Applications consoles. The Storage console provides a standard set of tools for maintaining the system's disk drives. These tools include the Disk Management tool, the Disk Defragmenter utility, and a Logical Drives utility.

2. **a, b, d.** (a) One way to access the Task Manager in Windows 2000 is to right-click the system tray and select Task Manager from the pop-up contextual menu. Then, select the application from the list on the Applications tab and press the End Task button. If prompted, press the End Task button again to confirm the selection. (b) The Ctrl+Alt+Del key combination opens the Windows Security menu screen, which offers Task Manager as an option. Select the application from the list on the Applications tab and press the End Task button. If prompted, press the End Task button again to confirm the selection. (d) Pressing Ctrl+Shift+Esc accesses the Windows 2000 Task Managers. Select the application from the list on the Applications tab and press the End Task button. If prompted, press the End Task button again to confirm the selection.

3. **d.** When an application hangs up in a Windows 2000 operating system, you can access the Task Manager window and remove it from the list of tasks.

4. **b.** The Backup utility can be accessed through the Start/Programs/Accessories/System Tools path. Select the Restore tab on the Backup Welcome screen. Supply the file and path of where the restore should come from in the dialog boxes. Click the Next button to continue with the Restore operation.

5. **b.** In a full or total backup process, the entire contents of the designated disk are backed up. This includes directory and subdirectory listings and their contents. This backup method requires the most time each day to back up, but also requires the least time to restore the system after a failure.

6. **b.** The system configuration utility is useful in controlling which programs will automatically be loaded at startup.

7. **c.** The icons for backup, ScanDisk, and defrag are located in the Programs/Accessories/System Tools path.

8. **d.** CHKDSK /F can be used to convert lost file units into files that can be investigated, and removed if necessary. In some cases, the converted file is a usable data file that can be rebuilt for use with an application.

9. **c.** The defragmentation process optimizes the operation of the disk drive by reorganizing its data into logically contiguous blocks. With data being arranged in this manner, the system does not need to reposition the drive's read/write heads as many times to read a given piece of data. Therefore, a heavily used drive becomes more efficient and faster.

10. **d.** To determine what resources the system already has in use, click the Computer icon at the top of the Device Manager display. The Computer Properties page provides ways to view and reserve system resources. Through this page, you can click radio buttons to display the system's usage of four key resources: IRQ channels, DMA channels, I/O addresses, and memory addresses.

11. **c.** The Backup and Restore utility has been included in Windows 9x systems and in Windows 2000/XP systems. This utility is not automatically installed when Windows is set up. If the user decides to install this feature, the actual Backup file (BACKUP.EXE) is placed in the c:\Program Files\Accessories directory.

12. **a.** When a red *X* appears at the device's icon, the device has been disabled due to a user-selection conflict.

13. **c.** The Standard operation checks the folders and files on the drive for errors; the Thorough operation also examines the disk's physical surface for problems besides the folders and files on the drive.

14. **b.** The defragmentation utility executes the DEFRAG.EXE program to optimize the disk drive operation by reorganizing its data into logically contiguous blocks. The system becomes more efficient and faster by eliminating the repositioning of the drive's read/write heads when reading a given piece of data.

15. **a.** The defragmentation process optimizes the operation of the disk drive by reorganizing its data into logically contiguous blocks. With data being arranged in this manner, the system does not need to reposition the drive's read/write heads as many times to read a given piece of data.

16. **c.** The CHKDSK (Check Disk) command is a command-line utility that has remained in use with Windows 3.x, 9x, NT, 2000, and XP and is used to recover (and remove, if necessary) lost allocation units from the hard drive.

17. **a.** Windows 2000 and Windows XP include two Registry editors: RegEdit and RegEdt32. Both utilities enable you to add, edit, and remove Registry entries and to perform other basic functions. However, specific functions can be performed only in one editor or the other.

18. **b.** The Device Manager will display an exclamation point (!) inside a yellow circle whenever a device is experiencing a direct hardware conflict with another device. The nature of the problem is described in the device's Properties dialog box.

19. **d.** When a device conflict is suspected, just click the offending device in the device listing in the Device Manager screen, make sure that the selected device is the current device, and then click the Resources tab in the selected device's properties screen to examine the conflicting device's list.

20. **a.** The System Monitor is used to track the performance of key system resources for both evaluation and troubleshooting purposes. If system performance is suspect but there is no clear indication of what might be slowing it down, the System Monitor can be used to determine which resource is operating at capacity, thereby limiting the performance of the system.

21. **a.** The Signature Verification Tool (SIGVERIF.EXE) is used to check files to determine whether Microsoft has signed them. It also determines whether the files have been modified since they were signed.

22. **a.** There are at least three methods to defrag a disk. You can right-click on the drive icon in My Computer, select Properties from the menu, and then click Defragment Now under the Tools tab. Another way to do it is to use the Start/Settings/Control Panel/Administrative Tools path, and then double-click Computer Management. The last method is to go through the Start/Programs/ Accessories/System Tools path, and then select Disk Defragmenter.

23. **b.** The defragmentation process optimizes the operation of the disk drive by reorganizing its data into logically contiguous blocks. With data being arranged in this manner, the system does not need to reposition the drive's read/write heads as many times to read a given piece of data. Therefore, it becomes more efficient and faster.

24. **a.** In an incremental backup operation, the system backs up those files that have been created or changed since the last backup. Restoring the system from an incremental backup requires the use of the last full backup and each incremental backup taken since then. This method requires the least amount of time to back up the system but the most amount of time to restore it.

25. **c.** The Backup and Restore utility is not automatically installed when Windows is set up. If the user decides to install this feature, the actual Backup file (BACKUP.EXE) is placed in the `c:\Program Files\Accessories` directory. Windows also creates a shortcut icon for the Backup utility in the `C:\Windows\Start Menu\Programs\Accessories\System Tools` directory.

26. **b.** The Computer Management Storage Console provides a standard set of tools for managing the system's disk drives in Windows XP.

27. **c.** By default, the command-line version of ScanDisk runs automatically during startup whenever the operating system detects that the system has not been shut down correctly.

28. **d.** Run the CHKDSK /F command periodically to recover lost allocation file units from a hard drive. In some cases, the converted file is a usable data file that can be rebuilt for use with an application. This command is often used before running a drive defragmentation program.

29. **b.** The Backup utility is located in the C:\Program Files\Accessories applet in Windows 9x and is located in C:\WINNT\SYSTEM32 in Windows NT/2000/XP.

30. **b.** The simplest way to access the HDD tools in Windows 9x is to open My Computer and right-click on the icon for the hard disk drive you want to use. Next, select the Properties option from the pop-up menu. Then, simply click on the Tools tab to gain access to the three most useful Windows HDD utilities: ScanDisk, Backup, and Defrag.

31. **c.** In Windows NT, Windows 2000, and Windows XP, the Close Program dialog window is referred to as the Task Manager. This utility can be used to determine which applications in the system are running or stopped, as well as which resources are being used. You can also determine general microprocessor and memory usage levels.

32. **d.** In Windows 2000 and Windows XP, significant events (such as system events, application events, and security events) are routinely monitored and stored. These events can be viewed through the Event Viewer utility enabling you to review conflicts and problems that have occurred over time. This tool is located under the Control Panel/Administrative Tools/Computer Management path.

33. **b.** The Windows 2000/XP System Information utility provides five subfolders of information about the system. These folders include a System Summary, a list of Hardware Resources being used, a list of I/O Components in the system, a description of the system's current Software Environment, and a description of the Windows Internet Explorer.

34. **a.** To activate the Windows XP System Restore Wizard, navigate the Start/All Programs/Accessories/System Tools path, and then select the System Restore option from the menu.

35. **d.** All of the options presented except the System Information database gets backed up in a Windows 2000/XP System State Data backup operation.

Operating System Domain 2.0: Installation, Configuration, and Upgrading

Objective 2.1: Identify the procedures for installing Windows 9x/Me, Windows NT 4.0 Workstation, Windows 2000 Professional, and Windows XP.

1. What is the minimum amount of RAM required for Windows 95?

❏ a. 32MB
❏ b. 8MB
❏ c. 16MB
❏ d. 4MB

Quick Answer: **311**
Detailed Answer: **313**

2. What are the minimum hardware requirements for installing Windows 98 onto a standard desktop PC?

❏ a. 80486DX/66 CPU, 8MB RAM, 120MB HDD space
❏ b. 80486DX/66 CPU, 16MB RAM, 170MB HDD space
❏ c. 80386DX/33 CPU, 4MB RAM, 20MB HDD space
❏ d. Pentium CPU, 16MB RAM, 225MB HDD space

Quick Answer: **311**
Detailed Answer: **313**

3. What are the minimum, recommended, and preferred amounts of memory specified to start Windows 95?

❏ a. 4MB, 8MB, 16MB
❏ b. 2MB, 4MB, 8MB
❏ c. 8MB, 16MB, 32MB
❏ d. 16MB, 32MB, 64MB

Quick Answer: **311**
Detailed Answer: **313**

4. What are the minimum, recommended, and preferred CPU specifications for running Windows 95?

Quick Answer: **311**
Detailed Answer: **313**

- ❑ a. 8088, 80286, 80386DX
- ❑ b. 80286, 80386DX, 80486DX
- ❑ c. 80386DX, 80486DX, Pentium
- ❑ d. 80486DX, Pentium, Pentium II

5. Windows 9x requires that _____ partition exist on the drive where it is being installed.

Quick Answer: **311**
Detailed Answer: **313**

- ❑ a. an NTFS
- ❑ b. a FAT16
- ❑ c. a FAT32
- ❑ d. an HPFS

6. The _____ utility is located on the Windows 2000 Installation CD and should be run on the system before installing the operating system to verify that the system's hardware is compatible with Windows 2000.

Quick Answer: **311**
Detailed Answer: **313**

- ❑ a. HCL.EXE
- ❑ b. CHECKUPGRADEONLY
- ❑ c. ACL.EXE
- ❑ d. UPGRADE.EXE

7. The minimum microprocessor listed for installing Windows 2000 Professional is _____.

Quick Answer: **311**
Detailed Answer: **313**

- ❑ a. Pentium III 233
- ❑ b. Pentium II 133
- ❑ c. Pentium 133
- ❑ d. Pentium 4 750

8. What is the file type used to store files on the Windows 9x distribution CD?

Quick Answer: **311**
Detailed Answer: **313**

- ❑ a. .ZIP
- ❑ b. .EXE
- ❑ c. .CAB
- ❑ d. .TAR

9. What is the minimum amount of RAM needed to install Windows 2000 Professional?

Quick Answer: **311**
Detailed Answer: **313**

- ❑ a. 32
- ❑ b. 64
- ❑ c. 128
- ❑ d. 256

Quick Answer: **311**
Detailed Answer: **313**

10. What type of file system should you put on a partition if you intend to dual-boot Windows 9x and Windows NT off that partition?

- ❏ a. FAT
- ❏ b. FAT32
- ❏ c. NTFS
- ❏ d. HPFS

Quick Answer: **311**
Detailed Answer: **314**

11. Which Windows 2000 Professional start file is used to start a Windows 2000 install from a 32-bit operating system?

- ❏ a. WINNT16
- ❏ b. WINNT
- ❏ c. WINNT32
- ❏ d. WIN2K

Quick Answer: **311**
Detailed Answer: **314**

12. Which command is used to start a Windows 2000 installation from a 16-bit operating system?

- ❏ a. WINNT32
- ❏ b. WIN2K
- ❏ c. WINNT16
- ❏ d. WINNT

Quick Answer: **311**
Detailed Answer: **314**

13. What are the minimum hardware requirements needed to install Windows 2000 Professional?

- ❏ a. Pentium 75 CPU, 32MB RAM, 650MB HDD space
- ❏ b. Pentium 133 CPU, 64MB RAM, 650MB HDD space
- ❏ c. Pentium 100 CPU, 64MB RAM, 650MB HDD space
- ❏ d. 80486DX/66 CPU, 32MB RAM, 650MB HDD space

Quick Answer: **311**
Detailed Answer: **314**

14. What should you do if you encounter hardware devices not listed on the Windows 2000 HCL?

- ❏ a. Devices not directly supported by the Windows 2000 HCL cannot be installed.
- ❏ b. Use a driver from a similar model from the same manufacturer in the Add New Hardware Wizard's list of supported devices.
- ❏ c. Install the device without drivers.
- ❏ d. Download appropriate drivers from the device manufacturer's Web site.

. . . .

15. What is the minimum hard disk space requirement for installing Windows XP Professional in a PC system?

- ❏ a. 2GB with 650MB of free space required
- ❏ b. 2GB with 1.5GB of free hard disk space required
- ❏ c. 2GB on a 2GB partition required
- ❏ d. 2GB with 2GB partition required

Quick Answer: **311**
Detailed Answer: **314**

16. What is the minimum amount of RAM that needs to be installed in the system to install Windows XP Professional?

- ❏ a. 128MB
- ❏ b. 32MB
- ❏ c. 64MB
- ❏ d. 256MB

Quick Answer: **311**
Detailed Answer: **314**

17. Microsoft typically releases patches in the form of updates, or in collections that include additional functionality or new device drivers, that they refer to as _____.

- ❏ a. service packs
- ❏ b. OEM patches
- ❏ c. releases
- ❏ d. updates

Quick Answer: **311**
Detailed Answer: **314**

18. Your network has an RIS server in it and you need to install multiple copies of Windows XP throughout the network. The computers in the network all have different configurations and components to deal with, so you can't efficiently perform an unattended install script for them. How does the presence of the RIS server help you conduct the installations you need to perform?

- ❏ a. You can configure the clients with RIS client software to download a Windows XP image from the Remote Installation Services (RIS) server as desired.
- ❏ b. You can configure the Remote Installation Services (RIS) server to detect the RIS client on other computers as they log onto the network and automatically conduct a Windows XP installation on them.
- ❏ c. You can configure the Remote Installation Services (RIS) server to conduct a Windows XP installation on the other network computers when requested—provided they have the RIS client installed on them.
- ❏ d. With the Remote Installation Services (RIS) server in the network, you can boot up other systems as RIS clients that can download the Windows XP image from the server.

Quick Answer: **311**
Detailed Answer: **314**

19. You are preparing to conduct a department-wide disk-cloning operation to install Windows XP. Which Windows tool is used to prepare the reference computer for cloning?
    - ❏ a. RIPrep
    - ❏ b. Unattend.exe
    - ❏ c. Sysprep
    - ❏ d. Ghost

Quick Answer: **311**
Detailed Answer: **314**

20. You are preparing to install Windows XP Professional on a computer across the network. You are working at the local computer that is the destination for the new operating system. Where should you configure the installation routine to obtain the Windows XP system files?
    - ❏ a. In the \I386 folder on the destination computer
    - ❏ b. In the \I386 folder on the distribution server
    - ❏ c. In the \Windows folder on the distribution server
    - ❏ d. In the \Windows folder on the distribution CD in the server

Quick Answer: **311**
Detailed Answer: **314**

21. What is the minimum microprocessor requirement for installing Windows XP?
    - ❏ a. Pentium 4 1GHz or compatible
    - ❏ b. Pentium II 300MHz or compatible
    - ❏ c. Pentium III 800MHz or compatible
    - ❏ d. Pentium II 233MHz or higher or compatible

Quick Answer: **311**
Detailed Answer: **315**

22. _____ speed mismatches can cause OS installation failures.
    - ❏ a. Bus
    - ❏ b. RAM
    - ❏ c. Microprocessor
    - ❏ d. Disk drive

Quick Answer: **311**
Detailed Answer: **315**

23. What should be checked before installing Windows 2000?
    - ❏ a. The hardware manufacturer's Web sites for updated device drivers
    - ❏ b. The expiration date for the operating system
    - ❏ c. The speed of the hard disk drive
    - ❏ d. Your Internet connection

Quick Answer: **311**
Detailed Answer: **315**

24. _____ partition must be located on the HDD in order to install Windows 95.
    - ❏ a. A CDFS
    - ❏ b. An NTFS
    - ❏ c. A FAT
    - ❏ d. An HPFS

Quick Answer: **311**
Detailed Answer: **315**

Objective 2.2: Identify steps to perform an operating system upgrade from Windows 9x/Me, Windows NT 4.0 Workstation, Windows 2000 Professional, and Windows XP.

1. What type of utilities can prevent Windows operating system upgrades from occurring?

   - ❏ a. Compression/archive
   - ❏ b. Encryption
   - ❏ c. Antivirus
   - ❏ d. Multiple OS loader

   Quick Answer: **311**
   Detailed Answer: **315**

2. Which of these methods can be used to upgrade a Windows 95 computer to Windows 2000? (Select all that apply.)

   - ❏ a. Open the command prompt and navigate to the CD-ROM drive, change to the I386 subdirectory, enter the command **SETUP**, and then click on Install Windows 2000.
   - ❏ b. Boot to the desktop, insert the Windows 2000 CD, and then click on Install Windows 2000.
   - ❏ c. Open the command prompt and navigate to the CD-ROM drive, change to the I386 subdirectory, and then enter the command **WINNT32**.
   - ❏ d. Open the command prompt, navigate to the CD-ROM drive, enter the command **SETUP**, and then click on Install Windows 2000.

   Quick Answer: **311**
   Detailed Answer: **315**

3. Which type of Windows XP upgrade enables the installer to specify the installation partition, installation folder, language options, and file system type to be used?

   - ❏ a. An Express upgrade
   - ❏ b. A Custom upgrade
   - ❏ c. An Interactive upgrade
   - ❏ d. A Partial upgrade

   Quick Answer: **311**
   Detailed Answer: **315**

4. You are preparing to clean install a new copy of Windows XP on a network computer in your company. However, the user wants to retain his My Documents, My Pictures, Desktop, and Favorites folders, along with his display properties, mapped network drives, network printers, browser settings, and folder options. What can you do to achieve both goals?

Quick Answer: **311**
Detailed Answer: **316**

❑   a. Access the Windows XP User State Migration Tools (USMT) to transfer the user configuration settings and files to a clean Windows XP installation without going through the upgrade process.

❑   b. Run the Windows XP Recovery Process utility to move the files to a server on the network and then reinstall them after the operating system installation has been completed.

❑   c. Run the Windows XP Automatic System Recovery (ASR) utility to move the files to a server on the network and then reinstall them after the operating system installation has been completed.

❑   d. Run the Windows XP Backup/Restore utility from NTBACKUP to move the files to a server on the network and then reinstall them after the operating system installation has been completed.

5. Which Windows operating system versions can be upgraded directly to Windows XP? (Select all that apply.)

Quick Answer: **311**
Detailed Answer: **316**

❑   a. Windows 2000 Professional
❑   b. Windows NT 4.0 Workstation
❑   c. Windows 98
❑   d. Windows NT 3.51

6. How can you find out what version of the operating system is running in Windows 9x?

Quick Answer: **311**
Detailed Answer: **316**

❑   a. Click Start, select Settings, and then click Properties.
❑   b. Right-click on the desktop and select Properties.
❑   c. Click Start, select Settings, click Control Panel, and then choose Windows Properties.
❑   d. Right-click My Computer and select Properties.

7. How can the current version of Windows be displayed? (Select all that apply.)

   ❏ a. Open Windows Explorer, click on the Help menu, and then select About Windows.

   ❏ b. Open Windows Explorer and then click on the File menu and select Properties.

   ❏ c. Right-click on My Computer and select Properties from the contextual menu.

   ❏ d. Right-click on the desktop and select Properties from the contextual menu.

Quick Answer: **311**
Detailed Answer: **316**

8. You are upgrading your Windows 98 machine to Windows 2000 Professional. You have a modem that is not on the Windows 2000 compatibility list. What should you do first?

   ❏ a. Install Windows 2000 anyway.

   ❏ b. Go to the Internet and look for the latest driver.

   ❏ c. Do not upgrade the system.

   ❏ d. Buy a new modem that is on the list.

Quick Answer: **311**
Detailed Answer: **316**

9. Which command can be used to install Windows 2000 Professional from a Windows NT 3.51 machine?

   ❏ a. `INSTALL.EXE`

   ❏ b. `WINNT.EXE`

   ❏ c. `UPGRADE.EXE`

   ❏ d. `WINNT32.EXE`

Quick Answer: **311**
Detailed Answer: **316**

10. Which command can be run from the command line of a Windows 95a machine to upgrade it to Windows 2000 Professional?

    ❏ a. `WINNT32.EXE`

    ❏ b. `WINNT.EXE`

    ❏ c. `UPGRADE.EXE`

    ❏ d. `INSTALL.EXE`

Quick Answer: **311**
Detailed Answer: **316**

11. Which file is used to install Windows 2000 from a Windows NT 4.0 machine?

    ❏ a. Winnt.exe

    ❏ b. Winnt32.exe

    ❏ c. Win.com

    ❏ d. Win.exe

Quick Answer: **311**
Detailed Answer: **316**

Objective 2.3: Identify the basic system boot sequences and boot methods installed for Windows 9x/Me, Windows NT 4.0 Workstation, Windows 2000 Professional, and Windows XP.

1. What three files, at a minimum, are required to start Windows 9x to the command prompt?

   - ❏ a. IO.SYS, MSDOS.SYS, and NTLDR
   - ❏ b. COMMAND.COM, AUTOEXEC.BAT, and CONFIG.SYS
   - ❏ c. IO.SYS, WIN.COM, and AUTOEXEC.BAT
   - ❏ d. IO.SYS, MSDOS.SYS, and COMMAND.COM

Quick Answer: **311**
Detailed Answer: **316**

2. The correct loading sequence for the following Windows NT startup files is _____.

   - ❏ a. NTLDR, NTDETECT, BOOT.INI, NTOSKRNL
   - ❏ b. NTLDR, BOOT.INI, NTDETECT, NTOSKRNL
   - ❏ c. BOOT.INI, NTDETECT, NTLDR, NTOSKRNL
   - ❏ d. NTDETECT, NTOSKRNL, NTLDR, BOOT.INI

Quick Answer: **311**
Detailed Answer: **317**

3. During startup, the memory of a computer is tested by the _____.

   - ❏ a. CPU
   - ❏ b. CMOS setup program
   - ❏ c. POSTs
   - ❏ d. Interrupt Controller

Quick Answer: **311**
Detailed Answer: **317**

4. The video BIOS _____.

   - ❏ a. replaces the system BIOS for video operations
   - ❏ b. is an extension of the system BIOS
   - ❏ c. acts independently from the system BIOS
   - ❏ d. is unaware of the system BIOS, and vice versa

Quick Answer: **311**
Detailed Answer: **317**

5. Which function key can be used to alter the MS-DOS boot process?

   - ❏ a. F5
   - ❏ b. F4
   - ❏ c. F1
   - ❏ d. F11

Quick Answer: **311**
Detailed Answer: **317**

6. Which files must be present on an MS-DOS boot disk? (Select all that apply.)

Quick Answer: **311**
Detailed Answer: **317**

- ❑ a. IO.SYS
- ❑ b. MSDOS.SYS
- ❑ c. COMMAND.COM
- ❑ d. CONFIG.SYS

7. What is the order of execution for the files involved in the MS-DOS boot process?

Quick Answer: **311**
Detailed Answer: **317**

- ❑ a. IO.SYS, MSDOS.SYS, CONFIG.SYS, AUTOEXEC.BAT, COMMAND.COM
- ❑ b. IO.SYS, MSDOS.SYS, CONFIG.SYS, COMMAND.COM, AUTOEXEC.BAT
- ❑ c. IO.SYS, MSDOS.SYS, COMMAND.COM, CONFIG.SYS, AUTOEXEC.BAT
- ❑ d. MSDOS.SYS, IO.SYS, CONFIG.SYS, COMMAND.COM, AUTOEXEC.BAT

8. What type of error message is produced when no valid MBR is found in a system?

Quick Answer: **311**
Detailed Answer: **317**

- ❑ a. Non-System Disk or Disk Error
- ❑ b. Invalid Media Type
- ❑ c. No Partition Found
- ❑ d. Disk Not Found

9. Which symptom would the POST not identify?

Quick Answer: **311**
Detailed Answer: **317**

- ❑ a. CMOS RAM
- ❑ b. Keyboard
- ❑ c. Hard drive
- ❑ d. A RAM chip that fails at high temperature

10. Which of the following is true regarding the boot sector?

Quick Answer: **311**
Detailed Answer: **317**

- ❑ a. It always contains the Master Boot Record (MBR).
- ❑ b. It contains the disk's partition table.
- ❑ c. It resides on each disk partition.
- ❑ d. It contains the root directory.

11. The old Last Known Good Hardware Configuration settings are not replaced until _____.

Quick Answer: **311**
Detailed Answer: **317**

- ❑ a. a user logs on to the system
- ❑ b. a user shuts down the operating system
- ❑ c. a user boots the operating system
- ❑ d. a user logs off the system

12. Which file is not required to boot the Windows NT 4.0 operating system?

    ❑ a. BOOT.INI

    ❑ b. NTLDR

    ❑ c. OSKRN.EXE

    ❑ d. NTDETECT.COM

Quick Answer: **311**
Detailed Answer: **317**

13. When you restart Windows 2000 using the Safe Mode with the command prompt option, which of the following files are you executing?

    ❑ a. DOSSTART.BAT

    ❑ b. CONFIG.EXE

    ❑ c. MSDOS.EXE

    ❑ d. CMD.EXE

Quick Answer: **311**
Detailed Answer: **318**

14. Which of these files does not need to be present to boot Windows NT/2000?

    ❑ a. NTLDR

    ❑ b. BOOT.INI

    ❑ c. NTDETECT.COM

    ❑ d. KERNEL.EXE

Quick Answer: **311**
Detailed Answer: **318**

15. How can a Windows 9x system be started when it will not boot normally? (Select all that apply.)

    ❑ a. F5

    ❑ b. F8

    ❑ c. `WIN /V:X`

    ❑ d. `WIN /D:N`

Quick Answer: **311**
Detailed Answer: **318**

16. What is the function key used to access the Startup menu in Windows 9x so that Safe Mode can be selected?

    ❑ a. F11

    ❑ b. F5

    ❑ c. F1

    ❑ d. F8

Quick Answer: **311**
Detailed Answer: **318**

17. When should standard Safe Mode be used?

    ❑ a. When an application will not start from the Desktop or the command line

    ❑ b. When Windows displays a Registry Failure error message

    ❑ c. When Windows does not start after the Starting Windows... message appears

    ❑ d. When Windows needs to load Real Mode drivers for a device instead of its embedded virtual drivers

Quick Answer: **311**
Detailed Answer: **318**

18. Which file must be present on the Startup disk to provide real-mode access to CD-ROM drives?
    - ❑ a. CDROM.INF
    - ❑ b. MSCDEX.COM
    - ❑ c. MSCDEX.EXE
    - ❑ d. CDROM.EXE

Quick Answer: **311**
Detailed Answer: **318**

19. Which items are loaded in Safe Mode?
    - ❑ a. BOOT.INI, CONFIG.SYS
    - ❑ b. NTDETECT, BOOT.INI, NTLDR
    - ❑ c. Standard mouse, standard keyboard, standard VGA drivers
    - ❑ d. Standard network adapter, standard mouse, standard keyboard

Quick Answer: **311**
Detailed Answer: **318**

20. To locate and install a missing or corrupt Windows 98 file from the distribution CD, use the _____.
    - ❑ a. SUBTRACT.EXE program
    - ❑ b. COMPACT.EXE program
    - ❑ c. LOCATE.EXE program
    - ❑ d. EXTRACT.EXE program

Quick Answer: **311**
Detailed Answer: **318**

21. What conditions indicate that the Step-by-Step Startup mode should be used in Windows 2000?
    - ❑ a. When an application will not start from the Desktop or the command line
    - ❑ b. When Windows does not start after the Starting Windows... message appears
    - ❑ c. When Windows stops responding after a remote network has been accessed
    - ❑ d. When Windows displays a Registry Failure error message

Quick Answer: **311**
Detailed Answer: **318**

22. What are two methods of creating an ERD in Windows 2000?
    - ❑ a. During setup
    - ❑ b. Using the Backup utility
    - ❑ c. Using the Add/Remove Programs utility
    - ❑ d. Using the Startup Disk utility

Quick Answer: **311**
Detailed Answer: **319**

23. What is the RDISK command used for in a Windows NT 4.0 system?
    - ❑ a. Restore a backup.
    - ❑ b. Create an ERD.
    - ❑ c. Restore a file system to a previous good condition.
    - ❑ d. Make a backup to a disk.

Quick Answer: **311**
Detailed Answer: **319**

24. Which command is used to create Setup disks in Windows NT 4.0?

❑   a. `WINNTCD /O`
❑   b. `WINNT /OX`
❑   c. `MAKEBT`
❑   d. `MAKEBT32`

25. What is the utility used to retrieve a file from a cabinet (.CAB) archive file located on the Windows 98 distribution CD?

❑   a. COPY
❑   b. RESTORE
❑   c. EXT
❑   d. EXPAND

26. Which file must be present on the Windows 9x Startup disk to provide CD-ROM support?

❑   a. CDFS.SYS
❑   b. CDDRVR.SYS
❑   c. MSCDDVR.EXE
❑   d. MSCDEX.EXE

27. Which of these files is included on the Windows 9x Startup disk?

❑   a. WIN.COM
❑   b. FDISK.EXE
❑   c. PAGEFILE.SYS
❑   d. NTLDR

28. What are the two methods for creating Emergency Start disks in Windows 9x?

❑   a. Select the option during installation.
❑   b. In the Add/Remove Programs Properties window, select the Startup Disk tab.
❑   c. `format a: /c`
❑   d. Right-click on the desktop and select Create System Disk.

29. What command can you use from the command line to show a listing of all the Windows 9x bootup switches?

❑   a. `WIN /HELP`
❑   b. `WIN ?`
❑   c. `WIN /?`
❑   d. `WIN /H`

30. Which of these function key commands is associated with booting to standard Safe Mode?

 □ a. F8
 □ b. Shift+F5
 □ c. F6
 □ d. F5

Quick Answer: **311**
Detailed Answer: **319**

31. Under what conditions would you select a Safe Mode Command Prompt Only option for starting a computer?

 □ a. When the system fails to start in standard Safe Mode
 □ b. When the system fails to start in Step-by-Step Confirmation mode
 □ c. When the System Recovery tool will not start Windows
 □ d. When the Emergency Repair Disk will not start Windows

Quick Answer: **311**
Detailed Answer: **319**

32. Which of these function key commands is associated with booting to the Startup menu?

 □ a. Shift+F5
 □ b. F8
 □ c. F6
 □ d. F5

Quick Answer: **311**
Detailed Answer: **319**

33. When in Safe Mode, the BOOTLOG.TXT file has to be initiated with the _____ option.

 □ a. Logged Mode
 □ b. Command Prompt
 □ c. Network Support
 □ d. Step-by-Step Confirmation

Quick Answer: **311**
Detailed Answer: **320**

34. MSCDEX.EXE assigns a logical drive letter to _____.

 □ a. the floppy drive
 □ b. the primary active partition
 □ c. an extended partition
 □ d. a CD-ROM drive

Quick Answer: **311**
Detailed Answer: **320**

35. The real-mode driver normally associated with a CD-ROM drive is _____.

 □ a. CDDRIVE.COM
 □ b. MSCDEX.EXE
 □ c. CDX.EXE
 □ d. CDROM.EXE

Quick Answer: **311**
Detailed Answer: **320**

36. Using a Windows XP Professional workstation, which of the following functions does the Recovery Console perform?

   ❑   a.   Recovers the system remotely
   ❑   b.   Copies files to the hard disk where the system files are located
   ❑   c.   Restores a computer to a previous state without losing data
   ❑   d.   Configures, optimizes, and troubleshoots the network system

Quick Answer: **311**
Detailed Answer: **320**

37. Your Windows XP system refuses to start up. You have been unable to recover the system using other methods, including Safe Mode, Last Known Good Configuration mode, and the Recovery Console. What else can be done in a Windows XP system to recover the system?

   ❑   a.   Run the Automated System Recovery (ASR) backup operation.
   ❑   b.   Run the Automated System Recovery (ASR) restore operation.
   ❑   c.   Run the Windows XP Repair Disk program (RDISK.EXE) from the command line of the ASR disk.
   ❑   d.   Run the Windows XP recovery program WINNT /ox at the command prompt.

Quick Answer: **311**
Detailed Answer: **320**

38. Under what conditions should you consider manually establishing a Restore Point? (Select all that apply.)

   ❑   a.   Whenever you can't get into Safe Mode to reconfigure the driver loading process
   ❑   b.   Before you install a new software program and it creates problems with the system that uninstalling the software does not resolve
   ❑   c.   Anytime you need to get back to a point where you know the system was functioning correctly.
   ❑   d.   Before you update a driver and it appears to cause problems with the system that rolling back the driver does not resolve

Quick Answer: **311**
Detailed Answer: **320**

Objective 2.4: Identify procedures for installing and adding a device, including loading, adding, and configuring device drivers, and required software.

1. A Windows .PIF file _____.

Quick Answer: 312
Detailed Answer: 320

  ❑ a. defines program information for Windows-based programs

  ❑ b. identifies Pure Information Files for the Windows Program Manager

  ❑ c. identifies Physical Inventory Files for the Windows Program Manager

  ❑ d. defines requirements for DOS application programs running in Windows

2. How are printer drivers installed in Windows 9x if the particular device is not listed in the standard Windows driver listings?

Quick Answer: 312
Detailed Answer: 321

  ❑ a. Locate the appropriate .INF file and select Install after right-clicking the file.

  ❑ b. Locate the appropriate .INF file and double-click the file.

  ❑ c. Install a similar driver from the manufacturer that is listed.

  ❑ d. You cannot install unlisted devices drivers.

3. Which procedure can be used for installing a network printer in Windows 9x?

Quick Answer: 312
Detailed Answer: 321

  ❑ a. Start/Settings/Printers, navigate to the remote network printer, and then right-click on it and select Install from the pop-up menu.

  ❑ b. Start/Settings/Control Panel/Printers, navigate to the remote network printer, and then right-click on it and select Install from the pop-up menu.

  ❑ c. Open Network Neighborhood, navigate to the remote network printer, and then right-click on it and select Install from the pop-up menu.

  ❑ d. Start/Run, navigate to the remote network printer, highlight it, and click the OK button.

4. What are the required features of a print server in Windows 9x?

Quick Answer: **312**
Detailed Answer: **321**

- ❑ a. Remote network computer, printer drivers preinstalled, printer settings preconfigured, access controlled by the primary domain controller
- ❑ b. Remote network computer, printer drivers preinstalled, printer settings preconfigured, printer services shared over the network
- ❑ c. Remote network computer, printer drivers preinstalled, printer settings preconfigured, printer services shared over the network, TCP/IP installed
- ❑ d. Remote network computer, printer services shared over the network

5. Which Windows 9x service loads files to memory for later printing?

Quick Answer: **312**
Detailed Answer: **321**

- ❑ a. Networking
- ❑ b. Print spooler
- ❑ c. Protected storage
- ❑ d. Printer

6. Where and how are the settings changed for a printer under the Windows 9x operating system? (Select two correct answers.)

Quick Answer: **312**
Detailed Answer: **321**

- ❑ a. Start/Settings/Printers, select the printer, click the File menu, and select Properties.
- ❑ b. Start/Run/Printers, select the printer, click the Tools menu, and select Properties.
- ❑ c. My Computer/Printers, right-click on the printer, and select Properties from the contextual menu.
- ❑ d. My Computer/Printers, select the printer, click the File menu, and select Settings.

7. What are the methods of printing documents in Windows 9x? (Select all that apply.)

Quick Answer: **312**
Detailed Answer: **321**

- ❑ a. Right-click the file and choose Print from the contextual menu.
- ❑ b. Highlight the file, click on the File menu, and select Print.
- ❑ c. Drag and drop the file onto the Printer icon.
- ❑ d. Open the file and select Print from the Edit menu.

8. Where can you access the Print Manager in Windows 9x? (Select all that apply.)

Quick Answer: **312**
Detailed Answer: **321**

- ❑ a. Start/Settings/Control Panel/Printers
- ❑ b. My Computer/Printers
- ❑ c. Start/Settings/Printers
- ❑ d. Network Neighborhood/Printers

Quick Answer: **312**
Detailed Answer: **321**

9. What utility can be used to make older Microsoft applications compatible with the Windows 9x operating system?

- ❑ a. Wincompt
- ❑ b. Mscompat
- ❑ c. Doscompt
- ❑ d. Mkcompat

Quick Answer: **312**
Detailed Answer: **322**

10. What is the function of the DOSSTART.BAT file?

- ❑ a. Serves no function in Windows
- ❑ b. Makes DOS commands available under Windows
- ❑ c. Loads virtual-mode DOS drivers
- ❑ d. Loads real-mode DOS drivers

Quick Answer: **312**
Detailed Answer: **322**

11. You are running an MS-DOS application under Windows 9x and its display has taken up the full screen. What can you do if you wish to switch to another application while this MS-DOS program is running?

- ❑ a. Alt+Tab
- ❑ b. Ctrl+Tab
- ❑ c. Ctrl+End
- ❑ d. Alt+F4

Quick Answer: **312**
Detailed Answer: **322**

12. What are the various methods of launching an application in the Windows 9x environment? (Select all that apply.)

- ❑ a. Start/Programs, select the application's entry, and then select the shortcut to the executable file.
- ❑ b. Start/Run, enter the full path and filename to the executable file, and then click the OK button.
- ❑ c. Browse to the application's folder in Windows Explorer, and then double-click the application's executable file.
- ❑ d. Browse to the application's folder in Windows Explorer, click on the executable file to highlight it, and then click the Edit menu and select the Open option.

13. You have an employee who is hearing impaired and needs visual warning messages. Where do you set these up?

Quick Answer: **312**
Detailed Answer: **322**

   ❏   a.   Under Visual Warnings in Control Panel
   ❏   b.   Under Accessibility Options in Control Panel
   ❏   c.   In Window Display Properties
   ❏   d.   Dr. Watson

14. If installed, where are those options that enable users with physical challenges to use a Windows 9x computer?

Quick Answer: **312**
Detailed Answer: **322**

   ❏   a.   Right-click on My Computer and then click the Accessibility tab.
   ❏   b.   Start/Settings/Control Panel/System and then click the Accessibility tab.
   ❏   c.   Start/Settings/Control Panel and then open the Accessibility Options utility.
   ❏   d.   Right-click on the Taskbar and select Properties from the contextual menu, and then click the Accessibility tab.

15. Where is the tool that enables you to set up an application that does not feature an automated installation utility in Windows 9x?

Quick Answer: **312**
Detailed Answer: **322**

   ❏   a.   Right-click on My Computer and select Properties from the contextual menu, and then click on the Add/Remove Programs tab.
   ❏   b.   Start/Settings/Control Panel, and then open Add/Remove Programs.
   ❏   c.   Start/Settings/Control Panel/System, and then click on the Add/Remove Programs tab.
   ❏   d.   Right-click on the desktop and select Properties from the contextual menu, and then click on the Add/Remove Programs tab.

16. What are your options for installing drivers not directly supported by the Windows 9x operating system? (Select two correct answers.)

Quick Answer: **312**
Detailed Answer: **322**

   ❏   a.   Obtain an OEM installation disk or CD for the device that has the Windows 9x drivers.
   ❏   b.   Devices not directly supported by Windows cannot be installed.
   ❏   c.   Use a driver from a similar model from the same manufacturer in the Add New Hardware Wizard's list of supported devices.
   ❏   d.   Attempt to locate the specific device in the Add New Hardware Wizard's list of supported devices.

Quick Check

17. If Plug and Play is not working for a particular device, how can the Windows 9x system be configured to use it?

Quick Answer: **312**
Detailed Answer: **322**

   ❑ a. Reboot the computer after the hardware installation has been accomplished.
   ❑ b. It can't be configured if the device is not PnP compatible.
   ❑ c. Use the manufacturer's Setup disk and perform a manual configuration.
   ❑ d. Allow the operating system to autodetect it.

18. Before installing a new piece of hardware in a Windows 2000 system, what precaution should be taken?

Quick Answer: **312**
Detailed Answer: **322**

   ❑ a. The Windows 2000 HCL should be consulted to make sure that the device is listed on it.
   ❑ b. The device's driver should be checked to ensure that it has been signed by Microsoft.
   ❑ c. The device's operating speed should be examined to make sure that it will run at Windows 2000–compatible speeds.
   ❑ d. The BIOS should be flashed to make sure that it has the latest hardware support information.

19. Where are device drivers not supplied directly from Microsoft usually located?

Quick Answer: **312**
Detailed Answer: **323**

   ❑ a. On the Windows OS installation CD
   ❑ b. On the device manufacturer's Web site
   ❑ c. At http://www.microsoft.com/downloads/search.asp
   ❑ d. At http://www.windrivers.com/

20. Since your company upgraded its machines to Windows XP, you have encountered numerous problems in which employees have loaded manufacturer's drivers for equipment that did not work in the new environment. You need to stop this from occurring. What should you do?

Quick Answer: **312**
Detailed Answer: **323**

   ❏   a. Access the Driver Signing Options page located under the Control Panel/System icon/Hardware tab/Driver Signing button to establish how the system responds when it detects an unsigned driver. Set the option to Substitute.

   ❏   b. Access the Driver Signing Options page located under the Control Panel/System icon/Hardware tab/Driver Signing button to establish how the system responds when it detects an unsigned driver. Set the option to Warn.

   ❏   c. Access the Driver Signing Options page located under the Control Panel/System icon/Hardware tab/Driver Signing button to establish how the system responds when it detects an unsigned driver. Set the option to Disable.

   ❏   d. Access the Driver Signing Options page located under the Control Panel/System icon/Hardware tab/Driver Signing button to establish how the system responds when it detects an unsigned driver. Set the option to Block.

21. What is the most common type of file that can be installed by an application that will damage the operation of another application attempting to use the same file?

Quick Answer: **312**
Detailed Answer: **323**

   ❏   a. .COM
   ❏   b. .EXE
   ❏   c. .DLL
   ❏   d. .CAB

22. Which of the following describes the process used to install a second microprocessor in a Windows XP system?

Quick Answer: **312**
Detailed Answer: **323**

   ❏   a. Access the Microprocessor applet in the Control Panel and select the Update Driver option from the menu. Then choose the driver for the new processor from the list.

   ❏   b. Access the Add New Hardware applet in the Control Panel and select the Update Driver option from the menu. Then choose the driver for the new processor from the list.

   ❏   c. Access the Device Manager and expand the Computer node. Then, right-click on the existing HAL and select the Update Driver option from the menu.

   ❏   d. Access the Windows Component utility in the Add/Remove Programs applet and highlight the Symmetrical Multiprocessing (SMP) option in the menu. The SMP Wizard will detect the new processor and load the proper SMP drivers for it.

Objective 2.5: Identify procedures necessary to optimize the operating system and major operating system subsystems.

1. Under Windows 2000, what is the name of the virtual-memory swap file?

    ❏   a.   SWAP.SYS

    ❏   b.   PAGEFILE.SYS

    ❏   c.   WIN386.SWP

    ❏   d.   WINSWAP.SWP

Quick Answer: **312**
Detailed Answer: **323**

2. What steps can be performed to optimize the operation of a system running a Windows 98 operating system? (Select two correct answers.)

    ❏   a.   Create a supplemental CD-ROM cache.

    ❏   b.   REM out unneeded items (such as SMRTDRV) in the CONFIG.SYS and AUTOEXEC.BAT files.

    ❏   c.   Establish a fixed disk cache for faster access.

    ❏   d.   Delete CONFIG.SYS and AUTOEXEC.BAT.

Quick Answer: **312**
Detailed Answer: **323**

3. The virtual-memory file in Windows 98 is _____.

    ❏   a.   WIN386.SWP

    ❏   b.   PAGEFILE.SYS

    ❏   c.   IO.SYS

    ❏   d.   AUTOEXEC.BAT

Quick Answer: **312**
Detailed Answer: **323**

4. What action does the operating system take when it runs out of available RAM?

    ❏   a.   It writes data to virtual memory.

    ❏   b.   It writes data to the hard disk drive.

    ❏   c.   It writes data to memory addresses that are not used frequently.

    ❏   d.   It writes data to cache.

Quick Answer: **312**
Detailed Answer: **323**

5. What effect can active commands in a CONFIG.SYS, AUTOEXEC.BAT, or .INI file have on the operation of an advanced Windows operating system?

    ❏   a.   It runs better with older devices.

    ❏   b.   It runs faster.

    ❏   c.   It runs better with older programs.

    ❏   d.   It runs more slowly.

Quick Answer: **312**
Detailed Answer: **323**

6. What function does the VCACHE utility perform in a
   Windows 9x system?

   Quick Answer: **312**
   Detailed Answer: **323**

   ❑   a. It creates and manages a RAM cache.
   ❑   b. It creates and manages the HMA.
   ❑   c. It creates and manages a disk cache in RAM.
   ❑   d. It creates and manages the UMB.

7. What is the virtual-memory file used by Windows
   NT/2000/XP specifically called?

   Quick Answer: **312**
   Detailed Answer: **324**

   ❑   a. Pagefile
   ❑   b. Winswp.386
   ❑   c. Swap file
   ❑   d. Winswp.XP

8. What part does the hard-disk drive play in Windows 9x
   memory management?

   Quick Answer: **312**
   Detailed Answer: **324**

   ❑   a. The swap file is located on the hard disk drive.
   ❑   b. Real memory storage is on the hard disk drive.
   ❑   c. The memory registers are located on the hard disk drive.
   ❑   d. The page file is located on the hard disk drive.

9. Where in Windows 2000/XP can you optimize the virtual-
   memory management?

   Quick Answer: **312**
   Detailed Answer: **324**

   ❑   a. Help and Support Center
   ❑   b. Programs/Accessories/System Tools
   ❑   c. System Tools/Control Panel/Advanced tab
   ❑   d. Control Panel/System

10. Which of the following can be done to enhance the efficiency
    of a Windows 9x system?

    Quick Answer: **312**
    Detailed Answer: **324**

    ❑   a. Establish a supplemental cache for the A: drive.
    ❑   b. Install a longer power supply cable.
    ❑   c. Establish a supplemental cache for the CD-ROM.
    ❑   d. Remove the power supply fan.

11. What Windows 9x/Me utility can be used to view a system's
    memory allocation so that an optimization plan can be
    designed?

    Quick Answer: **312**
    Detailed Answer: **324**

    ❑   a. Sysinfo
    ❑   b. RAMEN
    ❑   c. MEM
    ❑   d. ScanDisk

12. Which of the following utilities can be used to optimize the performance of the Windows 2000/XP system?

- ❑ a. Report
- ❑ b. Defragmenter
- ❑ c. Help
- ❑ d. Smartdrv

Quick Answer: **312**
Detailed Answer: **324**

13. Which utilities can you use to improve system performance by removing or repairing crossed-linked files that take up disk space? (Select two correct answers.)

- ❑ a. Defrag
- ❑ b. ScanDisk
- ❑ c. Check Disk
- ❑ d. Cleanup

Quick Answer: **312**
Detailed Answer: **324**

14. Which of the following will decrease VCACHE system performance in Windows Me?

- ❑ a. Smartdrv
- ❑ b. Loadhigh.exe
- ❑ c. Himem.sys
- ❑ d. ScanDisk utility

Quick Answer: **312**
Detailed Answer: **324**

15. What utility is used in Windows XP to improve performance by removing temporary files created by the operating system and Internet?

- ❑ a. ScanDisk
- ❑ b. Bootdisk
- ❑ c. Cleanup
- ❑ d. Trash Can

Quick Answer: **312**
Detailed Answer: **324**

16. What is the name of the component found in Windows 9x/Me that can be used to optimize the computer for someone who has physical challenges?

- ❑ a. Accessibility Options
- ❑ b. Physical Challenge Options
- ❑ c. Support Options
- ❑ d. Help Options

Quick Answer: **312**
Detailed Answer: **324**

17. Where in Windows XP can you find the Defragmenter utility for optimizing the hard drive?

- ❑ a. Control Panel/System Tools
- ❑ b. Administrative Tools/Computer Management Console
- ❑ c. Control Panel/Computer Management Tools
- ❑ d. Administrator Management Console

Quick Answer: **312**
Detailed Answer: **324**

Quick Check Answer Key

Objective 2.1

1. d
2. b
3. a
4. c
5. b
6. b
7. c
8. c
9. b
10. a
11. c
12. d
13. b
14. d
15. a
16. c
17. a
18. d
19. c
20. b
21. d
22. b
23. a
24. c

Objective 2.2

1. c
2. b, c, d
3. b
4. a
5. a, b, c
6. d
7. a, c
8. b
9. d
10. b
11. b

Objective 2.3

1. d
2. b
3. c
4. b
5. a
6. a, b, c
7. b
8. a
9. d
10. c
11. a
12. c
13. d
14. d

15. a, b, d
16. d
17. c
18. c
19. c
20. d
21. d
22. a, b
23. b
24. b
25. c
26. d
27. b
28. a, b
29. c
30. d
31. a
32. b
33. a
34. d
35. b
36. b
37. b
38. b, c, d

Objective 2.4

1. d
2. a
3. c
4. b
5. b
6. a, c
7. a, b, c
8. a, b, c
9. d
10. d
11. a
12. a, b, c
13. b
14. c
15. b
16. a, d
17. c
18. a
19. b
20. d
21. c
22. c

Objective 2.5

1. b
2. a, b
3. a
4. a
5. d
6. c
7. a
8. a
9. d
10. c
11. c
12. b
13. b, c
14. a
15. c
16. a
17. b

Answers and Explanations

Objective 2.1

1. **d.** The Windows 95 system must be at least an 80386DX or higher machine, operating with at least 4MB of RAM.

2. **b.** To install Windows 98, the system hardware must be at least an 80486DX/66 or higher machine, operating with at least 16MB of RAM. The system should also possess a modem, a mouse, and a 16-color VGA monitor or better. Typical installations use between 170 and 225MB of disk space.

3. **a.** The minimum RAM requirement is 4MB with 8MB being the recommended option; but 16MB, 32MB, or 64MB is preferred for running Windows 95.

4. **c.** The 80386DX is the listed minimum microprocessor for running Windows 95, and the recommended processor is the 80486DX, but the Pentium processors are actually the preferred microprocessor for running Windows 95.

5. **b.** Windows 95 must be installed in an existing FAT16 partition (that is, one formatted by an operating system, such as MS-DOS, or Windows 3.x). This prevents it from being mistakenly installed over some other type of operating system, such as Windows NT, or Novell NetWare OS.

6. **b.** Before installing Windows 2000 Professional from the CD, it is recommended that the Windows 2000 version of the checkupgradeonly be run. This file checks the system for possible hardware compatibility problems and is located on the installation CD under \i386\winnt32.

7. **c.** The minimum hardware requirements for installing Windows 2000 Professional on a PC-compatible system are 133MHz Pentium (P5 equivalent or better), 64MB RAM (4GB maximum), and 650MB or more free HDD space on a 2GB drive.

8. **c.** In addition to the necessary system files required to start the system in a minimal, real-mode condition, the Windows 98 Startup disk provides a number of diagnostic programs that are stored in the .CAB file format. They can be pulled out of the cabinets using the EXTRACT.EXE program.

9. **b.** The minimum hardware requirements for installing Windows 2000 Professional on a PC-compatible system are 133MHz Pentium (P5 equivalent or better), 64MB RAM (4GB maximum), and 650MB or more free HDD space on a 2GB drive. A VGA Monitor is also required.

10. **a.** The FAT file system is supported by both Windows 9x and Windows NT systems. Therefore, it is recommended that logical drives in a Windows 9x and Windows NT dual-boot system be formatted with the FAT system.

11. **c.** When upgrading from a 32-bit operating system, such as Windows NT 4.0 to a Windows 2000 Professional system, Winnt32.exe should be executed to start the installation.

12. **d.** In the case of upgrading to Windows 2000 Professional from 16-bit operating systems, such as Windows 3.x, the Winnt command should be used to start the installation.

13. **b.** The minimum hardware requirements for installing Windows 2000 Professional on a PC-compatible system are 133MHz Pentium (P5 equivalent or better), 64MB RAM (4GB maximum), and 650MB or more free HDD space on a 2GB drive. A VGA Monitor is also required.

14. **d.** If your system has hardware devices that are not on the Windows 2000 HCL, contact the manufacturers to determine whether they have new, updated Windows 2000 drivers for their device. Many peripheral makers post their latest drivers and product compatibility information on their Internet Web sites, so their customers can download them.

15. **a.** The minimum hardware requirement of HDD space for installing Windows XP Professional on a PC-compatible system is 2GB with 650MB of free space required, with 2GB of free hard disk space recommended. A 1.5GB partition size is required, with 2GB recommended. Additional disk space is required for installing over a network. The maximum hard disk space supported for a partition is 2TB.

16. **c.** The minimum requirement of RAM for installing Windows XP Professional on a PC-compatible system is 64MB required, with 128MB recommended. The more memory installed, the better. Maximum supported RAM is 4GB.

17. **a.** Microsoft typically releases patches in the form of updates, or in collections that include additional functionality or new device drivers, that they refer to as *service packs*.

18. **d.** Remote Installation Services (RIS) is used to conduct RIS image-based Windows XP installations across the network. This system involves establishing an RIS server in the network and then booting up systems as RIS clients that can download the image from the server. These images can be CD-based images or Remote Installation Preparation (RIPrep) images created with the Windows RIPrep Wizard.

19. **c.** The Sysprep tool is used to prepare the reference computer for cloning.

20. **b.** The installer must have access to the operating system's installation files. This primarily means the equivalent of the \I386 folder on the distribution CD. In network settings, the operating system files are placed on a distribution server and executed from the destination (receiving) computer.

21. **d.** The minimum hardware requirements for installing Windows XP Professional on a PC-compatible system include a Pentium II 233MHz or higher (or a compatible) processor required.

22. **b.** The memory speed mismatch or mixed RAM-type problem produces a Windows Protection Error message during the installation process. This error indicates that the operating system is having timing problems that originate from the RAM memory used in the system.

23. **a.** Make certain to check the Hardware Compatibility List to ensure that your hardware is compatible with Windows 2000. If the hardware is not listed, contact the hardware vendor, or check the hardware manufacturer's Web site to determine whether they support Windows 2000/XP before starting the installation.

24. **c.** Windows 9x draws from the existing FAT structure when it is being installed. Therefore, an interruption or a crash during the installation process can leave the system with no workable operating system in place. If this occurs, you must boot the system from a bootable floppy disk and reinstall Windows 9x from that point.

Objective 2.2

1. **c.** Active antivirus software might prevent Windows from being installed on a system. These utilities see the changes to the new operating system's core files as a virus activity and will work to prevent them from occurring. Any antivirus programs should be disabled prior to running Windows Setup. The program can be re-enabled after the setup process has been completed.

2. **b, c, d.** (b) Upgrading a Windows 95 computer to Windows 2000 can be accomplished by selecting the Install Windows 2000 option if the system detects the Windows 2000 Professional distribution CD in the drive. (c) When upgrading a Windows 95 computer to Windows 2000 at the command prompt, navigate to the location of the Winnt32.exe file (for example, d:\i386\), and then execute the file. (d) To upgrade a Windows 95 computer to Windows 2000, insert the Windows 2000 Professional distribution CD in the CD-ROM drive first. If the system doesn't detect the CD in the drive, start setup through the Run command.

3. **b.** There are two types of Windows XP upgrades—express and custom. An express upgrade will automatically upgrade the existing Windows installation and maintain all current settings. A custom upgrade enables the installer to specify the installation partition, installation folder, language options, and file system type to be used.

4. **a.** Windows XP has special tools called the User State Migration Tools (USMT) that administrators can use to transfer user configuration settings and files from systems running Windows 9x and NT systems to a clean Windows XP installation. This enables user information to be preserved without going through the upgrade process.

5. **a, b, c.** Computers running Windows 98, Windows Me, Windows NT Workstation 4.0 (with Service Pack 5 installed), or Windows 2000 Professional can be upgraded directly to Windows XP. However, systems running Windows 95 or Windows NT Workstation 3.51 operating systems cannot upgrade directly to XP. Instead, they must have intermediate upgrades to bring them up to a Windows version that does support direct upgrading to Windows XP.

6. **d.** In order to determine the current version of a Windows operating system running on a computer, alternate-click on the My Computer icon, select the Properties option from the pop-up menu, and select the General tab of the System Properties window.

7. **a, c.** (a) One way to get the version of Windows is to open Windows Explorer and then select About Windows in the Help menu. (c) In order to determine the current version of a Windows operating system running on a computer, alternate-click on the My Computer icon, select the Properties option from the pop-up menu, and select the General tab of the System Properties window.

8. **b.** Contact the manufacturer to determine whether it has new, updated Windows 2000 drivers for the modem. Many peripheral makers post their latest drivers and product-compatibility information on their Internet Web sites, where their customers can download them.

9. **d.** The WINNT32.EXE program is designed to run under a 32-bit operating system and will not run from the command line. It is used to initiate clean installs from Windows 9x or Windows NT to Windows 2000 or Windows XP.

10. **b.** From a 16-bit operating system, such as DOS or Windows 95a, you must run the WINNT.EXE program from the command line to initiate the installation of Windows 2000.

11. **b.** The WINNT32.EXE program is designed to run under a 32-bit operating system and will not run from the command line. It is used to initiate upgrades from Windows 9x or Windows NT to Windows 2000 or Windows XP.

Objective 2.3

1. **d.** IO.SYS, MSDOS.SYS, and COMMAND.COM are required to boot Windows 9x to the command prompt.

2. **b.** The correct order of file execution for Windows NT/2000/XP startups is: NTLDR, (mini-file), BOOT.INI, NTDETECT, NTOSKRNL.

3. **c.** During startup, the memory of a computer is tested by the POST test. In addition to the RAM and ROM memory units, the POST test also checks the operation of the microprocessor, disk drive units, the keyboard, and the video display.

4. **b.** Advanced video cards contain Video BIOS code, either in a ROM IC, or built directly into the video controller ASIC. The IBM EGA and VGA standards allow for onboard ROM that uses addresses between C0000h and C7FFFh in the reserved BIOS extension area.

5. **a.** The special function keys available during the MS-DOS Startup are F5 (also Left Shift key), to skip CONFIG.SYS and AUTOEXEC.BAT files; and F8, to proceed through the CONFIG.SYS and AUTOEXEC.BAT files one step at a time, waiting for confirmation from the user.

6. **a, b, c.** IO.SYS, MSDOS.SYS, and COMMAND.COM are the main portions of Microsoft's FAT-based operating systems and have to be present on an MS-DOS boot disk.

7. **b.** After both being moved into memory, IO.SYS runs MSDOS.SYS to load memory- and file-management functions. Afterward, IO.SYS uses CONFIG.SYS found in the root directory to reconfigure the system. COMMAND.COM, loaded by IO.SYS, then searches for AUTOEXEC.BAT in the root directory and carries out the commands listed in the file.

8. **a.** If the BIOS does not locate the Master Boot Record in one of the indicated drives, it simply displays a Non-System Disk or Disk Error, or ROM BASIC Interpreter Not Found message on the screen.

9. **d.** During the POST test, the operation of the keyboard, hard disk drive, and CMOS RAM is tested. But a RAM chip that fails at high temperature could not be detected at this stage.

10. **c.** The boot sector found on any logical disk holds information about how the disk is organized.

11. **a.** The Last Known Good Hardware Configuration mode of Windows NT startup causes the system to start up using the configuration information that it recorded the last time a user successfully logged on to the system. This configuration information is not replaced until a user actually logs on to the system.

12. **c.** There is no OSKRNL.EXE file in Windows NT.

13. **d.** When restarting Windows 2000 in Safe Mode with the command prompt, the CMD.EXE is being executed.

14. **d.** NTLDR, BOOT.INI, and NTDETECT.COM are involved in the Windows 2000 startup process. KERNEL.EXE is not one of the Windows 2000 system files.

15. **a, b, d.** (a) Pressing the F5 function key while the Starting Windows 9x message is displaying onscreen will boot the system to the Safe Mode. (b) Pressing the F8 function key while the Starting Windows 9x message is displaying onscreen will boot the system to the Step-by-Step Confirmation Mode. (d) When Windows 9x refuses to start up, a number of options are available for starting it from the command line. Starting Windows using the WIN command with a /D switch is often helpful in isolating possible areas of the operating system as problem sources. The /D:N switches start Windows in Safe with Networking Mode.

16. **d.** The Windows 9x Startup menu can be obtained on a nonstarting system by holding down the F8 function key when the Starting Windows 9x message is displaying onscreen. The menu offers several startup options including Normal, Logged, Safe, Step-by-Step Confirmation, and Command Prompt Modes.

17. **c.** Safe Mode should be used when: The system does not start after the Starting Windows message is displayed; when the system stalls repeatedly or for long periods of time; when the system cannot print to a local printer after a complete troubleshooting sequence; when the system has a video display problem; and whenever the system slows down noticeably or does not work correctly.

18. **c.** The real-mode CD-ROM driver (that is, MSCDEX.EXE) should be included in the Windows 9x Emergency Startup Disk to provide CD-ROM support for access to the utilities on the Windows distribution CD.

19. **c.** In Safe Mode, the minimal device drivers (keyboard, mouse, and standard-mode VGA drivers) are active to start the system. However, the CD-ROM drive will not be active in Safe Mode.

20. **d.** The Windows 98 Emergency Startup Disk features a new Extract command (EXT.EXE) to work with EXTRACT.EXE. The Extract command is used to pull necessary files from the cabinet (.CAB) files on the Windows 98 distribution CD.

21. **d.** A classic symptom that calls for running the Step-by-Step Confirmation startup option is when a Registry Failure error message is displayed. This mode enables you to specifically identify the Registry as the source of the problem so that it can be repaired or restored to an operating condition.

22. **a, b.** (a) The Windows 2000 Setup routine prompts you to create an ERD during the installation process. (b) The Windows 2000 ERD can be created using the Windows 2000 Backup utility that can be located through the Programs/Accessories/System Tools path.

23. **b.** The Repair Disk program (RDISK.EXE) can be used to create an ERD after Windows NT 4.0 is installed. To do so, select the Run option from the Start menu, enter the CMD command in the Run dialog box, and then type **rdisk** at the command prompt.

24. **b.** To create Setup disks under Windows NT 4.0, you must install the Windows NT distribution CD in the system and type **WINNT /ox** at the command prompt.

25. **c.** The Windows 98 Emergency Startup Disk features a new Extract command (EXT.EXE) to work with EXTRACT.EXE. The Extract command is used to pull necessary files from the cabinet (.CAB) files on the Windows 98 distribution CD.

26. **d.** The real-mode CD-ROM driver (that is, MSCDEX.EXE) should be included in the Windows 9x Emergency Startup Disk to provide CD-ROM support for access to the utilities on the Windows distribution CD.

27. **b.** In addition to creating a startup floppy disk, Windows 95 transfers a number of diagnostic files to the disk, including FDISK.EXE.

28. **a, b.** (a) During the Windows 9x setup operation, the software provides an option for creating an Emergency Startup Disk called Emergency Start disk. This option should be used for every Windows 9x installation. (b) An Emergency Start disk can be created through the Control Panel's Add/Remove Programs icon. This option is normally used to create a new Startup disk after new hardware has been installed, or when configuration information has been changed.

29. **c.** Using a question mark as a switch with the WIN command (WIN /?) shows a listing of all the switches associated with the WIN command.

30. **d.** Safe Mode can be accessed by pressing the F5 function key while the Starting Windows 9x message is displaying onscreen.

31. **a.** You normally resort to using the Command Prompt Only mode when the system fails to start in standard Safe Mode.

32. **b.** The Windows 9x Startup menu can be obtained on a nonstarting system by holding down the F8 function key when the Starting Windows 9x message is displaying onscreen.

33. **a.** The Logged option of the Windows 9x Startup menu attempts to start the system in normal mode, but keeps an error log file, BOOTLOG.TXT. This log file, which can be read with any text editor or printed out on a working system, contains the steps performed and the outcome.

34. **d.** MSCDEX.EXE is the real-mode CD-ROM driver. It assigns a logical drive letter to a CD-ROM drive.

35. **b.** MSCDEX.exe is the real-mode CD-ROM driver in Windows 95 and is one of the real-mode CD-ROM drivers in Windows 98. It should be included in the Emergency Startup Disk to provide CD-ROM support for access to the utilities on the Windows distribution CD in Safe Mode.

36. **b.** The Recovery Console can copy files from a floppy disk, CD, or another hard disk to the hard disk used for booting, enabling you to replace or remove files that might be affecting the boot process. Because of the security features in Windows 2000 and Windows XP, you are only granted limited access to certain files on the hard drive.

37. **b.** In Windows XP, the Emergency Repair Disk has been replaced by the ASR tool, which is used to back up and restore the system state information, along with all the files stored on the system volume. The ASR feature is considered to be the last resort that is used when you have been unable to recover the system using other methods, including Safe Mode, Last Known Good Configuration Mode, and the Recovery Console.

38. **b, c, d.** You should actually create a Restore Point any time you are making changes to the system that might make it unstable or that might disable it. Restore Points can be created manually as a method of preserving the current state of the operating system prior to performing management activities including (**b**) when you are installing a new software program and it creates problems with the system that uninstalling the software does not resolve, (**c**) any time you need to get back to a point where you know the system was functioning correctly, and (**d**) when you are updating a driver and it appears to cause problem with the system that rolling back the driver does not resolve.

Objective 2.4

1. **d.** A PIF file is a file created to serve as a bridge between an MS-DOS–based application and the Windows environment in older versions of Windows. These files contain information about how much memory the application requires and which system resources it needs.

2. **a.** If the printer is not recognized as a model supported by the Windows 9x driver list, OEM drivers can be installed from a device manufacturer's installation disk, which contains the OEMSETUP.INF file. After locating the appropriate .INF file, simply right-click on the file and select the Install option from the context-sensitive menu.

3. **c.** To install a network printer, access the Network Neighborhood icon on the desktop, select the remote computer's network name, right-click on the remote unit's printer name, and select the Install option. After the remote printer has been installed, the local computer can access it through the Network Neighborhood icon.

4. **b.** If the physical printer is connected to a remote computer, referred to as a print server, the remote unit must supply the printer drivers and settings to control the printer. Likewise, the print server must be set up to share the printer with the other users on the network.

5. **b.** In Windows 9x, the Print Manager function and its support components have been integrated into a single print-processing architecture called the *print spooler*. The print spooler loads files to memory for later printing. Data is only moved to the printer when it is ready. Therefore, the system is never waiting for the printer to digest data that has been sent to it.

6. **a, c.** (a) The setting changes for any printer can be made through the Printers option under the Start menu's Settings entry. Just highlight the desired printer and select its Properties entry from the File menu. (c) The settings for any printer can be changed through the My Computer icon on the desktop. Just double-click on the Printer folder, right-click on the desired printer, and select its Properties entry from the pop-up menu.

7. **a, b, c.** (a) One method to print documents in Windows 9x is to right-click on a file and select the Print option in the pop-up menu. The file can be located in either My Computer or Windows Explorer. (b) To print documents in Windows 9x, you can locate and highlight the file in Windows Explorer or My Computer, and then click on the File menu and select Print. (c) Documents can be dragged and dropped onto a printer icon in the Printers folder in the Network Neighborhood listing or on the desktop. Obviously, this option can be performed with both local and remote networked printers.

8. **a, b.** The Printers folder can be accessed from Start/Settings/Printers, My Computer/Printers, or Control Panel/Printers.

9. **d.** The Make Compatible utility establishes compatibility between the application and the operating system. This utility can be executed by typing `mkcompat.exe` in the Run dialog box.

10. **d.** When Windows is restarted in MS-DOS mode, a batch file named DOSSTART.BAT runs automatically. It is used to load real-mode DOS drivers for devices such as mice, sound cards, or joysticks.

11. **a.** If an MS-DOS application takes up the entire screen in Windows 9x, it will be necessary to press the Alt+Tab key combination to switch the screen to another application.

12. **a, b, c.** (a) To launch an application in the Windows 9x environment, you may select the Programs entry from the Start menu, click the folder where the desired application is, and then double-click its filename. (b) Another method to launch an application in the Windows 9x environment is to enter the full path- and filename of the executable file in the Run dialog box, and then click the OK button. (c) Or, to launch an application in the Windows 9x environment, browse to the application's folder in Windows Explorer, and then double-click the application's executable file.

13. **b.** Accessibility Options contains programs that modify the operations of the Windows keyboard, audio, and video output for use by those who have physical conditions that inhibit their use of the computer. When Accessibility Options is installed, the icon appears in the Control Panel.

14. **c.** When Accessibility Options is installed, the icon appears in the Control Panel. This option uses 4.6MB of disk space when it is installed.

15. **b.** Windows 9x offers the user assistance in installing new programs. The Add/Remove Programs icon under the Start/Settings/Control Panel is used to install new programs automatically.

16. **a, d.** (a) If Windows 9x does not support the device, obtain an OEM installation disk or CD for the device that has the Windows 9x drivers. It will be necessary to click the Have Disk button in the Hardware Installation Wizard window and supply the file's location to complete the installation process if the driver disk does not have an AutoStart function. (d) If the wizard does not detect the hardware, the user can attempt to locate the device in the Add New Hardware Wizard's list of supported devices.

17. **c.** If Windows 9x does not support the device, it will be necessary for the user to perform manual configurations by clicking the Have Disk button during the Hardware Installation Wizard routines to load drivers supplied by the device's manufacturer.

18. **a.** To determine what components Windows 2000 supports, it is necessary to consult the Hardware Compatibility List to make sure that the device is listed on it.

19. **b.** Contact the device's manufacturer for appropriate Windows drivers. It is a good idea to regularly check the manufacturer's Web site for updated drivers that can simply be downloaded.

20. **d.** On the Windows XP Driver Signing Options page, you can establish how the system should react when it detects an unsigned driver. The Block option will not permit any unsigned drivers to be loaded into the system.

21. **c.** .INI and .DLL are common types of files that can be installed by an application, but become a source of conflict with new software added to the system.

22. **c.** If you upgrade a system to use additional processors, or you upgrade the existing processors on a multiprocessor board, you will need to update the HAL file. Access the Device Manager and expand the Computer node. Then, right-click on the existing HAL and select the Update Driver option from the menu.

Objective 2.5

1. **b.** The Windows 2000 virtual-memory swap file, named pagefile.sys, is created when the operating system is installed to optimize the system's performance by distributing the swap-file space between multiple drives. Its default size is typically set at 1.5 times the amount of RAM installed in the system.

2. **a, b.** (**a**) Establishing a supplemental cache for the CD-ROM drive can enhance the efficiency of a Windows 98 system. (**b**) Any unneeded commands in the CONFIG.SYS and AUTOEXEC.BAT files have the potential to reduce system performance. Removing them will optimize the system performance.

3. **a.** The Windows 98 virtual-memory file is WIN386.SWP. Its size is variable and is dynamically assigned. Windows 98 swap drives do not require contiguous drive space and can be established on compressed drives that use virtual device drivers.

4. **a.** When an operating system runs out of available RAM, it shifts data to the virtual-memory swap file on the disk drive.

5. **d.** If a Windows 9x system has a CONFIG.SYS, AUTOEXEC.BAT, or .INI file that has been held over from a previous operating system, it will run more slowly because of some unneeded commands in these files. Check the CONFIG.SYS and AUTOEXEC.BAT files for SMARTDRV and any other disk cache software settings. Remove these commands from both files to improve performance. Also, remove any Share commands from the AUTOEXEC.BAT file. The SYSTEM.INI, WIN.INI, PROTOCOL.INI, CONFIG.SYS, and AUTOEXEC.BAT files can be modified through the System Editor (Sysedit) in Windows 9x.

6. **c.** The VCACHE driver establishes and controls a disk cache in an area of RAM as a storage space for information read from the hard disk drive, CD-ROM, and other drives and file operations.

7. **a.** Pagefile is the name of the virtual-memory file used by Windows NT/2000/XP specifically. The Pagefile shifts data between RAM memory and the disk in 4KB pages. This theoretically provides the operating system with a total memory space that equals the sum of the system's physical RAM and the capacity of the hard disk drive.

8. **a.** A heavily used, heavily fragmented hard drive can affect the system's virtual memory (in particular, the swap file) and produce memory shortages as well.

9. **d.** You can increase the performance of Windows 2000/XP by manipulating the size and placement of their virtual-memory swap file. Pagefile manipulation in Windows 2000/XP can be done in the Control Panel's System applet.

10. **c.** Establishing a supplemental cache for the CD-ROM drive can enhance the efficiency of a Windows 9x system.

11. **c.** The MEM utility is used to determine how much memory is actually in the system and how it is organized so that you can free up as much conventional memory as possible to optimize your system.

12. **b.** You can optimize the performance of Windows 2000/XP by defragmenting the system drives.

13. **b, c.** You can improve system performance by removing or repairing crossed-linked files that take up disk space with the Checkdisk or the ScanDisk utility.

14. **a.** The SMARTDRV function from older operating systems will inhibit dynamic VCACHE operation and slow the system down.

15. **c.** The Windows XP Cleanup utility can be used to identify optional applications and certain types of temporary files that are not required and remove them.

16. **a.** The Accessibility Options utility is used for the physically challenged and contains programs that modify the operations of the Windows keyboard, audio, and video.

17. **b.** The Windows XP Defragmenter utility is available through the Administrative Tools/Computer Management Console.

Operating System Domain 3.0: Diagnosing and Troubleshooting

Objective 3.1: Recognize and interpret the meaning of common error codes and startup messages from the boot sequence.

1. How are problems associated with the Windows NT boot sequence corrected?

   - ❑ a. Boot to the Emergency Startup Disk and run sys c:.
   - ❑ b. Restore system files from the ERD.
   - ❑ c. Copy needed files from the Windows NT distribution CD.
   - ❑ d. Boot to the Emergency Startup Disk and run restore c:.

   Quick Answer: **336**
   Detailed Answer: **337**

2. What are the effects of checking the Disable Virtual Memory setting in Windows 9x?

   - ❑ a. The mouse stops working.
   - ❑ b. The operating system runs slowly.
   - ❑ c. Applications will not start.
   - ❑ d. The operating system fails to start.

   Quick Answer: **336**
   Detailed Answer: **337**

3. You have just encountered a Bad or Missing COMMAND.COM error. How should it be corrected? (Select two correct answers.)

   - ❑ a. Boot to an Emergency Startup Disk. At the command prompt, type **format c: /s**.
   - ❑ b. Boot to an Emergency Startup Disk. At the command prompt, type **fdisk /mbr**.
   - ❑ c. Boot to an Emergency Startup Disk. At the command prompt, type **SYS C:**.
   - ❑ d. Boot to an Emergency Startup Disk. At the command prompt, type copy **a:\command.com c:\command.com**.

   Quick Answer: **336**
   Detailed Answer: **337**

Quick Check

4. Where do you go and how do you correct HIMEM.SYS errors in Windows 9x?

Quick Answer: **336**
Detailed Answer: **337**

- ❏ a. `C:\WINDOWS`; check CONFIG.SYS for the line
  `DEVICE=C:\WINDOWS\HIMEM.SYS`
- ❏ b. `C:\DOS`; check AUTOEXEC.BAT for the line
  `DEVICE=C:\DOS\HIMEM.SYS`
- ❏ c. `C:\WINDOWS`; check AUTOEXEC.BAT for the line
  `DEVICE=C:\WINDOWS\HIMEM.SYS`
- ❏ d. `C:\DOS`; check CONFIG.SYS for the line
  `DEVICE=C:\DOS\HIMEM.SYS`

5. What shortcut key is used to single-step through the bootup process?

Quick Answer: **336**
Detailed Answer: **337**

- ❏ a. F11
- ❏ b. F5
- ❏ c. F1
- ❏ d. F8

6. Which shortcut keys are used to skip normal startup operations in the Windows 95 bootup process? (Select two correct answers.)

Quick Answer: **336**
Detailed Answer: **337**

- ❏ a. F5
- ❏ b. F8
- ❏ c. F1
- ❏ d. F11

7. Which command is commonly used to repair the error Missing Command Interpreter?

Quick Answer: **336**
Detailed Answer: **337**

- ❏ a. `copy a:\command.com c:\command.com`
- ❏ b. `fdisk /mbr`
- ❏ c. `format c: /c`
- ❏ d. `command.com c:xcopy`

8. Where do you go and how do you correct HIMEM.SYS errors in MS-DOS?

Quick Answer: **336**
Detailed Answer: **337**

- ❏ a. `C:\DOS`; check CONFIG.SYS for the line
  `DEVICE=C:\DOS\HIMEM.SYS`
- ❏ b. `C:\DOS`; check AUTOEXEC.BAT for the line
  `DEVICE=C:\DOS\HIMEM.SYS`
- ❏ c. `C:\WINDOWS`; check CONFIG.SYS for the line
  `DEVICE=C:\WINDOWS\HIMEM.SYS`
- ❏ d. `C:\WINDOWS`; check AUTOEXEC.BAT for the line
  `DEVICE=C:\WINDOWS\HIMEM.SYS`

9. What action should logically be taken as the first step when a
   Disk Boot Failure error message is received during bootup?

   - ❑ a. Replace the hard disk drive.
   - ❑ b. Replace the disk drive controller.
   - ❑ c. Boot the system from a floppy and type **SYS C:**.
   - ❑ d. Replace the floppy disk drive.

10. How do you correct a problem identified by an error message
    about a particular line in a CONFIG.SYS or
    AUTOEXEC.BAT file?

    - ❑ a. Delete the CONFIG.SYS or AUTOEXEC.BAT file.
    - ❑ b. Use SYSEDIT to correct the line in the file.
    - ❑ c. At the command prompt, type **SYS C:**.
    - ❑ d. Reinstall Windows.

Objective 3.2: Recognize when to use common diagnostic utilities and tools.

1. You have a boot sector virus. Someone tells you to boot with a
   clean disk and type **FDISK /MBR**. What does this do?

   - ❑ a. This repartitions your hard drive to clear the virus.
   - ❑ b. This replaces the Master Boot Record on the hard drive,
             leaving the rest of the files intact.
   - ❑ c. Nothing—/mbr is not a valid switch.
   - ❑ d. This moves the virus to the Recycle Bin.

2. If you install a new video card in a Windows XP machine and
   the display is skewed when the system is started, what action
   should you take to gain control of the system?

   - ❑ a. Restart the system and select the Safe Mode option from the
             Advanced Options menu.
   - ❑ b. Restart the system and select the Last Known Good Hard-
             ware Configuration option from the Advanced Options menu.
   - ❑ c. Restart the system and select the Normal option from the
             Advanced Options menu
   - ❑ d. Restart the system and select the VGA mode from the
             Advanced Options menu.

3. Windows 2000 Recovery Console does all the following except
   _____.

   - ❑ a. copy files
   - ❑ b. control startup of services
   - ❑ c. format volumes
   - ❑ d. uninstall programs

Quick Check

4. When dealing with a disk operating system startup problem, which tools can be useful in isolating the cause of the problem? (Select two correct answers.)

Quick Answer: **336**
Detailed Answer: **338**

❏ a. Emergency Startup Disks
❏ b. Defragmenter
❏ c. Single-step startup procedures
❏ d. ScanDisk

5. The Emergency Repair process is designed to _____ and cannot be of assistance in repairing application or data problems.

Quick Answer: **336**
Detailed Answer: **338**

❏ a. repair the desktop configuration
❏ b. repair the file system
❏ c. repair the network configuration
❏ d. repair the operating system

6. What utility can be used to restore the Windows XP Registry from a backup if you cannot boot to a GUI?

Quick Answer: **336**
Detailed Answer: **338**

❏ a. Backup
❏ b. Regback
❏ c. Recovery Console
❏ d. ScanReg

7. Which Windows 9x utility can be used to restore backup copies of the Registry to the system?

Quick Answer: **336**
Detailed Answer: **339**

❏ a. Backup
❏ b. Restore
❏ c. ScanReg
❏ d. Regback

8. What types of problems is the MSCONFIG.EXE utility used for?

Quick Answer: **336**
Detailed Answer: **339**

❏ a. Registry configuration
❏ b. System configuration
❏ c. Network configuration
❏ d. Desktop configuration

9. Which log file is not generated automatically during the Windows startup process?

Quick Answer: **336**
Detailed Answer: **339**

❏ a. BOOTLOG.TXT
❏ b. SETUPLOG.TXT
❏ c. DETLOG.TXT
❏ d. DETCRASH.LOG

10. What is the proper path to activate the Windows XP System Restore Wizard?

Quick Answer: **336**
Detailed Answer: **339**

❏   a.   Start/All Programs/Administrative Tools/Backup
❏   b.   Start/All Programs/Administrative Tools/System Restore
❏   c.   Start/All Programs/Accessories/System Tools
❏   d.   Start/All Programs/Backup/System Restore

11. What command is used to view hidden system files?

Quick Answer: **336**
Detailed Answer: **339**

❏   a.   `attrib -r -s -h c:\*.sys`
❏   b.   `attrib +r +s +h c:\*.sys`
❏   c.   `fa -r -s -h c:\*.sys`
❏   d.   `fa +r +s +h c:\*.sys`

12. What command should be used in order to manipulate .CAB files?

Quick Answer: **336**
Detailed Answer: **339**

❏   a.   `EDIT.COM`
❏   b.   `EXTRACT.EXE`
❏   c.   `DEBUG.EXE`
❏   d.   `EXPAND.EXE`

Objective 3.3: Recognize common operational and usability problems and determine how to resolve them.

1. Give two reasons an Internet connection message would request a username and password all the time.

Quick Answer: **336**
Detailed Answer: **339**

❏   a.   The user is entering an invalid computer name.
❏   b.   The user's Internet account has been canceled.
❏   c.   The user is using Netscape Navigator instead of Internet Explorer.
❏   d.   The user is entering invalid username or password information.

2. Which Windows 9x utility can be used to close down an application that has stalled?

Quick Answer: **336**
Detailed Answer: **340**

❏   a.   Add/Remove Programs
❏   b.   Close Program
❏   c.   Task Manager
❏   d.   There isn't a utility for closing down a stalled application

· ·

3. You change the display properties on a Windows 9x machine. You can hear the machine boot up fine and know that it is working, but you have no display on the screen. What can you do to shut down the computer and enter Safe Mode without losing any data?

Quick Answer: **336**
Detailed Answer: **340**

- ❑ a. Press the Reset button on the computer.
- ❑ b. Press Ctrl+Alt+Del twice.
- ❑ c. Press Alt+F4 and then Enter.
- ❑ d. Unplug the computer from the wall outlet.

4. A user accidentally removes files from his removable drive and they don't show up in the Recycle Bin. What's the problem?

Quick Answer: **336**
Detailed Answer: **340**

- ❑ a. Files on removable disks are deleted immediately.
- ❑ b. The Recycle Bin has reached its capacity and must be emptied before anything else can be stored.
- ❑ c. The removable disk is bad.
- ❑ d. The user inserted the wrong disk when trying to retrieve the files.

5. You want to use a printer connected to another computer running Windows 9x in the network. What must that other computer have enabled to permit you to print through it?

Quick Answer: **336**
Detailed Answer: **340**

- ❑ a. Port Sharing
- ❑ b. Network Printing
- ❑ c. Print Sharing
- ❑ d. File Sharing

6. A user can look at the contents of the folder in Windows 2000 but cannot open the files or rename them. What permission do they have enabled?

Quick Answer: **336**
Detailed Answer: **340**

- ❑ a. Read
- ❑ b. List
- ❑ c. Execute
- ❑ d. Modify

7. On a Windows 2000 computer, you have forgotten the Administrator password and have not created other accounts with Administrator privileges. What should you do?

Quick Answer: **336**
Detailed Answer: **340**

- ❑ a. Reset the CMOS.
- ❑ b. Restart the computer.
- ❑ c. Reinstall Windows 2000.
- ❑ d. Reinstall the Service Pack.

8. In a networked printing operation, if a file prints directly from the local computer (print server), which of the following could prevent printing from a remote computer?

Quick Answer: **336**
Detailed Answer: **340**

    ❑ a. The printer is not set to Network mode.
    ❑ b. The local printer has a bad port.
    ❑ c. The local printer has a bad print driver.
    ❑ d. The network path setting is incorrect.

9. In Windows 9x, how do you test the print spooler if the printer won't print?

Quick Answer: **336**
Detailed Answer: **340**

    ❑ a. Use ScanDisk to check the disk integrity.
    ❑ b. Print directly to the printer port.
    ❑ c. Change the printer cable.
    ❑ d. Print from the DOS command line.

10. Which of the following is the correct network pathname?

Quick Answer: **336**
Detailed Answer: **340**

    ❑ a. \\SERVER_name\COMPUTER_name\USER_name
    ❑ b. \\COMPUTER_name\SHARE_name
    ❑ c. \\USER_name\COMPUTER_name\SHARE_name
    ❑ d. \\COMPUTER_name\USER_name\SHARE_name

11. What is a common reason for not seeing a remote printer in Windows 9x Network Neighborhood?

Quick Answer: **336**
Detailed Answer: **340**

    ❑ a. File and printer sharing not enabled
    ❑ b. Inadequate access rights
    ❑ c. Improper printer name
    ❑ d. No driver loaded

12. How is a UNC path created from a local computer to a remote printer, or a directory located on a remote computer?

Quick Answer: **336**
Detailed Answer: **341**

    ❑ a. \\Computer_name\shared_resource_name
    ❑ b. //computer_name/shared_resource_name
    ❑ c. \\shared_resource_name
    ❑ d. //shared_resource_name

13. How is the operation of the Windows 9x print spooler tested when the printer will not print?

Quick Answer: **336**
Detailed Answer: **341**

   ❑ a. Start/Settings/Printers, click on the Printer icon to highlight it, click on the File menu and select Properties, and then click on the Print Test Page button.

   ❑ b. Start/Settings/Printers, right-click on the Printer icon and select Properties, click on the Details button, select Spool Settings, and select the Print Directly to Printer option.

   ❑ c. Start/Settings/Printers, right-click on the Printer icon and select Properties, and then click on the Print Test Page button.

   ❑ d. Start/Settings/Printers, right-click on the Printer icon and select Properties, click on the Advanced tab, and then select the Print Directly to Printer option.

14. How are hidden and system files displayed in the Windows 2000 environment?

Quick Answer: **336**
Detailed Answer: **341**

   ❑ a. Start/Programs/Accessories/System Tools/Folder Options/View tab, and then select the Show Hidden Files and Folders option.

   ❑ b. Open Windows Explorer/Tools/Folder Options/View tab, and then select the Show Hidden Files and Folders option.

   ❑ c. Start/Settings/Control Panel/System/Folder Options/View tab, and then select the Show Hidden option.

   ❑ d. Open Windows Explorer/Tools/Folder Options, and then locate and select the Show Hidden Files and Folders option.

15. When applications will not start in Windows 2000, what items should be looked for? (Select all that apply.)

Quick Answer: **336**
Detailed Answer: **341**

   ❑ a. Conflicting DLL files

   ❑ b. Incorrect application properties

   ❑ c. Incompatibility with operating system

   ❑ d. Missing or corrupt Registry entries

16. What two types of deleted files do not appear in the Recycle Bin?

Quick Answer: **336**
Detailed Answer: **341**

   ❑ a. Files from removable storage devices

   ❑ b. System files

   ❑ c. Files from remote devices

   ❑ d. Hidden files

Quick Check

17. What happens when the Ctrl+Alt+Del keys are pressed twice?

❑ a. The computer shuts down.
❑ b. The computer restarts.
❑ c. The Close Program window opens.
❑ d. The currently running application will shut down.

Quick Answer: **336**
Detailed Answer: **341**

18. What methods can be used to access an MS-DOS application's properties?

❑ a. Click on the filename to highlight it and then select Properties from the Tools menu.
❑ b. Click on the filename to highlight it and then select Properties from the View menu.
❑ c. Click on the filename to highlight it and then select Properties from the Edit menu.
❑ d. Right-click on the filename and select Properties from the Contextual menu.

Quick Answer: **336**
Detailed Answer: **341**

19. Where is the Dr. Watson utility information stored in the system?

❑ a. \Program Files\Drwatson*.WLG
❑ b. \Drwatson*.WLG
❑ c. \Windows\Drwatson*.WLG
❑ d. \Windows\System\Drwatson*.WLG

Quick Answer: **336**
Detailed Answer: **341**

20. What is the function of the Dr. Watson utility?

❑ a. It detects and logs an application failure.
❑ b. It analyzes virus activity.
❑ c. It analyzes system failures.
❑ d. It detects and logs unauthorized user access.

Quick Answer: **336**
Detailed Answer: **342**

21. What are the two possible functions associated with the Alt+F4 key combination?

❑ a. Stop an application or open the Shutdown menu.
❑ b. Stop an application or restart the computer.
❑ c. Open the Close Program window or open the Shutdown menu.
❑ d. Switch the active window or open the Shutdown menu.

Quick Answer: **336**
Detailed Answer: **342**

22. How is a stalled application cleared in the Windows 9x environment?

    ❑ a. Press Ctrl+Alt+Del, select Task Manager, highlight all nonresponding applications, and click End Task.

    ❑ b. Press Ctrl+Alt+Del and close all nonresponding applications.

    ❑ c. Start/Settings/Control Panel/Add-Remove Programs, select the offending program, and then click Remove.

    ❑ d. Start/Programs/Accessories/System Tools/System Manager and close all nonresponding applications.

Quick Answer: **336**
Detailed Answer: **342**

23. Which command-line utility can be used to convert the disk drive file system from FAT to FAT32?

    ❑ a. CONVTER.EXE

    ❑ b. CONVERT.EXE

    ❑ c. CNVRT1.EXE

    ❑ d. CVT1.EXE

Quick Answer: **336**
Detailed Answer: **342**

24. How is disk drive performance optimized?

    ❑ a. Convert the file system to FAT16.

    ❑ b. Clean up to improve free disk space.

    ❑ c. Run ScanDisk.

    ❑ d. Run the Defrag utility.

Quick Answer: **336**
Detailed Answer: **342**

25. How does a Trojan virus attack a system?

    ❑ a. It appears to be a normal program.

    ❑ b. Code is added to a legitimate program.

    ❑ c. It replaces a disk's original boot-sector code.

    ❑ d. The attack occurs when a document is opened.

Quick Answer: **336**
Detailed Answer: **342**

26. Where is the Dr. Watson utility?

    ❑ a. Start/Programs/Accessories/System Tools and then select Dr. Watson.

    ❑ b. Start/Settings/Control Panel/Administrative Tools and then double-click Dr. Watson.

    ❑ c. Start/Programs/Accessories/System Tools, select System Information, and then select Dr. Watson in the Tools menu.

    ❑ d. Start/Programs/Accessories and then select Dr. Watson.

Quick Answer: **336**
Detailed Answer: **342**

27. Which Windows 9x utility can be used to monitor the operation of application packages and log any errors?

    ❑ a. Report Tool

    ❑ b. Dr. Watson

    ❑ c. Conflict Manager

    ❑ d. ScanDisk

Quick Answer: **336**
Detailed Answer: **342**

28. Which of the following are types of viruses? (Select all that apply.)

   ❑ a. Boot-sector virus

   ❑ b. File system virus

   ❑ c. Macro virus

   ❑ d. Trojan horse virus

Quick Answer: **336**
Detailed Answer: **343**

29. What type of system is more susceptible to a virus?

   ❑ a. A networked computer

   ❑ b. A standalone computer

   ❑ c. A laptop computer

   ❑ d. A personal digital assistant

Quick Answer: **336**
Detailed Answer: **343**

30. Which of the following presents the least likely cause of computer virus infections?

   ❑ a. Shareware programs

   ❑ b. Bulletin board software

   ❑ c. User-copied software

   ❑ d. Shrink-wrapped original software

Quick Answer: **336**
Detailed Answer: **343**

31. One of your applications fails to start when you click on its icon on the desktop. What action should you take to correct this problem?

   ❑ a. Right-click on the icon and open the application's Properties to check its executable filename and path information.

   ❑ b. Right-click on the desktop and select the Properties option from the pop-up menu to check for proper command syntax and path information.

   ❑ c. Move into the Control Panel and open the Add/Remove Software applet so that you can use the Add/Remove Software Wizard to repair the icon link to the application.

   ❑ d. Try to execute the application's Install file from the Windows Explorer.

Quick Answer: **336**
Detailed Answer: **343**

32. How does a macro virus attack a system?

   ❑ a. The attack occurs when an infected document is opened.

   ❑ b. It adds code to a legitimate program.

   ❑ c. It appears to be a normal program.

   ❑ d. It replaces a disk's original boot-sector code.

Quick Answer: **336**
Detailed Answer: **343**

Quick Check Answer Key

Objective 3.1

1. b
2. d
3. c, d
4. a
5. d
6. a, b
7. b
8. a
9. c
10. b

Objective 3.2

1. b
2. d
3. d
4. a, c
5. d
6. c
7. c
8. b
9. a
10. c
11. a
12. b

Objective 3.3

1. b, d
2. b
3. c
4. a
5. c
6. b
7. c
8. d
9. b
10. b
11. a
12. a
13. b
14. b
15. a, b, d
16. a, c
17. b
18. d
19. c
20. a
21. a
22. b
23. d
24. d
25. a
26. c
27. b
28. a, c, d
29. a
30. d
31. a
32. a

Answers and Explanations

Objective 3.1

1. **b.** The Emergency Repair Disk provides another troubleshooting tool that can be used when Safe Mode and the Recovery Console do not enable you to repair the system. If you have already created an ERD, you can start the system with the Windows NT Setup CD or the Setup floppy disks, and then use the ERD to restore core system files.

2. **d.** If the system locks up and does not start, the swap file might have become corrupted, or the Virtual Memory setting might have been changed to Disabled. In either case, you must reinstall Windows 9x to correct the problem.

3. **c, d.** (c) To restore COMMAND.COM, start the system using the Emergency Startup Disk. At the command prompt, type **sys c:** to copy the IO.SYS, MSDOS.SYS, and COMMAND.COM files onto the hard disk. (**d**) To restore the COMMAND.COM file from the command line, start the system from the startup disk and use the Copy command to transfer the file manually. The COMMAND.COM file's read-only, system, and hidden attributes must be removed so that it can be manipulated within the system.

4. **a.** With Windows 9x, the HIMEM.SYS statement must be present in the \WINDOWS directory and must be the correct version for the operating system to run. Use the System Editor to check the syntax and correctness of the entry in the CONFIG.SYS file. In a system that has been upgraded to Windows 9x, there can be as many as three different versions of HIMEM.SYS present.

5. **d.** F8 is used to single-step through the bootup process.

6. **a, b.** (a) F5 will boot the system to Safe Mode. (**b**) F8 will bring the system into the Startup menu.

7. **b.** The Missing Command Interpreter error can be repaired by restoring the boot record and operating system files to the hard disk. In a FAT environment, if the boot disk contains a copy of the FDISK command, you can use the FDISK /MBR command to restore the hard drive's Master Boot Record, along with its partition information.

8. **a.** The device=c:\dos\himem.sys command loads the DOS extended memory driver. This driver manages the use of extended memory installed in the system so that no two applications use the same memory locations at the same time.

9. **c.** When a Disk Boot Failure error message is received during bootup, the Master Boot Record has been lost or corrupted. Boot the system from a boot disk and check to see whether the architecture of the disk is intact. If yes, use the sys c: command to copy the IO.SYS, MSDOS.SYS, and COMMAND.COM system files from the boot disk to the hard disk drive.

10. **b.** To correct a problem identified by an error message about a particular line in a CONFIG.SYS or AUTOEXEC.BAT file, use one of the system's text editors, such as SYSEDIT, to correct the designated line in the file, reload the indicated file with a known good copy, and restart the computer.

Objective 3.2

1. **b.** In a FAT environment, if the boot disk contains a copy of the FDISK command, you can use the FDISK /MBR command to restore the hard drive's Master Boot Record, along with its partition information, and leave the rest of the files intact.

2. **d.** The VGA mode option was introduced into the Windows NT/2000/XP line expressly for the purpose of managing video driver problems. Under this option, the system starts normally except that it loads the standard Windows VGA display driver that every VGA adapter should run with.

3. **d.** You can use the Recovery Console to perform tasks such as copying files to the hard disk used for booting; controlling the startup state of services; adding, removing, and formatting volumes on the hard disk; repairing the MBR or boot sector of a hard disk or volume; and restoring the Registry. It cannot be used to uninstall programs.

4. **a, c.** When dealing with starting up a disk operating system, four tools can prove very useful to help you isolate the cause of startup problems. They are error messages and beep codes, clean boot disks (Emergency Startup Disks), single-step startup procedures, and system log files.

5. **d.** The emergency repair process is designed to repair the operating system in which you can repair the boot sector, replace the system files, and repair the startup files.

6. **c.** Every time you back up the system state data with Windows XP Backup, a copy of the Registry is placed in the \Repair\RegBack folder. By copying the entire contents of this folder or only particular files to \System32\Config, you can restore the Registry to the same condition as the last time you performed a system state data backup.

7. **c.** If a Windows 9x system fails to start up after installing some new software or hardware component, run the Registry Checker utility to return the Registry to its previous condition. Just type `ScanReg /Restore` at the MS-DOS prompt to view a list of available backup copies. Generally, the most recent version should be selected for use.

8. **b.** If a startup problem disappears when the system is started using any of the Safe Modes, use the System Configuration utility (MSCONFIG.EXE) to isolate the conflicting items. Of course, you might need to enter this command from the command line.

9. **a.** The BOOTLOG.TXT file contains the sequence of events conducted during the startup of the system. The original BOOTLOG.TXT file is created during the Windows 9x setup process. You can update the file by pressing the F8 key during startup, or by starting Windows 9x with a `WIN /b` switch. It is not updated automatically each time the system is started.

10. **c.** To activate the Windows XP System Restore Wizard, navigate the Start/All Programs/Accessories/System Tools path, and then select the System Restore option from the menu. The Welcome screen will be displayed. After you have confirmed the Restore Point, the system will conduct the rollback and the system will automatically restart.

11. **a.** The `Attribute` command can be used to verify that the hidden system files have been successfully copied to the disk (that is, `attrib -r -s -h c:\*.sys` to make them visible and to remove their read-only, system, and hidden status).

12. **b.** In addition to the necessary system files required to start the system in a minimal, real-mode condition, the Windows 98 Startup disk provides a number of diagnostic programs that are stored in the .CAB file format. The .CAB files can be pulled out of the cabinets using the EXTRACT.EXE program.

Objective 3.3

1. **b, d. (b)** Most accounts are paid for on a monthly schedule. If the account isn't paid up, the ISP might cancel the account and deny access to the user. If the user attempts to log on to the account regardless of the cancelation, he will repeatedly be asked to enter his account name and password until a predetermined number of failed attempts has been reached. **(d)** Forgetting or misspelling either the user's account name or password will result in the ISP rejecting access to the Internet. If the user attempts to log on to the account regardless of the rejection, he will repeatedly be asked to enter his account name and password until a predetermined number of failed attempts has been reached.

2. **b.** If the Windows 9x system locks up, or an application stalls, it is often possible to regain access to the Close Program dialog box by pressing the Ctrl+Alt+Del key combination. When the Close Program dialog box is onscreen, you can close the offending application and continue operating the system without rebooting.

3. **c.** If the Alt+F4 combination is pressed when no applications are active, the Windows Shut Down menu will appear on the display. This will enable you to conduct an orderly shutdown or restart of the system.

4. **a.** Files and folders deleted from a removable disk are permanently deleted. They don't show up in the Recycle Bin.

5. **c.** If you want to use a printer connected to another computer running Windows 9x in the network, the printer must be shared with the network users. The print server should appear in the Windows 9x Network Neighborhood window of the remote computer. If the local computer cannot see printers at the print server station, print sharing cannot be enabled there.

6. **b.** When users of a Windows 2000 system complain that they can see files in a folder but cannot access any of the files, they might have been assigned the List permission at the folder level. The List permission enables users to view the contents of the folder only, denying them all other permissions, including Read and Execute.

7. **c.** If you have forgotten the Administrator password and you have not created any other accounts with Administrator privileges, you must reinstall Windows 2000.

8. **d.** When printing cannot be carried out across the network, verify that the local computer and the network printer are set up for remote printing. In the Windows operating systems, this involves sharing the printer with the network users with a correct network path setting.

9. **b.** If a printer is not printing in Windows 9x, check the print spooler to see whether it causes the problem. Select the Print Directly to the Printer option in the Spool Setting dialog box through the printer's properties window. If the print job goes through, there is a spooler problem. If not, the hardware and printer driver are suspect.

10. **b.** The correct format for the UNC network printer pathname is \\computer_name\shared_device_name.

11. **a.** The local computer that the printer is connected to, referred to as the print server, should appear in the Windows 9x Network Neighborhood window of the remote computer. If the local computer cannot see files and printers at the print server station, file and print sharing may not be enabled there. Inadequate access rights will not prevent you from "seeing" the printer.

12. **a.** The correct format for the UNC network printer or directory pathname is \\computer_name\shared_resource_name, where the shared resource can be a device or a directory/file.

13. **b.** If a printer is not printing in Windows 9x, check the print spooler to see whether any particular type of error has occurred. Right-click on the printer's icon, select Properties, and then open the Details page. From this point, click on Spool Settings and select the Print Directly to the Printer option. If the print job goes through, there is a spooler problem. If the printer will not print under this setting, the printer hardware and printer driver are suspect.

14. **b.** Windows 2000, by default, does not display hidden or system files in Explorer. To see hidden or system files in Windows 2000, open the Windows Explorer, click Tools, click Folder Options, click the View tab, and then select the Show Hidden Files and Folders option.

15. **a, b, d.** (**a**) Windows 2000 retains the DLL structure. Corrupted or conflicting DLL files prevent applications from starting. (**b**) As with other GUI-based environments, Windows 2000 applications hide behind icons. The properties of each icon must correctly identify the filename and path of the application's executable file; otherwise, Windows will not be able to start it. (**d**) Most applications require Registry entries in order to run. If these entries are missing or corrupt, the application will not start.

16. **a, c.** (**a**) Files and folders deleted from removable storage devices are permanently deleted and cannot be recovered. (**c**) You cannot recover an item deleted by another user in the network. Files and folders deleted from remote devices do not appear in the Recycle Bin.

17. **a.** Pressing the Ctrl+Alt+Del key combination can activate the Close Program utility. When the Close Program dialog box is onscreen, you can restart the system by pressing Ctrl+Alt+Del again.

18. **d.** To access a DOS application's properties in Windows 9x, locate the program through My Computer or through the Windows Explorer interfaces, right-click on its filename, and select the Properties option from the pop-up menu.

19. **c.** When activated, Dr. Watson intercepts the software actions, detects the failure, identifies the application, and provides a detailed description of the failure. The information is automatically transferred to the disk drive and stored in the \Windows\Drwatson*.WLG file. You can view and print the information stored in the file from a word processor.

20. **a.** When activated, Dr. Watson intercepts the software actions, detects the failure, identifies the application, and provides a detailed description of the failure. The information is automatically transferred to the disk drive and stored in the \Windows\Drwatson*.WLG file. You can view and print the information stored in the file from a word processor.

21. **a.** Pressing Alt+F4 in an application stops the application and moves to the next active application in the task list. If the Alt+F4 combination is pressed when no applications are active, the Windows Shut Down menu will appear on the display. This will enable you to conduct an orderly shutdown or restart the system.

22. **b.** If a Windows 9x system locks up, or an application stalls, it is often possible to regain access to the Close Program dialog box by pressing the Ctrl+Alt+Del key combination. When the Close Program dialog box is onscreen, you can close the offending application and continue operating the system without rebooting.

23. **d.** If the system is running a FAT16 drive, you can free up additional space by converting it to a FAT32 drive. The command-line utility for this is CVT1.EXE.

24. **d.** A heavily used, heavily fragmented hard drive can affect the system's virtual memory and produce memory shortages as well. Run the Defrag utility to optimize the storage patterns on the drive.

25. **a.** A Trojan horse appears to be a legitimate program that might be found on any system. Trojan horse viruses are more likely to do damage by destroying files, and they can cause physical damage to disks.

26. **c.** Dr. Watson can be started through the Tools menu in the System Information screen. This option is located in the Programs/Accessories/System Tools path.

27. **b.** The main tool for isolating and correcting GPFs is the Dr. Watson utility provided in all Windows versions. As the system operates, Dr. Watson monitors the code moving through the system and logs its key events in the DRWATSON.LOG file. When a system error occurs, the log contains a listing of the events that were going on, up to the time of the failure.

28. **a, c, d.** (a) A boot-sector virus copies itself onto the boot sector of floppy and hard disks. The virus replaces the disk's original boot-sector code with its own code. This enables it to be loaded into memory before anything else is loaded. Once in memory, the virus can spread to other disks. (c) A macro virus hides in the macro programs of word processing document files. These files can be designed to load when the document is opened or when a certain key combination is entered. In addition, this type of viruse can be designed to stay resident in memory after the host program has been exited, or it might just stop working when the infected file is terminated. (d) A Trojan horse appears to be a legitimate program that might be found on any system. Trojan horse viruses are more likely to do damage by destroying files, and they can cause physical damage to disks.

29. **a.** A networked or online computer has more opportunity to contract a virus than a standalone unit because viruses can enter the unit over the network or through the modem.

30. **d.** One of the most effective ways to reduce the odds of a machine being infected by a virus is to buy shrink-wrapped original software from a reputable source.

31. **a.** When an application does not start after clicking its desktop icon, the first action you should take is to check its Properties. These properties can be accessed by right-clicking on the icon and selecting the Properties option from the pop-up menu that appears.

32. **a.** A macro virus hides in the macro programs of word processing document files. These files can be designed to load when the document is opened or when a certain key combination is entered. This type of virus can be designed to stay resident in memory after the host program has been exited, or it might just stop working when the infected file is terminated.

Operating System Domain 4.0: Networks

Objective 4.1: Identify the networking capabilities of Windows.

Given configuration parameters, configure the operating system to connect to a network.

1. Which of the following is not a valid network type?
   - ❏ a. LAN
   - ❏ b. WAN
   - ❏ c. MAN
   - ❏ d. NAN

Quick Answer: **359**
Detailed Answer: **360**

2. Which system can be classified as a RING topology?
   - ❏ a. Ethernet
   - ❏ b. ARCnet
   - ❏ c. Token Ring
   - ❏ d. Fiber-link

Quick Answer: **359**
Detailed Answer: **360**

3. Which type of network only lets its clients transmit data when they have a turn?
   - ❏ a. Ethernet
   - ❏ b. Token Ring
   - ❏ c. ARCnet
   - ❏ d. Fiber-optic

Quick Answer: **359**
Detailed Answer: **360**

4. How many computers are required to implement a true LAN?
   - ❏ a. One
   - ❏ b. Two
   - ❏ c. Three
   - ❏ d. Four

Quick Answer: **359**
Detailed Answer: **360**

5. What describes the pathway used to manually establish IP address and Subnet Mask settings in Windows 2000?

- ❏ a. Start/Settings/Network and Dial-Up Connections/desired connection/Properties/TCP/IPProperties
- ❏ b. Start/Settings/Network and Dial-Up Connections/TCP/IP adapter/Properties
- ❏ c. Start/Control Panel/TCP/IP adapter/Properties
- ❏ d. Start/Control Panel/Network and Dial-Up Connections/TCP/IP Properties

6. What describes the pathway used to manually establish IP Address and Subnet Mask settings in Windows 9x?

- ❏ a. Start/Settings/Control Panel/Network/TCP/IP Properties
- ❏ b. Start/Settings/Network/TCP/IP adapter/Properties
- ❏ c. Start/Control Panel/TCP/IP adapter/Properties
- ❏ d. Start/Control Panel/Network/TCP/IP Properties

7. What path would you follow to enable DHCP on a client workstation running Windows 9x?

- ❏ a. Start/Settings/Control Panel/Network/Client for Microsoft Networks/DHCP
- ❏ b. Start/Settings/Control Panel/System/Device Manager/Network Adapters/Properties
- ❏ c. Start/Settings/Control Panel/Network/TCP/IP Properties
- ❏ d. Start/Settings/Network and Dial-Up Connections/Connection/Properties/Internet Protocol (TCP/IP) Properties

8. You are called to a site where the user complains that he cannot access the network on his machine, which has just been upgraded to Windows 2000 Professional. When you arrive, you instantly notice that the My Network Places icon is missing from the desktop. Which of the following is the most likely cause of this condition?

- ❏ a. No network drivers were installed during the Windows 2000 installation process.
- ❏ b. There is no problem; you simply need to run the Windows 2000 Connection Wizard from the Control Panel.
- ❏ c. The computer is not networked.
- ❏ d. The icon has been dropped in the Recycle Bin by mistake and should be retrieved.

9. Which of the following protocols was designed to be used with a Novell network?

- ❑ a. TCP/IP
- ❑ b. IrLAN
- ❑ c. IPX/SPX
- ❑ d. NetBEUI

Quick Answer: **359**
Detailed Answer: **360**

10. Windows 9x includes what type of networking as its default?

- ❑ a. Peer-to-peer
- ❑ b. Client/server
- ❑ c. Token Ring
- ❑ d. Ethernet

Quick Answer: **359**
Detailed Answer: **360**

11. A customer is trying to dial into his LAN network; he can connect but cannot browse the network. What is the most likely cause of this problem?

- ❑ a. NetBEUI is not installed.
- ❑ b. PPP is not set up correctly.
- ❑ c. There is no Master Browser computer set up on the network.
- ❑ d. There are two Master Browser computers set up on the network.

Quick Answer: **359**
Detailed Answer: **361**

12. Which of the following is not a valid computer name for a Windows 2000 computer using a TCP/IP network?

- ❑ a. Production-John-Smith
- ❑ b. Station-0451
- ❑ c. Z
- ❑ d. John Smith 0451

Quick Answer: **359**
Detailed Answer: **361**

13. In a Windows 98 network, which items can be set through the Network icon in Control Panel? (Select all that apply.)

- ❑ a. Protocols
- ❑ b. Adapters
- ❑ c. Modem properties
- ❑ d. Clients

Quick Answer: **359**
Detailed Answer: **361**

14. _____ is required to navigate a local area network when using a RAS dial-up connection.

- ❑ a. IPX
- ❑ b. NetBEUI
- ❑ c. TCP/IP
- ❑ d. PPP

Quick Answer: **359**
Detailed Answer: **361**

15. What type of network operating system does NetBEUI belong to?

Quick Answer: **359**
Detailed Answer: **361**

   ❑   a. Internet
   ❑   b. NetWare
   ❑   c. Windows
   ❑   d. Intranet

16. Where can the TCP/IP protocol be manually installed in Windows 9x?

Quick Answer: **359**
Detailed Answer: **361**

   ❑   a. In the Network Component Type screen through the Dial-Up Connections page
   ❑   b. In the Select Network Component Type screen through the Network Configuration page
   ❑   c. In the Protocol Installation Screen through the Local Area Connection page
   ❑   d. In the Protocol screen of the Network Configuration page protocol

17. Which of the following will not cause a mapped drive to disappear from a system when it is shut down and restarted?

Quick Answer: **359**
Detailed Answer: **361**

   ❑   a. The mapped folder is no longer shared.
   ❑   b. The name of the mapped folder has been changed.
   ❑   c. The path to the mapped folder has changed.
   ❑   d. The host computer for the mapped folder is turned off.

18. How is the UNC format applied to shared resources?

Quick Answer: **359**
Detailed Answer: **361**

   ❑   a. //shared_resource_name
   ❑   b. //host_name/shared_resource_name
   ❑   c. \\shared_resource_name
   ❑   d. \\host_name\drive_path\shared_resource_name

19. Which of the following is a valid computer name for a Windows 9x workstation connected to a LAN?

Quick Answer: **359**
Detailed Answer: **361**

   ❑   a. MY COMPUTER
   ❑   b. THERECANBEONLYONE
   ❑   c. H-1-T-H-3-R-3
   ❑   d. TERMINAL 4

20. What are the specifications for setting up computer names in Windows 2000?

Quick Answer: **359**
Detailed Answer: **362**

   ❑   a. Up to 255 characters, A to Z, 0 to 9, hyphens, no spaces
   ❑   b. Up to 15 characters, A to Z, 0 to 9, hyphens, no spaces
   ❑   c. Up to 63 characters, A to Z, 0 to 9, hyphens, no spaces
   ❑   d. Up to 256 characters, A to Z, 0 to 9, hyphens, no spaces

21. What does the DOS command SHARE.EXE do?

   ❏ a. Enables file sharing over a network

   ❏ b. Allows multiple users to access a network printer

   ❏ c. Allows multiple users to log in to a single workstation

   ❏ d. Allows multiple users to share the same Internet connection

Quick Answer: **359**
Detailed Answer: **362**

22. Where would you go in a Windows 2000 system to establish parameters for local and wide area networking?

   ❏ a. Network Neighborhood

   ❏ b. Network and Dial-Up Connections

   ❏ c. My Network Places

   ❏ d. Network Control Panel

Quick Answer: **359**
Detailed Answer: **362**

23. How can you access the Add Printer Wizard in Windows 2000? (Select all that apply.)

   ❏ a. Start/Settings/Printers and then click the Add Printer icon

   ❏ b. Start/Programs/Accessories/Windows Explorer/Printers and then click the Add Printer icon

   ❏ c. Double-click My Network Places on the desktop, and then double-click Computers Near Me

   ❏ d. Control Panel/Printers and then click the Add Printer icon

Quick Answer: **359**
Detailed Answer: **362**

24. Which network items can be set through the Windows 2000 Network and Dial-up Connections applet's Local Area Connection properties? (Select all that apply.)

   ❏ a. Adding the DNS service

   ❏ b. Configuring network protocols

   ❏ c. Configuring network adapter cards

   ❏ d. Enabling the TCP/IP troubleshooting tools

Quick Answer: **359**
Detailed Answer: **362**

25. A graphical object that acts as a link to a share point on a remote unit is called _____.

   ❏ a. a sprite

   ❏ b. a window

   ❏ c. an alias

   ❏ d. an access port

Quick Answer: **359**
Detailed Answer: **362**

26. A _____ is an existing shared resource located on a remote system.

   ❏ a. remote service

   ❏ b. network service

   ❏ c. network share

   ❏ d. remote device

Quick Answer: **359**
Detailed Answer: **362**

Quick Check ✓

27. For Windows XP, the Local Connections properties window offers two tabs not available in the Windows 2000 version. What are the two tabs called?

   ❑ a. Advanced and Authentication
   ❑ b. Authentication and Encryption
   ❑ c. Advanced and Encryption
   ❑ d. General and Advanced

Quick Answer: **359**
Detailed Answer: **362**

28. You are installing a Windows XP Professional computer in a network environment that includes Novell NetWare servers. What action do you need to perform to make it possible for the Windows XP machine to communicate with those servers?

   ❑ a. Install the NetWare for Windows protocol on the client.
   ❑ b. Install the Client Service for NetWare (CSNW) option on the client.
   ❑ c. Install the Client Service for NetWare (CSNW) option on the servers.
   ❑ d. Install the Windows XP Universal Communications Protocol on the client.

Quick Answer: **359**
Detailed Answer: **362**

29. You have purchased a new copy of Windows XP Professional because it offers an onboard firewall feature that you want to use for Internet access on your home network. Where is the Windows XP firewall utility located?

   ❑ a. The Network and Dial-Up Connections/Advanced Settings button
   ❑ b. The Network and Dial-Up Connections/Advanced tab
   ❑ c. The Local Area Connections/Authentication tab
   ❑ d. The Local Area Connections Properties/Advanced tab

Quick Answer: **359**
Detailed Answer: **362**

30. What TCP/IP utility is commonly used to test a remote network node to see if it is active?

   ❑ a. IPCONFIG
   ❑ b. ARP
   ❑ c. PING
   ❑ d. WINIPCFG

Quick Answer: **359**
Detailed Answer: **363**

31. Which of the following TCP/IP utilities can be used to identify the IP address of a site when you are given a DNS domain name?

   ❑ a. NETSTAT
   ❑ b. NET VIEW
   ❑ c. TRACERT
   ❑ d. NBTSTAT

Quick Answer: **359**
Detailed Answer: **363**

32. Which TCP/IP utility can be used to locate a slow router on a wide area network, such as the Internet?

    ❑ a. ARP
    ❑ b. TRACERT
    ❑ c. NETSTAT
    ❑ d. IPCONFIG

Quick Answer: **359**
Detailed Answer: **363**

33. Where do you enter the command to run a TCP/IP utility program?

    ❑ a. At the command prompt
    ❑ b. On the TCP/IP Properties window
    ❑ c. In the dialog box that appears when you double-click the file tcpip.com
    ❑ d. From the dialog box in the Network Neighborhood Control Panel

Quick Answer: **359**
Detailed Answer: **363**

34. You have a new workstation with a known valid IP address but it cannot browse the network. What utility can you use to check connectivity to a nearby computer?

    ❑ a. PING
    ❑ b. IPCONFIG
    ❑ c. NETSTAT
    ❑ d. ARP

Quick Answer: **359**
Detailed Answer: **363**

35. What network utility shows the route taken to a given destination?

    ❑ a. NETSTAT
    ❑ b. ARP
    ❑ c. TRACERT
    ❑ d. NBTSTAT

Quick Answer: **359**
Detailed Answer: **363**

36. Which of the following network utilities are used to identify the IP address of a remote known network location? (Select all that apply.)

    ❑ a. TRACERT
    ❑ b. PING
    ❑ c. ARP
    ❑ d. NETSTAT

Quick Answer: **359**
Detailed Answer: **363**

37. Which TCP/IP utility can be used to display the path of a transmission across a network?

    ❑ a. PING
    ❑ b. NETSTAT
    ❑ c. TRACERT
    ❑ d. NSLOOKUP

Quick Answer: **359**
Detailed Answer: **363**

. . . .

38. Which two TCP/IP utilities display the address of a known remote location?

Quick Answer: **359**
Detailed Answer: **363**

❑ a. PING
❑ b. NETSTAT
❑ c. IPCONFIG
❑ d. NSLOOKUP

39. Where are TCP/IP utilities run from?

Quick Answer: **359**
Detailed Answer: **363**

❑ a. Start/Run
❑ b. Command prompt
❑ c. Start/Program Files/Accessories/System Tools
❑ d. Start/Settings/Control Panel/Network

40. Which Windows tools are employed to check out network-related problems?

Quick Answer: **359**
Detailed Answer: **363**

❑ a. TCP/IP utilities
❑ b. DHCP utilities
❑ c. WINS utilities
❑ d. DNS utilities

41. Which TCP/IP utilities show the host IP address? (Select all that apply.)

Quick Answer: **359**
Detailed Answer: **364**

❑ a. IPCONFIG
❑ b. NSLOOKUP
❑ c. NETSTAT
❑ d. WINIPCFG

42. Which TCP/IP utilities can be used to release and renew IP address information from a DHCP server?

Quick Answer: **359**
Detailed Answer: **364**

❑ a. IPCONFIG
❑ b. TRACERT
❑ c. PING
❑ d. NETSTAT

43. When you attempt to access another computer on the network, you can't see any folders or directories. What is most likely to be the cause of this problem?

Quick Answer: **359**
Detailed Answer: **364**

❑ a. Your computer has a missing or corrupted network protocol.
❑ b. Your computer needs a network adapter.
❑ c. The other computer is password protected.
❑ d. The other computer has no shared drives or folders.

44. In general, what is the first TCP/IP tool used to begin troubleshoot network connectivity problems?
    - ❑ a. IPCONFIG
    - ❑ b. ARP
    - ❑ c. NET VIEW
    - ❑ d. PING

Quick Answer: **359**
Detailed Answer: **364**

45. What does the presence of a light on the NIC card indicate?
    - ❑ a. The NIC sees network traffic.
    - ❑ b. It is downloading data.
    - ❑ c. It is uploading data.
    - ❑ d. The NIC driver is functioning.

Quick Answer: **359**
Detailed Answer: **364**

46. What problems can cause computers or resources to not appear on the network?
    - ❑ a. Incompatible protocols loaded
    - ❑ b. Incorrect computer name
    - ❑ c. Insufficient access rights
    - ❑ d. Incompatible file management systems

Quick Answer: **359**
Detailed Answer: **364**

Objective 4.2: Identify the basic Internet protocols and terminologies. Identify procedures for establishing Internet connectivity.

1. What file transfer protocol is traditionally used to download a file from the Internet?
    - ❑ a. HTTP
    - ❑ b. TELNET
    - ❑ c. FTP
    - ❑ d. HTTPS

Quick Answer: **359**
Detailed Answer: **364**

2. What part of the URL is designated by suffixes such as .com, .gov, .mil, and .edu?
    - ❑ a. Host name
    - ❑ b. Top-level domain
    - ❑ c. Domain
    - ❑ d. FQDN

Quick Answer: **359**
Detailed Answer: **364**

3. What protocol is typically used to transfer large files over a remote network connection?

- ❏ a. NNTP
- ❏ b. DTP
- ❏ c. HTTP
- ❏ d. FTP

Quick Answer: **359**
Detailed Answer: **364**

4. What programming language is used to create all Internet Web pages?

- ❏ a. C++
- ❏ b. HTML
- ❏ c. HTTP
- ❏ d. Java

Quick Answer: **359**
Detailed Answer: **364**

5. Which of the following configuration information is not needed in order to set up an email account?

- ❏ a. DNS server name or IP address
- ❏ b. Email account name
- ❏ c. SMTP server name or IP address
- ❏ d. POP3 server name or IP address

Quick Answer: **359**
Detailed Answer: **365**

6. Which of the following protocols permits a network server to assign an IP address to a network node?

- ❏ a. RAS
- ❏ b. DNS
- ❏ c. DHCP
- ❏ d. WINS

Quick Answer: **359**
Detailed Answer: **365**

7. Which of the following is not an advantage of using TCP/IP as your network protocol?

- ❏ a. No one owns the rights to it.
- ❏ b. It provides encrypted data transmission.
- ❏ c. It can service networks that include a wide variety of computer types.
- ❏ d. It is very resistant to hacking.

Quick Answer: **359**
Detailed Answer: **365**

8. What type of protocol is normally used to access a World Wide Web server?

- ❏ a. HTTP
- ❏ b. FTP
- ❏ c. GOPHER
- ❏ d. NTFS

Quick Answer: **359**
Detailed Answer: **365**

9. Internet service providers _____.

    ❑ a. install modems

    ❑ b. provide Internet addresses

    ❑ c. install cable

    ❑ d. create Internet browsers

Quick Answer: **359**
Detailed Answer: **365**

10. What language is used to create the pages that make up the Web?

    ❑ a. HTML

    ❑ b. C++

    ❑ c. Java

    ❑ d. Net

Quick Answer: **359**
Detailed Answer: **365**

11. What type of protocol is commonly associated with the World Wide Web?

    ❑ a. PPP

    ❑ b. TCP/IP

    ❑ c. FTP

    ❑ d. HTTP

Quick Answer: **359**
Detailed Answer: **365**

12. Dynamic IP addressing is performed by _____.

    ❑ a. LMHOST

    ❑ b. IMAP

    ❑ c. DHCP

    ❑ d. DNS

Quick Answer: **359**
Detailed Answer: **365**

13. What protocol supports dial-up, Ethernet, and Token Ring networking?

    ❑ a. RAS

    ❑ b. UDP

    ❑ c. TCP/IP

    ❑ d. IPX

Quick Answer: **359**
Detailed Answer: **365**

14. What are the advantages of using the TCP/IP protocol? (Select all that apply.)

    ❑ a. It can be used on any network topology.

    ❑ b. It is common to most operating systems.

    ❑ c. It is encrypted.

    ❑ d. It is nonproprietary (no one owns it).

Quick Answer: **359**
Detailed Answer: **365**

15. What does TCP/IP do? (Select two correct answers.)

   ❑ a. It enables messages to be fragmented and reassembled.

   ❑ b. It enables messages to be routed to a specific computer.

   ❑ c. It bundles data into network packets.

   ❑ d. It provides basic encryption to data packets.

Quick Answer: **359**
Detailed Answer: **366**

16. What is TCP/IP?

   ❑ a. Protocol used on the Internet

   ❑ b. Protocol used to send email

   ❑ c. Protocol used to enable remote interrupt masking

   ❑ d. Protocol used to send remote network commands

Quick Answer: **359**
Detailed Answer: **366**

17. On a Microsoft-based LAN, what is the preferred naming service?

   ❑ a. DNS

   ❑ b. LMHOST

   ❑ c. NetBIOS

   ❑ d. WINS

Quick Answer: **359**
Detailed Answer: **366**

18. What modem string command will turn off the dialing sound?

   ❑ a. M1

   ❑ b. M0

   ❑ c. S0

   ❑ d. S1

Quick Answer: **359**
Detailed Answer: **366**

19. Windows 9x uses which function to share dial-up connections?

   ❑ a. RAS

   ❑ b. UDP

   ❑ c. TAPI

   ❑ d. TCP/IP

Quick Answer: **359**
Detailed Answer: **366**

20. In Windows 2000, the dialing rules for modems are established in the _____ path.

   ❑ a. Start/Programs/System Tools/Modem Options

   ❑ b. Start/Settings/Control Panel/Phone and Modem Options

   ❑ c. My Computer/Options/Dial-Up Options

   ❑ d. My Network Places/Dial-Up Connections/Options

Quick Answer: **359**
Detailed Answer: **366**

21. To create a dial-up connection in Windows 2000, you should access the _____.

Quick Answer: **359**
Detailed Answer: **366**

   ❑ a. Network Settings entry in the Control Panel

   ❑ b. Make New Connections icon in the My Computer Network Connection folder

   ❑ c. New Network Connection icon in the My Computer window

   ❑ d. Remote Access Services icon in the Control Panel

22. You are installing a new network for a company. They recently acquired workstations with the Windows XP Professional operating system, and have a hub and a DSL modem. Due to costs, the company does not wish to pay for a new server or a router, but would still like to have the Internet available to all workstations, and would therefore be willing to pay for extra cabling and network interface card costs. Which of the following is the best solution for this scenario?

Quick Answer: **359**
Detailed Answer: **366**

   ❑ a. Establish ICS.

   ❑ b. Employ VMM.

   ❑ c. Install a LAN adapter.

   ❑ d. Activate ACL.

23. Which of the following Windows XP new features can be applied with the Windows ICS service to provide Internet access to multiple computers through a single connection?

Quick Answer: **359**
Detailed Answer: **366**

   ❑ a. IPSec

   ❑ b. RDP

   ❑ c. MMC

   ❑ d. ICF

24. Your friend is setting up the Internet Connection Firewall utility in his new Windows XP Professional machine, and he wants to make sure that his email can be sent and received. What does he need to know in order to make sure these services can pass through the firewall?

Quick Answer: **359**
Detailed Answer: **367**

   ❑ a. Open TCP/UDP port 144.

   ❑ b. Open TCP/UDP ports 20 and 21.

   ❑ c. Open TCP/UDP ports 25 and 110.

   ❑ d. Open TCP/UDP port 80.

25. You have purchased a new copy of Windows XP because you want to use its Internet Connection Sharing (ICS) feature to provide a central Internet connection for your home computer network. Where is the ICS feature located in Windows XP?

Quick Answer: **359**
Detailed Answer: **367**

   ❏   a. Access Network Connections, select the connection to be shared, and then select the Change Settings of This Connection option from the Network Tasks pane. On the Advanced tab, enable the Allow Other Network Users to Connect Through This Computer's Internet Connection setting.

   ❏   b. Click on Start/Settings and select the Network and Dial-Up Connections option. Right-click the connection to be shared and then select the Properties option from the pop-up menu. Under the Internet Connection Sharing tab, select the Enable Internet Connection Sharing for This Connection check box.

   ❏   c. Click on Start/Local Network Connections. Right-click the connection to be shared and then select the Properties option from the pop-up menu. Under the Internet Connection Sharing tab, select the Enable Internet Connection Sharing for This Connection check box.

   ❏   d. Click on the Internet icon in the Control Panel, select the Internet Connection Sharing option from the menu, and designate the computers to provide connection sharing with.

26. What are the possible reasons that I could log in to my Internet account yesterday, but it won't work today? (Select all that apply.)

Quick Answer: **359**
Detailed Answer: **367**

   ❏   a. Thunderstorm
   ❏   b. Incorrect username or password
   ❏   c. Password has expired
   ❏   d. Failure to pay fee

Quick Check Answer Key

Objective 4.1

1. d
2. c
3. b
4. c
5. a
6. a
7. c
8. c
9. c
10. a
11. a
12. d
13. a, b, d
14. b
15. c
16. b
17. a
18. d
19. c
20. c
21. a
22. b
23. a, d
24. a, b, c
25. c
26. c
27. a

28. b
29. d
30. c
31. c
32. b
33. a
34. a
35. c
36. a, b
37. c
38. a, d
39. b
40. a
41. a, d
42. a
43. d
44. a
45. a
46. a

Objective 4.2

1. c
2. b
3. d
4. b
5. a
6. c
7. b

8. a
9. b
10. a
11. d
12. c
13. c
14. a, b, d
15. a, c
16. a
17. d
18. b
19. c
20. b
21. b
22. a
23. d
24. c
25. a
26. b, d

Answers and Explanations

Objective 4.1

1. **d.** Unlike NAN, LAN (local area network), WAN (wide area network), and MAN (metropolitan area network) are valid network types.

2. **c.** Token Ring is a token-passing protocol operating on a ring topology.

3. **b.** Token Ring is a token-passing protocol operating on a ring topology. Only the node possessing the token can have control of the Token Ring LAN.

4. **c.** In concept, a minimum of three stations must be connected to have a true LAN. If only two units are connected, point-to-point communications software and a simple null modem can be employed.

5. **a.** In Windows 2000, the TCP/IP settings are established through the Start/Settings/Network and Dial-Up Connections/desired connection/Properties/TCP/IP Properties path. You can then set the desired method of obtaining an IP address automatically, from a DHCP server, or manually, by specifying a static IP address.

6. **a.** In Windows 9x, the TCP/IP settings are established through the Start/Settings/Control Panel/Network/TCP/IP Properties path. You can then click on the IP Address tab to set the desired method of obtaining an IP address automatically, from a DHCP server, or manually, by specifying a static IP address.

7. **c.** The Dynamic Host Configuration Protocol (DHCP) service dynamically assigns IP addresses to the server's clients. This service must be located on both the server and the client computers. In Windows 9x, the path to the TCP/IP Properties window is Start/Settings/Control Panel/Network/TCP/IP Properties.

8. **c.** If the My Network Places window is empty, or if its icon is missing, networking connections have not been established. If this is the case, you must correctly configure networking on the local unit to connect to any other computers on the network.

9. **c.** IPX/SPX is a Novell network protocol for LANs.

10. **a.** In Windows 9x, the peer-to-peer local area networking function is an integral part of the system.

11. **a.** NetBEUI is required to support dial-up RAS connections through a modem. The RAS service uses NetBEUI to navigate through a connected LAN network. Both the calling client and the receiving server must be running NetBEUI. If either one does not have NetBEUI active, the client will be able to connect with the LAN, but will not be able to navigate through it.

12. **d.** In Windows 2000 using the TCP/IP protocol, computer names can range up to 63 characters in length and should be made up of the letters A through Z, numbers 0 through 9, and hyphens. The names cannot contain any blank spaces.

13. **a, b, d.** Protocols, adapters, clients, and services can be set through the Network icon in Control Panel. Clicking on the Add button in the Network Configuration page brings up the Select Network Component Type screen where those four networking components can be configured.

14. **b.** NetBEUI is required to support dial-up RAS connections through a modem. The RAS service uses NetBEUI to navigate through a connected network. Both the calling client and the receiving server must be running NetBEUI. If either one does not have NetBEUI active, the client will be able to connect with the LAN, but will not be able to navigate through it.

15. **c.** In a Windows network, the set of rules that govern the exchange of data between computers is the NetBIOS Enhanced User Interface (NetBEUI) protocol. This protocol works in most purely Windows networks, so another protocol is rarely called for.

16. **b.** The protocols for a particular type of network (such as TCP/IP) in which the computer is being used must be installed manually. Clicking the Add button in the Network Configuration page brings up the Select Network Component Type screen. One of the four network component types on that screen is the protocol.

17. **a.** If a red *X* appears on the icon of a properly mapped drive, this indicates that the drive is no longer available. Its host computer might be turned off, the drive might have been removed, or it might no longer be on the same path. If the drive was mapped to a particular folder and the foldername has been changed, the red *X* will also appear.

18. **d.** The path to the shared resource contains the remote computer's name and shared resource name (directory or printer). It also must be expressed using the Universal Naming Convention (UNC) format. The format begins with a pair of backslashes (\\). Each name in the path is separated by a single backslash.

19. **c.** Valid computer names in Windows 9x can be up to 15 characters in length and cannot contain any blank spaces.

20. **c.** In Windows 2000 using the TCP/IP protocol, computer names can range up to 63 characters in length and should be made up of the letters A through Z, numbers 0 through 9, and hyphens. The names cannot contain any blank spaces.

21. **a.** The SHARE.EXE command provides file-sharing and file-locking capabilities for files on a local hard disk drive. These capabilities enable multiple users to access the same file at the same time in a networked or multitasking environment.

22. **b.** Network and Dial-Up Connections provides several key functions associated with local and wide area networking. It is used to install new network adapter cards and change their settings, change network component settings, and to install TCP/IP.

23. **a, d.** (a) To access the Add Printer Wizard using the Start menu in Windows 2000, move to the Settings entry, click on Printers, and then double-click the Add Printer icon. (d) In Windows 2000, the Add Printer Wizard can be accessed through the Control Panel/Printers path.

24. **a, b, c.** The functions associated with the Windows 2000 Local Area Connections Properties include adding, removing, or configuring network services (such as DNS, WINS, and DHCP), network protocols, and network adapter cards.

25. **c.** In Windows 2000 and XP, the My Network Places enables the user to create shortcut icons to network shares on the desktop. The new My Network Places icon acts as an alias to link the system to the share point on the remote unit.

26. **c.** A network share is an existing shared resource (printer, drive, modem, or folder) located on a remote system. The My Network Places icon in Windows 2000 and XP enables the user to create shortcut icons to network shares on the desktop.

27. **a.** The Windows XP Local Connections properties window offers two tabs not available in the Windows 2000 version. These are the Advanced tab and the Authentication tab. The Advanced tab is used to enable the Windows XP Internet Connection Firewall. The Authentication tab is used to configure Authentication protocols.

28. **b.** In Windows XP systems, you must install the Client Service for NetWare (CSNW) option to provide the Windows client with the capability to communicate with NetWare servers.

29. **d.** The Windows XP Local Area Connections Properties Advanced tab is used to enable the Windows XP Internet Connection Firewall. This feature is embedded in Windows XP so that it can act as an Internet firewall for itself or for a local area network attached to it.

30. **c.** The PING utility is used to check the status of a connection. A packet is sent to a specified address, and returned to your machine, provided the specified address is active. If it is not, you will receive a message saying that the transaction has timed out.

31. **c.** In a LAN environment, you will need to know the IP address, or the name of a computer in the network to which you can direct the PING. TRACERT can be used to identify the IP address of a known network address. It displays the host name, IP address, and round-trip time for each hop including the destination site in the path.

32. **b.** The TRACERT utility traces the route taken by ICMP packets sent across the network and displays the host name, IP address, and round-trip time for each hop in the path. Because the TRACERT report shows how much time is spent at each router along the path, it is helpful to determine where network slow-downs are occurring.

33. **a.** All TCP/IP utilities are controlled by commands entered and run from the command prompt.

34. **a.** PING is a tool used to check connectivity between network devices, such as between workstations or between workstations and servers.

35. **c.** TRACERT enables you to display the route, and a hop count, taken to a given destination. The route taken to a particular address can be set manually using the ROUTE command.

36. **a, b.** In a LAN environment, you will need to know the IP address, or the name of a computer in the network to which you can direct the PING. Both PING and TRACERT can be used to identify the IP address of a known network address.

37. **c.** TRACERT enables you to display the route, and a hop count, taken to a given destination.

38. **a, d.** (a) PING enables you to verify connections to remote hosts. You can use the command to test both the name and IP address of the remote unit. (d) NSLOOKUP is a Windows 2000/XP TCP/IP utility that can be entered at the command prompt to query Internet (DNS) name servers for information about hosts and domains.

39. **b.** All TCP/IP utilities are controlled by commands entered and run from the command prompt.

40. **a.** When TCP/IP is installed in a Windows 9x, Windows 2000, or Windows XP system, a number of TCP/IP tools are automatically installed with it to check out network-related problems.

. . . .

41. **a, d.** (a) IPCONFIG enables you to determine the current TCP/IP configuration (MAC address, IP address, and subnet mask) of the local computer. It also can be used to request a new TCP/IP address from a DHCP server. IPCONFIG is available in both Windows 98 and Windows 2000. Windows 95 did not support IPCONFIG. (**d**) WINIPCFG is a GUI version of the IPCONFIG command available only in Windows 95. The various command-line switches available with the IPCONFIG command are implemented in graphical buttons.

42. **a.** The IPCONFIG utility can be started with two important option switches, /renew and /release. These switches are used to release and update IP settings received from a DHCP server.

43. **d.** If you can browse the network but cannot use certain resources in other locations, sharing is not turned on in the remote unit or the local unit does not have proper access rights to that resource.

44. **a.** IPCONFIG enables you to determine the current TCP/IP configuration (MAC address, IP address, and subnet mask) of the local computer. With these TCP/IP configuration settings, you can troubleshoot network connectivity problems.

45. **a.** The presence of the light indicates that the NIC sees network traffic.

46. **a.** If the network cannot be seen in the Network Neighborhood, the network protocols and drivers should be checked through the Control Panel's Network icon.

Objective 4.2

Identify procedures for establishing Internet connectivity. In a given scenario, configure the operating system to connect to and use Internet resources.

1. **c.** The File Transfer Protocol (FTP) is used to upload files to and download files from the Internet. Large files take considerably less time to send and download than through an email server.

2. **b.** A top-level domain defines the type of organization associated with an Internet address. It can be .com (commercial businesses), .edu (educational institutions), .gov (government agencies), .org (nonprofit organizations), .net (networking organizations), .mil (military establishments), or .int (international organizations).

3. **d.** The File Transfer Protocol (FTP) is used to upload and download files to and from an FTP server. Large files take considerably longer to send to and download from an FTP server than from an email server.

4. **b.** HTML (Hypertext Markup Language) provides a way to code a document so that it can be displayed on the World Wide Web.

5. **a.** When setting up an email account, you must supply the configuration information (email account name, password, POP3 Server address, and SMTP Server address).

6. **c.** DHCP is an Internet protocol that can be used by a network server to automatically assign IP addresses to devices on a network using TCP/IP.

7. **b.** TCP/IP does not support encryption.

8. **a.** HTTP is a client/server protocol used to send and receive files on the Internet. A client, which can be any network workstation or a standalone computer connected to the Internet through an ISP, sends a request to a Web server for files contained at the server. The server responds to the request by sending the files to the client.

9. **b.** ISPs are companies that provide the technical gateway to the Internet. These companies own blocks of access addresses that they assign to their customers to give the customer an identity on the network.

10. **a.** HTML, Hypertext Markup Language, provides a way to code a document so that it can be displayed on the World Wide Web.

11. **d.** The World Wide Web (WWW) is a menu system that ties together Internet resources from around the world. Web servers inventory the Web's resources. To access a Web site, the user must place the desired URL on the Internet. Each URL begins with the letters http://. These letters stand for Hypertext Transfer Protocol, and identify the address as a Web site.

12. **c.** The Dynamic Host Configuration Protocol (DHCP) is an Internet protocol that can be used to automatically assign IP addresses to devices on a network using TCP/IP. Using DHCP simplifies network administration because software, rather than an administrator, assigns and keeps track of IP addresses.

13. **c.** TCP/IP can be used on any topology (Ethernet, Token Ring, and dial-up). Therefore, different types of computers can exchange data across a network using the TCP/IP protocol.

14. **a, b, d.** (a) The TCP/IP protocol can be used on any network topology, such as Ethernet and Token Ring. Therefore, different types of computers can exchange data across a network using the TCP/IP protocol. (b) The TCP/IP protocol was so widely accepted by the Internet community that virtually every network operating system supports it, including Apple, MS-DOS/Windows, Unix, Linux, OS/2, and even networked printers. (d) The U.S. Department of Defense originally developed the TCP/IP protocol as a hacker-resistant, secure protocol for transmitting data across a network. Because the U.S. government developed TCP/IP, no one actually owns the TCP/IP protocol.

15. **a, c.** (**a**) The TCP/IP packet is designed primarily to allow for message fragmentation and reassembly. It exists through two header fields, the IP header and the TCP header, followed by the data field. (**c**) TCP/IP calls for data to be grouped together in bundles called network packets.

16. **a.** The primary protocol used on the Internet is the Transmission Control Protocol/Internet Protocol (TCP/IP). No matter what type of computer platform or software is being used, the information can move across the Internet in the form of TCP/IP packets.

17. **d.** Although DNS is the naming service used by the Internet, it is not the only name-resolution service used with PCs. In the case of Windows LANs, the Microsoft-preferred naming system is the Windows Internet Naming Service (WINS).

18. **b.** An M0 setting should turn the volume on the modem off so that it is quiet when connecting to the Internet.

19. **c.** Windows 9x applications can cooperatively share the dial-up connections through its Telephony Application Programming Interface (TAPI). This interface provides a universal set of drivers for modems and COM ports to control and arbitrate telephony operations for data, faxes, and voice.

20. **b.** For Windows 2000 to connect to a network or dial-up connection, it must know what rules to follow to establish the communication link. These rules are known as the *dialing rules*. In Windows 2000, the dialing rules are configured through the Phone and Modem Options icon in the Control Panel.

21. **b.** To create a dial-up connection in Windows 2000, click the Make New Connection icon in the My Computer/Network Connections folder. This action will open the Windows 2000 Network Connection Wizard that guides the connection process.

22. **a.** Sharing an Internet connection enables several computers to be connected to the Internet through a single dial-up connection. These connections can be made individually, or simultaneously. To establish Internet Connection Sharing (ICS), you must log on to the computer using an account that has Administrator rights.

23. **d.** When combined with the Windows ICS service, the XP firewall can be configured to provide Internet access to multiple computers through a single connection. ICF should be enabled on the shared external connection to secure communication for all internal clients.

24. **c.** The ICF function can be configured with filters to enable specific traffic to enter the network, such as Web or FTP services running on the internal network that must be made available to external customers. Then you can configure a filter to open the firewall to let just that service pass through. For email SMTP and POP3 services the port settings involved are 25 and 110.

25. **a.** To establish Internet Connection Sharing (ICS), you must log on to the computer using an account that has Administrator rights. In Windows XP, access the Network Connections, select the connection to be shared, and then select the Change Settings of This Connection option from the Network Tasks pane. On the Advanced tab, enable the Allow Other Network Users to Connect Through This Computer's Internet Connection setting.

26. **b, d.** (**b**) The ISP establishes an Internet access account for each user. These accounts are based on the user's account name and password that are asked for each time the user logs on to the account. (**d**) If the Internet access account isn't paid up, the ISP might cancel the account and deny access to the user.

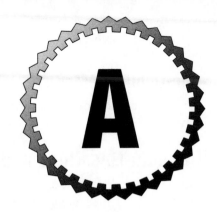

CD Contents and Installation Instructions

The CD features an innovative practice test engine powered by MeasureUp™, giving you yet another effective tool to assess your readiness for the exam.

Multiple Test Modes

MeasureUp practice tests are available in Study, Certification, Custom, Adaptive, Missed Question, and Non-Duplicate question modes.

Study Mode

Tests administered in Study Mode enable you to request the correct answer(s) and explanation to each question during the test. These tests are not timed. You can modify the testing environment *during* the test by selecting the Options button.

Certification Mode

Tests administered in Certification Mode closely simulate the actual testing environment you will encounter when taking a certification exam. These tests do not enable you to request the answer(s) and/or explanation to each question until after the exam.

Custom Mode

Custom Mode enables you to specify your preferred testing environment. Use this mode to specify the objectives you want to include in your test, the timer length, and other test properties. You can also modify the testing environment *during* the test by selecting the Options button.

Missed Question Mode

Missed Question Mode enables you to take a test containing only the questions you have missed previously.

Non-Duplicate Mode

Non-Duplicate Mode enables you to take a test containing only questions not displayed previously.

Random Questions and Order of Answers

This feature helps you learn the material without memorizing questions and answers. Each time you take a practice test, the questions and answers appear in a different randomized order.

Detailed Explanations of Correct and Incorrect Answers

You'll receive automatic feedback on all correct and incorrect answers. The detailed answer explanations are a superb learning tool in their own right.

Attention to Exam Objectives

MeasureUp practice tests are designed to appropriately balance the questions over each technical area covered by a specific exam.

Installing the CD

The minimum system requirements for the CD-ROM are

➤ Windows 95, 98, Me, NT 4.0, 2000, or XP

➤ 7MB disk space for the testing engine

➤ An average of 1MB disk space for each test

To install the CD-ROM, follow these instructions:

NOTE If you need technical support, please contact MeasureUp at 678-356-5050 or email support@measureup.com. Additionally, you'll find Frequently Asked Questions (FAQs) at www.measureup.com.

1. Close all applications before beginning this installation.

2. Insert the CD into your CD-ROM drive. If the setup starts automatically, go to step 6. If the setup does not start automatically, continue with step 3.

3. From the Start menu, select Run.

4. In the Browse dialog box, double-click Setup.exe. In the Run dialog box, click OK to begin the installation.

5. On the Welcome screen, click Next.

6. To agree to the Software License Agreement, click Yes.

7. On the Choose Destination Location screen, click Next to install the software to `C:\Program Files\Certification Preparation`.

8. On the Setup Type screen, select Typical Setup. Click Next to continue.

9. After the installation is complete, verify that Yes, I Want to Restart My Computer Now is selected. If you select No, I Will Restart My Computer Later, you will not be able to use the program until you restart your computer.

10. Click Finish.

11. After restarting your computer, choose Start, Programs, MeasureUp, MeasureUp Practice Tests.

12. Select the practice test and click Start Test.

Creating a Shortcut to the MeasureUp Practice Tests

To create a shortcut to the MeasureUp practice tests, follow these steps.

1. Right-click on your Desktop.

2. From the shortcut menu, select New, Shortcut.

3. Browse to `C:\Program Files\MeasureUp Practice Tests` and select the MeasureUpCertification.exe or Localware.exe file.

4. Click OK.

5. Click Next.

6. Rename the shortcut MeasureUp.

7. Click Finish.

After you have completed step 7, use the MeasureUp shortcut on your Desktop to access the MeasureUp practice test.

Technical Support

If you encounter problems with the MeasureUp test engine on the CD-ROM, please contact MeasureUp at 678-356-5050 or email support@measureup.com. Technical support hours are from 8:00 a.m. to 5:00 p.m. EST Monday through Friday. Additionally, you'll find Frequently Asked Questions (FAQs) at www.measureup.com.

If you'd like to purchase additional MeasureUp products, call 678-356-5050 or 800-649-1MUP (1687), or visit www.measureup.com.

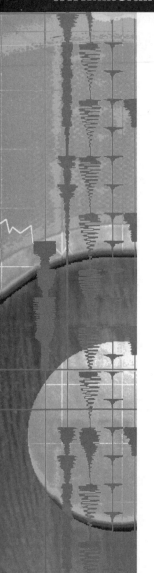